Roman Military Architecture on the Frontiers

Armies and Their Architecture in Late Antiquity

*Rob Collins, Matthew Symonds
and Meike Weber*

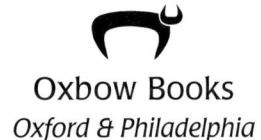

Oxbow Books
Oxford & Philadelphia

Published in the United Kingdom in 2015 by
OXBOW BOOKS
10 Hythe Bridge Street, Oxford OX1 2EW

and in the United States by
OXBOW BOOKS
908 Darby Road, Havertown, PA 19083

© Oxbow Books and the individual authors 2015

Hardcover Edition: ISBN 978-1-78297-990-6
Digital Edition: ISBN 978-1-78297-991-3

A CIP record for this book is available from the British Library

Library of Congress Cataloging-in-Publication Data

Collins, Rob, 1977-
  Roman military architecture on the frontiers : armies and their architecture in late antiquity / Rob Collins, Matt Symonds and Meike Weber.
       pages cm
  Includes bibliographical references.
  ISBN 978-1-78297-990-6 (hardback)
 1. Fortification, Roman. 2. Military architecture--Rome. 3. Rome--Military antiquities. I. Symonds, Matthew F. A. II. Weber, Meike. III. Title.
  UG405.C65 2015
  725'.180937--dc23
                                                         2015022492

All rights reserved. No part of this book may be reproduced or transmitted in any form or by any means, electronic or mechanical including photocopying, recording or by any information storage and retrieval system, without permission from the publisher in writing.

Printed in the United Kingdom by Berforts Information Press

For a complete list of Oxbow titles, please contact:

UNITED KINGDOM
Oxbow Books
Telephone (01865) 241249, Fax (01865) 794449
Email: oxbow@oxbowbooks.com
www.oxbowbooks.com

UNITED STATES OF AMERICA
Oxbow Books
Telephone (800) 791-9354, Fax (610) 853-9146
Email: queries@casemateacademic.com
www.casemateacademic.com/oxbow

Oxbow Books is part of the Casemate Group

Front cover: Gasr Kh 14 in the Wadi Kharab (in the Tripolitanian pre-desert), © John Dore, used with the kind permission of his estate.

CONTENTS

List of Figures and Tables v
List of Contributors vii
Acknowledgements viii
List of Abbreviations ix

1. Late Roman military architecture: An introduction 1
   Rob Collins and Meike Weber

2. Making sense of the frontier armies in late antiquity: An historian's perspective 6
   Conor Whately

3. Economic reduction or military reorganization? Granary demolition and conversion in later 4th-century northern *Britannia* 18
   Rob Collins

4. Late Roman military buildings at Binchester (Co. Durham) 32
   David Petts

5. Fourth-century fortlets in Britain: sophisticated systems or desperate measures? 46
   Matthew Symonds

6. The late Roman coastal fort of Oudenburg (Belgium): Spatial and functional transformations within the fort walls 62
   Sofie Vanhoutte

7. The legionary fortress of Vindobona (Vienna, Austria): Change in function and design in the late Roman period 76
   Martin Mosser

8. The dwindling legion: Architectural and administrative changes in Novae (Moesia inferior) on the threshold of late antiquity 90
   Martin Lemke

9. Severan *Castra*, Tetrarchic *Quadriburgia*, Justinian *Coenobia*, and Ghassanid *Diyarat*:
   Patterns of transformation of *limes Arabicus* forts during late antiquity   98
   Ignacio Arce

10. *Castra* or *centenaria*? Interpreting the later forts of the North African frontier   123
    Alan Rushworth

11. In defence of the late empire   140
    David Breeze

LIST OF FIGURES AND TABLES

List of Figures

Figure 3.1: Hadrian's Wall in the 4th century
Figure 3.2: The *horreum* structures from the principal sites under consideration
Figure 3.3: The 3rd and 4th century plans of the double-granary at Housesteads
Figure 3.4: The 4th century plans of Building XV at Housesteads
Figure 3.5: The 4th and 5th century plans of the east and west granaries at Vindolanda
Figure 3.6: The sequence of transformation of the granaries at Birdoswald
Figure 3.7: A visualization of the second timber structure at Birdoswald as a hall

Figure 4.1: Location plan of Binchester Roman fort
Figure 4.2: A geophysical survey of Binchester, showing the earlier and later phases of fort
Figure 4.3: An outline plan of the Phase 1 barrack block
Figure 4.4: A vertical photograph of excavations within the barrack area at Binchester
Figure 4.5: An outline plan of the Phase 2 barrack block
Figure 4.6: The *Vicus* bath-house under excavation

Figure 5.1: The Yorkshire fortlets and the Nunnery on Alderney
Figure 5.2: The possible late Roman fortlets on the west coast
Figure 5.3: The core of the southern enclosure wall at Hen Waliau
Figure 5.4: The north rampart at Caer Gybi
Figure 5.5: The north-west bastion at Caer Gybi
Figure 5.6: The north-east bastion at Caer Gybi
Figure 5.7: The robbed-out remains of the corner tower at Burrow Walls
Figure 5.8: The northern length of extant masonry at Burrow Walls
Figure 5.9: The late Roman installations on the Carlisle–York Highway

Figure 6.1: The location of Oudenburg fort, along with other military installations of the *Litus Saxonicum*
Figure 6.2: An aerial view of Oudenburg
Figure 6.3: The city center of Oudenburg showing the location of the different excavation campaigns on the fort area
Figure 6.4: A simplified excavation plan of the fifth fort period
Figure 6.5: A view of the *hypocaust* floor from the fifth fort period
Figure 6.6: A section through the double well of the 4th century AD
Figure 6.7: The large wooden water-basin, 4.5 m square
Figure 6.8: An excavation plan of the fifth fort period

Figure 7.1: Vindobona – the Late Roman legionary fortress with sites numbered
Figure 7.2: The Acaunus altar from Vindobona
Figure 7.3: The western *intervallum* and *via sagularis* of the Vindobona legionary fortress
Figure 7.4: A map of Pannonia I and the eastern part of Noricum ripense
Figure 7.5: Late Roman graves and stamped tiles sites of Vindobona
Figure 7.6: 1st- to 3rd-century tombstone findspots

Figure 8.1: Novae in late antiquity
Figure 8.2: Novae: the military hospital with the courtyard house
Figure 8.3: The courtyard house in Sector 4
Figure 8.4: Late antique portico looking towards the south, Sector 12

Figure 9.1: A map of the *Limes Arabicus*
Figure 9.2: A plan of Qasr al-Hallabat
Figure 9.3: Qasr al-Hallabat Sequence of the evolution of the complex
Figure 9.4: Deir el Kahf, plan
Figure 9.5: Khirbet el-Khaw
Figure 9.6: Khirbet es-Samra
Figure 9.7: Umm al-Jimal
Figure 9.8: Qasr el-Ba'ij
Figure 9.9: Qasr al-Hayr al Gharbi (*Hauliaram*)
Figure 9.10: (a) Deir an-Nasrani; (b) Qasr Burqu
Figure 9.11: Qasr Burqu

Figure 9.12: Monastery of St. Mary, Mt. Gerizim, Neapolis-Nablus (Palestine)
Figure 9.13: Castrum-Lavra of St. Catherine in Sinai
Figure 9.14: Khirbet al-Kerak, identified as Sinnabra
Figure 9.15: *Kastron* at Al-Andarin / Androna
Figure 9.16: Qasr Ibn-Wardan. The so-called 6th-century 'Barracks'
Figure 9.17: Civil Forts. (a) Istabl Antar and (b) Kastron at Androna / Anderin
Figure 9.18: Roman (and Persian) forts that served as inspiration for Arab fortified residences
Figure 9.19: (a) Ed-Dur Fort (*chantier F*) (UAE); (b) Jabal Says 6th-century pre-Umayyad (Ghassanid?) fort; (c) Kh. el-Bayda (Hauran, Syria)

Figure 10.1: A map of late Roman military sites in Mauretania Caesariensis, Sitifensis and eastern Numidia
Figure 10.2: Late Roman forts and fortlets in North Africa
Figure 10.3: The Tripolitanian fortlet of Benia bel-Recheb
Figure 10.4: Forts and fortlets in the *limes* commands of western Tripolitania and southern Byzacena
Figure 10.5: Plans of a range of courtyard towers (*gsur*)
Figure 10.6: A typical courtyard tower: Gasr Kh 41 in the Wadi Kharab

List of Tables

Table 2.1: Disposition of auxiliaries in the Moesias in AD 138
Table 2.2: Disposition of auxiliaries in the Moesias in AD 170
Table 2.3: The legions of the Moesias listed in the *Antonine Itinerary*
Table 2.4: The legions in the *Notitia Dignitatum*
Table 2.5: The units listed in the *Notitia Dignitatum* for the Moesias

Table 3.1: Summary of changes to granaries at selected Wall forts in the late Roman period
Table 3.2: Summary of palaeobotanical evidence from Wall granaries

Table 7.1: Construction periods of the legionary fortress in Vindobona

Table 9.1: A comparison of enlarged forts and single-phase fortifications from the *Limes Arabicus*

LIST OF CONTRIBUTORS

Dr Ignacio Arce
Director
Spanish Archaeological Mission to Jordan

Prof David Breeze
Honorary Professor
Durham, Edinburgh and Newcastle Universities

Dr Rob Collins
Newcastle University

Dr Martin Lemke
University of Warsaw

Dr Martin Mosser
Stadtarchäologie Wien

Dr David Petts
Durham University

Dr Alan Rushworth
The Archaeological Practice
Newcastle University

Dr Matthew Symonds
Editor
Current Archaeology
Newcastle University

Sofie Vanhoutte
Flemish Heritage Institute

Dr Meike Weber
Cambridge University

Dr Conor Whately
University of Winnipeg

ACKNOWLEDGEMENTS

This volume originated with the session "You call that a *principia*?" at the 22nd International Congress of Roman Frontier Studies, in Ruse (Bulgaria) in 2012. Ordinarily, sessions papers are published in the proceedings of that esteemed congress, but the editors of the present volume wanted to expand on the conference session, as well as offering longer papers so that sufficient detail could be presented to the reader. Suffice to say, we (the editors) are pleased with the volume, and are especially grateful to the contributors for their excellent and timely work.

LIST OF ABBREVIATIONS

AAA	Gsell, S. (1911) *Atlas Archéologique de l'Algérie*. Paris and Algiers. N.B. Site entries are given as AAA (map sheet):(site entry)
AE	*L'Année épigraphique*
CIL	*Corpus Inscriptionum Latinarum*
ILAf	*Inscriptions latines d'Afrique*. Cagnat, R., Merlin, A. and Chatelain, L. (1923) Paris
ILS	*Inscriptiones Latinae Selectae*. Dessau, H. (1892–1916) Berlin
IMS	*Inscriptions de le Mésie Supérieure*
IRT	*Inscriptions of Roman Tripolitania*. Reynolds, J. M. and Ward Perkins, J. B. (1952) Rome and London
Itin Ant	*Itineraria provinciarum Antonini Augusti*. Cuntz, O. (1929) *Itineraria Romana*, I, 1–85 Leipzig, Teubner
ND	*Notitia Dignitatum* (ed.) O. Seeck, (1876) Berlin
ND Occ.	*Notitia Dignitatum omnium in partibus Occidentis*
ND Or.	*Notitia Dignitatum omnium in partibus Orientalis*
P.Oxy	*Papyrus Oxyrhynchus*
RGZM	*Römisch-Germanishcen Zentralmuseums*
RIB	Collingwood, R. P. and Wright, R. G. (1995) *Roman Inscriptions of Britain Volume 1 Inscriptions on Stone*. Stroud, Sutton
RMD	*Roman Military Diplomas*
RMR	Fink, R. O. (1971) *Roman Military Records on Papyrus*. Cleveland

1

LATE ROMAN MILITARY ARCHITECTURE: AN INTRODUCTION

Rob Collins and Meike Weber

Introduction

The Roman army was one of the most astounding organizations in the ancient world, and much of the success of the Roman empire can be attributed to its soldiers. Archaeological remains and ancient texts provide detailed testimonies that have allowed scholars to understand and reconstruct the army's organisation and activities. This interest in the army has traditionally worked in tandem with the study of Roman frontiers. Historically, the early imperial period, and in particular the emergence of the frontiers, has been the focus of research. During those investigations, however, the remains of the later Roman army were also frequently encountered, if not always understood. Recent decades have brought a burgeoning interest in not only the later Roman army, but also late antiquity more widely.

The late Roman army was a vital and influential element in the late antique empire. Having evolved through the 3rd century and been formally reorganized under Diocletian and Constantine, the *limitanei* guarded the frontiers, while the *comitatenses* provided mobile armies that were fielded against external enemies and internal threats. The transformation of the early imperial army to the late antique army is documented in the rich array of texts from the period. Law compilations, like the Theodosian Code, provide specific cases related to various military matters. Military manuals, such as Vegetius' *Epitoma rei militaris*, provide idealized accounts of the structure, support systems, and deployment of the army. Histories, like the *Res Gestae* of Ammianus Marcellinus, provide broader accounts of political and military activity. Further detail can be found in letters from the Abinnaeus archive or ostraca from the arid climates of the empire. Last, but certainly not least, is the alluring-but-"complicated" source that is the *Notitia Dignitatum*. This document provides a list of offices in the later Roman empire in the decades around AD 400, but its original function is still debated, and internal inconsistencies and amendations beg more questions than they answer. A number of reliable accounts present detailed overviews of the late Roman army (e.g. Elton 1996; Nicasie 1998; Serantis and Christie 2013), as well as studies that contextualize the later military and warfare more broadly (Whitby 2007; Lee 2007).

Detailed studies of the archaeological remains of these late Roman soldiers and their garrisons, however, still most commonly take the form of a dedicated site report (e.g. Wilmott 1997), or a summary overview with a chronological or geographical focus (e.g. Reddé *et al.* 2006). Site reports detail the remains of buildings or structures of later Roman phases, but of necessity focus on the site itself. Summary overviews are also extremely useful, but generally consolidate the evidence for concurrent occupation at sites and relate them back to tactical or strategic concerns for the Roman emperor or his *magistri* (Mackensen 1999; von Petrikovits 1971). Johnson (1983) took a different approach, focusing instead on the physical attributes of fortification during the later Roman Empire. This overall emphasis on fortification and distribution also has a tendency to draw on the *Notitia Dignitatum* in an attempt to determine both the identity of a site, or series of sites, as well as the resident garrison(s), though criticisms of this approach have been voiced (Kulikowski 2000). Such approaches neatly underscore the difficulties late Roman military archaeologists face: the absence of generally uniform military installations and seemingly imprecise terminology from documentary sources contrasts with a propensity for inscriptions during the 1st to 3rd centuries and more uniform military remains that have bequeathed a confident and often quite specific understanding of the early Roman army (see Whately, this volume). Given the ambiguities and generalities of documentary sources, detailed study of the archaeological remains provides the best means of understanding the realities of life for the late Roman soldier across all parts of the later Empire.

Late Roman military architecture

Stone-built military installations were erected across the Roman Empire wherever and whenever an installation was intended to function for the long-term. In the frontiers, this sense of permanence and consolidation is usually attributed to the reign of Hadrian (117–138), although earlier and later installations were also built in stone. The exact form and layout of larger installations, auxiliary forts and legionary fortresses, varied in detail, but the general template is well established. A square or rectangular enclosure with rounded corners had a large, double gateway in each of its four walls, with longer walls also containing secondary gates. The defences were supplemented with square corner and interval towers that projected into the interior of the fort. The curtain was generally backed with an earth rampart. Inside the fort or fortress, the space was divided into front (*praetentura*), middle, and rear (*retentura*) ranges. The principle buildings – the headquarters (*principia*), the commanding officer's house (*praetorium*), and the "granaries" (*horrea*) – were located in the central range, sometimes alongside optional extras, such as a hospital (*valetudinarium*). The T-shaped layout of the main roads – the *via praetoria* and *via principalis* served to guide traffic through the main gates to these buildings. Other buildings, mostly barracks but also workshops and stables, among others, were located in the front and rear ranges. This combination of distinctive features makes forts and fortresses not only easily recognizable for archaeologists, but it also allows site plans and layouts to be projected with a fair degree of confidence when circumstances only allow for small areas of excavation. Vienna (see Mosser, this volume) is an excellent example of this.

Subsequent evolution through the 2nd and 3rd centuries resulted in this reassuringly predictable plan being redrawn. Forts and fortresses that had already been built were adapted or modified, generally in terms of the refurbishment or reconstruction of its buildings, although some structures were demolished and replaced with new buildings, and roads were repaved. In the later 2nd and 3rd century, new forts and fortresses did not adhere as strictly to the rules established in the previous decades and century. Enclosures and curtains no longer had to conform to a rectangular or square plan, with polygonal and even curvilinear curtains appearing. There were fewer gates, while towers were built projecting boldly beyond the curtain. An alternative to the tower, the solid bastion, was also employed at some sites to serve as an elevated strongpoint on the curtain wall. Furthermore, curtain walls were built free-standing, without the traditional rampart backing. Many of these features are seen in the 3rd-century forts of the Saxon Shore of Britain. This is not to say that forts of a more regular plan did not exist. The *quadriburgium* form, generally square with large projecting corner towers, gates centrally placed on opposing walls, and high free-standing curtain walls were built across the southern and eastern stretches of the Empire, generally during the Tetrarchy. What is significant about this form is the general lack of internal structures, or the more limited remains of any such buildings.

The 4th century witnessed the culmination of the architectural adaptations and novelties of the preceding 3rd century. Existing fortifications were modified in any number of ways. Surplus gates were blocked and converted, or demolished outright. Existing gates were adapted or rebuilt with more sophisticated, defendable features, including a single portal, the addition of wing walls or by recessing the gate inwards from the curtain wall. Old interval or corner towers were replaced with new projecting towers or bastions of square-, apsidal-, semi-circular-, or fan-shaped plans. Internal buildings were retained, but refurbishment or replacement proved less conservative than in previous centuries, and there were significant changes in construction styles. At many forts and fortresses, there is clear evidence that the fortifications were reduced, resulting in a smaller enclosure being embedded within the plan of the previous fort, as at Aquincum.

Newly-built sites of the 4th century incorporate all these features, alongside a penchant for erecting internal buildings against the interior of the curtain wall. The central space at the heart of the fort or fortress interior may also be occupied by structures, but in many instances the fort interior appears to be left open, as at Altrip and Alzey. The interior buildings may have been completed in stone, but there are also indications that stone was used more sparingly and that timber and other bio-degradable materials were generally used, for example in Britain's Saxon Shore forts (Pearson 2002). Significantly, there does not appear to be a standardized internal layout, nor can the internal structures always be identified. Therefore, in contrast to the installations of the early empire, the buildings and plans of later imperial fortifications often cannot be identified or extrapolated with much confidence.

In addition to these changes in the fabric of forts and fortresses, the 4th century saw increased frequency in the construction of smaller installations, namely fortlets. While these erections are primarily associated with Valentinian (364–375) and his brother Valens (364–378), they drew upon centuries of Roman experience of building such smaller structures (see Symonds, this volume). In form, they typically employed a small sub-square or irregular quadrangular enclosure with projecting towers or bastions.

Internal structures could be built against the interior of the curtain, and/or in a freestanding structure located in the centre of the interior.

Regardless of whether these new installations were large fortresses, forts, or small fortlets, the positioning of these fortifications shows an emphasis on tactical defensive use of topography and landscape. This is not to say that strategic siting was not employed in earlier centuries, as it clearly was. But the focus was on garrisoning a strategic location within a broader network of military sites rather than occupying a site based primarily on its defensive merits. Analysis of the new late antique fortifications makes it clear that the defensive position of the fortification was fundamental to its choice of location, a trend that continues to gain in importance over the course of the 5th century.

A number of observations can be made in relation to the archaeology of the late Roman army and its installations. First, there is this increased emphasis on defence. While this is not observed consistently across the empire, the fact that it occurs at all is worth noting. Secondly, the construction of numerous fortlets, new-style smaller forts, and the reduction of pre-existing forts and fortresses point to smaller garrison sizes, more widely dispersed through the landscape. Third, these features of late Roman military architecture can be found across the empire, but the frequency and density are extremely variable. The new 4th-century installations and most sophisticated defensive architecture can generally be found along the Rhine and Danube frontiers, while Hadrian's Wall appears to be essentially relict, incorporating very few 3rd- and 4th-century adaptations and evolutions in military building. Thus, the structural remains of the *limitanei* stress a regionality that is more pronounced than in the 2nd and 3rd centuries. A further conclusion to be drawn from these observations is that there is an increased sense of insecurity. Breaking up larger garrisons into smaller installations allows more ground to be observed; enhancing the defensive architecture of these installations suggests that the Romans anticipated that they would be attacked directly and might need to defend themselves from their ramparts rather than meet the enemy in the field. Additionally, a number of non-military options were regularly employed across frontiers, including building projects, embassies, trade or subsidy concessions, hostage exchange, and assassination, or a combination of any of these (Heather 2001). Despite the great wealth of the imperial elite, and the flourishing artistic and literary expression and theological developments of late antiquity (Brown 1971), there was a greater awareness of frontier (in)security that can be observed in documentary sources as much as in the archaeology (Graham 2006).

On top of these fairly basic observations are a number of more complex criticisms of current approaches and interpretations. The later Roman empire is often viewed through the lenses of decline or barbarian migration (for recent overviews: Heather 2005; Ward Perkins 2005; Halsall 2007; Goldsworthy 2009; Christie 2011). Therefore, the shrinking or abandonment of extra-mural settlements outside forts and fortresses is often linked to a perceived deterioration in security. The fact that at least some of the occupants of these extra-mural populations are believed to have taken residence inside the fortification walls introduces a further complication. Related to this are documented instances of barbarian migration, and considerable ink has been spilled over the presumption that the changes in 4th century military remains were due to the settlement of barbarian *foederati* with distinctive national traditions. How do we distinguish between a soldier and a civilian, or a Roman from a barbarian in the later Roman frontiers? Is it a blurring of the material culture, or is it a fallacy of our own modern categories, preoccupations, and expectations? These presumptions and biases must be addressed in their own right so that the archaeology of the later Roman frontiers and their soldiers and other occupants can be interpreted on their own merits.

As discussed above, there has been less synthetic coverage of later Roman frontiers, making the detailed comparison of later frontiers more of an exercise in cherry-picking based on inconsistent publication rather than a more objective assessment (Collins 2012, 140–150). As a result, there has perhaps been an over-reliance on the dating offered by those sites that have been excavated. The frequency with which one encounters Diocletianic, Constantinian, Valentinianic, and Theodosian phasing accords well with documentary sources and narrative history, but seems suspiciously convenient when compared to the evidence we have for the continued building sequences of 2nd-century installations, which often do not correlate with historical event horizons. Furthermore, there is a tendency to rely on the *Notitia Dignitatum* to identify late Roman remains, particularly in regions where there has only been limited excavation. Underlying this problem is the general dearth of complete or near-complete late Roman fort plans supported by excavation. Archaeological survival and preservation of late antique deposits are one factor, as these later deposits are stratigraphically closer to modern ground surfaces and thus more vulnerable to disturbance. However, bias within Roman frontier studies toward the foundation of frontiers over previous decades and centuries has been as influential as the actual survival of remains.

Conclusion

Many of the issues raised above are rehearsed in the present volume, and neatly articulated by contributors with a mastery of the evidence from sites and regions where they have excavated or investigated in detail. Whately provides an excellent starting point, in a rapid but sweeping overview of documentary sources, and the difficulties that can be encountered when these sources are applied to a specific region, in this case Moesia; the frustrations of the *Notitia Dignitatum* and other sources are abundantly clear. Following this consideration of the written sources, coverage is extended into each major frontier zone of the Empire, from northern *Britannia* (Collins; Petts; Symonds) to the Rhine and Danube (Vanhoutte; Mosser; Lemke), over to the *Limes Arabicus* (Arce) and finally to North Africa (Rushworth).

The military remains of *Britannia* are well known, and interpretation of the late antique phases of occupation were invigorated by the discovery of the famous timber hall sequence at Birdoswald (Wilmott 1997). Collins reviews this sequence at the granaries of Birdoswald and other sites along Hadrian's Wall, exploring the chronology of changes to this fundamental "military" building and the implications it has for our understanding of supply in the 4th and 5th centuries. Petts provides the evidence from recent excavations at the fort of Binchester, south of Hadrian's Wall, exploring the sequence of a structure that started as a barrack, but which may have ended as something very different. Symonds mulls the evidence for late Roman fortlets in Britain, identifying the range of architecture employed at these sites, and exploring how they fit into the defence of the diocese.

Vanhoutte, Mosser, and Lemke provide us with detailed accounts of a Saxon Shore fort at Oudenburg, and the legionary fortresses at Vindobona and Novae, respectively. Site phasing is often reliant on the sequences of individual buildings, which may undergo radically different use in the 4th century and beyond than in preceding centuries. The ability to definitely claim military use of these buildings also becomes a point of interest, and the increasing evidence for the presence of women and children inside the defensive circuit is also notable. Historical narratives are also taken into account, while the impacts of barbarian incursions are considered.

The Eastern frontiers, given the different climatic considerations and the presence of the Sasanid Persian empire contrasts to some extent with the European frontiers of the Roman empire. In this region, the arid landscape and the need for water was a stronger influence in the long-term settlement of the region in the centuries both preceding and following the Roman empire. Arce identifies a "double frontier" here, in which a centuries-old sedentary-nomadic frontier ultimately corresponded with the Roman military one. Thus it is perhaps unsurprising to see that the Roman military sites established in the region had a long currency, and Arce emphasizes that these installations had complex lives that outlasted their Roman creators. These sites experienced recurrent frontier roles, albeit with different functions under different political circumstances.

Rushworth provides an excellent overview for North Africa, attempting to reconstruct the hierarchy of military sites in Numidia and Tripolitania in particular. Regionality, or rather provincialism, becomes an apparent theme, particularly in comparing the 4th century deployment, both in terms of the archaeology and insights from textual sources such as inscriptions and the *Notitia*. Interpretation is further complicated by imprecise or variable late Roman usage of the term *centenaria*. Finally, David Breeze offers a summary of the contents of this volume, drawing on his extensive experience of Rome's frontiers to draw together the key themes that challenge the archaeologists of the later Roman frontiers.

It is the aim of this volume to demonstrate that while scholars grappling with the late Roman army may want for the rich corpus of inscriptions and easily identifiable military installations that service colleagues immersed in the high empire, they have risen to the challenge. Their research is revealing a dynamic, less-predictable force that was adapting to a changing world, in terms of both external threats and its own internal structures. The dynamism and ingenuity of the late Roman army provides a breath of fresh air after the suffocating uniformity of its forbears.

Bibliography

Brown, P. (1971) *The World of Late Antiquity*. London, Thames and Hudson.

Christie, N. (2011) *The Fall of the Western Roman Empire: An Archaeological and Historical Perspective*. London, Bloomsbury.

Collins, R. (2012) *Hadrian's Wall and the End of Empire*. New York, Routledge.

Elton, H. (1996) *Warfare in Roman Europe AD 350–425*. Oxford, Clarendon.

Goldsworthy, A. (2009) *The Fall of the West: The Death of a Roman Superpower*. London, Phoenix.

Graham, M. (2006) *News and Frontier Consciousness in the Late Roman Empire*. Ann Arbor, University of Michigan Press.

Heather, P. (2001) The Late Roman art of client management: imperial defence in the fourth century west. In W. Pohl, I. Wood, and H. Reimitz (eds) *The Transformation of Frontiers, From Late Antiquity to the Carolingians*, Transormation of the Roman World 10, 15–68. Boston, Brill.

Heather, P. (2005) *The Fall of the Roman Empire: A New History*. London, Macmillan.

Johnson, S. (1983) *Late Roman Fortifications*. London, Batsford.

Kulikowski, M. (2000) The *Notitia Dignitatum* as a historical source. *Historia* 49, 358–377.

Lee, A. D. (2007) *War in Late Antiquity: A Social History*. Oxford, Blackwell.

Nicasie, M. J. (1998) *Twilight of Empire: The Roman Army from the Reign of Diocletian until the Battle of Adrianople*. Amsterdam, Gieben.

Pearson, A. (2002) *The Roman Shore Forts: Coastal Defences of Southern Britain*. Stroud, Tempus.

von Petrikovits, H. (1971) Fortifications in the northwestern Roman Empire from the third to the fifth centuries AD. *Journal of Roman Studies* 61, 178–218.

Reddé, M, Brulet, R, Fellmann, R, Haalebos, J-K, and

von Schnurbein, S. (eds) (2006) *L'architecture de la Gaule Romaine: Les Fortifications Militares*. Bordeaux, MSH-Ausonius.

Serantis, A. and Christie, N. (eds) (2013) *War and Warfare in Late Antiquity: Current Perspectives*. Leiden, Brill.

Whitby, M. (2007) Army and society in the late Roman world: a context for decline? In P. Erdkamp (ed.) *A Companion to the Roman Army*, 515–531. Oxford, Blackwell.

Wilmott, T. (1997) *Birdoswald, Excavations of a Roman fort on Hadrian's Wall and its successor settlements: 1987–92*. London, English Heritage.

2

MAKING SENSE OF THE FRONTIER ARMIES IN LATE ANTIQUITY: AN HISTORIAN'S PERSPECTIVE

Conor Whately

Introduction

The army of the early and high empire was stationed across the Roman Empire from Britain to Jordan, with legionaries and auxiliaries housed at its limits. Much of what we know about the identity and organization of those units rests on the epigraphic evidence, though the literary and material evidence are also of considerable value. By the late empire, however, we are in a different world. Challenges to the empire's territorial integrity emerged on the Rhine, Danube, Black Sea coast, and in the east, with many enemies (Goths, Huns, Sasanid Persians) wreaking havoc for decades. In general, the combat duties of soldiers were now apportioned to *comitatenses*, who campaigned, and *limitanei*, stationed on the frontiers, not to mention barbarian federate armies. Those *limitanei* were, like their imperial-era predecessors, still stationed across the frontiers, though not always in the same places as before.

Much of the complexity inherent in the military history of the period is the direct result of the evidence. There are familiar items to students of the earlier imperial period like the classicizing *Res Gestae* of Ammianus Marcellinus, the papyri, such as those that make up the Abinnaeus Archive (Bell *et al.* 1962), detailed excavation reports for select portions of the frontier such as Britain, and the coinage. There is also much that is new; students of the late Roman military must come to grips not only with the change in the epigraphic habit, but also with the legal material such as the *Theodosian Code* (Mommsen and Meyer 1905; Pharr 1952); a proliferation, of sorts, of hoards; even hagiographical accounts, such as Eugippius' *Life of Saint Severinus* (mid-5th century); and the problematic register known as the *Notitia Dignitatum* (late 4th / early 5th century). Thus, while the frontier armies are well-trodden ground, and a not inconsiderable amount of work has already been carried out on some of the generalities (Van Berchem 1952; Jones 1964; Elton 1996; Nicasie 1998; Richardot 2005; Scharf 2005; Gardner 2007; and Collins 2012, among others), gaps remain.

In this chapter, we explore the structural changes in the frontier armies from around AD 250–400 in light of the evidence, with the *Notitia Dignitatum* as the focus. The emphasis is on the complexity of the picture this late antique evidence gives us, especially in relation to what we know about the earlier imperial era (*c*.27 BC–AD 250) Roman military on the frontiers. To highlight the difficulties that the later evidence poses to our understanding of the organization of the late Roman frontier armies, we will be making an explicit comparison with that of the earlier empire. We will focus our attention on one region particularly well documented for both the early and late empire: the lower Danube. We begin with a discussion of the evidence with regard to its nature, quality, and variety; then turn to the organizational features of the Roman military on the lower Danube; and we finish with a brief sojourn to the southeastern frontier in modern day Jordan and el-Lejjūn.

The nature of the evidence for frontier armies in late antiquity

We begin with the evidence for frontier soldiers in late antiquity. Like other aspects of late antique military history, the quantity and quality varies widely. It should be noted too that, as we will see, important pieces of evidence for some facets of the late Roman military are less useful for the frontier armies and their soldiers than others.

The textual evidence

The most important textual evidence is that provided by the late antique historians, with the most notable works for the period under review being the late 4th-century *Res Gestae* of Ammianus Marcellinus and the early 6th-century *New History* of Zosimus, among others. As a group, the historians are especially noteworthy for what they have to say about the wars and campaigns of the 4th and 5th centuries. Although truthfulness is the avowed aim of most of these historians, their understanding of this tends to be varied, and it often differs quite widely from ours; moreover, their conception of military history was also often quite different from ours. Ammianus, for instance, was writing within the parameters of a classical or classicizing history. This meant writing military and political history, but with a certain set of characteristics, such as prologues, ethnographic digressions, and battle exhortations (Fornara 1983). When it comes to the minutiae of military history, the material of especial relevance for this discussion, such as the names and size of units and the positioning and tactics of enemy forces, we also tend to be on shaky ground, for ancient historians prefer to focus on great leaders when describing a conflict. Procopius, for example, often gives misleading figures, in part to exaggerate barbarian forces and highlight the performance of the leading general Belisarius (Hannestad 1960), and tends to use vague or general terms when naming or referring to individual units (Müller 1912; Whately forthcoming A); he is not alone in this (cf. Müller 1905 on Ammianus Marcellinus). This tendency diminishes the value of the historians for reconstructing the precise technical aspects of the late Roman army, even if they are important for other aspects of military history.

The epigraphic evidence

Much of what we know about military affairs in the imperial period comes from the many inscriptions that survive from the era. The situation is rather different in late antiquity, however. Many of the inscriptions that survive from this period are dedicatory inscriptions that hint at military activity (Kennedy and Falahat 2008). Trombley (1997) analysed a number of inscriptions that contain this sort of material, chiefly dedicatory inscriptions on a host of structures, from religious architecture to city walls in Syria (cf. Sarantis forthcoming). What we do not have, however, are the funerary inscriptions and the military diplomas that are so valuable to our understanding of the Roman imperial frontier armies.

The papyrological evidence

Late antiquity is well served with respect to papyri, the majority of which come from Egypt, though there are significant collections from Petra in Jordan (Fiema 2007) and Nessana in Israel/Palestine (Kraemer 1958). Those from Egypt tend to come from sites to the south, such as Oxyrhynchus, Aphrodito, and Syene. Thus, much of the epigraphic evidence hails from frontier regions, so seemingly providing us with valuable insight into the workings and daily operations of select groups of frontier soldiers, even if there is some doubt about how representative this Egyptian evidence is for other frontier armies. Perhaps the most notable collection concerns the 4th-century officer Abinnaeus (Bell, Martin Turner, and Van Berchem 1962). This collection includes letters addressed to Abinnaeus from concerned citizens, and lists of goods for purchase. The Panopolis Archive (Skeat 1964) is also worthy of note, and its two papyri are, among other things, concerned with provisions for the soldiers.

The legal evidence

The legal compilation most relevant for us is the 5th-century *Theodosian Code*. Book seven of the *Theodosian Code* is specifically concerned with military affairs. It includes legislation on military clothing (7.6), recruits (7.13), and river patrols on the Danube (7.17). Laws of relevance appear elsewhere: for example, 5.6 on the estates of soldiers, 6.14 which deals with the counts of military affairs (*comites rei militaris*), and 6.36 on military *peculium* (essentially property). In this collection there are a handful of laws that are especially valuable for the information they contain about frontier soldiers. Novel 24.1 in the *Theodosian Code* is concerned with the return of land to the *limitanei*. This imperial pronouncement, dated to September of 443, was reused in the *Code of Justinian* (11.20). Incidentally, in the aftermath of the conquest of Vandal Africa, Justinian ordered the deployment of *limitanei*, an event captured in a piece of Justinianic legislation found in the *Justinianic Code* (1.27.2.8; cf. Proc. *Wars*, 4.8.21). As with all of the evidence discussed herein, the legal evidence must be read with the specific context of the individual piece of legislation borne in mind (Millar 2006, 7–13).

The *Notitia Dignitatum*

Arguably the most significant single piece of evidence for the organization of the Roman military in late antiquity is the inestimably problematic *Notitia Dignitatum*. It provides a list of all the civil and military offices, including those of the eastern and westerns halves of the empire. It dates to some time before 430, but its function may have been bureaucratic rather than utilitarian (Brennan, pers. comm.). The two halves of the document (eastern and western) are dated differently, with the eastern half dated to around 394, and the western to the 420s, most likely; the document as a whole seems to have been a product of the west (Brennan 1996, 1998a). The *Notitia* contains a vast and multitudinous array of late Roman military regiments, and these often differ in significant ways from the more familiar garrisons of the high empire, who served in the legions and auxiliary units that dotted Rome's frontiers. It also happens to be our most "complete" account of the late Roman Empire's frontier soldiers. Thus, the *Notitia* has been used to elucidate the organization of the armed forces (Hoffman 1969–1970; Brennan 1998b; Scharf 2005; Collins 2012, 38–54; Pollard 2013). Valid concerns have been raised about the text, however, particularly since we are poorly informed about its context (Brennan 1996; Brennan 1998a; Kulikowski 2000). In addition, we are not clear about its purpose; some see it as an ideological document (Brennan 1996), while others prefer to see it as an official document (Jones 1964). Some sort of middle ground is likely the best course of action when it comes to its interpretation (Brennan 1998a), even if serious doubts have been raised about its utility, particularly concerning the western section (Kulikowski 2000).

The evidence as a whole

These are the types of evidence most useful to our understanding of soldiers on the late Roman frontiers. Although select issues with this evidence were highlighted above, taken together, and on the surface, this evidence would seem to provide us with a rich and varied picture of this frontier soldiery. A closer look, however, reveals that while this is undoubtedly true, the material is far more complex than it at first seems.

Frontier armies in late antiquity: The Lower Danube

In the central part of this chapter the focus is on one region, Moesia. It has been chosen, in part, because of the amount of evidence that exists about its military history, both early imperial and late imperial. This is especially true, for example, with respect to the *Notitia*, for the portion concerned with Moesia has been preserved, unlike that for Germany I. A close examination of the evidence for the region illustrates the difficulties of the evidence with respect to late Roman frontier armies.

Legiones *and* **auxiliae** *in early and high imperial* **Moesia**

Across the vast empire the most heavily fortified of regions were Britain, the Rhine, the Danube, and Syria. The survival of thousands of inscriptions (primarily in Latin) combined with a handful of choice passages in the works of the historians Josephus, Tacitus, and Cassius Dio has meant that we are relatively well informed about the disposition of the legions and auxiliary units on those frontiers (and others) throughout the period from Augustus to Severus Alexander.

Much discussion of the organization of imperial-era frontier armies has centred on which units, amongst legions and auxiliaries, were in a region at a given time, and what changes, if any, have taken place.

As regards the legions, for the early and high imperial period we have no less than four lists (of varying quality) that provide the legionary disposition of the empire as a whole at a range of times, from Augustus / Tiberius through to Elagabalus / Severus Alexander. Given our emphasis on late antiquity, it is the last two that are most useful. There is an inscription from Rome, which lists all of the empire's legions (ILS 2288); and there is an account in Cassius Dio's *History* that compares the legionary disposition of the reign of Augustus with that of his own day (Cass. Dio 55.23–24). The existence of these lists, and a host of additional material, such as funerary inscriptions, means that we can chart with some accuracy the movement of legions in and out of the provinces over a 200 or so year span.

Turning to the material of value for the troop dispositions of Roman Moesia towards the end of the 2nd century, the inscription (ILS 2288) from Rome, dated to around 161, gives the following legions for the Moesias: the *legio I Italica*, the *legio V Macedonica*, and the *legio XI Claudia* in Moesia Inferior; the *legio IIII Flavia* and the *legio VII Claudia* were in Moesia Superior. A few decades later, around 220 (between 211 and 222), Cassius Dio provided a comparable, updated list in his *History*; he says that in his day only 19 of the 23 or 25 legions that existed under Augustus were still in action (Cass. Dio 55.23.2). According to him, the legionary disposition of the two Moesias in Dio's lifetime was as follows: the *legio I Italica* and the *legio XI Claudia* in Moesia Inferior; and the *legio IIII Flavia* and the *legio VII Claudia* in Moesia Superior (Cass. Dio 55.23.3–24.1). The legion missing from that list but present in the earlier inscription is the *legio V Macedonica*, which had moved from Moesia Inferior to Dacia (Cass. Dio 55.23.3).

We know a great deal about the auxiliary units of the Moesias too, and in some cases we even know which units were in a province on a specific day. This is due in large part to the survival of the military diplomas, which list all those units that had soldiers eligible for discharge in a province at a particular time. For example, CIL 44 and 45, for Moesia Inferior, are dated to August 12, AD 99, and list 6 *alae* (cavalry wings) and 13 *cohortes* (infantry cohorts) each. In fact, there are at least 75 published diplomas from the Moesias, in varying states of preservation, and as a result we are well informed about the auxiliary garrison of the provinces. Diplomas that detail auxiliary units only cover a period of nearly 100 years; the earliest one for the Moesias dates to AD 75 (RGZM 1 – united Moesia), and the latest one to 161 (RMD 1.55 – Moesia Superior). The information from these diplomas, as well as a handful of additional inscriptions, allows us to establish the auxiliary garrison for the two provinces as a whole, Moesia Inferior and

Table 2.1: Disposition of auxiliaries in the Moesias in AD 138

Moesia Inferior	Moesia Superior
ala I Pannoniorum et Gallorum,	ala I Claudia nova miscellanea,
ala Gallorum Atectorigiana,	ala I Gallorum Flaviana,
ala I Vespasiana Dardanorum,	cohors V Gallorum,
ala I Flavia Gaetulorum,	cohors V Hispanorum,
ala II Hispanorum Aravacorum,	cohors I Montanorum,
cohors I Lusitanorum,	cohors I Antiochensium,
cohors I Flavia Numidarum,	cohors I Cretum,
cohors I Germanorum,	cohors III campestris,
cohors I Bracaraugustanorum,	cohors II Gallorum,
cohors I Lepidiana,	cohors III Brittonum,
cohors II Flavia Brittonum,	cohors I Lusitanorum,
cohors II Chalcidenorum,	cohors I Pannoniorum
cohors II Mattiacorum,	
cohors II Bracaraugustanorum,	
cohors I Cilicum sagittaria,	
cohors I Thracum Syriaca,	
cohors I Claudia Sugambrorum veterana	

Table 2.2: Disposition of auxiliaries in the Moesias in AD 170

Moesia Inferior	Moesia Superior
ala I Pannoniorum et Gallorum,	ala I Claudia nova miscellanea,
ala Gallorum Atectorigiana,	ala I Gallorum Flaviana,
ala I Vespasiana Dardanorum,	cohors II Aurelia nova Sacorum,
ala I Flavia Gaetulorum,	cohors I Aurelia nova Pasinatum,
ala II Hispanorum Aravacorum,	cohors II Aurelia nova milliaria equitata,
cohors I Lusitanorum,	cohors I Aurelia Dardanorum,
cohors I Germanorum,	cohors II Aurelia Dardanorum,
cohors I Bracaraugustanorum,	cohors V Hispanorum,
cohors I Lepidiana,	cohors I Montanorum,
cohors II Flavia Brittonum,	cohors I Antiochensium,
cohors II Chalcidenorum,	cohors I Cretum,
cohors II Mattiacorum,	cohors II Gallorum,
cohors II Bracaraugustanorum,	cohors III Brittonum,
cohors I Cilicum sagittaria,	cohors I Pannoniorum
cohors I Thracum Syriaca,	
cohors I Claudia Sugambrorum veterana	

Moesia Superior, for various points in the first and second centuries. For example, we can determine the auxiliary garrison of the provinces for the years 138 and 170, all the while charting the respective changes in the intervening years, and to a lesser degree the ones that follow. Thus we find the disposition in Table 2.1 for the two Moesias in AD 138 (Whately, forthcoming).

By AD 170 the auxiliary garrison was nearly identical, with the one difference being the absence of the *cohors I Flavia Numidarum*, which had moved to the east, and Lycia and Pamphylia in particular (CIL 16.128; RMD 1.67, 5.438; Matei-Popescu 2010, 225). With respect to Moesia Superior, the cavalry disposition of the province was the same. The infantry cohort disposition, on the other hand, had changed. The *cohors II Aurelia nova Sacorum, cohors I Aurelia nova Pasinatum, cohors II Aurelia nova milliaria equitata, cohors I Aurelia Dardanorum,* and the *cohors II Aurelia Dardanorum* were all new additions, possibly established by Marcus Aurelius (HA *Marc.* 21.7; cf. AE 1952, 191, CIL III.8251, CIL III.14537). The *cohors V Gallorum* and the *cohors I Lusitanorum* had left. In sum, we find the following auxiliary disposition for the two Moesias in AD 170 (Table 2.2):

The wide variety and sheer abundance of evidence from the imperial period means we are well placed to establish organizational change in frontier armies over the course of the early and high imperial periods. The discussion above was just a sample of what this evidence tells us.

Table 2.3: The legions of the Moesias Listed in the Antonine Itinerary

Legion	Location	Reference
legio XIII Gemina	Ratiaria	*It. Ant.* 219.3
legio V Macedonica	Oescus	*It. Ant.* 220.5
the *legio I Italica*	Novae	*It. Ant.* 221.4
legio XI Claudia	Durostorum	*It. Ant.* 223.4
legio I Iovia	Troesmis	*It. Ant.* 225.2
legio II Herculia	Noviodunum	*It. Ant.* 226.1

The regiments of the *legiones, equites*, and *auxiliares* in late antique Moesia

We now shift to the lower Danube in late antiquity. What we find are a number of similarly named units, such as the legions, as well as a host of new and unfamiliar ones. In addition, relative certainty in charting changes in disposition, amongst other things, gives way to uncertainty and complexity as we are forced to grapple with the *Notitia Dignitatum*, in contrast to the evidence from the early empire.

The legiones *in late antique Moesia*

By the 3rd century the kind of evidence that had been so abundant and useful earlier, like the Latin inscriptions, disappear, with the exception of the material (the odd reference in a literary text and a handful of inscriptions) naming the Aurelian cohorts. The only document that tells us anything about the garrison of Moesia in the 3rd century is the problematic *Antonine Itinerary*. This pseudo-gazetteer might originally have been produced during the reign of Caracalla, though in the form that we have it probably dates to the reign of Diocletian, or shortly thereafter. What is relevant for our purposes is the information it includes about legionary emplacement. Thus, among the baffling multitude of roads and sites along the Roman transportation network, it lists the legions based at the relevant locations.

As regards the Moesias, the *Antonine Itinerary* lists the following legions and camps (Table 2.3). Of those legions, the *legiones I Italica* and *XI Claudia* remained stationary, while the *legiones I Iovia* and *II Herculia* were new additions. The *legio V Macedonica* which had moved to Dacia around AD 168 had likely returned to the Moesias following the abandonment of Dacia in AD 271. When it did return to Moesia Inferior it did not go back to its former base at Troesmis, but rather to its earlier Moesian base at Oescus (*Itin. Ant.* 220.5).

The missing legions from the *Antonine Itinerary* are the *legio IIII Flavia* and the *legio VII Claudia*. Additionally, no significance is attached to the two Upper Moesian legionary sites of Singidunum, which itself is absent, and Viminacium. Bojović has demonstrated, however, that the *legio IIII Flavia* was based at Singidunum at least until the reign of the emperor Constantine (Bojović 1996, 66ff). As regards Viminacium, we have a few inscriptions from the end of the 2nd century and beginning of the 3rd century that refer to the legion (IMS II.12; IMS IV.44; CIL III.14507; CIL III.14509). Thus, it is unlikely that the *legio VII Claudia* left its base at Viminacium before the end of Severus Alexander's reign.

The next significant piece of evidence with respect to troop structures is the aforementioned *Notitia Dignitatum*. The garrison of the Moesias is in four sections, all of which are in the *pars Orientis* and under the following generals: the *Dux Scythiae* (*ND or.* 39), the *Dux Moesiae secundae* (*ND or.* 40), the *Dux Moesiae primae* (*ND or.* 41), and the *Dux Daciae ripensis* (*ND or.* 42). These commands correspond to late Roman provinces (Moesia I, Dacia Ripensis, Moesia II, and Scythia Minor). The earlier Moesian legions are still in existence: the *legio I Italica* and the *legio XI Claudia* were in Moesia Secundae (*ND or.* 40.30–35); the *legio IIII Flavia* and the *legio VII Claudia* in Moesia Primae (*ND or.* 41.30–32). There were additional legions in Dacia ripensis, the *legio V Macedonica* and the *legio XIII Gemina* (*ND or.* 42.31–39), and Scythia Minor, the *legio II Herculia* and the *legio I Iovia* (*ND or.* 39.29–35). As noted above, two of the additional legions had been based in Dacia (across the Danube), and when the territory was abandoned in the second half of the 3rd century (around 271), they were shifted to the newly created province of Dacia ripensis (*ND or.* 42).

The addition of four legions seems straightforward enough. There are complications, however, for the *legio V Macedonica* and the *legio XIII Gemina* from Dacia ripensis are both listed under the *comes limitis Aegypti* (*ND or.* 38.14–15). Details such as this reveal a lot about changes in the legions. Around AD 295 a vexillation (detachment) of Balkan legions was deployed in Egypt, and it seems likely that these two legions were part of this detachment (P.Oxy 43; Pollard 2013, 14–15). Those legionary detachments then kept the title and stayed put, an implausible act a century or more earlier. With only the *Notitia* to go on, we would not have been able to guess when those two legions moved to Egypt. The same could be said for the move of the *legiones V Macedonica* and *XIII Gemina* to Dacia ripensis around 271 (Eutr. 9.15). There are also issues with the legions that had been in the Moesias before late antiquity, such as the *legio I Italica*. A *legio I Italica* composed of *pseudocomitatenses* appeared further east serving under the *Magister Militum per Orientem* (*ND or.* 7.53). Thus, yet another unit must have been transferred to the east, and at some point become part of this particular field army. This points towards the fragmentation of the original *legio I Italica*. Getting back to Moesia II, the legion was based in two different places, Novae and Sexagintaprista (*ND or.* 40.30–31, 32). As for the new legions, they are usually attributed to Diocletian. Tomlin (2008, 154) notes, "the *Ioviani* and *Herculiani*

Table 2.4: The legions in the Notitia Dignitatum

Legion	Location
legio I Iovia	Noviodunum and Accissum
legio II Herculia	Troesmis, Axiopolis, and Iprosmis
legio I Italica	Novae and Sexagintaprista
legio XI Claudia	Durostorum and Transmarisca
legio IV Flavia	Singidunum
legio VII Claudia	Viminacium and Cuppae
legio V Macedonica	Variana, Cebrus, and Sucidava
legio XIII Geminae	Aegeta, Transdrobeta, Burgus Novus, Zernis, and Ratiaria

were named after the gods of Diocletian and Maximian". This gives us a *terminus post quem* of 284 for the creation of the *legiones I Iovia* and *II Herculia* (cf. Veg. *Mil.* 1.57; Tomlin 2000, 161). Furthermore, the presence of the two legions in the *Antonine Itinerary* lends some credence to this supposition.

If we take stock of the legions as depicted in the *Notitia*, what we are left with is the image of a regiment that had fragmented in no small measure. While many familiar units remained – the *I Italica* and the *XI Claudia* for example – much had changed. Several of the legions, including both those that had been in the region for hundreds of years and those that were more recent arrivals, had fragmented. Thus, the legionary disposition of the region was as described in (Table 2.4).

There are no less than 20 locations for only eight legions. The evidence of the *Antonine Itinerary* suggests only a 100 years or so earlier these legions had individual bases – they had not yet been split up. What is more, one of those legions, or a part, was redesignated to a field role, for, as noted above, there was a *legio I Italica* of *pseudocomitatenses*. This type of legion was first reported in 365 and the title "*pseudocomitatenses*" itself was given to frontier legions that became field ones (Elton 2007, 275–276; cf. Brennan 2007, 212). Thus, where before we had one legion, with detachments possibly deployed for other tasks in the vicinity and beyond (RMR 63; AE 1984, 805), we now had several legions with the same name, strewn across the region and beyond, each led by its own prefect.

There is one further pair of legions which might have been based in the region in the 4th century, and which are referred to in the *Notitia*. Under the command of the *magister militum per Thracias* were two *legiones comitatenses*, the *Constantini Dafnenses* and the *Ballistarii Dafnenses* (*ND or.* 8.45, 46). Although no longer part of the frontier armies of the region, their very names suggest that they once had been, for there was a site across the Danube from Transmarisca called Dafne. When these units were withdrawn is another matter, and not something we can determine (Brennan 1980, 556).

The equites, *and* auxiliares *in late antique Moesia*

In the earlier Roman imperial period the legions, of course, were not the only regiments operating on Rome's frontiers. There were others, namely the auxiliaries, who are absent from the Moesian section of the *Notitia*. The auxiliaries had either disappeared, or become something else, and it is by examining these units that we get a clearer image of the change in the organization of the frontier armies. Indeed, a glance at the units for the respective sections of the Moesias will highlight the seeming abundance of new and unfamiliar units (Table 2.5).

Excluding the legions, the *Notitia* lists 15 regiments in Scythia, 17 in Moesia II, 20 in Moesia I, and 18 in Dacia ripensis. What can we infer from these data?

In this table we find all sorts of unfamiliar regiments, including a number of *cunei equitum*, variously named units of *milites*, as well as variously named units of *auxilia*. The only signs of the familiar *alae* and *cohortes* appear as supplementary units listed under Moesia II, namely the *cohors quarta Gallorum* in Rhodope (*ND or.* 40.46), and the *cohors prima Aureliana* and the *cohors tertia Valeria Bacarum* in Thrace (*ND or.* 40.48–49). Two of these *cohortes* might have been in the region before, for there was a *cohors I Bracaraugustanorum* (the closest equivalent to the *cohors tertia Valeria Bacarum*) based in Moesia Inferior, and all of the *cohortes Aureliae* (the closest equivalent to the *cohors prima Aureliana*) based in Moesia Superior. With respect to the regiment of Gauls, there had been *cohortes IIII Gallorum* in Raetia (CIL 16.94, 117, 183) and Tingitana (CIL 16.161, 165) during the high imperial period. By and large, however, we are dealing with new and different units; the majority of the *alae* and *cohortes* of the earlier empire are gone, and this despite the fact that they feature in a number of other provinces, with several *alae* based in Egypt (*ND or.* 28.24–34), several *cohortes* based in Syria (*ND or.* 32–35), and several in Britain (*ND occ.* 40), for example. Additionally, the new units of *cunei*, *milites*, and *auxilia* are not simply renamed versions of the older units, for but one of these new units preserves an element of the nomenclature of the old units: the several *cunei equitum sagittariorum* were archers, like the earlier *cohors I Cilicum sagittaria*.

Table 2.5: The units listed in the Notitia Dignitatum for the Moesias

Dux Scythiae (*or.* 39)	Dux Moesiae Secundae (*or.* 40)	Dux Moesiae Primae (*or.* 41)	Dux Daciae Ripensis (*or.* 42)
cun eq scutariorum,	cun eq scutariorum,	cun eq Constantiacorum,	cun eq Dalmatarum Fortensium,
cun eq solensium,	cun eq solensium,	cun eq promotorum,	cun eq Dalmatarum Divitensium,
cun eq stablesianorum,	cun eq armigerorum,	cun eq sagittariorum,	cun eq scutariorumm,
cun eq catafractariorum,	cun eq II armigerorum,	cun eq Dalmatarum,	cun eq Dalmatarum,
cun eq armigerorum,	cun eq stablesianorum,	aux Reginenses,	cun eq stablesianorum,
cun eq Arcadum,	mil praeuentores,	aux Tricornienses,	cun eq Constantinianorum,
mil nauclarii,	mil Constantini,	aux Novenses,	aux Miliarensium,
mil superuentores,	mil Dacisci,	aux Margense,	aux I Daciscorum,
mil Scythici,	mil III nauclarii,	aux Cuppense,	aux Crispitiense,
mil II Constantini,	mil novenses,	aux Gratianense,	aux Mariensium,
mil I Constantiani,	mil I Moesiaci,	aux Taliatense,	aux Claustrinorum,
mil V Constantiani,	mil Moesiaci,	aux Aureomontanum,	aux II Daciscorum,
mil I Gratianenses	mil IV Constantiani,	mil exploratorum ,	mil exploratorum
	mil Cimbriani,	mil Vincentiensium	
	mil nauclarii altinenses		

The complexity of the evidence and the difficulty it poses to our understanding of frontier army organization is even more apparent when we look closer at unit nomenclature, which provides important clues to the earlier imperial units (Meyer 2013, 3–11). For the late imperial regiment names, while useful, can be difficult to interpret (cf. Tomlin 2008, 154), even when the meaning of the name itself might seem to be comparatively straightforward. Case in point, there are two units of *nauclarii* on the lower Danube, the *Milites nauclarii* from Scythia (*ND or.* 39.20) and the *Milites nauclarii Altinenses* from Moesia II (*ND or.* 40.28), and their name *nauclarii* might indicate that the soldiers in question were marines, if the name is an abbreviated form of *nauicularius*, "belonging to the navy" (Souter 1949, 263). There is, potentially, some comparative evidence. Book 7 of the *Theodosian Code*, the portion of the compilation concerned with military affairs, contains a piece of legislation, title 17, specifically concerned with "River Patrol Craft on the Danube" and dated to Jan. 28, 412 (cf. Elton 1996, 100), around the time of the publication of the *Notitia Dignitatum*; so our *nauclarii* marines might be identified with these, even though no mention is made of the soldiers or the particular bases. On the other hand, these two vague references, one to soldiers in the *Notitia* and the other to ships in the *Theodosian Code*, do not match up as easily as we might like. The *Code* deals with the fleet, while the *Notitia*, in these instances, deals with naval soldiers (marines). If there is a connection between the *Notitia* and the *Code* with respect to naval matters then, it is more likely between the fleets mentioned at Margus and Viminacium under the *Dux Moesiae primae* and the *limes Mysiacus* of the *Code*, and the fleet at Inplateypegiis under the *Dux Scythiae* and the Scythia of the *Code*.

Sometimes the *Notitia* explicitly tells us – via nomenclature – what kinds of soldiers (infantry vs. cavalry) made up these regiments; in other instances we have to infer this from their names or from other sources. The *cunei equitum*, for instance, were cavalry, and of the 67 non-legionary regiments, 29 were cavalry (*cunei equitum*). Of those 29 cavalry regiments, there is room for greater specificity with a handful. In Scythia we find a *cuneus equitum catafractariorum* (*ND or.* 39.16), and in Moesia I we find two *cunei equitum sagittariorum* (*ND or.* 41.14, 17). That is one unit of cataphracts, heavily armoured horsemen (and their horses), and two units of horse-archers, both soldier types that became increasingly common in late antiquity (Elton 2007, 294–295). After those three units, matters become muddled. Other possible examples of specialized cavalry might include the regiments of *cunei equitum scutariorum* (*ND or.* 39.12; 40.11–12, 16; 41.15, 20), *cunei equitum stablesianorum* (*ND or.* 39.14, 15; 40.17; 41.19), and *cunei equitum armigerorum* (*ND or.* 39.17; 40.14). Both the *armigeri* and the *scutarii* were imperial bodyguards from the *scholae palatinae*, whom Constantine had replaced the praetorians with (Elton 2007, 280). We are less certain about the so-called *stablesiani* (cf. Rance 2012). There are also the *cunei equitum promotorum* in Moesia I (*ND or.* 41.13, 16), which were legionary cavalry that had been detached from their parent units in the 4th century (Brennan 1980, 554; Brennan 1998b; Elton 2007, 279).

Having covered the cavalry regiments, that leaves the infantry regiments (generally called *auxiliares*), again legionaries aside. These *auxiliares* were split between two groups of regiments, the *auxilia*, found in Scythia and Moesia II, and *milites,* found in Moesia I and Dacia ripensis, both likely infantry (Elton 1996, 99). These in turn, like their cavalry counterparts, had an array of names, though in their case there is considerable more certainty. The majority of the names pertain to either a people or a place in a similar way to their imperial era forerunners, the auxiliary *cohortes*. Thus, the *milites Scythici* (*ND or.* 39.22) and the *milites Dacisci* (*ND or.* 40.21) are likely named after people, the Scythians, and Dacians, while the *auxilium Novenses* (*ND or.* 41.23) and the *auxilium Crispitiense* (*ND or.* 42.25) are named after places, Ad Novas and Crispitia respectively. It should be noted, however, that we seem to have their unofficial names, which incorporate the location of the garrisons, rather than the official ones (Elton 2007, 272); in those instances, without independent evidence, we cannot hope to recover their official titles.

Regiments with vaguer names still include the *milites superventores* (*ND or.* 39.21) and the *milites praeventores* (*ND or.* 40.19), whose identities are uncertain, and who both feature in Ammianus Marcellinus, though only in passing (Amm. Marc. 18.9.3). There are also the *auxilium Miliarensium*, the *auxilium Mariensium*, and the *auxilium Claustrinorum*, all found in Dacia ripensis (*ND or.* 42.23, 26, 27). The first of that group would seem to be associated with the earlier auxiliaries classified as *milliaria*, such as the *cohors I Flavia Hispanorum milliaria* attested in Moesia Superior on September 16, AD 93 (CIL 16.39). These units were composed of around 1000 men rather than the more typical 500 of the earlier imperial era (called quingenary) (cf. Rankov 2007, 54). Perhaps the title *Miliarensium* refers to the size of the unit (*c.*1000 men) in late antiquity as well. There are several other such examples throughout the *Notitia*, such as the *Ala secunda Miliarensis* in Arabia (*Not. dign. or.* 37.28). The *auxilium Mariensium* and the *auxilium Claustrinorum* are harder to pin down. These names might refer to a people, though if so – a remote possibility – the location or characteristics of the *Mariensium* and the *Claustrinorum* are unknown.

The chronology of garrison changes in late antique Moesia

The identities of the units aside, we still need to account for the chronology of the changes in the regiments in the region, even if some attention has already been devoted to changes to the legions. As noted, the epigraphic habit changed, and so the inscriptions that were invaluable for the history of the legions and auxiliary units in the imperial era do not exist. Furthermore, some imperial era historians also provided registers of the empire's legions (Tac. *Ann.* 4.5; Cass. Dio 55.23–24). However, as important as the late antique historians like Ammianus are for specific details of battles, campaigns, and wars, they are far less useful when it comes to structures. Ammianus regularly refers to *legiones* and *auxiliares*, but only in the most general of terms (cf. Amm. Marc. 14.11.15, 30.2.6), and he is the only extant historian who discusses pertinent matters (military affairs) in any detail.

We could also look for signs of change in other evidence, such as the papyrological evidence and the textual evidence. With respect to the former, there is an aforementioned papyrus which attests to changes in the disposition of the regiments in Egypt that has some bearing on the situation on the Danube at the end of the 3rd century (P.Oxy. 43; Pollard 2013, 14–15). With respect to the latter, there is the evidence of John the Lydian (mid-6th century), who claims that Constantine took troops from Scythia and Moesia and transferred them to Asia (*Mag.* 2.10); this would seem to support the slightly earlier (early 6th century) claims of Zosimus (2.34). It might even be worth reconsidering the *Res Gestae* of Ammianus, and in particular because of his account of the campaign and battle of Adrianople in 378. This battle had a marked impact on the late Roman populace (Lenski 1997), but also on the armies involved, with nearly two-thirds of the Roman forces involved perishing on the day (Amm. Marc. 13.18–19; cf. Lenski 2002, 339). Hoffmann (1969, 449–457) has speculated that 16 units from the eastern empire were destroyed, and that a further 6,000–12,000 men from other units perished. Much of the defeated Roman army, however, was likely drawn from the field army (*legiones comitatenses*, among others).

Another way to address chronology is to focus on the history of generic frontier troops as a whole like *limitanei* (also called *burgarii*, *castellani*, and *riparenses* / *rivarienses* – Elton 1996, 99; Elton 2007, 273–274), and then to apply this to specific regiments or regions. Late in the 1st century, the legions and auxiliary units became increasingly stationary, a process that had essentially been completed by the 2nd century. With these regiments now stationary, vexillations were often dispatched on campaigns rather than entire units, and it is the troops who were left behind that likely evolved into the *limitanei* (Nicasie 1998, 20). How we go from the stationary units based on the frontiers in the 2nd and early 3rd centuries to the clearly defined border troops of the middle of 4th century, however, is less clear.

The term *limitanei* itself is used in a handful of 4th-, 5th-, and 6th-century texts (discussed by Isaac 1988, 139–146). The writer of the *Historia Augusta* refers to *limitanei* in the context of the 3rd century (*HA Pescennius Niger* 7.7, *Sev. Alex.* 18.58.4, *Probus* 14.7, *Aurelianus* 38.4; Nicasie 1998, 18). As noted above, Zosimus alluded to Diocletian's stationing of units of *limitanei* throughout the empire (Zos. 2.34), and Malalas claimed that Diocletian stationed units of *limitanei* throughout the eastern frontier. There is also the account provided by the Latin panegyricist Eumenius (late 3rd century), who refers to Diocletian's use of border troops (*Pan. Lat.* 4.18.4; Isaac 1988, 141; Richardot 2005, 171). Festus, in his *Breviarium* (fourth quarter of the 4th century), claims that Galerius replenished his depleted troops in the midst of his war with the Sasanid Persians with *limitanei* from Dacia (Festus *Brev.* 25). Collectively, these disparate sources suggest that the border troops had been conceived by the end of the reign of Diocletian.

Ammianus Marcellinus refers to *limites* several times, but does not explicitly refer to *limitanei*. On the other hand, in his description of the emperor Julian's ill-fated expedition against Persia in 363, he notes that he brought along the commander of a limitanean unit, Victor the *Dux Osdruenae* (he means Osrhoene; *Dux Osrhoenae*, *ND or.* 35), and presumably his accompanying *limitanei* (Amm. Marc. 24.1.2). A few sections later he refers to the *Dux Aegypti* (Amm. Marc. 24.1.9; cf. *ND or.* 28 – *Comes limitis Aegypti*, 31 – *dux Thebaidos*). There is also some legislation in the *Theodosian Code* that refers to *limitanei*, either using the term specifically or a broadly comparable term. *Limitanei milites* are mentioned in a law published in the *Codex Theodosianus* dated to 363 (*Cod. Theod.* 12.1.56). A law from 40 years earlier (325) records *riparenses* (*Cod. Theod.* 7.20.4), soldiers that had the same function as *limitanei*. The term "*limitanei*" itself is conspicuously absent from the eastern section of the *Notitia*. In the western section it features primarily in regard to the troops in Africa. Thus, *limitanei* are specifically referred to as under the command of the *comes Africae* (*ND occ.* 25.20) and the *comes Tingitaniae* (*ND occ.* 26.12). All those units discussed so far from the *Notitia Dignitatum*, however, should be considered *limitanei*, even if they are not expressly called that, given the placement of a *dux* or *comes* in command over them.

It would also seem to make sense to look for clues within the *Notitia Dignitatum*; however, trying to determine changes in garrison on the basis of the *Notitia* alone is impossible, especially if chronological certainty of the sort we sometimes have for the imperial era is desired. Although we might have a good idea when the eastern section of the *Notitia* was compiled, namely around 394, it is often unclear whether what we have is a snapshot of that specific moment in time, or something more synchronic. The situation with respect to the *auxiliares* and *equites* in Moesias is a case in point. That two of the units of cavalry wedges (*cunei equitum*) and four of the units of *milites* (*Milites primi Constantiani, Milites secundi Constantini, Milites quarti Constantiani,* and *Milites quinti Constantiani*) bear some form of "Constantine" in their names might point towards their establishment during the reign of Constantine; it might, just as well, point towards the renaming of earlier units. On the other hand, the name Constantini might be associated with Constantius II, or Constantius Chlorus, for that matter – a name like "Constantiani" is rarely enough to go on. This name does not necessarily mean that the comparable units from the region were established, or at least relocated to the region, at that time. If we had an ancient register of the auxiliary garrison of Moesia Superior for 170 we would have the same problem: a handful of units (possibly) ascribed to Marcus Aurelius, and many more that are not. In that case we know that the other units had moved to the province much earlier and so were not also creations of Marcus Aurelius.

What about the other similarly named regiments, namely those named after other emperors? Other such names include forms of *Maximianae, Diocletianae, Valentianae,* and *Theodosianae*. With respect to the *Maximianae*, there is one under the *magister militum per Thracias* (*ND or.* 8.36), and another serving under the *dux Thebaidos* (*ND or.* 31.37). There are, for example, two units of *Diocletianae* serving under the *dux Thebaidos* (*ND or.* 31.33, 38), and one serving under the *dux Foenicis* (*ND or.* 32.34). There are a host of units of *Valentianae*, with at least two found in Arabia (*ND or.* 37.29, 30), and one in Armenia (*ND or.* 38.37), for example. There are also a number of *Theodosianae*, including two under the *magister militum per Thracias* (*ND or.* 8.27, 32), and four in Armenia (*ND or.* 38.18, 19, 32, 33). There are none of these listed in the Moesias, however, with the only command somewhat relevant being that of the *magister militum per Thracias*, and marginally so at best. Thus, while it might be possible in some provinces to determine approximately when regiments were transferred on this sort of information, such as the *ala Theodosiana* and the *ala Arcadiana* in Egypt (*ND or.* 28.20, 21; Pollard 2013; 28), this is not always the case.

In some instances, to determine the history of a unit's movements a consideration of other parts of the *Notitia* is in order, particularly when there are apparent discrepancies, as is the case with the *promoti*. As noted above, there were two *cunei equitum promotorum* in Moesia I (*ND or.* 41.13, 16). In fact, there are more of these *promoti* in other Danubian provinces: there are three in Pannonia II (*ND occ.* 32.25, 30, 38), two in Valeria (*ND occ.* 33.30, 36), and two in Pannonia I (*ND occ.* 34.16, 22). The absence of *promoti* in Scythia, Moesia II, and Dacia ripensis might be tied to the *promoti Illyriciani* found throughout the near east (*ND or.* 33.17, 34.19, 35.16, 36.20, 37.15), especially given the presence of a number of *promoti idigenae* (*ND or.* 33.19, 27; 34.23, 24; 35.18, 19; 36.23, 24; 37.18, 19) in addition to these *promoti Illyriciani*. The *promoti* were likely transferred from the lower Danube to the near east at some point in the 4th century (or at the very end of the 3rd century), with Brennan suggesting that it happened in the context of Galerius' campaigns against Persia (Brennan 1998b, 242–243).

Focusing on periods of known change across the late Roman military is another way to approach this. Thus, we might attribute most of the changes in deployment to Diocletian or Constantine, and the abundance of *Milites Constantini* (and the like) makes such a solution all the more attractive; moreover, a few ancient authors refer to the changes in Roman military organization carried about by those emperors. Zosimus credits Diocletian with solidifying the defences of the empire's forts and cities, and charges Constantine with allowing the barbarians to invade (Zos. 2.34.1–2). Malalas alludes to something similar, crediting Diocletian with fortifying the eastern frontier from Egypt to Persia in the north, and stationing *limitanei* under *duces* in those fortifications (Malalas 12.40). The other significant period of change came during the reigns of the emperors Valentinian and Valens (Amm. Marc. 26.5.1–3; Themistius *Or.* 10.136d–8b; Zos. 4.3.4–5; CIL 3.7494; AE 1978, 716; cf. Lenski 2002, 375; Whitby 2007, 142). The two emperors divvied up the empire's military, and a number of attempts have been made to explain what happened (Hoffmann 1969/1970, 122–130; Tomlin 1972; cf. Barlow and Brennan 2001, 238). Though there are problems with these ancient accounts – it is not as simple as "Diocletian emphasized the frontier while Constantine emphasized the mobile command" (cf. Brennan 2007) – it would make sense to attribute some changes in the frontier armies to the actions of these particular emperors.

The problems with determining precise chronology of changing unit attributions and dispositions would seem to be insurmountable, and this has been reflected in the scholarship, with some scholars suggesting that the Danube garrison as presented in the *Notitia* dated to before the reign of Valentinian (Hoffmann 1970, 151–152, n. 323), and others seeing it as a reflection of the garrison in the last decade of the 4th century (Zahariade 1988, 21–27, 181–185, 192; cf. Liebeschuetz 2007, 102). Try as we might, the evidence does not allow, with few exceptions, greater chronological certainty of the sort we had for the earlier imperial era.

Conclusion: Frontier fortresses and the case of el-Lejjūn

The aim of this paper has been to elucidate the complexity of late Roman military history by way of a discussion of the frontier armies of the period from 250 to 400, with a particular emphasis on the evidence, especially the *Notitia Dignitatum*. In addition, we have sought to address how this evidence shapes our picture of those armies, especially in relation to what we know about the earlier imperial-era Roman military.

To this point we have excluded the issue of the frontier bases presented in the *Notitia Dignitatum*. Some locations we know, others we do not, and in those cases it is often nearly impossible to do so. For a comparative example, we can look to late Roman Jordan and the southern frontier under the command of the *Dux Arabiae*, especially the fort of el-Lejjūn. El-Lejjūn was built in the late 3rd / early 4th century (Parker 2006, 538–552). Although we are well informed about the physical remains of the site thanks to the detailed excavation reports (Parker 2006), we are a little less certain about the identity and the nature of its inhabitants, the soldiers.

Most scholars accept that a unit of *limitanei*, the *legio IV Martia*, was based there (Parker 2006, 542–543). The evidence, however, is far from conclusive, for the history of the *legio IV Martia* is obscure. The unit does not appear in the aforementioned passage above from Cassius Dio that lists the legions of his time (44.23.2–55.24.4). Hoffmann (1969, 173–176; 1970, 69, n. 589) suggested that the legion might have been a creation of Galerius based on the similarity of its name, Martia, to Galerius' protective deity, Mars. Jumping ahead nearly 100 years, the legion is listed in the *Notitia Dignitatum* under the command of a prefect, who in turn is under the command of the *Dux Arabiae* (*ND or.* 37), and its base is given as Betthorus, which is otherwise unknown. At el-Lejjūn itself no evidence has been found to identify the unit based there with the *legio IV Martia*; rather, the evidence is circumstantial.

There is an inscription from Azraq (Jordan), just over 200km distant from el-Lejjūn, probably dated to the 290s (Speidel 1987, 217), on which six legions are mentioned including the *legio III Cyrenaica*, also listed under the *Dux Arabiae*, as well as a number of sites in the region, but not the *IV Martia*. Although hardly conclusive, the inscription implies that the *IV Martia* arrived in Arabia at some point in the 4th century. As regards the connection between Betthorus and el-Lejjūn, this hinges, at least in part, on the size of the site of el-Lejjūn, and the lack of an alternative site to identify Betthorus with. The modern name, el-Lejjūn, goes back to at least the 19th century, and alludes to the site's Roman origins (Kennedy 2004, 154). Its size is commensurate with one of the largest military sites in Jordan, Udruh, which we now know housed the *legio VI Ferrata* during the tetrarchy (Kennedy and Falahat 2008). If Udruh housed a legion then there is every reason to suppose that el-Lejjūn did too, rather than an unnamed auxiliary (or other) unit. Given the absence of another such site, el-Lejjūn would seem to be the most plausible to identify Betthorus with.

If we turn back to the lower Danube, we find plenty of comparative examples of identified sites and known garrisons, known sites without known garrisons, and known garrisons without known sites. For example, on the one hand Axiopolis (*ND or.* 39.21), Troesmis (*ND or.* 39.23), and Noviodunum (*ND or.* 32) and their garrisons (the *milites superventores*, the *milites secondi Constantini*, and the *legio primae Iovia*, among others) are known. On the other hand, the modern location of Cimbrianis (*ND or.* 40.27) is not known, even if its garrison is (*milites Cimbriani*; *ND or.* 40.27; cf. Ivanov 2012, 24–26). The material evidence and the textual/documentary evidence do not always fit together as neatly as we would like (cf. Whately 2013, 101–102), which further complicates our picture of frontier organization in the late Roman military.

There are close to 1000 regiments listed in the *Notitia*, and we have only been focusing on a select part of that total. Thus, whether any of this discussion is applicable to the wider empire and other frontiers is another matter. In some cases, as alluded to above, gaps in the *Notitia* itself make this difficult. In other cases, the information is comparable and so we are in a much better position.

The focus was on frontier armies. The conscious decision was taken to exclude other elements of the late Roman military that would have been based in the region such as the praesental army (Whitby 2007, 144), not to mention the armies of the *magister militum per Illyricum* and the *magister militum per Thracias* (*ND or.* 8, 9), which might have been stationed at sites such as Odessus, Marcianopolis, Naissus, Serdica, and Philippopolis (Whitby 2007, 144). These would only have added to the complex picture of the frontier armies in late antiquity that we now have.

Bibliography

Barlow, J. and Brennan, P. (2001) Tribuni Scholarum Palatinarum c. A.D. 353–364: Ammianus Marcellinus and the *Notitia Dignitatum*. *The Classical Quarterly* 51, 237–254.

Bell, H. I., Martin, V., Turner, E. G. and Van Berchem, D. (eds) (1962) *The Abinnaeus Archive: Papers of a Roman Officer in the Reign of Constantius II*. Oxford, Oxford University Press.

Bojović, D. (1996) Le Camp de la Légion IV Flavia à Singidunum. In P. Petrović (ed.) *Roman Limes on the Middle and Lower Danube*, 53–68. Belgrade, Archaeological Institute.

Brennan, P. (1980) Combined legionary detachments as artillery units in late-Roman Danubian bridgehead dispositions. *Chiron* 10, 553–567.

Brennan, P. (1996) The *Notitia Dignitatum*. In C. Nicolet (ed.) *Les Litteratures Techniques dans l'antiquité Romaine*, 147–178. Geneva, Fondation Hardt.

Brennan, P. (1998a) A User's Guide to the *otitia Dignitatum*: the Case of the *dux Armeniae*. *Antichthon* 32, 34–49.

Brennan, P. (1998b) Divide and fall: the separation of legionary cavalry and the fragmentation of the Roman Empire. In T. W. Hillard, R. A. Kearsley, C. V. E. Nixon, and A. M. (eds) *Ancient History in a Modern University*, 238–244. Cambridge, William Eerdmans.

Brennan, P. (2007) Zosimos 2.34.1 and "the Constantinian reform"; using Johannes Lydos to expose an insidious fabrication. In A. Lewin and P. Pellegrini (ed.) *The Late Roman Army in the Near East from Diocletian to the Arab Conquest*, 211–218. BAR International Series 1717, Oxford, Archaeopress.

Coello, T. (1996) *Unit Sizes in the Late Roman Army*. BAR International Series 645, Oxford, Archaeopress.

Collins, R. (2012) *Hadrian's Wall and the End of Empire: The Roman Frontier in the 4th and 5th Centuries*. London, Routledge.

Elton, H. (1996) *Warfare in Roman Europe AD 350–425*. Oxford, Oxford University Press.

Elton, H. (2007) Military forces. In P. Sabin, H. Van Wees, and M. Whitby (eds) *The Cambridge History of Greek and Roman Warfare. Volume II: Rome from the Late Republic to the Late Empire*, 270–309. Cambridge, Cambridge University Press.

Fiema, Z. T. (2007) The Byzantine military in the Petra papyri – a summary. In A. S. Lewin and P. Pellegrini (eds) *The Late Roman Army in the Near East from Diocletian to the Arab Conquest*, 313–319. Oxford, Archaeopress.

Fornara, C. W. (1983) *The Nature of History in Ancient Greece and Rome*. Berkeley, University of California Press.

Gardner, A. (2007) *Soldiers and Society in Late Roman Britain*. Walnut Creek, CA, Left Coast Press.

Hannestad, K. (1960) Les forces militaires d'après la guerre Gothique de Procope. *Classica et Mediaevalia* 21, 136–183.

Hoffman, D. (1969–1970) *Das Spätromische Bewegungsheer und die Notitia Dignitatum*. Düsseldorf, Rheinland-Verlag.

Isaac, B. (1988) The meaning of the terms Limes and Limintanei. *The Journal of Roman Studies* 78, 125–147.

Ivanov, R. (2012) The Roman Limes in Bulgaria (1st – 6th C. AD). In L. Vagalinski, N. Sharankov, and S. Torbatov (eds.) *The Lower Danube Roman Limes (1st – 6th C. AD)*, 23–42. Sofia, National Achaeological Institute with Museum, Bulgarian Academy of Sciences.

Jones, A. H. M. (1964) *The Later Roman Empire 284–602*. Oxford, Oxford University Press.

Kennedy, K. (2004) *The Roman Army in Jordan*, 2nd edition. London, The British Academy.

Kennedy, K. and Falahat, H. (2008) *Castra Legionis VI Ferratae*: a building inscription for the legionary fortress at Udruh near Petra. *Journal of Roman Archaeology* 21, 150–169.

Kraemer, C. J. (1958) *Excavations at Nessana, volume 3: the Non-Literary Papyri*. Princeton, Princeton University Press.

Kulikowski, M. (2000) The *Notitia Dignitatum* as a historical source. *Historia* 49, 358–377.

Lenski, N. (1997) Initium mali Romano imperio: contemporary reactions to the Battle of Adrianople. *Transactions of the American Philological Association* 127, 129–168.

Lenski, N. (2002) *Failure of Empire: Valens and the Roman State in the 4th c. A.D*. Berekely, University of California Press.

Liebeschuetz, W. (2007) The lower Danube region under pressure: from Valens to Heraclius. In A. G. Poulter (ed.) *The Transition to Late Antiquity on the Danube and Beyond*, 101–134. Oxford, Oxford University Press.

Matei-Popescu, F. (2010) *The Roman Army in Moesia Inferior*. Bucharest, Conphys Publishing House.

Meyer, A. (2013) *The Creation, Composition, Service and Settlement of Roman Auxiliary Units Raised on the Iberian Peninsula*. Oxford, Archaeopress.

Millar, F. (2006) *A Greek Roman Empire*. Berkeley, University of California Press.

Mommsen, T. and P. M. Meyer (1905) *Theodosiani Libri XVI*. Berlin, Deutsche Akademie der Wissenschaften.

Müller, A. (1905) Militaria aus Ammianus Marcellinus. *Philologus* 64, 573–632.

Müller, A. (1912) Das Heer Justinians nach Procop und Agathias. *Philologus* 71, 101–138.

Nicasie, M. J. (1998) *Twilight of Empire: the Roman Army from the Reign of Diocletian Until the Battle of Adrianople*. Amsterdam, J. C. Giegen.

Parker, S. T. (ed.) (2006) *The Roman Frontier in Central Jordan: Final Report on the* Limes Arabicus *Project, 1980–1989*. Washington, Dumbarton Oaks.

Pharr, C. (trans.) (1952) *The Theodosian Code*. Princeton, Princeton University Press.

Pollard, N. (2013) *Imperatores castra dedicaverunt*: Security, Army Bases, and Military Dispositions in Later Roman Egypt

(Later Third–Fourth Century). *The Journal of Late Antiquity* 6, 3–36.

Rance, P. (2012) The Third Equites Stablesiani at Cyrrhus. *Chiron* 42, 345–358.

Rankov, B. (2007). Military forces. In P. Sabin, H. Van Wees, and M. Whitby (eds.) *The Cambridge History of Greek and Roman Warfare. Volume II: Rome from the Late Republic to the Late Empire*, 30–75. Cambridge, Cambridge University Press.

Richardot, P. (2005) *La Fin de l'Armée Romaine 284–476*. Paris, Economica.

Sarantis, A. (forthcoming) *The Balkans During the Reign of Justinian*. Cambridge, Francis Cairns.

Scharf, R. (2005) *Der Dux Mogontiacensis und die Notitia Dignitatum*. Berlin, Walter de Gruyter.

Skeat, T. K. (1964) *Papyri from Panopolis in the Chester Beatty Library, Dublin*. Dublin, Chester Beatty Monographs.

Souter, A. (1949) *A Glossary of Later Latin to 600 A. D.* Oxford, Oxford University Press.

Speidel, M. (1987) The rise of the mercenaries in the third century. *Tyche* 2, 191–201.

Tomlin, R. (1972) *Seniores-Iuniores* in the late Roman field army. *American Journal of Philology* 93, 253–278.

Tomlin, R. (2000) The legions in the late empire. In R. J. Brewer (ed.) *Roman Frontiers and Their Fortresses*, 159–178. London / Cardiff, Society of Antiquaries of London.

Tomlin, R. (2008) A. H. M. Jones and the army of the 4th C. In D. M. Gwynn (ed.) *A.H.M. Jones and the Later Roman Empire*, 143–165. Leiden, Brill.

Trombley, F. (1997) War and society in rural Syria c. 502–613 A.D.: observations on the epigraphy. *Byzantine and Modern Greek Studies* 21, 154–209.

Van Berchem, D. (1952) *L'Armée de Dioclétien et la Réforme Constantinienne*. Paris, Imprimerie Nationale.

Whately, C. (forthcoming A) *Battles and Generals:Combat, Culture, and Didacticism in Procopius* Wars. Leiden, Brill.

Whately, C. (forthcoming B) Dispositions and strategy in the Moesias from Trajan to Commodus. In *Proceedings of Limes Congress XXII*.

Whately, C. (2013) War in Late Antiquity: secondary works, literary sources and material evidence. In A. Sarantis and N. Christie (eds.) *War and Warfare in Late Antiquity: Current Perspectives*, 101–151. Leiden, Brill.

Whitby, M. (1995) Recruitment in Roman armies from Justinian to Heraclius (*ca.* 565–615). In A. Cameron (ed.) *The Byzantine and Early Islamic Near East III: States, Resources, and Armies*, 61–124. Princeton, American Oriental Society.

Whitby, M. (2007) The late Roman army and the defence of the Balkans. In A. G. Poulter (ed.) *The Transition to Late Antiquity on the Danube and Beyond*, 135–161. Oxford, Oxford University Press.

Zahariade, M. (1988) *Moesia Secunda, Scythia şi Notitia Dignitatum*. Bucharest, Editura Academiei Republicii Socialiste România.

3

ECONOMIC REDUCTION OR MILITARY REORGANIZATION? GRANARY DEMOLITION AND CONVERSION IN LATER 4TH-CENTURY NORTHERN *BRITANNIA*

Rob Collins

Introduction

The Roman forts of Hadrian's Wall were built in the 2nd century and retained their basic form and layout well into the 4th century. This architectural conservatism is in stark contrast to the forts found in the other frontiers of the later Roman Empire, where many auxiliary forts of the Principate were refurbished and received upgrades to their defensive architecture or rebuilt in a smaller form inside the larger area of the Principate fort (Johnson 1983). Installations built *de novo* employed more sophisticated forms and layouts that further distinguished the military architecture of the Dominate. Seen in this light, the forts of Hadrian's Wall and the frontier zone of northern *Britannia* can be seen as relict. The Wall and broader frontier zone continued to be occupied at least until the early 5th century and perhaps later (Fig. 3.1), but beneath this general appearance of conservatism a number of changes are visible in the archaeology of the late frontier (Collins 2012). One of the more intriguing changes that occurred repeatedly along the Wall corridor in the later Roman period was the demolition or conversion of *horrea*, the granaries or storehouses that were found in every fort. Prior to these changes, the granaries from the Wall fit comfortably with evidence for granaries in other parts of Britain (Gentry 1976). This paper examines the evidence for *horreum* demolition / conversion along the Wall corridor in detail; *horrea* functioned primarily, though not exclusively, as warehouses for foodstuffs for fort garrisons, and the demolition or conversion of these buildings provides insight into the changing aspects of the *limitanei* of the Wall. Fundamentally, changes to the *horrea* indicate changes to the supply and economy not only of a single fort, but to the entire Wall corridor, as well as prompting further questions of what replaced the space and functions of the *horrea*?

Horrea demolition or conversion

A number of forts in the Wall corridor have provided evidence for partial or wholesale conversion of *horrea*. Along the Wall corridor, each fort typically was provided with two granaries placed in the central range immediately to the right or left of the *principia*. In some instances, a double-granary structure or its equivalent was provided instead, for example at Housesteads. In the late Roman period, one or both storehouses were completely demolished and or reworked for some other type of use. It is worth reviewing this evidence on a site-by-site basis where modern excavation or reassessment has provided a relatively clear sequence, namely at the forts of South Shields, Newcastle, Housesteads, Vindolanda, and Birdoswald (Fig. 3.2).

South Shields

While the fort at South Shields is not directly attached to Hadrian's Wall, it presumably served as the primary port for the Wall corridor at its eastern terminal on the mouth of the River Tyne. Notably, the fort was converted in the early 2nd century into a large supply-base with an estimated 24 granaries in the Severan period (Bidwell and Speak 1994, 20–33). The later 3rd and early 4th century, between 286

3. Economic reduction or military reorganization?

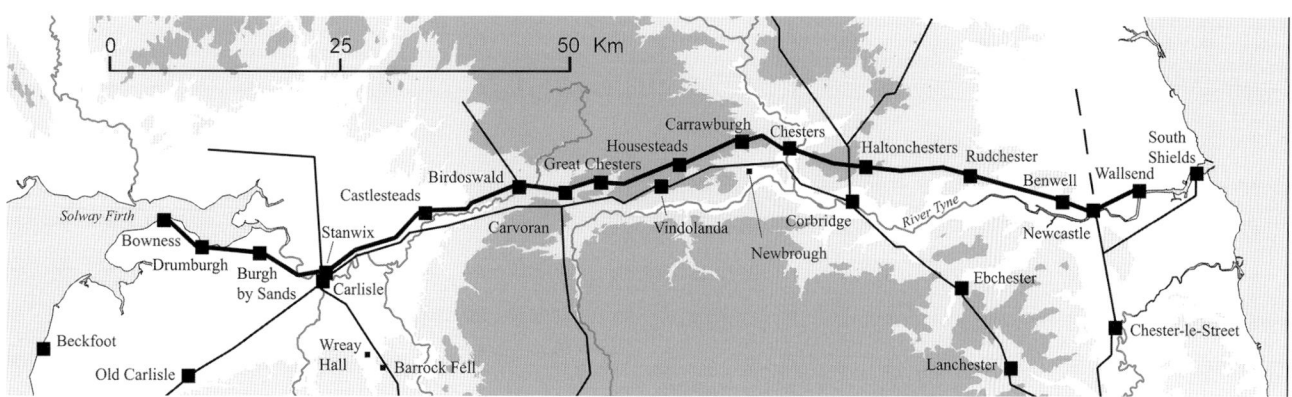

Figure 3.1: Hadrian's Wall in the 4th century, showing the locations of the forts along its length

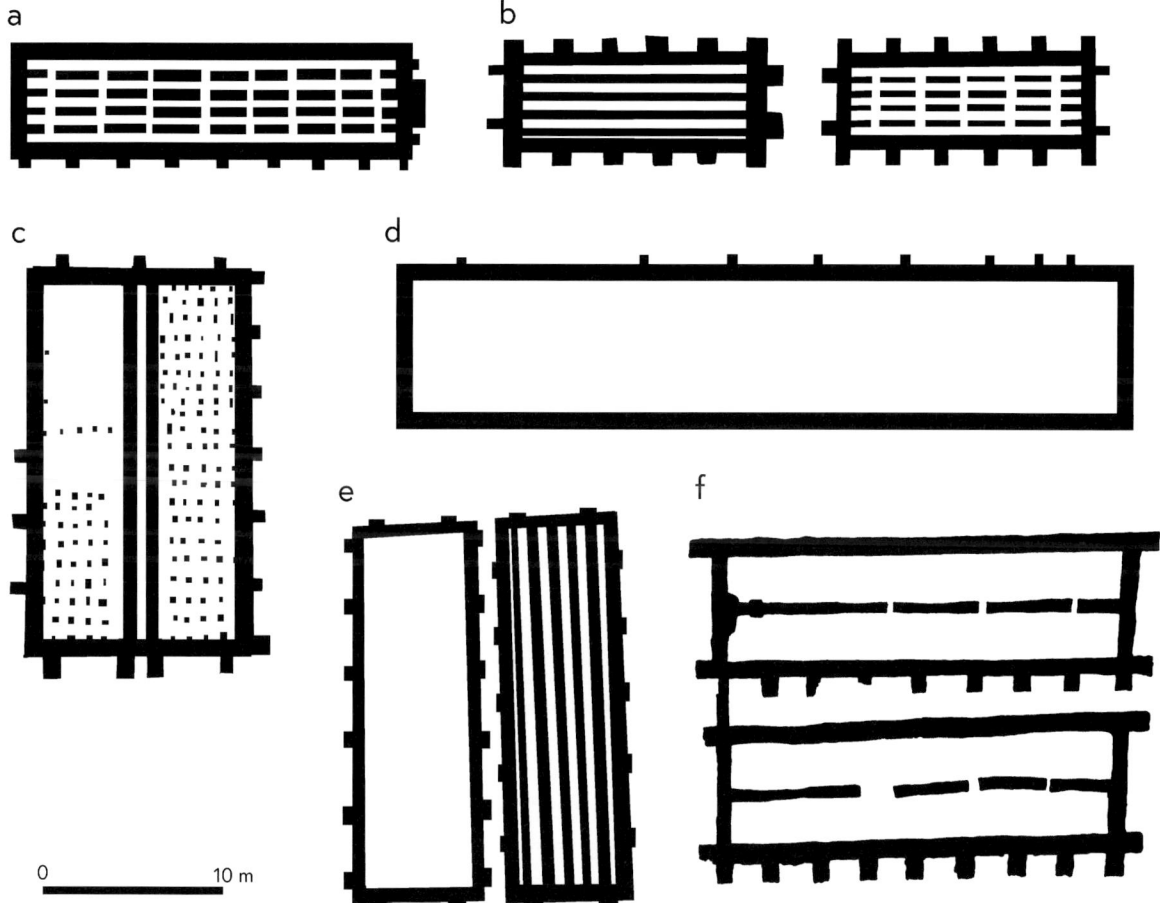

Figure 3.2: The horreum structures from the principal sites under consideration; a. South Shields forecourt granary; b. Newcastle east and west granaries; c. Housesteads "double" granary; d. Housesteads Building XV; e. Vindolanda east and west granaries; f. Birdoswald north and south granaries. After: Bidwell and Speak 1994; Snape and Bidwell 2002; Crow 2004; Rushworth 2009; Birley 2013b; Wilmott 1997

and 318, saw the conversion of the supply-fort back to a more "standard" layout for the period. The Severan granaries to the southeast of the *principia* in the *praetentura* were converted into barracks, though it is thought that the eight granaries to the northwest of the *principia* in the *retenura* were retained, as was the so-called forecourt granary, immediately behind the *principia*; but the double granary immediately beside the *principia* to its southwest was demolished and replaced with tile kilns (Bidwell and Speak 1994, 20–33). Unfortunately, no modern excavations have examined the granaries in the *retentura*, and it is uncertain how long these eight granaries were retained, as the raised floors of two of these were removed at some point (Dore and Gillam 1979, 42–44). Therefore, it seems likely that the forecourt granary was the primary granary for the garrison of South Shields in the 4th century.

The forecourt granary was first built in Period 5, during the early 3rd century conversion to a supply base of the forecourt of the *principia* of the earlier fort, and making use of three of the pre-existing *principia* walls (Bidwell and Speak 1994, 77). This granary was built in the standard rectangular shape, 22.2 × 4.6 m internally, externally buttressed only along the southwest and northeast walls, with the northeast wall also providing the location of the loading bay. The subfloor was composed of four rows of sleeper walls, simply built on a levelled surface and the stones of which were only bonded by a gritty clay. The granary floor consisted of sandstone slabs, and it is thought that the weight on this floor pushed some of the sleeper walls out of position.

The forecourt granary was retained through Period 6, which is when the building may have suffered from a fire, judging by the deposits of carbonized grain found in the subfloor space, which is aslo attested in the southeast quadrant of the fort. Period 7, probably starting in the early 4th century, saw the sealing of the previous sandstone slab floor with a layer of *opus signinum c.* 0.15 m thick. *Opus signinum* was not the normal choice of flooring for a granary, but it was used more widely at South Shields in the 4th century. This new flooring suggests the retention of the building as a granary, which continued until Period 8, at which point the *opus signinum* flooring was demolished, and the subfloor of the granary was filled in. The demolition work, with debris packed into the subfloor, indicates that only the floor was dismantled, and not the entire building due to the absence of other structural elements in the debris. A worn coin of Valens dating to 364–367, East Yorkshire coarsewares, a Crambeck ware mortarium, and a Fowler type D7 penannular brooch were found in the deposits relating to this infilling activity (Bidwell and Speak 1994, 103, 105). Demolition of the loading bay may also date to this time, but truncation of deposits from later Period 9 activity removed any clear dating evidence for this.

While the subfloor infilling can be confidently dated to *c.* 370 or later by the finds, it is uncertain what the use of the building was. Subsequent activity in Period 9 saw the granary walls demolished and paving from the surrounding streets quarried (Bidwell and Speak 1994, 105). Robber trenches, however, contained a number of fills containing artefacts that help date this activity, including a coin of Valentinian minted 367–375 and a fragmentary Fowler type D7 penannular brooch. Subsequently, the large quarry pit in the road outside the northeast end of the granary was repaved, and a Fowler type E penannular brooch was found in association with this paving (Bidwell and Speak 1994, 106). On this basis, forecourt granary demolition and / or robbing may have taken place as early as *c.* 375. However, on the presumption that the new function of the building with its infilled subfloor lasted longer than a few years, plus the demolition and quarrying activity, it is suggested that this activity extends the use of the building and its demolition into the 5th century, with the latest paving surface representing a subsequent phase of activity.

Newcastle

The fort at Newcastle was constructed in the later 2nd / early 3rd century on a small promontory immediately south of Hadrian's Wall. The size of this promontory restricted the fort size and impacted on the arrangement of its internal space. As a result, the granaries are sited north of the *via principalis* in a mirror arrangement to either side of the *via praetoria* creating an east and west granary, rather than being placed immediately beside the *principia*. Furthermore, the granaries are smaller than most of those found along the Wall, measuring 16.05 × 5.90 m externally. This size has been suggested as a feature of their date of construction, as units are thought to be smaller than in the early 2nd century (Bidwell and Snape 2002, 269–271). Both granaries were buttressed externally on all four walls, and the loading bays appear to be located at the end of the granary opposite the *via praetoria*. Despite the mirror arrangement of the granaries, there are small differences in their structures.

Both the east and west granaries have evidence for the infilling of the subfloor between the sleeper walls. In the east granary, an *opus signinum* floor was laid over the infill, with pottery from the fill providing a date of the late 3rd century at the earliest (McMaster 2002, 70–72). A timber porch and/or steps were added to the loading bay at the east end of the eastern granary, and the posthole fill contained fourth-century pottery (McMaster 2002, 72). The modifications to the porch and infilling of the granary subfloor can probably be dated to the same phase of activity.

The western granary also had its subfloor infilled. Overlying this was a deposit of dark soil with clay and mortar patches, and in places there was burnt material and charcoal, reddened clay and lumps of coal. The dark soil contained a sherd of painted Crambeck ware dated to AD 370 or later, providing a TPQ for the activity. A trench hearth was inserted in the centre of the structure near the western edge of the excavation, and this feature combined with the burnt material and coal suggests that the *horreum* was converted for industrial activity (Snape and Bidwell 2002, 62–66).

At some later date, when the western granary was no longer used, it appears to have been demolished. The walls were levelled at a height of four or five courses, and a drain or aqueduct was inserted, running northeast-southwest through the granary, across the *via principalis* and into the northeast corner of the *praetorium*. The drain fed a water tank made of stone slabs and set against the southern face of one of the southern buttresses of the granary. The whole system was inserted at some point after c. 370, but it predated the post-Roman cemetery phase (Snape and Bidwell 2002, 111–114). This activity is presumed to date to a point after which the western granary was robbed or collapsed, due to the different alignment of the drain relative to the Roman building plan, but this may be making too much of such a drastic reuse of the space; at best, the activity can be dated to the 5th to 7th centuries. The east granary was robbed of its stone, its eastern wall reduced to a height of one course, and deposits of mixed clay, rubble and mortar were found in the central area of the building lying over the subfloor infill (Snape and Bidwell 2002, 116). The deposits overlying the latest activities in both the east and west granaries contained human bone, mixed from the early medieval cemetery phase commencing c. 700 (Nolan 2010).

Housesteads

The fort of Housesteads was a primary fort attached to the curtain of Hadrian's Wall in the 120s AD; as such, the fort was built with a Hadrianic layout with a large single structure with a functional capacity of a double-granary built immediately to the north of the *principia*, internally measuring 23.75 × 13 m. Cleared in 1930, almost no record of this work under the National Trust was kept, and the following account has been based on subsequent interpretation of upstanding remains and what little archive remains (Birley 1952; Crow 2004, 55–57).

The original granary was buttressed on all four sides, with two doorways located in the western wall. A series of six large, stone piers ran east–west across the central length of the building, which probably supported the raised floor structure as well as the central roof ridge. There is no further evidence for a subfloor support structure, but there must have been some means of supporting a raised floor, as vents are found in the lowest courses of the north, west, and south walls; stone *pila* were added subsequently (Crow 2004, 56). Modification in the late 2nd or early 3rd century saw the addition of two stone-built walls across the middle length of the granary, immediately to the north and south of the piers of the original structure. It is thought that the southern dividing wall was erected first, as it incorporates the original pier bases into its structure, and then the piers were dismantled; the northern dividing wall was built next. The stone *pila* may have been inserted at this phase, as they are consistent in their form and layout in both the (now distinct) northern and southern granary (Crow 2004, 56); that said, the consistency could also be related to a reflooring episode that occurred between the original erection of the granary

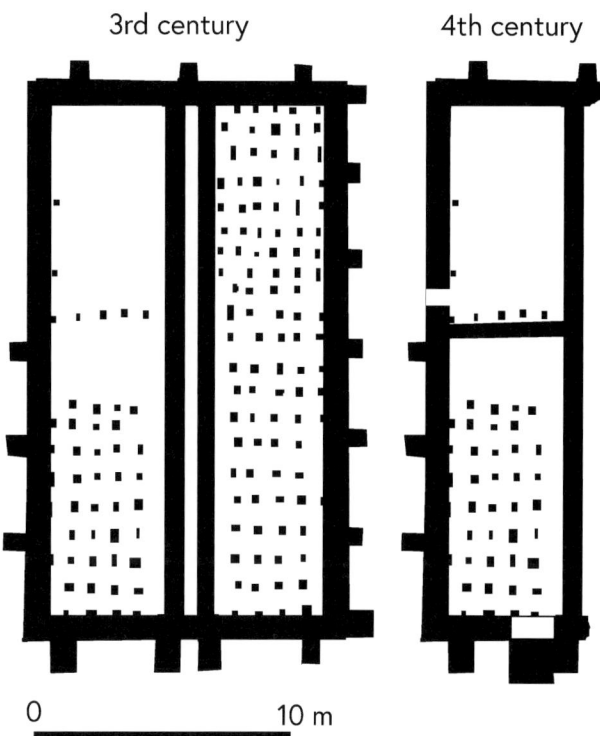

Figure 3.3: The 3rd and 4th century plans of the double-granary at Housesteads

and this phase of modification. Presumably, the dismantling of the piers and insertion of the new walls indicates that the former large granary should be seen as two distinct granaries with separate roofs.

Subsequent modification to these granaries is thought to date to the 4th century, but the nature of the 1930s clearance means that the dating is presumed rather than proven (Crow 2004, 95). The northern granary was little changed in form, and the threshold was relatively unworn; it has been suggested that this lack of modification may indicate that the structure became ruinous and collapsed, and that it was never subsequently repaired. The southern *horreum* was divided into two halves with the insertion of a north–south dividing wall across its width (Fig. 3.3).

The western half was probably rebuilt, as there are no exterior buttresses remaining in this part of the southern wall, in contrast to the other surviving walls of the primary granary. The underfloor was infilled and a flagged floor was laid (Birley 1952, 18), while a narrow door was inserted into the eastern end of the south wall to provide access to the building. This may indicate that the loading bay in the western wall was blocked. A "considerable amount of late pottery and the usual debris of occupation" were found on the flagged floor of the modified western half of the granary (Birley 1952, 18).

The east half continued to function as a *horreum*, but the stone piers were replaced by sleeper walls that were reported in Bosanquet's 1898 plan of the site, and a new entrance was inserted into the eastern wall, with access provided by large stone steps (Crow 2004, 95). The presumed collapse of the northern granary cannot be proven, but it does explain the lack of later modification to the structure. This is not simply a result of the 1930s clearance, as Bosanquet's plan notes the individual *pila* of the northern granary and the sleeper walls of the eastern half of the southern granary (Bosanquet 1898). While some storage capacity seems to have been retained in the late Roman period, it is interesting to note the change to presumed domestic occupation in the western half of the southern granary. Overall, this would indicate a reduction of storage capacity in the 4th century to approximately 25% of 3rd century capacity, except that a new storage structure seems to have been erected elsewhere in the fort.

East of the *principia* on the *via praetoria*, a new structure (Building XV), built at some point in the late 3rd or early 4th century, seems to have been used throughout the 4th century as another *horreum* (Leach and Wilkes 1962; Crow 2004, 92–94; Rushworth 2009, 133–135). Measuring 49 × 10.8 m, the lowest courses consist of large stone blocks laid alternately as headers and stretchers; these solid courses had no rubble core or fill, though the northern wall was built with similarly large stones facing a rubble core. Eight buttresses were incorporated into the foundations of the northern wall. Inside the walls, fills were laid to create a level base for flagging, and a series of monolithic post-settings were placed east–west down the central length, based on the discovery of one such stone in the eastern end of the building.

The building was accessed by a 1.5 m-wide doorway in the west wall fronting the *via principalis* and through the middle of the south wall from the *via praetoria* by an entrance 3 m wide, bearing wheel-ruts in the threshold. The construction date for the building is reliant upon a TPQ provided by a coin minted in 259–273 found sealed in a drain deposit of the building of the preceding phase, and a later-4th-century sherd of Huntcliff parchment ware mortarium found in the floor make-up at the building's eastern end. In the most recent assessment, Rushworth (2009, 133–135) indicated that the mortarium sherd may be an intrusion associated with remodeling of the eastern end of the building for the later bathsuite, and further expands on Crow's (2004, 89–91, 98–99) suggestion that fragmentary Tetrarchic inscription *RIB* 1613 should be associated with this structure. The scale and quality of construction suggests that this double-aisled structure had an upper story, and two post sockets positioned against the north wall could be taken as evidence of the rear posts of a staircase (Crow 2004, 93–94).

Subsequently, the eastern end wall of the building was dismantled and the flagged floor removed for a length of 14 m into the interior, while a new end-wall for the

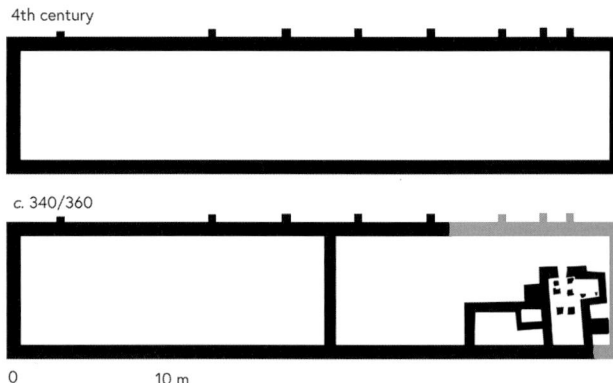

Figure 3.4: The 4th century plans of Building XV at Housesteads

storehouse was constructed 23 m from the former east end (Fig. 3.4). Within this area, a new bathsuite was constructed (Rushworth 2009, 171–173). The small block is L-shaped in plan and was built within the footprint of the storehouse, abutting the upstanding southern wall of the previous storehouse. The suite consisted of a *frigidarium* with a cold plunge bath and a *caldarium* with a hot bath, a stoke hole emerging out of the north wall of the latter. Tufa blocks for the vaulting were found, suggesting possible reuse of stone from the original external fort bathhouse. Fill overlying a drain system integrated with a drain from the bathblock contained a Huntcliff-type jar, providing a TPQ of 340 or later. However, the sherd of Crambeck parchment mortarium found in the makeup beneath the flagging of the storehouse to the west of the bathhouse, if intrusive from the phase of bathhouse construction, may push the erection of the structure to 360 or later.

Vindolanda

The granaries at Vindolanda were constructed c. 211–213 as integral components of stone fort II, and lay immediately to the west of the *principia*. The granaries ran north–south, with their gable-end fronting onto the *via principalis*, and can be distinguished as the east and west granaries. The eastern granary measured 25 × 7.5 m externally, while the western granary was slightly larger at 25 × 8 m. Both granaries were buttressed, but the western granary had six evenly spaced buttresses along its length and two on each short wall; the eastern granary also had two buttresses on each short wall but only five evenly spaced buttresses along its length. The eastern granary had a subfloor featuring four longitudinal sleeper walls, while the western granary had a solid subfloor consisting of a mixed matrix of rubble and clay; both granaries had flagstone floors placed over the subfloors but the subfloor structures suggests different uses for each building (Birley 2013b, 50–61).

The western granary appears to have suffered from a fire, evidenced by cracked and burnt flags and internal wall facing stones overlain by collapsed roof material; two coins found between the flags and sealed by the roof debris date to between 260–273 and provide the closest evidence for the date of this event (Birley 2013b, 60). The eastern granary floor was replaced in the early 4th century, evidenced by the shattered flags of the original floor overlain in the subfloor by an accumulated fill. A fill that had built up in the subfloor of the 3rd century and sealed by the shattered flags contained eight coins, seven of which dated to 268–273, but the latest was an issue of Constantine dating 332–333 (Brickstock 2013, table 1).

There is a suggestion that the superstructure of both granaries was rebuilt above the floor-level. New stone walls utilized clay bonding instead of lime mortar, and the facing stones were of variable quality. A new flagged floor was laid in the eastern granary, and the mixed size and reuse of flags probably contributed to the formation of a dark soil fill in the subfloor which contained a mix of artefacts, coins, and ceramics all dating to the mid to late 4th century in the northern half of the building. There were fewer objects in the subfloor deposits in the southern half of the building, suggesting a difference in the use of space within the granary. The western granary also had a new floor laid in the 4th century, but due to the solid subfloor, there is less evidence for dating except to note that there was a more even spread of material within and outside the western granary (Birley 2013b, 37–44). Perhaps the spread of 4th-century coins along the *via principalis* is related to the use and function of the granaries (Birley 2013b, 44).

Subsequently the western granary underwent a significant change (Birley 2013b, 25–27). A new structure was built over the southern half of the former granary, measuring 9.8 × 7.3 m (Fig. 3.5). This structure utilized the top of the south, east, and west walls of the former Roman granary and created a new wall across the former internal width. The new stone walls were bonded with mixed clay and rubble in the core, using diverse (non-uniform) but good quality facing stones. The new, north wall had a central doorway approximately 0.9 m wide. Inside lay a raised floor consisting of diverse monolithic *pila* fixed in place in by an *opus signinum* layer, and carrying a heavy flagstone floor. To the north of this new building, but still inside the footprint of the former granary was a cobbled surface covering the original granary floor and post-dating the construction of the new building. There was little dating evidence for the new structure or the cobbled surface; coins from inside the building dated to the mid-4th century, but perhaps more significant was that the mixed group of artefacts lacked any associated ceramics. On the basis of the datable evidence from the sequence of building activities, the new reduced-size storage building was erected in the mid-4th century, but a 5th century date is favoured by the excavators on the

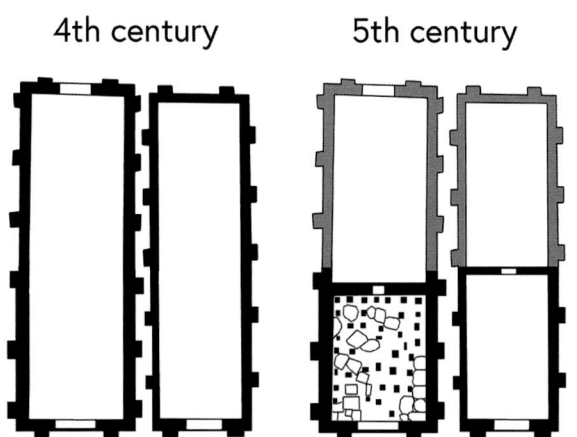

Figure 3.5: The 4th and 5th century plans of the east and west granaries at Vindolanda

basis of comparison of building technique with other post-Roman structures at Vindolanda and its aceramic deposits.

The eastern granary also saw a reduction in size after the late 4th century, presumably following a collapse or demolition of the structure (Birley 2013b, 31–32). Again, the southern half of the granary footprint was used, with new walls built over the southern, eastern, and western walls. The subfloor was completely infilled and the floor relaid, and a new northern wall was built across the width. This new structure measured 11 × 7 m. A hearth was found in the northeastern corner of the structure. There was no evidence for a paved yard to the north, as there was in the western granary, and unfortunately no direct dating evidence was encountered.

Birdoswald

While the fort at Birdoswald was Hadrianic in its construction, the pair of large stone granaries between the *principia* and the *porta principalis dextra* were erected in the early 3rd century, probably between 205 and 208 on the basis of the discovery of *RIB* 1909. The granaries lie east–west, parallel to the *via principalis*, and can be distinguished as the northern granary and southern granary; they also bear the same plan and construction, measuring 28.38 × 8.26 m with nine buttresses evenly spaced along the southern wall, and two buttresses supporting each gable-end wall (Wilmott 1997, 109–110).

In contrast to other granaries from the Wall corridor, the subfloor structure of both granaries at Birdoswald indicated a number of modifications that would have necessitated reflooring of each granary on at least four occasions (Wilmott 1997, 119–127). The initial subfloor arrangement consisted of a central longitudinal sleeper wall with timber posts to either side. These timber posts were replaced by

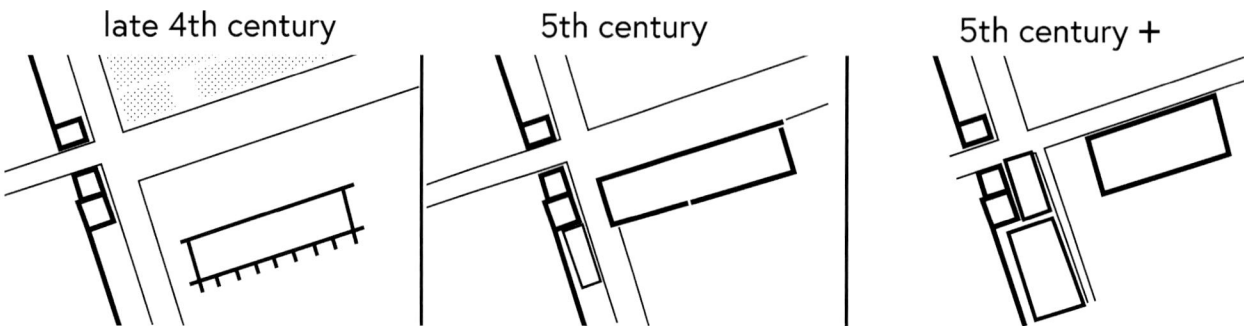

Figure 3.6: The sequence of transformation of the granaries at Birdoswald

monolithic stone *pila* in a second phase. The third phase saw the replacement of the posts, or rather the connection of posts with sleeper walls; these ran longitudinally in both granaries, though the west end of the southern granary also had a series of sleeper walls that ran laterally, north–south. The fourth phase saw the greatest change in subfloor structures. In the northern granary, the west end subfloor was infilled, creating a solid platform. In the southern granary, the central portion of the subfloor was modified to include sub-rectangular boxes of sleeper walls, which were then infilled. These last phases of modification are dated to the later 3rd century, on the basis of ceramics from subfloor fills. Given that the next major period of activity arguably began in the mid-4th century, this sequence of modification and reflooring of the granaries took place within a span of approximately 150 years.

Period 5, dating from the mid to late 4th century, saw the granaries undergoing a series of modifications, resulting in their changed function (Fig. 3.6). The southern granary had its entire subfloor filled in, and a new stone floor was laid over this. On the basis of the latest coins from the fill, this event can be dated to *c.* 350; however the ceramics from the fill suggest that a later date of *c.* 360–400 should be accepted (Hird 1997, 247–248; Bidwell 2005). Above the stone floor were secondary deposits of further flooring surfaces, and two successive hearths at the western end of the building; a coin dating 388–395 and a high proportion of late 4th-century ceramics suggests that this activity occurred in the later 4th century or perhaps even the early 5th century, followed by the collapse of the roof (Wilmott 1997, 203–205, 208, 209; Hird 1997, 249–250).

The northern granary appears to have suffered a roof collapse at the east end of the building, although there is evidence that the western end of the building (which also had the solid subflooring) remained in use. Ultimately, though, it too suffered a roof collapse, sealing a coin dating 350–353 (Wilmott 1997, 205–206, 208). Following the collapse of the roof, the northern granary appears to have been robbed of its building stone, and the subfloor was used for piecemeal refuse dumping. Coins and ceramics from these fills all generally date to the second half of the 4th century, with considerably less "residual" material than seen in the subfloor deposits of the southern granary. These almost certainly attest to the space being used for the episodic, contemporary rubbish disposal (Wilmott 1997, 208).

The northern granary was replaced with a large, timber post-built structure, with the remains of 19 postholes cut into the fabric of the granary walls, with five further postholes extending the length of the building a further 5 m west onto the *via sagularis* (Wilmott 1997, 212). A mix of facing stones and shale in a silt matrix formed a floor level for the building, and between the postholes and the floor surfaces, the building can be estimated to have had a footprint of 31.6 × 8m. It is uncertain how long this timber building was in use for, but it was replaced by a second timber building on a slightly different alignment. Post-pads indicated five pairs of timber uprights, placed over the central sleeper wall of the former northern granary and in the centre of the *via principalis*, probably to line up with the open portal of the west gate (Wilmott 1997, 214). While material was found in association with this sequence of timber structures, it is best understood as "residual" and not necessarily contemporary to the construction and use of the buildings. On the basis of the TPQ provided by dumping of the collapsed and robbed northern granary, these structures can date no earlier than 367–378, and Wilmott (1997, 217) suggests that the timber buildings were functional replacements for the final use of the southern granary, which collapsed at some point after 388–395. On either reckoning, however, it seems these timber structures were used in the 5th century and perhaps extended into the 6th century depending on the use-life of each timber structure (Fig. 3.7).

Other Sites

There are indications of changed use of granaries at other sites in the Wall corridor, though interpretation has been hindered for various reasons. At Benwell, the double *horreum* east of the *principia* was certainly altered in some fashion in the late Roman period, as excavations revealed

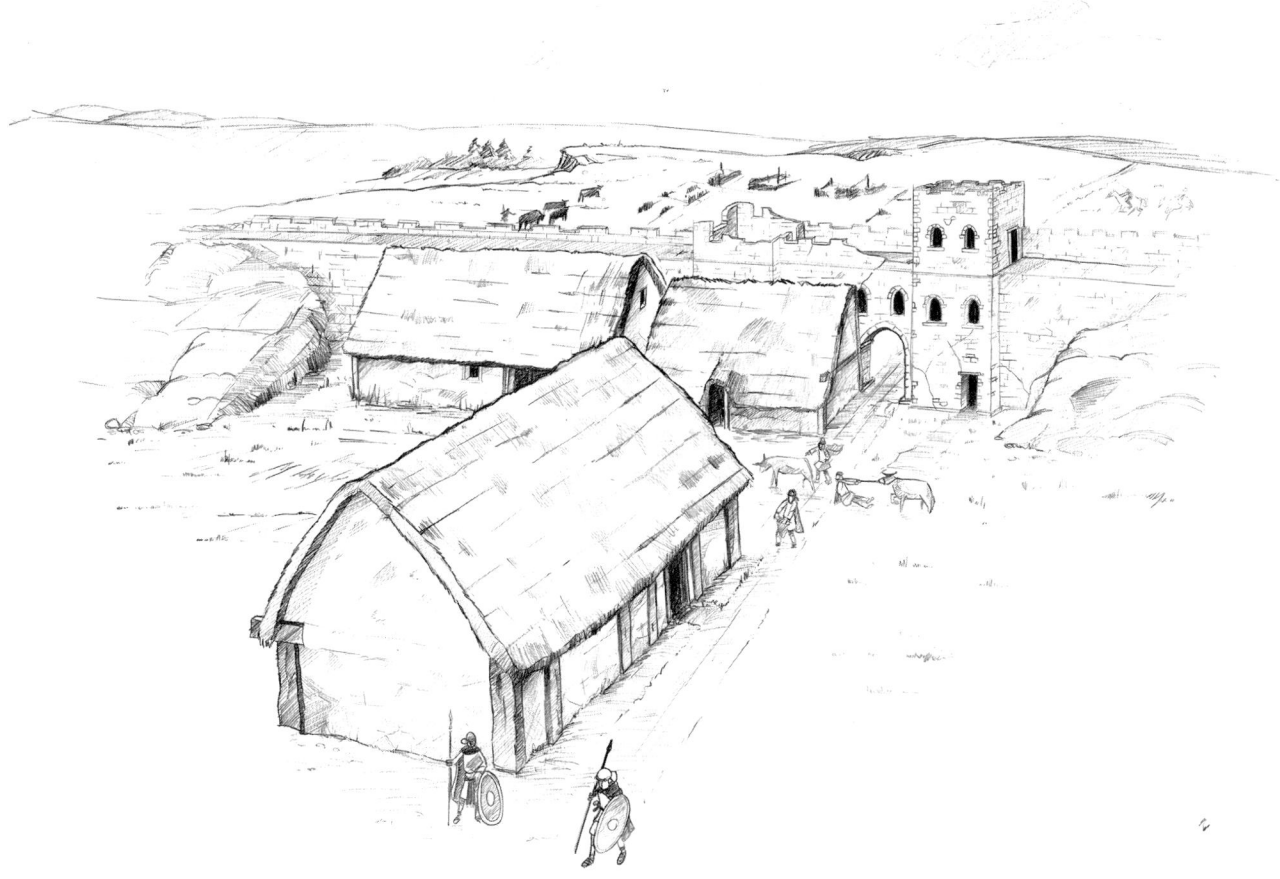

Figure 3.7: A visualization of the second timber structure at Birdoswald as a hall. Drawing by Mark Hoyle

demolition of the northern end of the double *horreum* down to the foundations, with the space subsequently replaced with a paved surface (Holbrook 1991, 43); unfortunately there was no evidence surviving subsequent to the demolition and paving activity.

Chesters has an intriguing range of evidence, but suffers from a lack of modern excavation. Geophysical survey suggests a "standard" granary in the central range to the west of the *principia*, and there is space for a pair of granaries (Bidwell 1999, Fig. 31). However, antiquarian excavation encountered a pair of granaries in the *retentura* south of the *principia* each measuring approximate 14.5 × 8.5 m. Reports of "defective" masonry probably indicate a very late Roman construction (Bruce 1884, 91).

At Stanwix, clay floors and the remains of timber buildings sealed the latest stone building and metalled surface deposits in both the area of the *horreum* and the barracks / stables (Esmonde Cleary 1998, 383). Unfortunately, these excavations have not been published, and a clearer statement of dating and interpretation cannot be offered.

In addition, the granaries at a number of sites have not been excavated, as at Carvoran or Bowness, or post-medieval and modern activity has truncated late Roman strata, as at Wallsend and Castlesteads.

Discussion

Table 3.1 provides a summary of the granaries described above, from which a number of points should be drawn out. Of the five sites reviewed in detail above, only Housesteads retained a storehouse structure that seemingly originated in the Hadrianic period, though the *horrea* at Newcastle were also original to the fort's foundation in the later 2nd or early 3rd century. The main granaries at South Shields, Vindolanda, and Birdoswald can be associated with Severan construction. Newcastle may also be a Severan construction, or was recent enough in its foundation not to have needed a Severan refurbishment, while the Hadrianic *horreum* at Housesteads may have been split into two "new" granaries during the same period.

Subsequent modification, excepting circumstances of fire, generally takes the form of the infilling of the subfloor, either in part or in whole. This occurs partially in both the

Table 3.1: Summary of changes to granaries at selected Wall forts in the late Roman period. e = early, l = late, c = century

Site	Granary	First built	Internal area	Subsequent changes	TPQ of changes	Remaining storage area
South Shields	Forecourt	e 3rd c	c. 102 m²	fire damaged?	l 3rd c	0 m²
				opus signinum surface laid	e 4th c	c. 102 m²
				subfloor infilled	c. 370	0 m²?
				demolished, quarried, and subsequent paving	5th c	0 m²
Newcastle	East	l 2nd/e 3rd c	c. 90 m²	subfloor infilled, *opus signinum* floor laid, timber porch added	l 3rd/4th c	0 m²
				demolition/robbing	5th c	0 m²
	West	l 2nd/e 3rd c	c. 90 m²	subfloor infilled, trench hearth inserted	c. 370	0 m²
				Demolished, drain inserted through foundations	5th c	0 m²
Housesteads	Hadrianic	120s	c. 309 m²	North granary	l 2nd/e 3rd c	c. 110 m²
				collapse?	4th c	0 m²
				South granary	l 2nd/e 3rd c	c. 110 m²
				insertion of dividing wall, new entrance	c. 350?	c. 60 m²
	Bldg XV	l 3rd/e 4th c	c. 425 m²	loss of eastern end to new bathblock	340/360	c. 246 m²
Vindolanda	East	c. 211	c. 160 m²	new floor laid	c. 330	c. 160 m²
				demolition?	c. 400?	0 m²
				new structure reuses southern portion	5th c	0 m²
	West	c. 211	c. 161 m²	fire	c. 275	0 m²
				rebuilt	c. 300	c. 161 m²
				demolition?	c. 400?	0 m²
				reduced size to southern portion	5th c	c. 58 m²
Birdoswald	North	c. 205	c. 156 m²	subfloor modifications	3rd c	c. 156 m²
				west end subfloor infilled	l 3rd c	c. 156 m²
				roof collapse at east end of building	c. 350	0 m²
				west end roof collapse, robbing, and dumping	c. 350	0 m²
				1st timber building	c. 390	0 m²
				2nd timber building	5th/6th c	0 m²
	South	c. 205	c. 156 m²	subfloor modifications	3rd c	c. 156 m²
				central section subfloor infilled	l 3rd c	c. 156 m²
				entire subfloor infilled	c. 360	c. 156 m²?
				subsequent refloorings	c. 390	0 m²
				roof collapse	5th c.	0 m²

northern and southern granaries at Birdoswald in the later 3rd century, where a solid subfloor does not necessarily indicate a non-storage role for the building. The western *horreum* at Vindolanda had a solid subfloor from its Severan construction. But such a feature probably does indicate that the building was not intended to store grains, for which greater ventilation would be required. Thus, buildings with a ventilated subfloor are generally perceived to have stored grains (Table 3.2).

It seems likely that *horrea* often had a second storey (Wilmott 1997, 137). The thickness of the walls, the use of buttressing, and evidence in some instances for

Table 3.2: Summary of palaeobotanical evidence from granaries at the sites in this paper

Site	Sample	Provenance	Results	Interpretation	Reference
South Shields	12236	3rd c. granary subfloor base	90% + grain; minor chaff & weeds; no germination or infestation	good storage conditions	van der Veen 1994
	12176	4th c. subfloor infill	very low counts of grain; weeds virtually absent	either more efficient processing and storage or not used as a granary	van der Veen 1994
Newcastle	multiple	3rd c. eastern granary subfloor	barley most abundant, followed by wheat, with minor presence of oats and other plant foodstuffs; absence of chaff; evidence of heather	grain from good quality crops, with possible shift from wheat to barley through 3rd c; heather could be stored for roofing, bedding, and/or as fuel	Huntley and Daniell 2002
Vindolanda	multiple (Level 2)	3rd c. fills of eastern granary subfloor	grains, mostly wheat, dominate, with minor contributions of grassland seeds, arable weeds, and chaff	good storage conditions, probably mostly used for grains	Huntley 2013
	multiple (Level 1)	4th c. fills of eastern granary subfloor	grains, mostly wheat, dominate, with a considerable presence of grassland seeds, and minor contributions of chaff, arable weeds, and tree/scrub seeds	increased presence of grassland seeds may indicate reduced presence of grains, or perhaps these samples were more disturbed	Huntley 2013
Birdoswald	multiple	3rd c. fills of southern granary	grains, mostly barley, dominate, with large amounts of barley chaff with wheat of secondary, some presence of wetland species	primarily grain storage, with possibility of local barley growth and processing, wet conditions	Huntley 1997

internal supports (as at Housteads Building XV) all provide supporting evidence for a second storey; upstanding remains at Trier, Rome, and Ostia also indicate that two-storey *horrea* were constructed. This doubles the area available for storage, and upper stories would have provided suitable ventilation for grains provided that structure could bear the weight. Significantly, there is no evidence for the insertion of wooden structures that would function as bins for loose grain, and cereals were almost certainly stored in sacks. Not only would this make transport easier, it makes the actual transfer and handling of the grain easier. Where a solid subfloor occurs from the original construction of the building, or a portion in conjunction with ventilated subfloors, a storage function for the building can still be presumed. Unsurprisingly, detailed sampling indicates zoned use of granary floors (e.g. Huntley and Daniell 2002; Huntley 2013).

The insertion of a solid subfloor across the entirety of a *horrea*, necessitating the removal of a previous floor surface and then replacing it, was still a considerable investment of time and labour. Such a drastic change signals the possibility of a more complete change of function for the building. Palaeobotanical evidence further underscores this, particularly at South Shields (van der Veen 1994; Table 3.2).

Evidence for complete demolition or drastically changed use of the granaries occurred at each of the five forts in this study. This left no obvious capacity for storage within these structures at South Shields (from *c.* 370), Newcastle (from *c.* 370) or Birdoswald (from *c.* 350–360). While the function of the former granary at South Shields is uncertain, as is the eastern granary at Newcastle, at Birdoswald both granaries appear to have been given over to more social functions. Around 370, the western granary at Newcastle had its subfloor infilled and the space appears to have been given over to industrial use. Half of the southern granary at Housesteads was given over to occupation presumably in the later 4th century, while it is assumed that the northern granary collapsed in the later 3rd or 4th century, quartering the storage capacity. In contrast, Vindolanda seems to have retained the storage capacity of both granaries (assuming that the west granary with its solid subfloor continued to function as a store) until the later 4th or early 5th century. The more significant change occurs in the 5th century when both granaries were demolished. The eastern granary was superseded by a domestic building on its footprint, while the western granary had a smaller *horreum* reconstructed over its southern half, fronted by a paved yard inside the northern half (Fig. 3.5).

While this may suggest a fairly substantial and consistent reduction in dedicated storehouses in the second half of the 4th century, such an impression may be misleading. The construction of Building XV at Housesteads in the Tetrarchic period, surpassed the capacity even of the large Hadrianic *horreum*, which still retained approximately 25% of its storage space (Table 3.1). At Vindolanda, the *principia* forecourt structures and veranda received raised floors, indicating an increased storage capacity within the fort, provided that these changes can be confidently dated to after *c.* 340 (Birley *et al.* 1936, 225–228). If these modifications are in fact later and attributed to the early 5th century, then these changes can be seen as an alternative to some of the lost capacity in the granaries. At Newcastle and Birdoswald, where both dedicated granaries were lost, it is feasible that new *horrea* were constructed elsewhere in the fort where there has not been any excavation.

This raises the question of how we should interpret the limited evidence at Chesters, where the granary and its presumed pairing immediately west of the *principia* were supplemented by a pair of smaller late Roman *horrea*. Were the original granaries demolished or reused, their function replaced by the smaller, later granaries? Or were these later *horrea* an increase in the storage capacity of the fort? Why would increased storage capacity be required?

Supply of the Wall *Limitanei*

At some level, all of these late granaries will have been linked to taxation and military supply; the question remains as to what scale. Apparent loss of storage capacity in the later 4th century at South Shields, Newcastle, and Birdoswald suggests a decrease in the scale of storage. This may relate to the size of the garrison and population at each fort, or to a declining need to import food and other supplies, if local or proximal provisioning was adequate. Garrison size and local carrying capacity, while linked, are best considered separately.

The original purpose of fort granaries was for the bulk storage of foodstuffs and other essential *materiél* to support the garrison of the Wall, with the vast majority of these supplies almost certainly imported from outside the frontier zone. Yet these stores were erected in conjunction with the establishment of Hadrian's Wall in the 120s. By the 4th century, nearly 200 years of military control would have established tried and tested supply arrangements. These may have been altered slightly with the late Roman reorganization of the tax system, introducing the *annonis militaris* and further codifying in law the preference for local-supply whenever possible (Rickman 1971, 283–290). Ceramic evidence serves to illustrate the *annona* was put into practice in the northern frontier zone; the main ceramic suppliers were the Yorkshire-kilns in the southeast corner of the frontier zone, and while there is evidence for limited quantities of wares from other British potteries, the importation of ceramics from outside of *Britannia* was extremely limited (Bidwell and Croom 2010).

Estimations of garrison size in the 4th century are notoriously difficult, but unit sizes of approximately 250–350 men are suggested as likely (Collins 2012, 51–54). Added to the unit strength is the non-soldier population, which by the 4th century had moved into the fort from the now abandoned extra-mural settlements (Birley 2013a; Hodgson 2014). At a conservative estimate, each Wall fort's total population would have numbered around 500 persons through much of the 4th century. Although the army was not obliged to provide food and supplies to the non-soldiers and dependents in the military community, their occupation inside the fort may still have put space at a premium. It therefore seems likely that any unnecessary structures would be demolished or converted, including *horrea*.

But could the Wall corridor provide enough food to support the military communities dispersed along the Wall? Roman agricultural terraces overlying *vicus* structures at Housesteads are testimony to local arable production in the 4th century, but the carrying capacity of the Wall corridor varied considerably. It was greatest in its eastern and western sectors, where the Tyne Valley and Solway Plain provided good farmland. The uplands were a different matter, however. A crude measure for the difference in upland and lowland agricultural value can be gained from the *Northumberland Lay Roll Subsidy of 1296*, where the ward of West Tynedale covering much of the central sector of the Wall and its hinterlands was assessed at £553 and the ward of East Tynedale covering most of the eastern sector of the Wall and its hinterlands was assessed at £1,430 (Fraser 1968, xxi). While agriculture at this date may have been more productive than during the later Roman period, it would not have been substantially different, and a case can be made for sizable arable production in the lowlands.

As a simple measure of potential, Manning (1975) calculated that in upland conditions with low crop yield, 2.56 km^2 (1 mi^2) of agricultural land would be required to meet the grain requirements of a Roman garrison of approximately 500 people. Certainly there was enough land with arable potential, but subtracted from this are the crops required by the farming community and land necessarily dedicated to growing fodder and pasture for livestock. So while there may have been a fair agricultural base for each fort population, it may still have been necessary to gather supplies from a larger area, if not importing from further afield. Indeed, the tax assessment in the 13th century for the entire county of Northumberland was a fraction of that for the North Riding of Yorkshire (Fraser 1968, xxi). Given the evidence for 4th-century ceramic supply dominated by the Yorkshire kilns and the infrastructure available to distribute those ceramics and their contents, it seems likely that Yorkshire may also have been the breadbasket for the northern frontier; the uplands, consisting of the Pennines and most of the lands to their west would have been well-suited for pasturage (Stallibrass pers. comm.). Forts such as Catterick, Binchester, and Piercebridge, located south of the Wall on Dere Street and at the interface of the eastern lowlands and central uplands may have been crucial within this supply gathering and redistribution network; indeed, this could very well explain the substantial evidence for the processing of cattle encountered at Binchester (Petts, this volume).

Perhaps the differential evidence of *horrea* space in the forts examined in this paper can be seen as an upland-lowland divide. Housesteads and Vindolanda, located in the centre of the Wall corridor, may have required a more substantial stockpile of foodstuffs like grains due to the limited arable potential of their locality. Birdoswald is at the western terminal of the upland central sector of the Wall, but may have had greater access to the arable lowlands to its west, freeing the fort from a need to retain large storehouses.

The construction of Building XV at Housesteads has been linked to the *annona militaris* and the reorganization of tax payment and collection and military pay under the Tetrarchs and subsequent emperors (Crow 2004, 98–99; Rushworth 2009, 307–309). The argument is that the retained storage function of the halved southern granary should still be understood as the garrison *horruem*, while the new Building XV was a public storehouse that received the taxes-in-kind supplied by civilians for the *annona militaris*, holding such quantities for subsequent redistribution along the Wall. There is the further suggestion that perhaps granaries at other Wall-forts functioned as public storehouses. While the hypothesis has merits, the basic premise should be explored further in particular, as to how such a system would relate to the infrastructure of the Wall corridor.

The fort at Housesteads seems an unlikely location for a collection point of the *annona militaris*, sitting on top of the craggy Whin Sill and detached from the main Stanegate road. Or does the Knag Burn gateway through the Wall at Housesteads indicate that collection was made from the population to the north of the Wall? Could enough tax / supplies be collected from the rural uplands of the central Wall sector to justify such a large storehouse?

If a suitable fort site was required in the central sector of Hadrian's Wall, then Vindolanda would be more appropriate, located on the Stanegate road that ran east–west to the south of the Wall. This need for storing the *annona* and seeing to its redistribution would provide a plausible explanation why Vindolanda retained both its granaries until the late 4th or early 5th century, as well as expanding on capacity by conversion of parts of the *principia*.

The western sector of the Wall has four prospective locations for *annona* collection points. The forts of Carlisle or Stanwix, located adjacent to the Roman town of Carlisle and also on a main road crossing north through the Wall, offer ideal sites. Unfortunately, there are insufficient data to argue for the presence of sizable granaries at either fort site in the 4th century; nor is there evidence for storehouses from the town of Carlisle. Birdoswald is another ideal candidate for an *annona* collection point; its position at the intersection of the Wall with the Maiden Way would facilitate collection from north of the Wall and further utilize the road network.

Yet, there is currently no evidence for the replacement of lost storage capacity at Birdoswald. The western sector may yet yield evidence supporting this model.

In the eastern sector, four sites merit attention: South Shields; Corbridge; Halton Chesters; and Chesters. As the presumed main port for the Wall corridor, South Shields was crucial for the transhipment of bulk goods for the Wall garrisons. While the forecourt granary seems to have been converted *c*. 370, the *horrea* in the *retentura* remain of potential interest. When and how were these granaries altered? The fort of Chesters was located on the Wall adjacent to the river North Tyne, and in more recent centuries this river valley provided a preferred route for accessing the Wall corridor from the north. The situation at Chesters has already been described above, and while nothing conclusive can be said, there is at least potential for increased storage capacity in the later Roman period.

Halton Chesters was built on the Wall just east of the Port Gate, which guarded the passage of the main north–south road through the Wall corridor, Dere Street; approximately one Roman mile north of Halton Chesters, another road, the Devil's Causeway branched northeast off of Dere Street. A granary was partially excavated to the west of the *principia* at Halton Chesters, which the original excavator claimed to have been destroyed by fire in the later 3rd century, with new 4th-century structures built over the site; modern reassessment is more cautious of this interpretation, and notes that there is no clear evidence for when the structure went out of use, though there may have been undated infilling of the subfloor (Dore 2010, 11–13).

The town of Corbridge was located at the intersection of Dere Street and the Stanegate on the River Tyne, and excavations in the early 20th century revealed urban storehouses at Sites 17W and 56 (Forster and Knowles 1910, 242–243; 1914, 292–297). While these structures were argued to be Severan in construction, the evidence is far from robust and their style of construction compares very favourably with Housesteads Building XV, suggesting a later construction (Rushworth 2009, 307). The two large granaries at Corbridge built facing onto the Stanegate in the later 2nd or early 3rd century probably continued in use into the 4th century on the basis of reported coins discovered, though evidence for late Roman use is ambiguous (Knowles and Forster 1909; Brassington 1975).

While the supply chain under the *annona* may have shortened, the provision of foodstuff could still be variable. A poor harvest, due to blight, weather or any other reason, would still create a shortfall in required supplies. Such failures could be localized, or could occur at the regional scale or greater, depending on the cause. In such circumstances, the capacity for collection and storage of provisions in bulk would still have been a pressing need for the frontier army, particularly in the more vulnerable uplands.

Conclusions

Taken at face value, only the town of Corbridge and the fort at Housesteads have clear evidence for substantial storehouse capacity for the *annona militaris*. The other key infrastructural sites in the Wall corridor simply do not provide enough evidence to support or disprove the hypothesis. Furthermore, the late Roman construction of a storehouse is only proven at Housesteads, though modification of the *principia* at Vindolanda sees the relocation of storage capacity to another building. On present evidence, South Shields, Newcastle, and Birdoswald have reduced storage capacity from *c.* 350–370.

Do these changes represent a reduction in imported supply, or is there a wider reorganization of supply to the Wall corridor in the later 4th century? The dating for the *horrea* at Housesteads and Vindolanda is crucial. Building XV at Housesteads was constructed in the Tetrarchic period; to that end, its original purpose may have been linked in with the *annona militaris*. However, its eastern end is demolished to accommodate a bathhouse in the mid to late 4th century, indicating that the entire building did not need to be retained for storage. While the overall capacity of the reduced Building XV was still quite considerable, it was still a sizable reduction.

Significantly, the changes to the granaries at each of these sites are different enough in date that we cannot ascribe them to a single event-horizon. The addition of storage suites to the *principia* at Vindolanda could have happened as early as the 340s, and the loss of the granaries at Birdoswald may begin as early as the 350s. South Shields and Newcastle both seem to have seen change around 370. The modifications at Housesteads are undated, but probably do not occur earlier than the 340s. Therefore, we cannot ascribe changes to the storage, and presumably supply of these forts to the final years of Roman administration of Britain, or even as a consequence of the Barbarian Conspiracy of 367. Rather, the impression gained is that alterations to *horrea* and storage conditions were made at each fort at the instigation of the local commander, rather than in response to a top-down directive from the *dux Britanniarum*.

Still, this conclusion leaves us asking further questions. To what extent was each fort supplied locally? And how much food had to be imported from further afield? Was retained or increased storage capacity at Corbridge, Chesters, Housesteads, and Vindolanda simply a means of anticipating arable failure or the need for arable imports in upland locations? Indeed, the answers to these questions further frame our understanding of the 5th-century use of the Wall forts in the aftermath of Britain's separation from imperial authorities, and any presumed fragmentation or collapse of the frontier.

Bibliography

Bidwell, P. (1999) *Hadrian's Wall 1989–1999*, Carlisle, Cumberland and Westmorland Antiquarian and Archaeological Society.

Bidwell, P. (2005) The dating of Crambeck parchment ware. *Journal of Roman Pottery Studies* 12, 15–21.

Bidwell, P. and Croom, A. (2010) The supply and use of pottery on Hadrian's Wall in the 4th century AD. In R. Collins and L. Allason-Jones (eds) *Finds from the Frontier*, 20–36. York: CBA.

Bidwell, P. and Snape, M. (2002) The history and setting of the Roman fort at Newcastle upon Tyne. *The Roman Fort at Newcastle upon Tyne*, Archaeologia Aeliana 5th series, 31, 251–283.

Bidwell, P. and Speak, S. (1994) *Excavations at South Shields Roman Fort, vol. 1*. Newcastle, Society of Antiquaries of Newcastle upon Tyne.

Birley, A. (2013a) The fort wall: A great divide? In R. Collins and M. Symonds (eds), *Breaking Down Boundaries: Hadrian's Wall in the 21st Century*, 85–104. JRA supplementary series 93, Rhode Island, Journal of Roman Archaeology.

Birley, A. (2013b) *The Vindolanda Granary Excavations*. Greenhead, Roman Army Museum Publications.

Birley, E. (1952) *Housesteads Roman Fort*. Department of Environment Official Guidebook, London, Her Majesty's Stationary Office.

Birley, E., Richmond, I., and Stanfield, J. (1936) Excavations at Chesterholm-Vindolanda. *Archaeologia Aeliana* 4th series, 8, 218–257.

Bosanquet, R. C. (1989) Excavations at Housesteads. *Proceedings of the Society of Antiquaries of Newcastle upon Tyne* 8, 247–254.

Brassington, M. (1975) A re-appraisal of the western enclave, Corstopitum. *Britannia* 6, 62–75.

Brickstock, R. (2013) Vindolanda 2008: The coins. In A. Birley *The Vindolanda Granary Excavations*, 121–167. Greenhead, Roman Army Museum Publications.

Bruce, J. C. (1884) *The Hand-book to the Roman Wall: A Guide to Tourists Traversing the Barrier of the Lower Isthmus*, 2nd edition, London, Alfred Russell Smith.

Collins, R. (2012) *Hadrian's Wall and the End of Empire*. New York, Routledge.

Crow, J. (2004) *Housesteads: A Fort and Garrison on Hadrian's Wall*. Stroud, Tempus.

Dore, J. and Gillam, J. (1979) *The Roman Fort at South Shields*. Newcastle, Society of Antiquaries.

Esmonde Cleary, S. (1998) Roman Britain in 1997: Hadrian's Wall, northern counties. *Britannia* 29, 381–389.

Fraser, C. M. (1968) *The Northumberland Lay Subsidy Roll of 1296*. Newcastle, Society of Antiquaries.

Forster, R. H. and Knowles, W. H. (1910) Corstopitum: Report on the excavations in 1909, *Archaeologia Aeliana* 3rd series, 6, 205–272.

Forster, R. J. and Knowles, W. H. (1914) Corstopitum: Report on the excavations in 1913, *Archaeologia Aeliana* 3rd series, 11, 279–310.

Gentry, A. P. (1976) *Roman Military Stone Built Granaries in Britain*. BAR British Series 32, Oxford, BAR.

Hird, L. (1997) The coarse pottery. In T. Wilmott *Birdoswald, Excavations of a Roman fort on Hadrian's Wall and its successor settlements: 1987–92*, 233–256. London, English Heritage.

Hodgson, N. (2014) The accommodation of soldiers' wives in Roman fort barracks – on Hadrian's Wall and beyond. In R. Collins and. F. McIntosh (eds) *Life in the Limes*, 18–28. Oxford, Oxbow.

Holbrook, N. (1991) A Watching Brief at the Roman Fort of Benwell-*Condercum* 1990. *Archaeologia Aeliana* 5th series, 19, 41–45.

Huntley, J. P. (1997) Macrobotanical evidence from the *horrea*. In T. Wilmott, *Birdoswald, Excavations of a Roman fort on Hadrian's Wall and its successor settlements: 1987–92*, 141–144. London, English Heritage.

Huntley, J. P. (2013) Vindolanda east granary samples. In A. Birley, *The Vindolanda Granary Excavations*, 99–116. Greenhead, Roman Army Museum Publications.

Huntley, J. P. and Daniell, J. (2002) The Charred Plant Remains. *The Roman Fort at Newcastle upon Tyne, Archaeologia Aeliana* 5th series, 31, 239–243.

Johnson, S. (1983) *Late Roman Fortifications*. London, Batsford.

Leach, J. and Wilkes, J. (1962) Excavations in the Roman fort at Housesteads. *Archaeologia Aeliana* 4th series, 40, 83–96.

Knowles, W. H. and Forster, R. H. (1909) Corstopitum: Report on the excavations in 1908. *Archaeologia Aeliana* 3rd series, 5, 305–423.

McMaster, A. (2002) The east granary. *The Roman Fort at Newcastle upon Tyne, Archaeologia Aeliana* 5th series, 31, 67–75.

Manning, W. H. (1975) Economic influences on land use in the military areas of the highland zone during the Roman period. In J. G. Evans, S. Limbrey, and H. Cleere (eds) *The Effect of Man on the Landscape: The Highland Zone*, 112–116. Nottingham, CBA.

Nolan, J. (2010) The early medieval cemetery at the Castle, Newcastle upon Tyne. *Archaeologia Aeliana* 5th series, 39, 147–287.

Rickman, G. E. (1971) *Roman Granaries and Store Buildings*. Cambridge, Cambridge University Press.

Rushworth, A. (2009) *Housesteads Roman Fort – the Grandest Station. Excavation and Survey at Housesteads, 1954–95, by Charles Daniels, John Gillam, James Crow and others*. Swindon, English Heritage.

Snape, M. and Bidwell, P. (2002) Excavations at Castle Garth, Newcastle upon Tyne, 1976–92 and 1995–6: the excavation of the Roman fort. *The Roman Fort at Newcastle upon Tyne, Archaeologia Aeliana* 5th series, 31, 1–249.

van der Veen, M. (1994) Grain from the forecourt granary and the charred grain from the courtyard house. In P. Bidwell and S. Speak (eds) *Excavations at South Shields Roman Fort*, vol. 1, 243–260. Newcastle, Society of Antiquaries.

Wilmott, T. (1997) *Birdoswald, Excavations of a Roman fort on Hadrian's Wall and its successor settlements: 1987–92*. London, English Heritage.

4

LATE ROMAN MILITARY BUILDINGS AT BINCHESTER (CO. DURHAM)

David Petts

Introduction

Over the last generation, the dominant paradigm for understanding the end of the Roman military frontier in Northern Britain has been transformed (Collins 2011; 2012; Petts 2013). Traditionally, the termination of Roman control was seen as a story of the progressive withdrawal of garrisons to support the various conflicts on the Continental mainland, leaving all forts and installations essentially empty by the final cessation of Roman coinage in the early 5th century. This perspective was based on a combination of the lack of clear contemporary documentary or epigraphic references to late 4th-century or early 5th-century military presence in northern Britain; the exception to this is the *Notitia Dignitatum*, a poorly understood and relatively opaque document. The influence of early medieval accounts, such as Gildas' *De Excidio* was also important to developing this narrative. The archaeological record also seemed to tell a story of progressive reduction in on-site activity at excavated sites. A more subtle understanding of the chronology of terminal occupation at many sites was frustrated by the end of coin supply, and the massive decline in ceramic supply, removing the twin pillars on which the dating of Roman sites relied.

From the early 1990s, however, it was increasingly realised that there *was* archaeological evidence for 5th-century activity on many forts in the frontier zone (Wilmott and Wilson 2000; Collins 2012). A key turning point was the excavations at Birdoswald (Cumbria) by Tony Wilmott, which revealed the presence of early medieval halls constructed over the former Roman granaries (Wilmott 1997; 2000; see also Collins, this volume). Significantly, it showed that there was evidence of continued activity, but that the construction techniques used and the wider architectural vocabulary utilised was very different from traditional Roman techniques, with the use of post-pads supporting timber structures rather than either mortared or clay-bonded stone walls. Developments in archaeological excavation techniques with a move towards more large-scale open area techniques, combined with this growing awareness of the more ephemeral nature of late activity on Roman sites and the increased use of radiocarbon dating (particularly the use of Bayesian statistical modelling) has meant that 5th century and later occupation on Roman sites is being increasingly recognised across the Northern frontier zone (Wilmott 2010).

This enhanced understanding of the extent of continuity of activity at Northern military sites in Britain is leading to exciting new perspectives on the dynamics of the transition from the Roman to early medieval world (e.g. Collins 2011; 2012; Petts 2013). However, there are still important interpretative challenges. One such key issue is the problem that although 5th-century activity has been widely identified at a regional scale, there is far less understanding of the spatial evolution of Roman military sites in this period at the level of the individual fort. Observations of 5th-century activity at sites are often limited to only one particular structure or zone of the site, most commonly the major administrative structures, such as *praetoria* or *principia*, which have tended to be the focus of research excavations.

As yet, there have been very limited cases where multiple observations of 5th-century activity at one site have allowed archaeologists to get a better handle on how the wider postulated social changes are being played out in terms of the changing spatial organisation and activity patterns within individual forts. This paper explores recent work at the Roman fort at Binchester (Co. Durham). Building on the identification of early to mid-5th-century activity within the *praetorium* in excavations carried out in the 1980s and early 1990s, a current campaign of excavation on a barrack block and also in the *vicus* is providing an opportunity to develop a wider understanding of the changing nature of activity across the site in the later 4th and 5th centuries AD.

The fort at Binchester

The Roman fort of Binchester lies just to the north of the modern town of Bishop Auckland (Co. Durham, UK) on a small gravel plateau overlooking the River Wear to its immediate west and south (Fig. 4.1). To its east the plateau is defined by the small but clearly defined valley of the Bell Burn which runs northwards to join the Wear. The plateau defined by these water courses is almost entirely occupied by the fort and its associated civilian settlement, though the movement of the Wear has caused severe landslips along the western side of the fort resulting in the loss of nearly one third of the fort and part of the *vicus* (Ferris 2011).

The key factor underlying the decision to build the fort here was the presence of the crossing of the Roman road now known as Dere Street over the River Wear. Dere Street was the main Roman road that originated at the supply base at Brough-on-Humber and ran north to the legionary headquarters at York, through North Yorkshire and southern County Durham to the town of Corbridge, then across Hadrian's Wall and advancing as far north as the Antonine Wall.

Binchester was just one of a series of forts that lay along the road between York and the Wall. These tended to protect and control the key river crossings: at Catterick the road crossed the Swale, at Piercebridge, the Tees. Binchester was the next fort north in the chain and to the north forts at Lanchester and Ebchester controlled access over the rivers Browney and Derwent, respectively. These rivers and their valleys also facilitated westwards movement into the remote uplands of the North Pennines, and the position of the fort was doubtless equally important in facilitating such lateral movements. The upland areas were probably important as a source of lead and possibly silver, with the protection of the production of lead itself probably the purpose of the remote fort at Alston (Cumbria). In addition to mineral wealth, the dales also comprised major areas of upland grazing, and as the altars from Eastgate (RIB 1041) and Bollihope Common (RIB 1042), in upper Weardale suggest, hunting pursuits for the military officers stationed in the region.

Binchester is attested as Vinovia or Vinovium in Ptolemy's *Geography*, the *Antonine Itinerary* and the *Ravenna Cosmography,* but does not appear in the *Notitia Dignitatum*. Although not subject to the same level of large-scale investigations as many of the Wall forts, Binchester has seen enough archaeological investigations to provide a fairly solid chronological framework within which we can understand its remains (Ferris 2010, 539–545). Although there are some upstanding earthworks of not inconsiderable height, particularly on the eastern edge of the fort, these do not belong to the earliest phase of activity. Instead, aerial photography and geophysical survey has demonstrated that the first fort on the site extended significantly to the north-east (Fig. 4.2). The precise dating of this initial phase is not clear. Although claims have been made for a date as early as the early AD 70s, it would perhaps sit better in the late AD 70s or AD 80. Certainly the limited excavation of this earlier fort suggests nothing more precise than a broad late-1st- or early 2nd-century date. Whatever the precise date, the most startling aspect of this early fort is its sheer size; at around 7 hectares it was one of the largest auxiliary forts from the northern frontier region in the 1st century AD. Binchester remained a substantial fort throughout its life, primarily because it was a cavalry fort; however, the scale of the earliest phase may indicate that, in its early stages at least, it functioned as a vexillation fortress.

This early, large phase of the fort appears to have operated until the early 2nd century. Even within this time it is clear that there major changes in the use of the fort. Excavations in the centre of the fort have revealed the presence of a substantial wooden building of later 1st-century date, presumably a *praetorium* or a *principia*. It was seemingly demolished and after a phase of refuse dumping there was evidence of significant iron working, followed by a further period of dumping of domestic refuse. These three periods of use seem to fit within *c*. AD 90 / 95 to AD 130. The lack of clear structural evidence for this late-1st-century and early 2nd-century phase suggest that much of the fort interior may have been given over to large-scale industrial production and the prime function of Binchester at this period is likely to have been for supply and logistical support for Roman installations and campaigns further north, rather than as a major garrison.

The return to the fort's primary purpose as a garrison appears to have taken place *c*. AD 130. The contraction of the overall size of the fort, with the north-eastern rampart moving westwards and forming the perimeter that was retained until the early 5th century probably dates to the AD 130s. By this point, Binchester was clearly an auxiliary base and was home to the *Ala Vettonum*, a Spanish cavalry unit, who are mentioned on a series of inscriptions recovered from the site (RIB 1028, 1035 and a new recent discovery from the *vicus*). It was also home at some point to a Frisian formation, the *Cuneus Frisiorum* (RIB 1036); the presence of a local detachment from Chester-le-Street (21 km to the north) is also indicated by their repeated mention on ceramic tiles (Ferris 2010, 422–423).

The *praetorium*

Until the recent new campaign of excavation at Binchester,

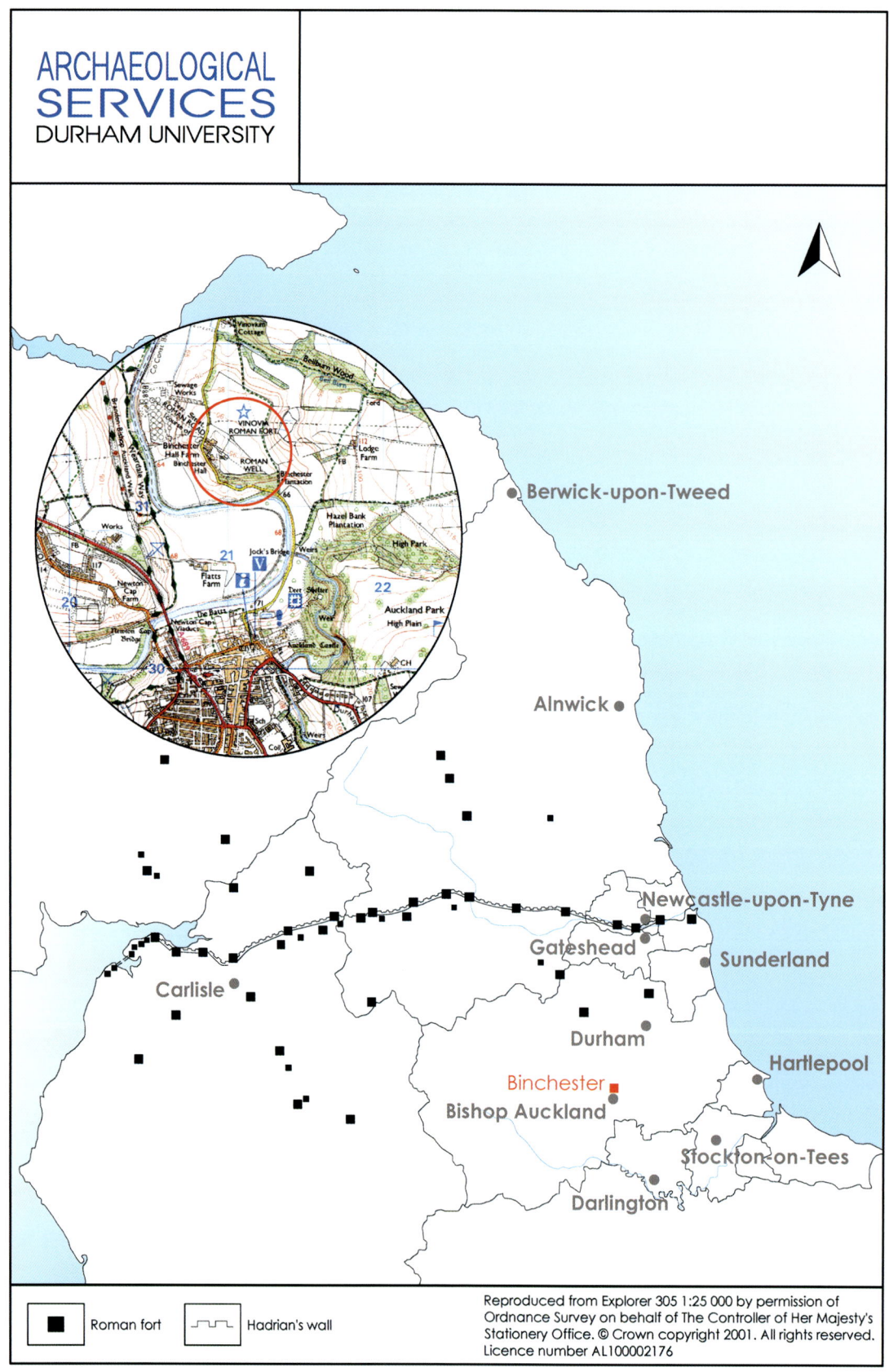

Figure 4.1: Location plan of Binchester Roman fort. Image credit: Durham University

4. Late Roman military buildings at Binchester (Co. Durham)

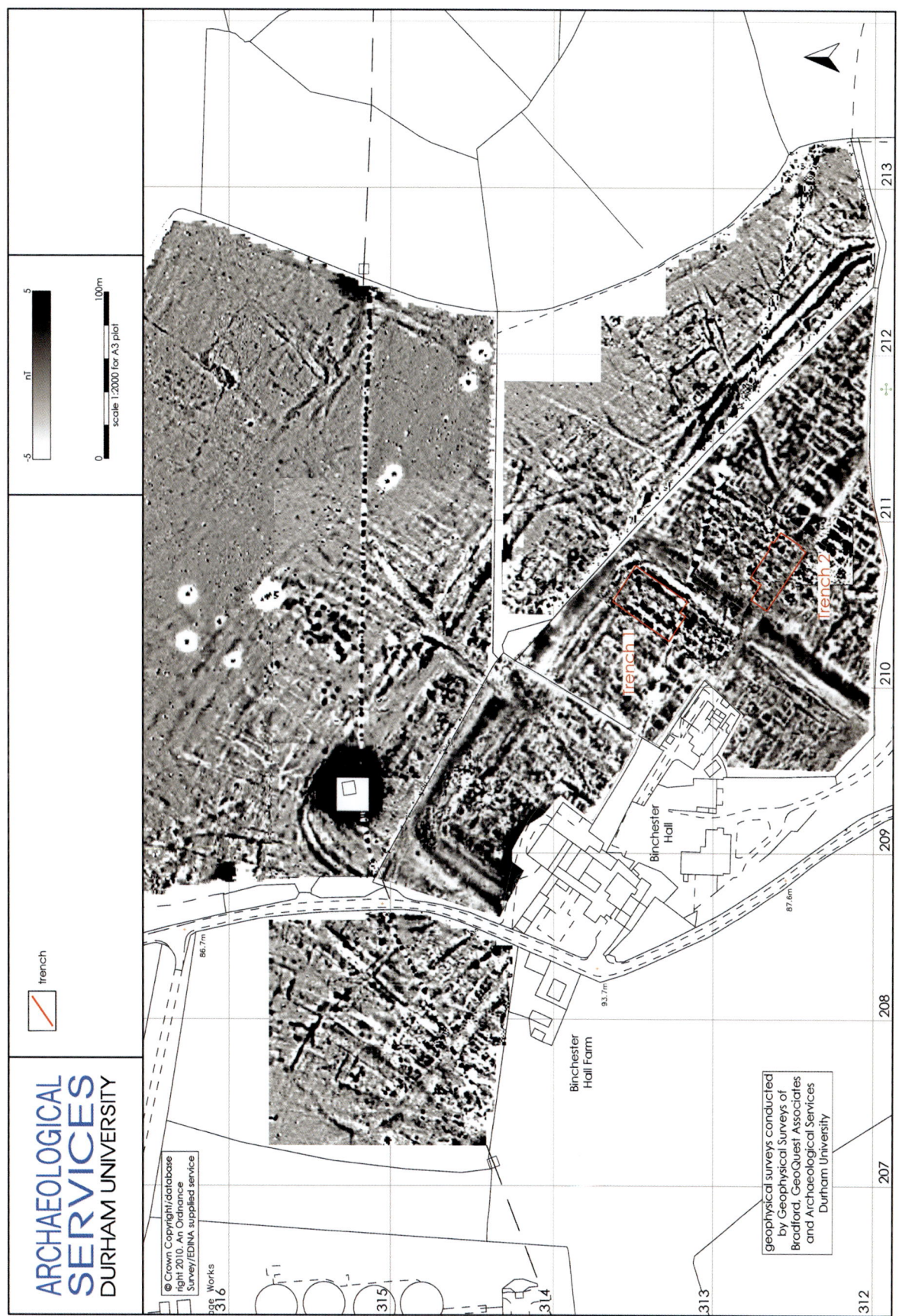

Figure 4.2: A geophysical survey of Binchester, showing the earlier and later phases of fort. Image credit: Durham University

the most significant archaeological investigation was the major exploration of the late Roman bath-house and associated *praetorium* that took place between 1976–1981 and 1986–1991. This revealed a well-preserved sequence of stratigraphy that ran from the earliest phase of occupation of the fort in the later 1st century AD through to the 5th century AD and beyond (Ferris 2010).

The earliest phases (Phases 1–2) were connected to the initial clearance in advance of the construction of the fort, and the erection of a timber building which may either have been a *praetorium* (prefiguring the later use of this area) or a *principia*. This appears to have been deliberately demolished *c*. AD 90–95. The following phases of activity (Phases 3–5) can be characterised as a period of dumping of refuse, including substantial quantities of butchered animal bone and pottery, as well as organic waste and sterile layers of clay, sand, and cobbles. Within these layers were also a series of industrial features, including hearths, hearth bases and furnaces. However, there was no indication of any permanent structures or buildings.

By the mid-2nd century AD, there was clearly a renewed phase of construction within the fort. The area previously given over to industrial activity and dumping became the site of a *praetorium* (Phase 6). This had very narrow stone walls, only *c*. 0.3 m wide, which may indicate that they were simply supporting a timber superstructure. This was partially demolished in the late 3rd century and replaced with a more substantially constructed all-stone *praetorium* (Phase 7). This was itself later demolished in the mid-4th century and replaced with a larger stone *praetorium* (Phase 8). This showed evidence for internal re-organisation and subsequent retraction and declining repair, before being turned over to industrial use, including a probable role as an abattoir (Phase 9). The precise chronology of Phases 8 and 9 is contested, with a key debate focusing on the extent to which activity continues into the 5th century (see below).

Barrack Block – Trench 1

Building on this important work on the *praetorium*, a new programme of research on Binchester commenced in 2009. Bringing together Durham University, Durham County Council, the Archaeological and Architectural Society of Durham and Northumberland and US partners, this further campaign of excavation was intended to look at two additional areas, with a trench (Trench 1) in the eastern corner of the fort and a trench located outside the fort just to the north of Dere Street, which sampled an area of the *vicus* (Trench 2). Both areas have produced important features, but in this paper the focus is on Trench 1 within the defences.

Trench 1 covered 42 × 26 m and was sited in order to expose an area of the fort where a typical barrack block might be located (Fig. 4.4). Within the excavated area the north-east and south-east edges included the interior scarp of the wall rampart, although the wall itself was only exposed in a limited number of areas, primarily at the point that a corner turret and latrine constructed against the wall were uncovered (see below). Two additional slots located the wall either side of the turret. It was noticeable that the gap between the wall and the intervallum roadway was very different on each rampart. On the north-east side, there was only a space of 4 m, but to the south-east the area of empty ground was over 5 m wide. This difference may be due to the fact that the south-east rampart must have comprised the original rampart of the early fort constructed in the late 1st century AD, whereas the north-east rampart was probably only erected following the contraction of the fort in the 2nd century.

The main structural feature was, as expected, a substantial rectangular structure that is clearly a late Roman barrack block. This was aligned northeast-southwest and at its greatest extent was approximately 12 m wide. It is not possible to determine its overall length as the southern end of the building extended beyond the edge of the excavated area, but it must have been at least 33 m. There is clear evidence of phasing within the barrack which will be explored below, although it is important to note that excavation and analysis is on-going so all conclusions, particularly with regard to dating, must remain provisional.

The earliest identified phase of structure is currently a clay-bonded stone structure with a footprint of less than 33 × 12 m (Fig. 4.3). This seems to have been divided along its length into ranges of paired rooms; *contubernia* on the western side and stables on the eastern side. The nature of the internal division between these two ranges of spaces is still to be resolved. There are a series of stone-lined post-holes and post-pads found within the floor surfaces associated with this earlier structure. However, it is not easy to identify any clear north–south alignments that could have formed the main internal dividing wall. An alternative partition is a central spine wall that ran along the length of the building slightly off-centre. This divided the barrack into two ranges, the one to the west of the central spine was 6 m in width, whilst the one to the east was 4 m wide. Frustratingly there are no solid stratigraphic relationships between any of the external walls or this central spine. The relationship between the northern gable end of the barrack and its eastern wall has been destroyed by a large late Roman pit, whilst an entrance at the western end of the north gable wall means there is no relationship with the western barrack wall; in any case, it is clear that the northern part of the western wall was rebuilt (see below). The central spine wall itself only butts up against the northern gable wall and is not bonded in.

The presence of three equally spaced hearths on the floor of the western range suggests that this area formed the main accommodation area. Crossing this eastern range at roughly equal distances (between 3 m and 4 m apart) are a series

4. Late Roman military buildings at Binchester (Co. Durham)

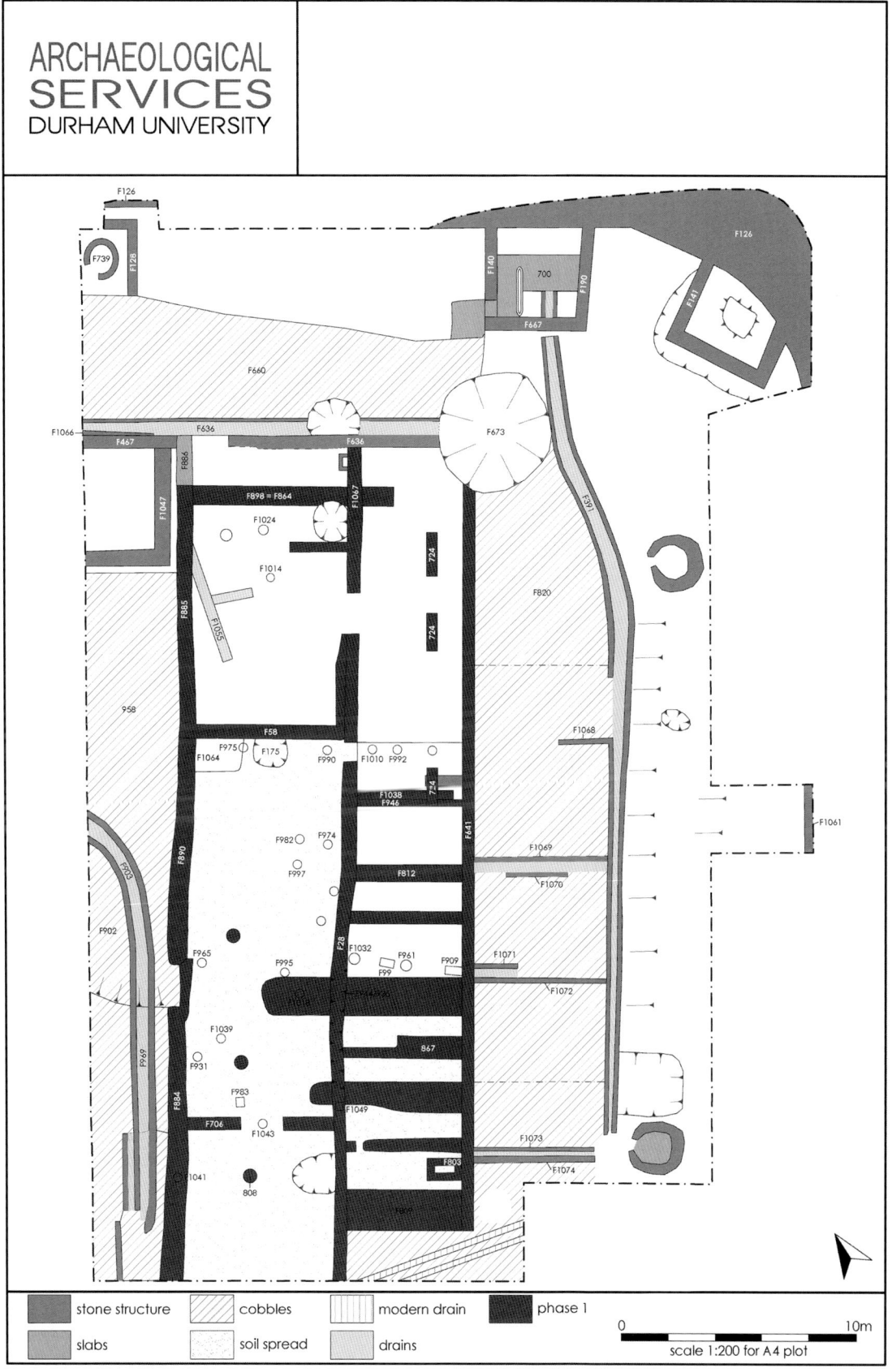

Figure 4.3: An outline plan of the Phase 1 barrack block. Image credit: Durham University

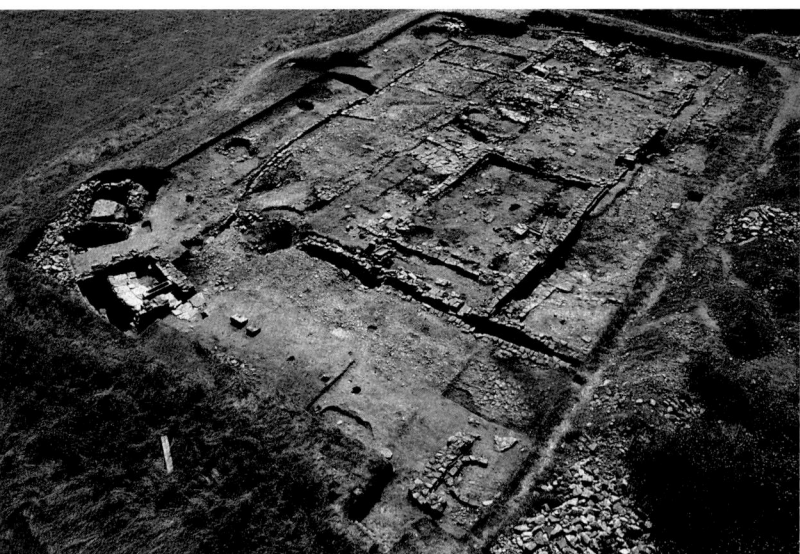

Figure 4.4: A vertical photograph of excavations within the barrack area at Binchester. Image credit: Durham University / Aerial Cam

of crude paved paths. These presumably provided access to the accommodation areas and in two cases this paving continues into the western half of the barrack; parallels can be found in all the 3rd- and 4th-century barracks at South Shields (Hodgson and Bidwell 2004, 137–139).

The series of paths and hearths imply that the barrack was divided into smaller rooms or compartments, and the stone-lined post-holes and post-pads mentioned earlier are likely to have had this function. There is one stone-built cross-wall towards the southern end of the barrack that does seem to separate two of the hearths, but there is no indication of other internal stone walls. In the eastern range of rooms a series of regularly spaces drainage channels were probably to expel horse urine and have parallels with similar examples from auxiliary cavalry barracks at sites such as Wallsend, as well as on the European mainland (Hodgson and Bidwell 2004, 130–132). It is clear that the Binchester barrack integrating the stables and *contubernia* are typical *Stallbaracken* ('stable-barracks') of the type found widely across the Empire (Sommer 1995). However, it is noticeable that these drains varied widely in size and constructional technique, which may be an indicator of a long period of use and possible reconstruction – although it is equally possible that not all these features were for horse urine, and some may have had a more general drainage function (Hodgson and Bidwell 2004, 139).

To the east of this barrack between the structure and the ramparts is an intra-vallum roadway. This was crossed by a series of lateral stone ridges. Their function is uncertain, but they are most likely to have facilitated drainage as they seem to spring from a roadside gully that ran along the eastern edge of the road.

At the northern end of the building the phasing is more complex, and as yet, still not fully resolved. It is here that the lack of clear stratigraphic relationships causes problems. Underlying the central spine and 2 m from the northern gable end is a cross-wall that butts up against the interior of the western barrack wall, but underlies the spine wall and projects into the eastern range of the building, but does not reach the eastern wall of the barrack. The western barrack wall, however, is clearly part of a single phase of construction that also includes the southern and part of an eastern wall, which underlies the central spine forming a discrete compartment in this part of the barrack. This might suggest that this compartment preceded the construction of the spine wall. However, there is a gap in the spine wall immediately to the south of the southern wall of the northern compartment. Although the wall north and south of this gap is clearly on the same alignment, there is no chronological link, and it is quite likely that the northern stretch of the spine wall is a later rebuild, although presumably there is an earlier phase contemporary with the southern stretch of spine wall that is still to be excavated.

It is probable that the cross-wall here may have been part of a larger structural unit that originally extended beyond the spine wall. The fact that this area seems to have formed a coherent and possibly higher status compartment in a later period is circumstantial evidence that this area might have been treated differently in an earlier phase. However, there is no southern or northern return to this cross-wall, although it is possible that this was in wood and so traces of it have not survived later activity.

It is clear that there is a secondary phase in which the occupied space within the barrack contracted significantly (Fig. 4.5). The eastern range of the barrack stopped being used; it is probable that it was deliberately demolished as

4. Late Roman military buildings at Binchester (Co. Durham)

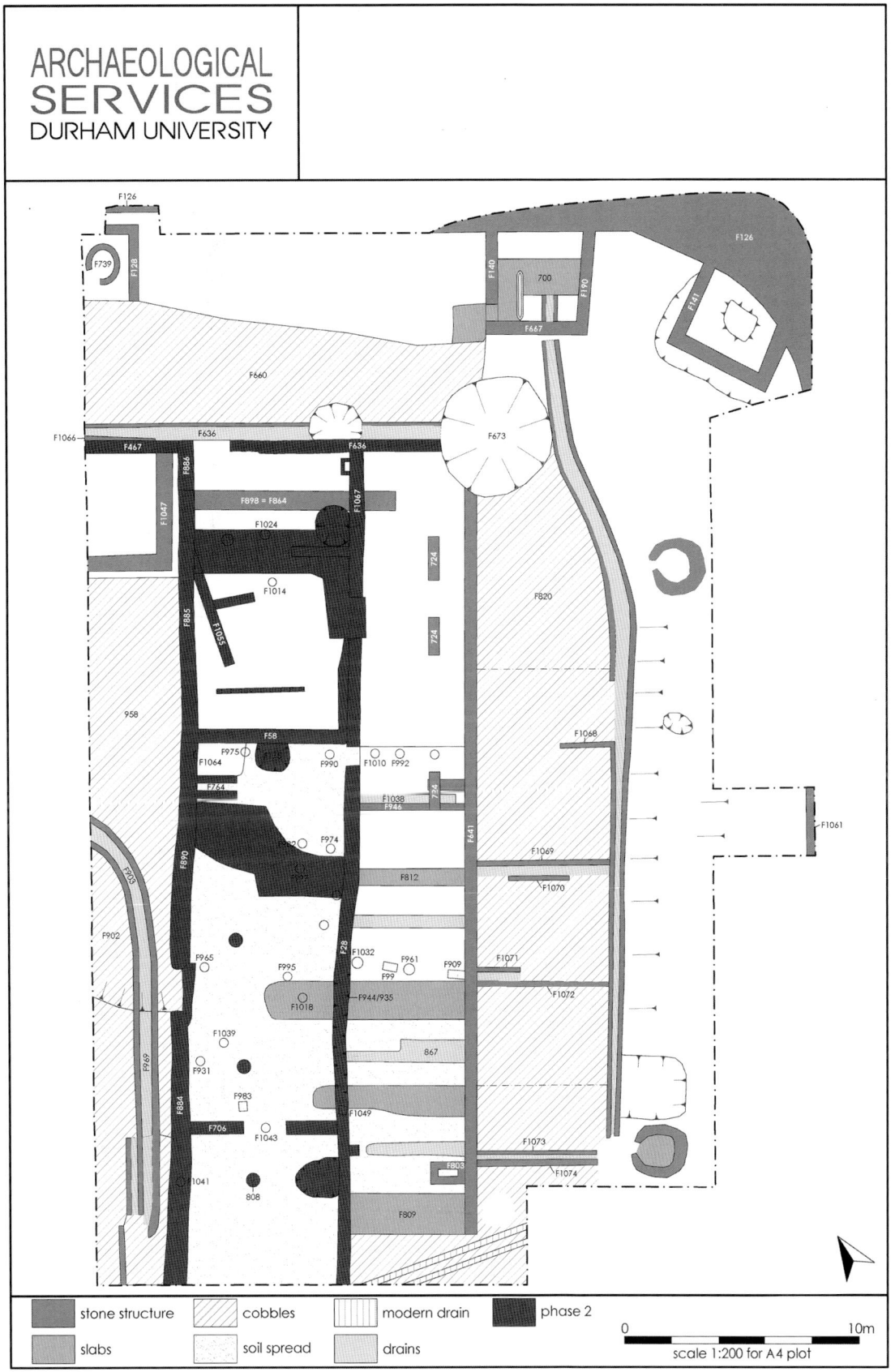

Figure 4.5: An outline plan of the Phase 2 barrack block. Image credit: Durham University

the tops of the eastern wall were at the same level as, and incorporated into, layers of gravel and cobbles that appear to have formed an area of hard-standing between the newly reduced barrack and the intra-vallum road. The resulting structure does not seem to have shrunk in length but was now only around 6 m wide. It is presumably contemporary with this reduction in size or subsequent to it that the northern compartment was rebuilt as a single phase of construction along its west and south and part of its eastern edge. It appears that the eastern wall of this compartment suffered some structural problems and was subsequently rebuilt. The constructional history at the very northern end of the structure is also complex. It is possible that the northern cross-wall previously mentioned may have formed the original northern gable of the structure. To the north of it, but to the south of the later gable wall, ran a stone-lined drainage gully. However, it appears that at a later date, the gable wall was moved about 2 m north and the drainage gully was rebuilt using the gable wall itself as its southern edge.

This northern compartment forms a discrete unit measuring roughly 6 × 11 m. There are two identifiable possible entrances. There is a door at the western end of the north gable; however it is not certain that this was used in this latest phase of occupation, as it is clear that the original internal floor level for this door was considerably lower than the floor level of the contracted barrack. At some point it appears that the internal rampart scarp to the immediate north of this doorway must have been built-up; the new line of the gully that incorporated part of the gable wall cut through the rampart dumping, which was at broadly the same level as the late phase floor. Indeed, there is some indication that this doorway may have been crudely blocked. The other entrance is in the eastern wall of the building and inside the building there is a clearly shaped stone hearthstone and an interior clay/gravel path. A stone-lined drainage gully and a cobbled surface lay in the southern half of the compartment. The gully is typical of those found in other auxiliary cavalry barracks and was used for draining stable areas. There is no clear division between this stable area and the northern, presumably residential, element of the compartment, although there is a stub of walling that projects westwards from the eastern wall; this may have acted as an internal divider, perhaps combined with a wooden partition or something more ephemeral such as a simple screen or curtain. To the north of this wall stub is a smaller space. In the north-eastern corner a stone basin was seated at floor level, but could easily have been used for washing. Just to the south of it is a small pit about 1 m wide. This partially cuts the cross-wall identifiable from the earlier phase. It is not clear whether it, in its turn, is cut by the rebuilt eastern wall of the compartment or simply butts up hard against it. A large stone drain was also constructed in the central area of the quarters that ran through the western wall and debouched into the street running along the western side of the barrack.

In the area of the barrack to the south of this northern compartment, the nature of continued activity is less clear. There is at least one large patch of stone paving forming a good quality floor in the centre of the building. It is not clear, though, whether the assumed internal division of this area into small compartments continued. The paved area is associated with a pit which has been placed hard up against the cross-wall marking the southern edge of the northern unit. This pit had several layers of superimposed stone-lining; the upper layers of this were contiguous with the associated paved flooring to the south.

Despite the broad characterisation of the structure as having two main phases, the earlier broad barrack with two ranges of rooms, and the later, narrower, single range barrack, it is clear that within this simple periodization that there is considerable chronological complexity. Walls from both phases show considerable evidence for reworking and reconstruction, varying widely along the length of individual walls. For example, it is possible that part of the southern end of the spine wall may at one stage have been constructed from timber uprights supported in a dug foundation packed with rocks. A broad comparison to this can be found at South Shields, where Phase 2B of the cavalry barrack was built largely in stone, but retained a front wall mainly of timber construction. A similar situation also occurred at Wallsend (Hodgson and Bidwell 2004, 143). Equally, the extensive range of flagstone, cobble and metalled surfaces, post-holes, post-pads, and drains attest to a long period of use and continued reworking of the structure.

Around the reduced barrack block was a heterogenous group of hollows, pits, and scoops. Many of these abutted the walls of the structure. The precise function of the original cut features may well have varied; for example, a large sunken feature lying against the northern gable wall was probably caused by subsidence from an undetermined feature underlying the barrack block, as were several major depressions along the western side of the barrack. Others were clearly deliberately cut, whilst some appear to have been little more than shallow depressions in the surface perhaps caused by normal wear and tear. However, all appeared to have become filled with deposits containing significant quantities of butchered animal bone (see below).

It is clear that at least one phase of the barrack block was roofed with stone tiles – many have been found across the site. However, plant macro-fossils from this trench indicate that there was a substantial quantity of heather at the site. A detailed environmental analysis of this material suggested that the harvest of heather was being actively managed, and it may have been used as a roofing material, as was common in the region in the medieval period, although it could well have been brought to Binchester as a fodder crop or bedding for the cavalry mounts (Joyce 2012).

Non-barrack activity

In addition to the main barrack block, a series of other features of probable late Roman date were identified within this trench. The most significant structure was a latrine block that lay just to the north-west of the eastern corner tower of the fort. This was built up against the interior of the fort wall and measured roughly 10 × 10 m. There were at least two phases of activity identifiable. Water was sluiced through the latrine via the roadside gully that ran along the edge of the intra-vallum roadway. This entered the latrine block through a hole in the southern wall and exited at a lower level through a carefully constructed arched conduit in the fort wall. The effluent clearly ended up deposited in the fort ditch. In winter months the quantity of water running through this system must have been enough to keep the system reasonably clear. This northern side of the fort lay downhill from the rest of the interior and as a consequence most internal rainwater run-off would have exited the fort via this latrine and any others located in a similar downhill location. However, in summer, there may not have been adequate rainfall to keep this system running effectively.

At some stage, it appears that the floor level of the latrine was raised, and along with it the associated gully for the water, which as a consequence did not run directly into the conduit through the wall. Although on the same alignment, a direct flow must have been replaced by a "soakaway" arrangement. The lining of the later phase of gully within the latrine incorporated re-used structural stone from elsewhere within the fort. Just to the south of the latrine block was a substantial pit, which in places retained hints of a timber lining. Although filled with butchered animal bone and other debris, this may have once functioned as a water hole and could have provided a supplementary source of water for the latrine when there was inadequate through-flow via the roadside gully.

The internal spatial organisation of the latrine was not complex. On the north side of the block, there was a large trench into which the gully ran. This was presumably covered by a timber or stone superstructure which held the latrine seats. Fragments of two stone seats were recovered from the fill of this trench, and a large stone with a rectangular hole which may have supported a vertical or horizontal timber support. Substantial subsidence underlying the flag-stone floor in the as yet incompletely excavated southern half of the latrine may indicate that another trench underlies it. It is possible that the raising of the interior floor level may have involved halving the latrine capacity.

Other features from the trench include a number of features built into the north-east rampart, which itself was predominantly constructed of yellow clay. In the western corner of the trench was half of a small structure that may have been the base of a turret or tower; although it may simply have been a small structure protecting the circular oven that lay within. Two further ovens have been identified in the south-west rampart. One, near the corner tower, is almost certainly Roman in date, although another towards the eastern corner of our trench is arguably of medieval date (see below). Between the north-eastern rampart and the northern gable of the barrack were a series of stone-lined post-holes running parallel to the rampart. These were roughly paired, although the match was not precise. These presumably formed some kind of simple wooden structure or pentice built against the rampart.

Chronology of Roman activity

As this project is still running, the post-excavation analysis is at an early stage and any thoughts about the chronology of the activity in the barrack must remain provisional. Nonetheless, it is possible to begin to explore some of the broad temporal parameters within which the later phases of activity in the barrack may have belonged.

The barrack block is unlikely to have had its origins before the first abandonment of the fort. This appears to have begun *c.* AD 90–95 / 100 and continued until *c.* AD 110 / 120–AD 120 / 130 (Phases 3–5; Ferris 2010, 32–42), with the fort being reoccupied in the Antonine period. It is at this stage that the fort is likely to have contracted from its earlier, more extensive, perimeter to the boundaries which appear to have defined the fort for the rest of its active life. It is possible that the subsidence found in several places in and around the barrack may have been caused by features related to the earliest phases of activity within the fort. The new *praetorium* of the revived fort was first erected as a half-timbered structure (Phase 6; mid 2nd to late 3rd century AD) and then as a stone structure (Phase 7; late 3rd to mid-4th century AD) (Ferris 2010, 42–52).

It is not clear that the sequence of activity in the *praetorium* can be used to calibrate the activity in the barrack, however, and the dates for the sequence of wooden to stone structures should not be used uncritically as a *terminus post quem* for the earlier stone-built phase of the barrack block. Hodgson and Bidwell also caution against using construction type as a chronological marker (Hodgson and Bidwell 2004, 144). Nonetheless, it may help to provide a chronological context for the Binchester barrack. It is not certain that there was a timber predecessor to the Binchester barrack. However, in a survey of auxiliary barracks by Nick Hodgson and Paul Bidwell, the transition from wooden to stone barracks in the northern frontier appears to have begun in the mid- to late 2nd century AD (Hodgson and Bidwell 2004, 142–144) At Wallsend, Hadrianic barracks constructed of timber were converted into stone post *c.* AD 160, whilst at South Shields two timber barracks were constructed *c.* AD 160 and replaced in stone before *c.* AD 200 (Hodgson and Bidwell 2004, 143). Although it is always difficult to generalise on the basis of poorly preserved structures and incomplete excavation, it does seem difficult to date the emergence of stone barracks before the second half of the 2nd century, perhaps giving the first phase of the Binchester barrack *c*. AD 150–160 as a conservative and circumstantial *terminus post quem*.

It is, at present, a challenge to date the apparent contraction of a barrack with two ranges of rooms to a single range. Although further analysis of the ceramics and artefactual assemblage will undoubtedly help to clarify the precise chronology of this transition, at the moment it is not possible to be more precise than suggesting a broad 3rd- or 4th-century date for this process. However, it is possible to make some suggestions about the date of its final use. There are two radiocarbon dates from the fill of the large pit/waterhole that cuts the junction of the north gable and the east wall of the larger phase of the barrack block. The first provides a date of 250–290 cal AD (5.1%), 320–540 cal AD (90.3%) (BETA-302143), the second, from lower in the sequence, provided a date of 127–248 cal AD (95.4%). Whilst one needs naturally to exercise caution in the interpretation of such dates, and in particular, be aware of the potential redeposition of materials in a complex and long-lived site, this would not be incompatible with the pit being dug and starting to fill up by the late 2nd or early 3rd century, although it is possible that given the size and clear evidence for long use and multiple recuts of the pit, that it was originally excavated before the barrack contracted and subsequently expanded in size. It is even feasible that the decision to remove the original eastern wall of the barrack block was caused by the pit causing subsidence or collapse in the north-east corner of the structure.

More generally, a very interim overview of the pottery assemblage from this trench seems to suggest continued activity within the area up until *c*. AD 370. The range of material recovered includes not surprisingly large quantities of East Yorkshire calcite gritted ware, Crambeck grey and parchment wares, as well as finewares, particularly Nene Valley colour-coats. The coinage from the excavations in the *praetorium* more or less ceases by Reece Period 19 (AD 364–378) (Reece 2010), and this is broadly reflected in the coin assemblage from both Trench 1 and the recent excavations in Trench 2, although a handful of Theodosian coins have been recovered indicating continued activity on the site in some form.

This dating evidence seems to combine to suggest a major period of change in this area of the site in the AD 360s or 370s. This contrasts partially with the evidence from the *praetorium*, because although coinage stops around this date there is evidence for later pottery use. In his report on the ceramics from the *praetorium* site, Jeremy Evans suggested that here pottery might still have been in use until the early 5th century, possible even as late as AD 420 / 430. Of course, it is possible that more detailed analysis of the pottery assemblage from the barrack might push back the date of the latest pottery into the late 4th or even early 5th century, but the evidence so far remains equivocal.

Despite the lack of precise dating and the clear need for further detailed analysis of the artefactual material, we might however cautiously advance a very basic chronology for the barrack. It is unlikely that the barrack would have been built in stone before *c*. AD 160, and the evidence from the earlier C14 date from the large pit that cuts the eastern wall/northern gable wall junction suggests a broadly late 2nd- or early 3rd-century date, we are probably looking at this period of use running from broadly the mid- to late 2nd century to perhaps the early 3rd century. The subsequent reduced size of the barrack probably commences early 3rd and may have continued in use until mid-4th century. However, one should acknowledge the limitations of using the date of the pit as indicating the date of the change in barrack plan and a later, perhaps considerably later, date for the retraction in the size of the structure is quite possible.

Does the lack of coinage and pottery from the barrack indicate that all activity had ceased in this area after AD370? It is clear from the *praetorium* that activity continued later into the later 4th century and beyond. From the AD 360s the *praetorium* and its bath suite declined in the level of its repair, and in Phase 9 the area saw large scale dumps of rubbish with some craft and butchery or slaughterhouse activities taking place within the *praetorium* rooms. This was then covered with dumped clay, rough paved surfaces associated with antler working (Ferris 2010, 82–91). The excavator of the *praetorium* has argued for a long chronology based on radiocarbon dates that takes Phase 9 from the very late 4th century to the mid-5th century (Ferris 2010, 82). This contrasts with a shorter and slightly earlier chronology proposed by Nick Hodgson, which places the commencement in the mid-4th century, contemporary with the latest coinage, with the first period of Phase 9 ceasing by cal AD 380–400, and the antler working phase by AD 390–430 (Hodgson 2013, 410).

A range of very similar activity is visible in and around the barrack, with large quantities of butchered animal bone being widely distributed around and to a lesser extent, within, the structure. The large pit associated with flagstone paving that butts up against the southern gable wall of the northern compartment contained substantial quantities of bone, including cattle skulls, as well as fragments of sawn antler. Crucially, this pit has produced two radiocarbon dates of 407–547 cal AD (SUERC-60237) and 422–576 cal AD (SUERC-60238), which are noticeably later than either of the proposed chronologies for the *praetorium* and are comparable for the dates from two late 5th-early 6th century Anglo-Saxon burials that lay over the sub-Roman activity. This would seem to indicate use of the barrack structure relatively late, although there has yet no evidence for earlier 5th century use, and it is not yet clear whether we are looking at continuity of activity or simply late re-use.

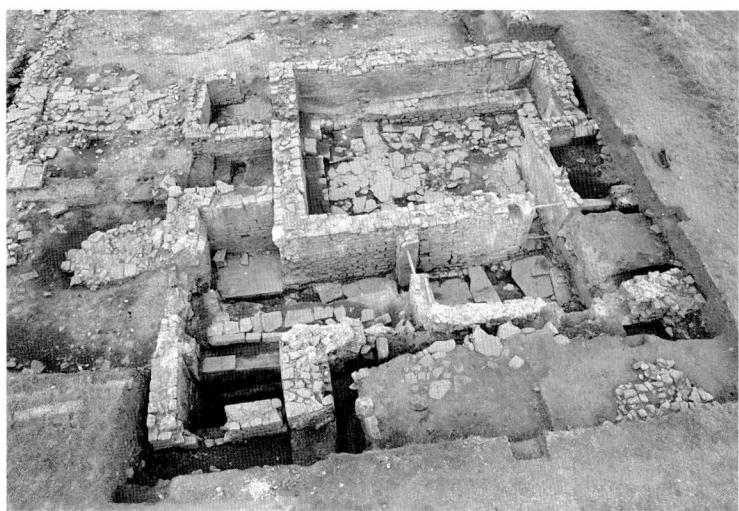

Figure 4.6: The Vicus bath-house under excavation. Image credit: Durham University

Later medieval activity

It is clear that there was activity of much later date within the trench. This could be seen most clearly in the construction of a building with stone-rubble walls that lay in the southern corner of the trench. This was on a slightly different alignment to the Roman fort and was clearly stratigraphically higher than much of the other activity within this trench. It was associated with a stone-lined oven that contained substantial quantities of charcoal. Although it was impossible to identify a direct stratigraphic relationship between the two, their spatial proximity and differences in the constructional techniques in this oven and the other ovens in this trench, suggest it may be contemporary with the building.

A small pit cutting through the intravallum roadway contained a leg of a fallow deer, which produced a radiocarbon date of AD 1181–1269. This pit was adjacent to a gully that cut across the site running from one of two adjacent pits inserted into the south-eastern rampart across the road and into the southern part of the barrack building. This portion of the barrack showed clear evidence for significant activity of medieval date. In places, the upper layers of the stone spreads overlying the eastern range of the building appear to have incorporated the tops of the barrack walls into them, suggesting that they were no longer upstanding. However, in other areas, there are indications that a medieval structure was built within the footprint of the barrack, potentially using the barrack walls as bases for later superstructures. There were a number of substantial pits cut into this area, which contained medieval green-glazed pottery.

There is nothing to suggest that this phase of activity dates to before the Norman Conquest. The earliest dating evidence (the radiocarbon date) and a long-cross penny of Henry III (ruled 1216–1273) imply a broadly late 12th- or 13th-century date for its commencement. The Boldon Book (written in 1183), a custumal account of rents and dues owed to the Bishops of Durham, records that the inhabitants of Binchester were obliged to attend the great hunt of the Bishops and supply a horse and a dog. Much of this medieval activity is seemingly contemporary with this record and is the first structural evidence of the buildings associated with this medieval estate. The articulated leg of fallow deer, a species specifically introduced by the Normans for hunting, should clearly be seen in the context of the documentary records of involvement in the hunt. The green-glazed pottery appears to indicate that activity continued in this area of the site until perhaps the 14th or 15th century AD.

Discussion

While still in need of further excavation and post-excavation analysis, the result of the current phase of investigation in Trench 1 is providing some useful insights into patterns of late Roman activity at Binchester and more widely in northern England. Although there is some evidence that activity in both the *praetorium* and the barrack may continue into the 5th century AD, it is noticeable that the major transition in the *praetorium* occurs in the AD 360s or 370s, when the house and baths fall out of use and are converted into an area for butchery and some basic industrial activity. On the basis of a superficial analysis of the coins and pottery from the barrack, a similar change appears to be occurring there. Intriguingly, similar changes might be underway in the *vicus*, where an exceptionally well-preserved bath-house falls out of use in the second half of the 4th century, probably around the AD 360s/370s on the basis of an initial analysis of the pottery assemblage from massive refuse deposits, which were dumped within the interior of this structure (Fig. 4.6).

Whilst Binchester occupies a key position in debates about on-going activity on Roman military sites in the 5th century, it is clear that there had been a major phase of change before the cessation of Roman control, in keeping with most other military sites on the northern frontier. Of course, it is likely that further chronological precision will be obtained following full post-excavation analysis. In particular, there is a need to better understand the chronological relationship between the sequences of activity in the three main excavated areas. For example, it is possible that the construction of the new bath-house in the *praetorium* in the AD 350s or 360s may post-date the cessation of activity in the *vicus* bath-house; indeed the two events may even be linked. If so, this would indicate interesting dynamics in the relationship between the fort and *vicus*, with potentially some *vicus* activities moving to within the fort.

The barracks themselves fit comfortably within the broad range of late Roman barracks known from the northern frontier, particularly the earlier phase stable barrack. It is harder to find direct comparanda for the later contraction of the structure, and it is noticeable that there is no sign of so-called "chalet" construction in this final phase of use. The reduction in size may be related to the widespread reduction in unit size known in the 4th century, although the admittedly circumstantial dating evidence for this change points to an earlier, 3rd-century date.

There are still key challenges for a further understanding of the late occupation at Binchester. Perhaps the most important is to refine the chronology of the final major stage of activity connected to the butchery of cattle and some other light industrial and craft activities. There are some important chronological issues at stake here. Key is the relationship between the butchery taking place in the *praetorium*, the barrack block, and the *vicus*. Currently dating would suggest that it terminates first in the vicus, then the *praetorium*, with the barracks faunal assemblage belonging to the later 5th century or later. Yet, this is based on only a few dates, and it is still not clear how representative they are of the wider intra-site chronology. It is still not clear how long each faunal assemblage took to build up, so it will be important to assess whether there is overlap or if the assemblages developed at different times, and whether there is any break in activity.

Until we can answer some of these issues, there are number of possible scenarios that may be at play here. Whatever the precise chronology, it is clear that there is a significant phase, or phases, of butchery at late and post-Roman Binchester. This might imply that a significant population was present for whom this meat was being prepared. Similar late Roman dumps containing substantial and broadly comparable faunal assemblages are known from late Roman Lincoln and have been interpreted as an indicator of continued economic complexity and by extension the presence of a reasonably substantial population (Dobney *et al.* 1998). However, at Binchester these faunal remains seemingly go hand in hand with a seeming decline in the use of coinage and pottery from the mid to late 4th century. There is virtually no evidence for contemporary structural remains that might be thought of as residential. So, where are the people? One possibility is that further post-excavation analysis will increase the proportion of later pottery and coinage in these assemblages, but the underlying question about where the population resided would remain. It may quite simply be that they lived elsewhere within the fort. The defended area is very large, and despite three trenches being excavated, we have sampled probably less than 1% of the entire fort and *vicus*.

It is also conceivable that the joints of meat being produced at Binchester were not intended for consumption on site, or even in the immediate locality. There are hints from the faunal assemblage that at least some of this meat was cured through drying or perhaps smoking, and could thus be easily transported elsewhere. If so, we may be seeing Binchester becoming some form of supply depot, which processed and prepared meat for consumption elsewhere (Collins 2012, 62). For example, excavation of the 4th-century coastal signal station at Filey (North Yorkshire) shows that it was being systematically provisioned from elsewhere and supplied with prepared joints, with little evidence for on-site butchery (Ottaway 2001).

Large-scale cattle slaughter would also result in the availability of substantial quantities of leather and hide, which would have multiple uses in a military context. In many ways, this activity could be seen as Binchester reverting to its previous role as a centre for military supply and production in the mid-2nd century AD (Phases 3–5 in the *praetorium*). Rather than seeing such activity as being an aspect of the transformation of the site from a Roman settlement to an early medieval centre, it may simply just be typical of the kind of activities for which forts may have been used by the Roman army.

If a longer chronology is preferred, pushing the bulk of the butchery into the very late Roman and early post-Roman period, then we still face similar interpretative issues. Where are the people for whom this meat is intended? Rather than being a part of a military supply chain, should this instead be seen as more socially embedded redistribution of food stuffs, perhaps by a proto-'warlord'? Even more fundamentally, how can we tell the difference between the two? There are of course a range of alternative scenarios for the latest phases at Binchester, which will hopefully be refined following further chronological analysis.

Acknowledgements

This paper is based on the results of fieldwork at Binchester carried out by Durham University, Archaeological Services, Durham University, Durham County Council, the Archaeological and Architectural Society for Durham and Northumberland and Vinovia, a non-profit organisation. Special thanks to Peter Carne and Matt Claydon from Archaeological Services Durham University and Nick Hodgson for his insight over the course of several site visits. Any errors remain the author's.

Bibliography

Birbeck, V. (2014) A *Time Team* evaluation at Binchester Roman Fort, County Durham. *Durham Archaeological Journal* 19, 23–32.

Collins, R. (2011) Military communities and the transformation of the frontier from the fourth to sixth centuries. In D. Petts and S. Turner (eds) *Early Medieval Northumbria: New Visions and New Directions*, 15–35. Studies in the Early Middle Ages 24, Brepols, Turnhout.

Collins, R. (2012) *Hadrian's Wall and the End of Empire: The Roman Frontier in the Fourth and Fifth Centuries*. London, Routledge.

Dobney, K., Ottaway, P., Kenward, H. and Donel, L. (1998) Down, but not out: biological evidence for complex economic organization in Lincoln in the late 4th century. *Antiquity* 72, 417–424.

Ferris, I. (2010) *The Beautiful Rooms are Empty: Excavations at Binchester Roman Fort: County Durham 1976–81 and 1986–1991*. Durham, Durham County Council.

Ferris, I. (2011) *Vinovia: the Buried Roman City of Binchester in Northern England*. Stroud, Amberley Press

Hodgson, N. (2013) Review of "*The Beautiful Rooms are Empty: Excavations at Binchester Roman Fort, County Durham 1976–1981 and 1986–1991*. By I.M. Ferris. Durham County Council, and *Vinovia: the Buried Roman City of Binchester in Northern England*. By I. M. Ferris. *Britannia* 44, 409–410.

Hodgson, N. and Bidwell, P. (2004) Auxiliary barracks in a new light: recent discoveries on Hadrian's Wall. *Britannia* 35, 121–157.

Joyce, J. (2012) *The charred plant remains from Hilly's Pit, Binchester Roman Fort, Bishop Auckland, Co. Durham: Evidence for plant resource use and human-environment interaction*. Unpublished MSc Dissertation, Department of Archaeology, Durham University.

Ottaway, P. (2001) Excavations on the site of the Roman signal station at Carr Naze, Filey, 1993–94. *Archaeological Journal* 157, 79–199.

Petts, D. (2013) Military and civilian: reconfiguring the end of Roman Britain in the north. *European Journal of Archaeology* 16(2), 314–335.

Sommer, C. S. (1995) "Where did they put the horses?" Uberlegungen zu Aufbau und Starke römischer Auxiliartruppen und deren Unterbringung in den Kastellen. *Provincialrömische Forschungen: Festschrift für Günter Ulbert zum 65. Geburtstag*, 149–168. Espelkamp, M. Leidorf.

Wilmott, T. (1997) *Birdoswald, Excavations of a Roman Fort on Hadrian's Wall and its successor settlements: 1987–92*. London, English Heritage.

Wilmott, T. (2000) The Late Roman transition at Birdoswald and on Hadrian's Wall. In T. Wilmott and P. Wilson (eds) *The Late Roman Transition in the North*, 13–23. BAR British Series 299, Oxford, British Archaeological Reports.

Wilmott, T. and Wilson, P. (eds) (2000) *The Late Roman Transition in the North*. BAR British Series 299, Oxford, British Archaeological Reports.

Wilmott, T. (2010) The late Roman frontier: a structural background. In R. Collins and L. Allason-Jones (eds) *Finds from the Frontier: Material culture in the 4th–5th centuries*, 10–16. CBA Research Report 162, London, CBA

5

FOURTH-CENTURY FORTLETS IN BRITAIN: SOPHISTICATED SYSTEMS OR DESPERATE MEASURES?

Matthew F. A. Symonds

Introduction

Fortlet defensive architecture in Britain reached its apogee during the 4th century AD. Although many of the 2nd-century fortlets known as milecastles on Hadrian's Wall appear to have endured in a recognisable form into the 4th century, elsewhere in Britain a new breed of fortlets emerged. Focused on the coastline, these installations incorporated advances in defensive technology pioneered on the European mainland, and represent the most sophisticated fortlets ever constructed in Britain. The most famous example of this late flowering of fortlet architecture is the chain of fortlets erected along the North Yorkshire coast in the final decades of the 4th century (Fig. 5.1). This cordon utilised hybrid installations, which fused fortlet and tower archetypes, to control landing grounds along a remote stretch of coastline. The prominence of the Yorkshire stations in the archaeological literature has, though, arguably eclipsed a more diverse group of small, 4th-century installations founded elsewhere in Britain. Among them are installations with defences incorporating elements that are both more, and substantially less, sophisticated than their counterparts in North Yorkshire.

Newly founded 4th-century fortlets in Britain occur both on the coast and inland along the road network, and may well have been more numerous than is currently accepted. The probably late Roman fortifications established on or near the Welsh coast at Caer Gybi and Hen Waliau, for example, resemble fortlets, but are rarely interpreted as such. Both these sites boast remarkably well-preserved masonry ramparts, which display conspicuous similarities in construction method (Wheeler 1924, 98). Despite this homogeneity, prevailing scholarly opinion holds that these installations served different purposes. As well as questioning this assertion, the following paper will consider whether vestiges of comparable masonry at Burrow Walls (Cumbria) could imply that late fortlets were deployed more widely along Britain's west coast than is currently appreciated. It will also examine the implications of a more rudimentary set of fortifications established on the main highway from Carlisle to York. When considered as a group, these late fortlets offer a unique insight into a complex and evolving security situation in northern England, and hint at a divergence between the degree of risk posed to military interests by internal and external threats.

The function of fortlets

Fortlets are best understood as a mechanism by which a small group of soldiers could be safely outposted away from their home base in areas where there were concerns about security. No universally accepted definition of a fortlet currently exists (see for example Mackensen 1987, 69; Walker 1989, 85), but during the first three centuries AD it seems appropriate to identify the absence of a *principia* as the key distinction between a fortlet and a fort (Frere and St Joseph 1983, 135). As the soldiers making up a fortlet garrison were on detachment duty, their formal unit headquarters lay elsewhere. This is not to suggest that individual fortlets had no administrative capability; study of road fortlets in the eastern Egyptian desert has emphasised their role in creating, copying, and circulating prodigious quantities of correspondence (Maxfield 1996). There is a difference, though, between a dedicated space for managing day-to-day military bureaucracy, and a formal headquarters building charged with ceremonial and ritual significance.

In practise most 1st- to 3rd-century fortlets are immediately distinguishable from forts by virtue of their

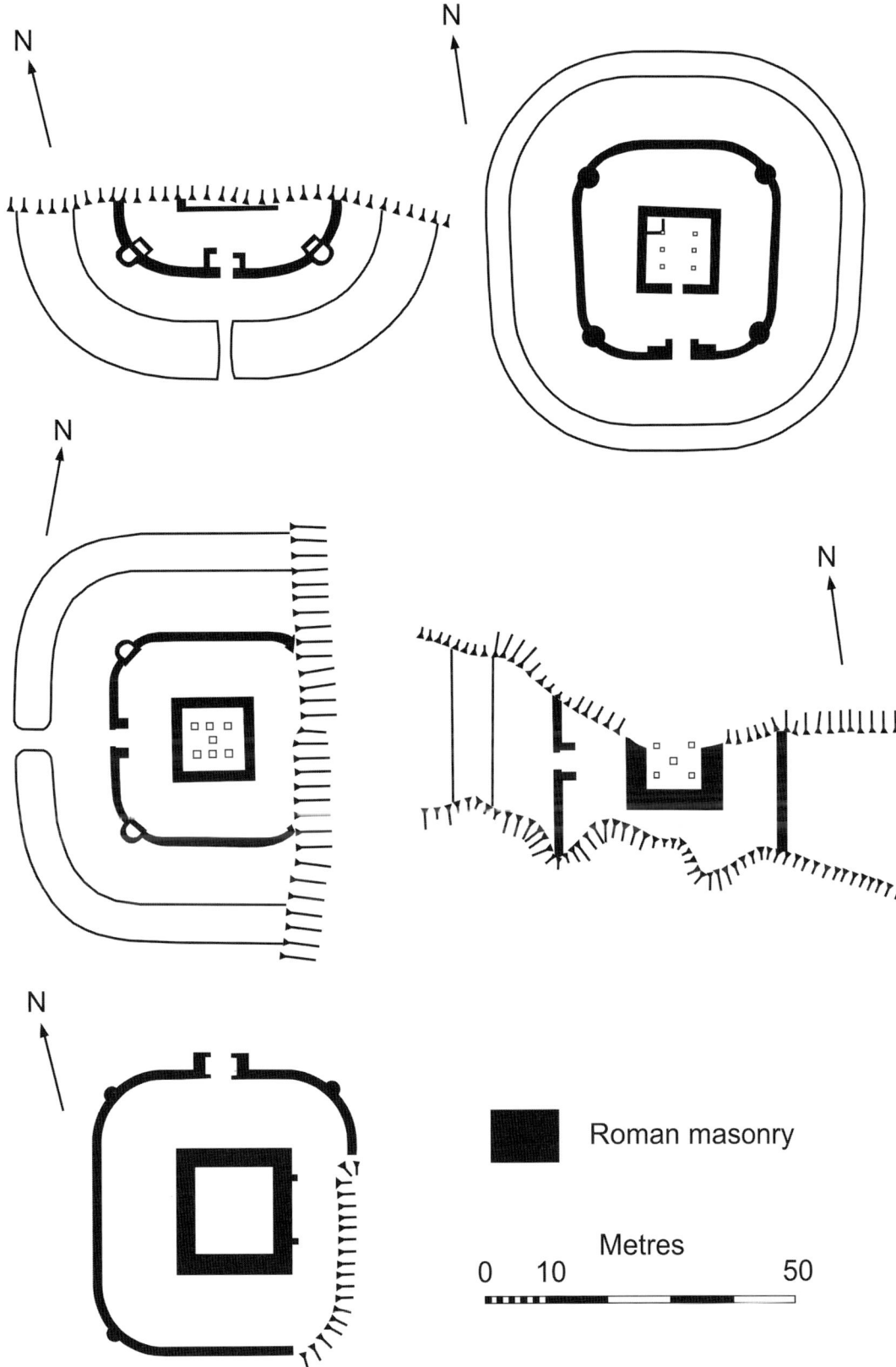

Figure 5.1: The Yorkshire fortlets and the Nunnery on Alderney. Clockwise from top left: Huntcliff, Goldsborough, Filey, and Scarborough. Bottom left: the Nunnery. After: Wilson 1991; Monaghan 2011

size. The space available within fortlets varied considerably during this period, with the smallest freestanding fortlets – that is fortlets not constructed as part of a formal frontier system – enclosing *c.* 200 m², while the very largest seemingly contain areas in excess of 4,200 m². This brings a handful of fortlets into the size-range of the smallest reduced forts on the Antonine Wall, creating ambiguity for sites such as Raeburnfoot (Dumfries and Galloway), which may be either a small fort or a large fortlet. Most freestanding fortlets founded in Britain during the 1st to 3rd centuries AD were, though, far smaller than forts and the greatest concentration of internal areas falls between 600m² and 1,200 m². The fluctuating size of freestanding fortlets reflects a high degree of design flexibility, which is probably a consequence of individual installations being tailored to the specific task its garrison was deployed to undertake. Distribution of freestanding fortlets across Britain is uneven, suggesting that they were built where and when they were needed, rather than as an automatic by-product of conquest. If so, the presence or absence of fortlets in any given region should have implications for our perception of the local security situation.

Using either the absence of a *principia* or installation size to distinguish fortlets from forts becomes more problematic in the 4th century, when readily identifiable headquarters buildings are no longer a staple of fort layouts. This transition is well illustrated on the Saxon Shore, where the early forts at Brancaster and Reculver, which were probably erected in the first half of the 3rd century (Pearson 2002, 14; 54), display traditional *principia*. Comparable headquarters buildings cannot be clearly associated with the developed, probably late-3rd-century, Saxon Shore forts boasting high ramparts studded with bastions. Equally, changes in unit strength seem to bring late forts on the European mainland closer in size to the range exhibited by 1st- to 3rd-century fortlets. On this basis it is possible that British sites such as Caer Gybi, and even the Yorkshire stations, could be perceived as small forts rather than fortlets (Hodgson 1997, 65; cf. Hind 2005, 17). Indeed, elsewhere in this volume installations that arguably display similarities to Caer Gybi are identified as forts (see Rushworth and Arce, this volume). Nevertheless, examples of late fort shrinkage, that is installations refortified with a reduced defended perimeter, are conspicuously rare in Britain. All of the fortifications considered here are distinct, in terms of size, from 2nd-, 3rd-, and early 4th-century forts that endured into the later 4th century.

It is not just a broad overlap in internal area that these small, late sites share with earlier fortlets. The bulk of fortlets constructed during the 1st to 3rd centuries lay along coastlines or river banks, roads, and linear frontiers. These are precisely the areas where installations of fortlet size were either founded or maintained in the 4th century. There is also continuity in the way that these early and late groups capitalised on the potential of the local terrain. Two mid-1st-century fortlets founded on the north Exmoor coast at Old Burrow and Martinhoe (Devon) dominate remote landing grounds in a manner that appears analogous to the location of the late 4th-century Yorkshire fortlets. This indication of a broad convergence of purpose, coupled with a continuing divergence of size from forts, makes it plausible to assert that these late installations are fortlets. If so, the proliferation of new installations during the 4th century contrasts with 3rd-century practise, when few fortlets in Britain away from Hadrian's Wall are known to have been occupied. This rash of fortlet building is explicable as a symptom of a new dimension to the threat faced by the Roman army.

Many late fortlets in Britain differ from their predecessors in one regard. Prior to the 4th century, stone fortlets were only constructed in large numbers on Hadrian's Wall. The widespread use of turf and timber elsewhere suggests that fortlets served as bases for small garrisons deployed to tackle local disruption that could be resolved within a limited timeframe. Once the problem was neutralised the fortlet would be decommissioned and the soldiers would return to their home unit, or units. As such, there was little need for durable installations. The increased use of stone in 4th-century fortlet defences may indicate that although the direct threat, in terms of the numbers involved, could still be effectively met by modest detachments of soldiers, the root cause of this activity was judged sufficiently intractable that it was beyond the garrisons' capability to resolve it permanently in the short term. This dovetails with the widely accepted belief that Britain was assailed by seaborne raiders in the 4th century (e.g. Mattingly 2007, 235), as the perpetrators' point of origin lay beyond a fortlet garrison's reach. While raiding parties could be intercepted on route, there was no military option to stem the flow at its source.

Stone coastal fortlets

One common feature shared by late stone fortlets on the British coast is that they occur in areas where such installations had not previously existed. They do not, though, adopt a uniform approach to securing the shoreline and there are indications of a divergence in technique between north Yorkshire and the west coast. There is not scope to offer a detailed commentary on the Yorkshire fortlets here, but it is important to provide an overview of the system. Four fortlet sites are known for certain at Filey, Scarborough, Goldsborough, and Huntcliff, while a fifth is implied by an inscription from Ravenscar, a sixth is often posited at Whitby, and traces of a seventh may have been unearthed at Seaton Carew in the 19th century. The former six sites all occupy high ground that dominates either landing grounds or, in the case of Goldsborough, the approaches to them. As well as placing the fortlet garrisons in a strong position to

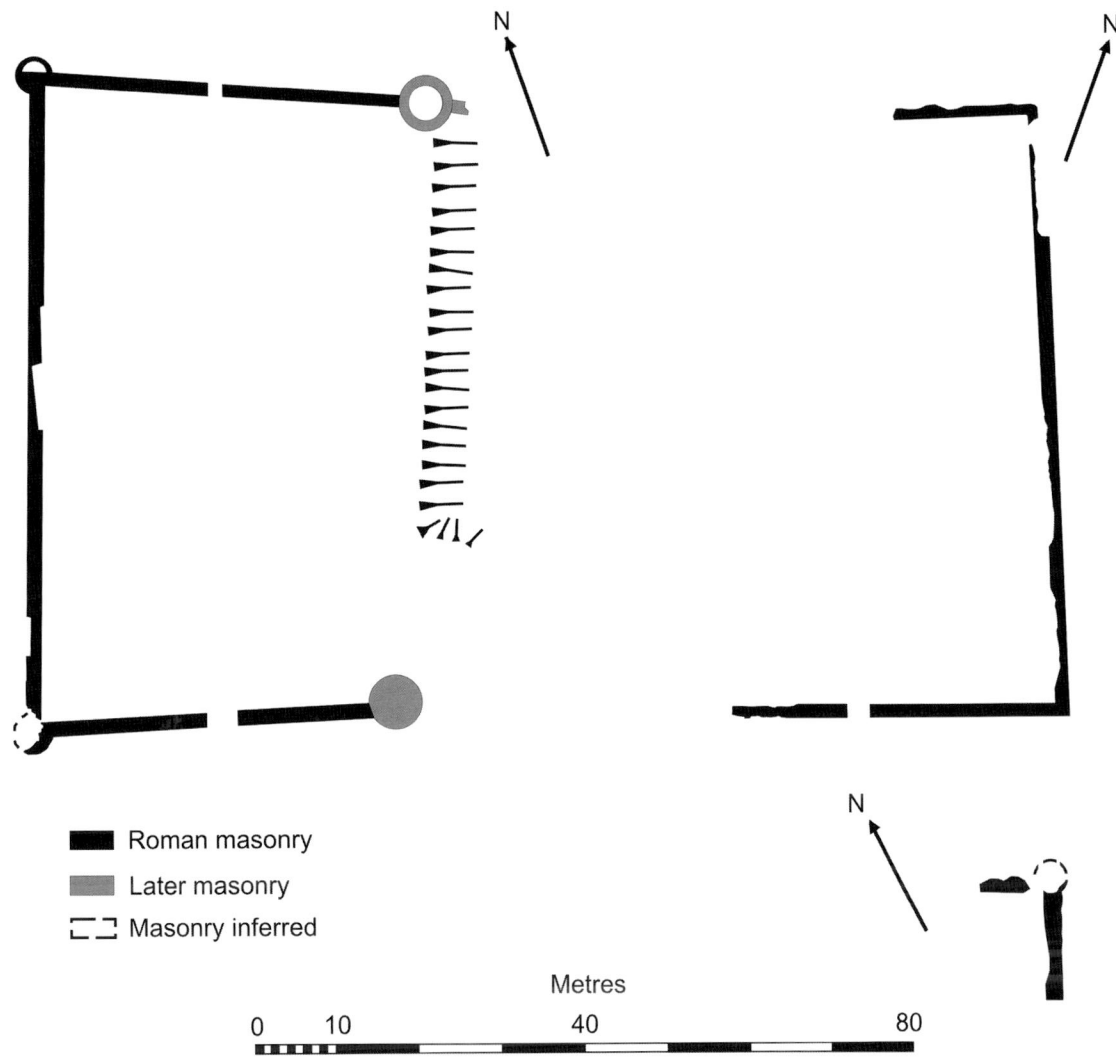

Figure 5.2: The possible late Roman fortlets on the west coast. Clockwise from top left: Caer Gybi, Hen Waliau, and Burrow Walls. After: Wheeler 1924; Boyle 1991; Bellhouse 1956

intercept raiders or pirates seeking to either land on or launch from the beaches, the conspicuous vantages crowned by the installations would have created a powerful visual deterrent.

Although the defensive architecture exhibited by the Yorkshire fortlets would have appeared impressive, in one regard it can be judged more imposing than practical. Despite the energy expended on erecting these edifices, the integrity of their ramparts was compromised by a failure to understand the concept of enfilading fire (Fig. 5.1). A jarring combination of mini bastions projecting from inflected rampart corners prevented defensive fire along the rampart face (Wilson 1991, 145). This failure to appreciate the basic purpose of a bastion was not replicated among otherwise similar fortifications on mainland Europe (see Hodgson 1997, 64), but it is more than a localised misunderstanding. A further installation built to the same specifications as the Yorkshire fortlets exists at the Nunnery, on the Channel island of Alderney (Johnston 1977, 31). Despite a striking commonality in design, the Nunnery displays a very different relationship to the terrain. Instead of commanding an elevated position, its builders elected to erect it just above beach height, directly adjacent to a natural harbour. Substituting a conspicuous vantage for immediacy to a potential mooring brings the setting of the Nunnery in line with the locations of Caer Gybi, Hen Waliau, and Burrow Walls.

The pair of installations at Caer Gybi and Hen Waliau in north Wales are rarely afforded comparable coverage to the Yorkshire fortlets in discussions of late Roman fortifications (Fig. 5.2). Founded respectively at Holyhead on Anglesey,

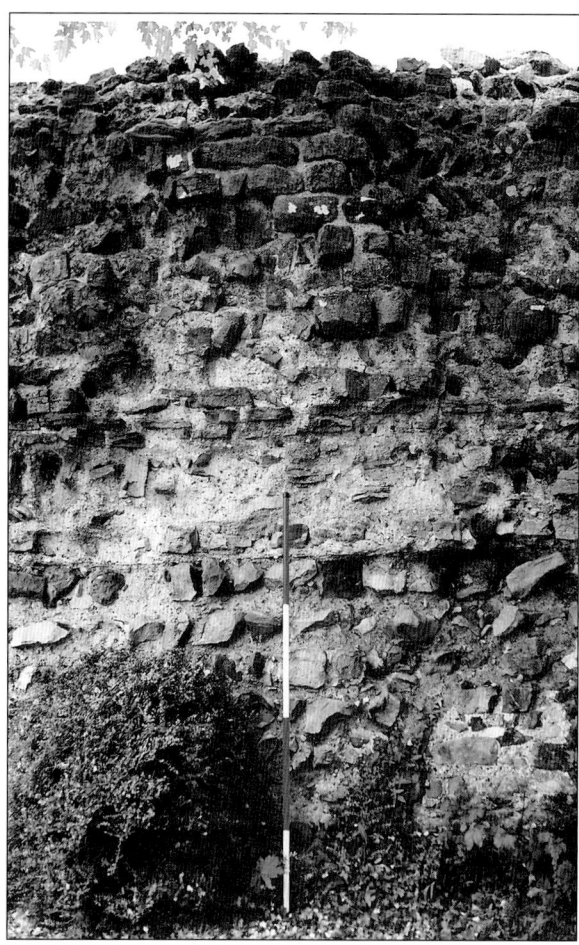

Figure 5.3: The core of the southern enclosure wall at Hen Waliau, seen from the south. Patches of herringbone work and two horizontal levelling courses can be seen in the masonry

and on the mainland overlooking the River Seiont 150m west of Caernarfon, both of these sites occupy natural ledges beside potential moorings (Wheeler 1924). Today Holyhead is a major terminal for ferries sailing to and from Ireland, while the River Seiont debouches into the Menai Strait – the channel severing Anglesey from the mainland – close to its southern mouth. Only Hen Waliau has produced enough dating evidence for even a tentative indication of its origin to be advanced. Two sherds of shell-tempered ware and one of Oxfordshire ware in undisturbed contexts sealed beneath the perimeter wall prompted the conclusion that "Hen Waliau must now be regarded a 4th-century construction" (Boyle 1991, 210).

Stretches of masonry enclosure wall still stand, in places, to a height of 5 m at Hen Waliau and 4 m at Caer Gybi. The facing stones survive at Caer Gybi, but most have been stripped away at Hen Waliau, exposing the wall core (Figs 5.3 and 5.4). One 18th-century commentator noted that this "discovers the peculiarity of the Roman masonry. It consists [partly] of regular courses disposed in zigzag fashion" (Pennant 1810, 412). Roman engineers did not hold a monopoly on this herringbone-work construction style, but at Hen Waliau the technique is combined with horizontal levelling courses, putlog holes, and coarse white mortar, all of which commonly occur in 4th-century fortifications in Britain (Wheeler 1924, 98). Caer Gybi has yet to produce independent dating evidence, but its build is sufficiently similar to Hen Waliau that most scholars agree it is plausible they belong to the same period (Wheeler 1924, 98–101; Boyle 1991, 211; Burnham and Davies 2010, 223). Despite this consensus that a broadly contemporary date is viable, it is widely believed that the two installations served

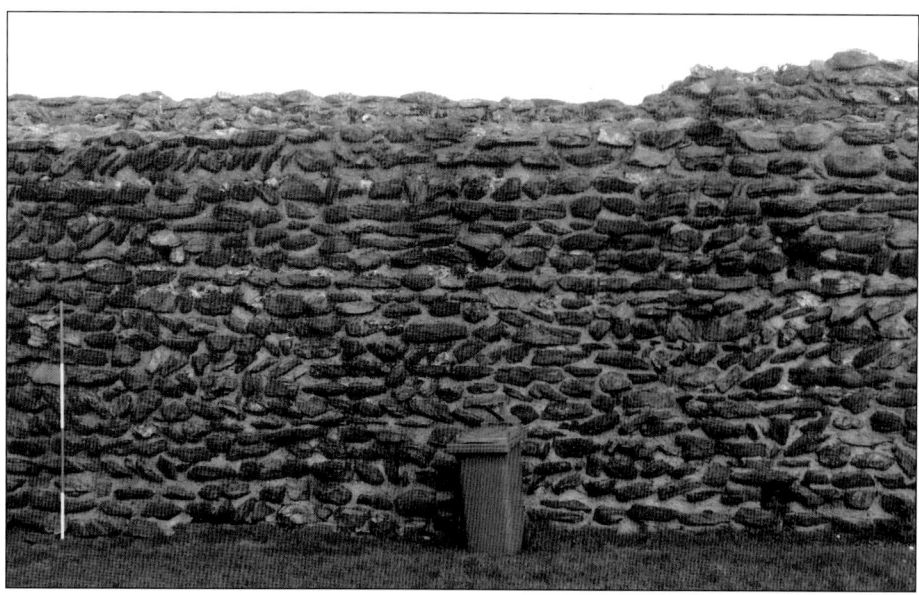

Figure 5.4: The north rampart at Caer Gybi, seen from the south. Levelling courses, putlog holes, and herringbone work are all visible. The parapet walk can be seen at the top

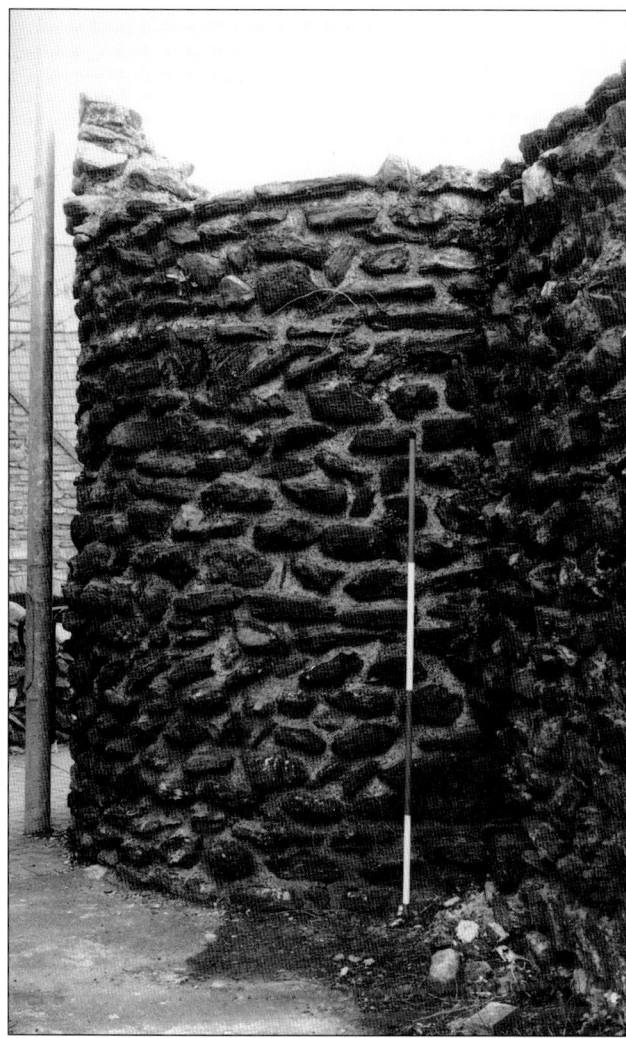

Figure 5.5: The north-west bastion at Caer Gybi, with the original facing stones still in situ

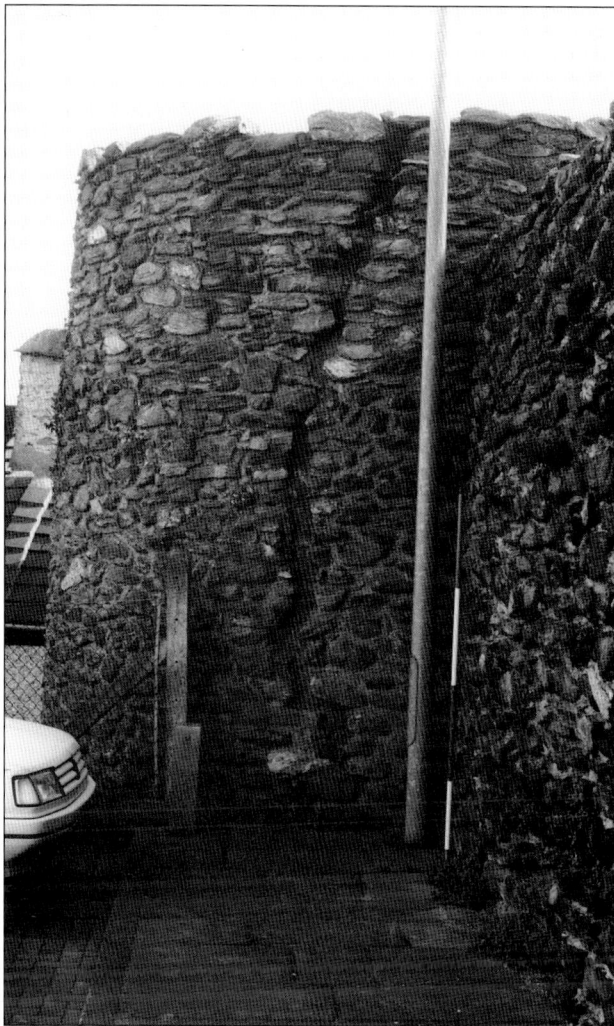

Figure 5.6: The north-east bastion at Caer Gybi. The clear difference in size and masonry from 5.5 shows that this bastion was completely rebuilt at a later date, presumably during the medieval period

different purposes (Boyle 1991, 211; Burnham and Davies 2010, 223).

Caer Gybi

Caer Gybi is generally perceived to be the only one of the pair to have an overtly military character. Its 1.5 m-wide ramparts survive on three sides, enclosing a rectangular plot of ground measuring 76 × 48 m. Projecting bastions were provided at the surviving north-west and south-west corners, as well as at the eastern ends of the extant north and south stretches of rampart (Burnham and Davies 2010, 216). Unlike the bastions on the Yorkshire coast, those at Caer Gybi would have been capable of providing enfilading fire along the rampart face (Fig. 5.2). The open eastern side of the perimeter now lies on a cliff edge, which presumably formed the coastline prior to the construction of the modern harbour. This prompted speculation that the missing length of rampart has been lost to erosion (Wheeler 1924, 98). A competing interpretation, however, holds that the side of Caer Gybi facing the coast was always open and that this is a British example of the "fortified landing sites" found on the far, "barbarian" side of the Rhine and Danube rivers (Collingwood and Richmond 1969, 55). These small installations are interpreted as a measure to ensure that Roman forces would not have to make opposed landings when they crossed the river. In order to expedite this, the installation ramparts appear to have been mostly or entirely open on the river side, so that boats could land within their walls. On this basis, Collingwood and Richmond argued that the Caer Gybi rampart originally extended to the east of the easterly bastions, carrying the curtain down to the shoreline (Collingwood and Richmond 1969, 55).

Evaluating these two competing interpretations of Caer Gybi is essential to understanding its purpose. Although there are traces of a rampart emerging from the north-east bastion and extending the defensive circuit towards the former shore, Wheeler pointed out that this bastion was completely rebuilt as a tower in the medieval period (Figs 5.5 and 5.6; Wheeler 1924, 98–99). The surviving stub of rampart projecting from it is likely to date to the same period. Indeed, the only bastion that appears to survive substantially in its original form lies at the north-west corner (Burnham and Davies 2010, 217). Leaving Caer Gybi open and therefore vulnerable on its seaward side must be considered questionable when the most obvious explanation for its presence is increased pressure on the coast due to maritime raiders. As Livens noted, the security of such a design "depends upon command of the sea" (Livens 1974, 336), a luxury that the very need for an installation implies could not be taken for granted. Circumstantial evidence that a lost east rampart did once close the perimeter is provided by the location of the gateway at the mid-point between the two bastions on the southern rampart. As gates are normally positioned at the centre of a stretch of rampart, this is exactly where it would be expected if the curtain did not originally extend further to the east. On this basis, Wheeler's conclusion that the installation served as "a small coastguard fort[let]" commanding a natural harbour, remains the most plausible explanation (Wheeler 1924, 101).

The notion that Caer Gybi served to enhance maritime security is supported by the presence of a tower to the east of the fortlet on Holyhead Mountain. This tower employed similar mortar to Caer Gybi and produced what appears to be a dispersed coin hoard deposited in the early AD 390s. The tower commands an extensive view, with Ireland visible to the west on a clear day. Crew concluded that the tower was probably "built in the late 4th century...together with Caer Gybi" (Crew 1981a, 35). He speculated that a mound of tumbled masonry at Pen Bryn Yr Eglwys on Carmel Head could represent a second such tower. This site lies on high ground to the north of Caer Gybi, at a point where the coastline turns sharply, exchanging a northerly course for an easterly one (Crew 1981b, 66). If a Roman tower stood on Pen Bryn Yr Eglwys, then combining its viewshed with that of the Holyhead Mountain tower would permit surveillance over "a substantial portion of the Irish Sea and Liverpool Bay" (Crew 1981a, 35).

Crew believed that "it is feasible that these two watch towers together with Caer Gybi, formed an independent element in the defences of the west coastline" (Crew 1981a, 35). Given that Holyhead was one of the closest parts of Roman Britain to Ireland, it would be well-placed to serve as a base for a detachment tasked with securing this stretch of the provincial waterways. The three sites could certainly have been designed as an integrated system to detect and intercept raiders before they could harass Roman shipping or make landfall in the Liverpool Bay area. The towers, set on high ground, provided the eyes of the system, while Caer Gybi, tucked unobtrusively in an inlet, protected a harbour. Maintaining the traditional split between towers and fortlets runs counter to the technique adopted on the Yorkshire coast, where the decision to combine them in a single installation forced the planners to chose between high ground and immediacy to a mooring. The Caer Gybi configuration permitted direct military control of both. Positioning the fortlet directly adjacent to a mooring could suggest that its garrison was equipped with boats, which would be necessary if they were to act on information received from the towers.

Hen Waliau

Despite boasting 1.9 m-wide walls, which enclosed an area of 70 × 50m and survive to a height of up to 5 m, Hen Waliau has been described as "not overtly defensive" (Casey *et al.* 1993, 6). Rather than being interpreted as a military installation, "a stores – or slave – compound" is generally judged to be "more plausible" (Livens 1974, 336). Two key symptoms of Hen Waliau's supposed defensive inferiority are the reported absence of a ditch and corner bastions (Fig. 5.2; Boyle 1991, 211). While it seems certain that no ditch was cut at Hen Waliau, this can hardly be used to emphasise its difference to Caer Gybi, as the latter was not provided with a ditch either (Griffiths 1954, 114). Whether bastions really were omitted from Hen Waliau remains contentious. Wheeler noted that three 19th-century observers refer to the vestiges of a tower at one or more of the corners (Wheeler 1924, 95–96). Among these commentators is Pennant, who related that "Near the corner of one of the walls is a heap of stones, the ruins of a tower; for on digging, some years ago, the foundations of a round one were discovered" (Pennant 1810, 412). The accuracy of these reports has been questioned in more recent times.

In Boyle's write up of investigations at Hen Waliau undertaken in the second half of the 20th century, he noted that the excavator of the compound's south-east corner in 1952 was "practically certain" that no tower ever stood there (Boyle 1991, 195). Boyle concluded Pennant was mistaken, suggesting that the key word in his account is "near", and that the pile of stones did not lie at precisely the corner of the enclosure walls. Instead of a round tower, Boyle argued that "[Pennant's] informant seems to have been referring to a free-standing structure, perhaps the well discovered close to the north-west angle in 1963" (Boyle 1991, 211). This possibility seems to be contradicted by Pennant's further statement that "[the tower] was paved, and in it were found the horn of a deer and the skeletons of some smaller animals;" suggesting that whatever this feature was, it was bottomed by the 19th-century investigators (Pennant 1810, 95). If so, a well would surely have been identified as such. In the absence of concrete evidence from the 1952 excavation it seems premature to dismiss the statements of Pennant and others, but even if bastions really were absent this does not prove that Hen Waliau had no military value. As will be discussed, 4th-century fortlets constructed along the Carlisle to York road appear to have been built without bastions, while the milecastles on Hadrian's Wall were never upgraded to incorporate this defensive refinement. As such, although it would be unusual to find a newly founded late fortlet built without bastions in a British coastal context, the military clearly had no qualms about reusing or even commissioning installations devoid of such features elsewhere during the 4th century.

Asserting Hen Waliau's defensive merit reinforces Wheeler's conclusion that it shared a common purpose with Caer Gybi. His reading was that "the purpose of both is scarcely in doubt; the coastal patrols both by sea and by land, must often have been glad of their shelter in those latter days when the black ships of Ireland swarmed eastward across the sea..." (Wheeler 1924, 101). The *Picti* and *Scotti* raiders who targeted Britain as Roman control collapsed were famously likened by Gildas to "dark swarms of worms that emerge from the narrow crevices of their holes when the sun is high and the weather grows warm" (*De Excidio Britanniae* xix). This evocative analogy raises the question of why additional installations were not raised elsewhere along the west coast to create a cordon comparable to that in Yorkshire. Even if Caer Gybi and Hen Waliau are accepted as part of a co-ordinated building programme, a token pair of installations signals a marked difference between the scale of late Roman fortlet construction on the north-east and west coasts. One possible explanation for this is that unlike North Yorkshire, there were forts and the legionary fortress at Chester controlling key locations on or near the west coast from the late 1st or 2nd century onwards. The enduring importance of these coastal installations is highlighted by Lancaster, which is the only fort in the northern military zone known to have been entirely rebuilt, complete with projecting towers, in the 4th century (Bidwell and Hodgson 2009, 87). It is conceivable, though, that one west-coast fortlet similar in style to Caer Gybi and Hen Waliau has been overlooked.

Burrow Walls

Today, the eponymous ruin at Burrow Walls (Cumbria) that stands within the footprint of an earlier Roman fort is regarded as medieval in origin (Breeze 2006, 410; Bellhouse 1956, 30). The ruins lie *c.* 1 km from the modern coastline on a natural platform overlooking the Siddick marshes, beside what was probably once the River Derwent channel (Blake 1956b, 42). This setting is reminiscent of Hen Waliau's location. The upstanding masonry consists of two stretches of wall that are *c.* 1.2 m wide, after being largely stripped of their facing stones, and which stand to a height of up to 3 m. The longest stretch of masonry can be traced for 12.2 m, while the shortest runs for 4.6 m (Fig. 5.2). It is impossible to judge with any confidence the original length of either stretch of wall, but it is clear that they were laid out at right angles, and linked by a projecting corner tower (Blake 1956a, 40). While it has long been stated that Roman material is visible in these walls, its presence is assumed to be the product of opportunistic recycling of material won from the earlier fort site (Breeze 2006, 410).

There are various reasons for believing that Burrow Walls is a medieval foundation. In particular there is a reference to Orme, an ancestor of the Curwen family, erecting a mansion house or peel tower at Burrow Walls in the 12th century. Denton, writing in 1610, identifies this residence with Burrow Walls when he notes that "the walls and ruins of his mansion house are to be seen there at Seaton to this day" (cited in Blake 1956a, 41). Jackson concurred, concluding that Orme "built himself a fortified dwelling, most probably of the usual peel tower type, on the edge of an acclivity sloping rapidly seawards, well suited both from its position and the abundance of stone offered by the neighbouring Roman Camp (which it is evident must have been at no great distance), for the erection of such a fortalice. The very name of 'Burrow Walls' seems to bear traces of this composite structure" (Jackson 1892, 290–291). Orme's tower, or mansion house, was subsequently abandoned by his descendent Patric, who took up residence at Workington. Blake has queried why Patric would abandon a masonry residence at Burrow Walls in favour of what was probably a timber hall at Workington, positing that an encroaching cliff face triggered by the eroding waters of the Derwent might have been the deciding factor.

Blake did note that the surviving masonry at Burrow Walls is excessive for a peel tower (Blake 1956a, 41–42). Even if the ruin does derive from a more substantial structure, further indications of a post-Roman origin can be found in references to "a winding staircase" and "wall slits, very narrow without and wide within, and circular bolt holes" visible in the fabric until 60 years prior to 1880, when their former presence was recorded (Dickinson 1879–1880, 22). Blake added that "a faint indication...of a newel staircase in the north-east corner" survives as a set of curving facing stones lining what would once have been the internal face of the corner tower (Fig. 5.7; Blake 1956a, 40). Chancellor Ferguson also noted that "in the early part of the century, Horsley said he could see nothing Roman about [Burrow Walls], and he found neither Roman coins nor stones" (Ferguson 1900, 51). Given this weight of evidence it is easy to see why a 4th-century date for the masonry is considered untenable.

Horsley's comments on Burrow Walls are, though, more nuanced than Ferguson's epitome implies. Horsley records that "The Borough walls, where the station is supposed to have been, is about a mile from the town... A good part of

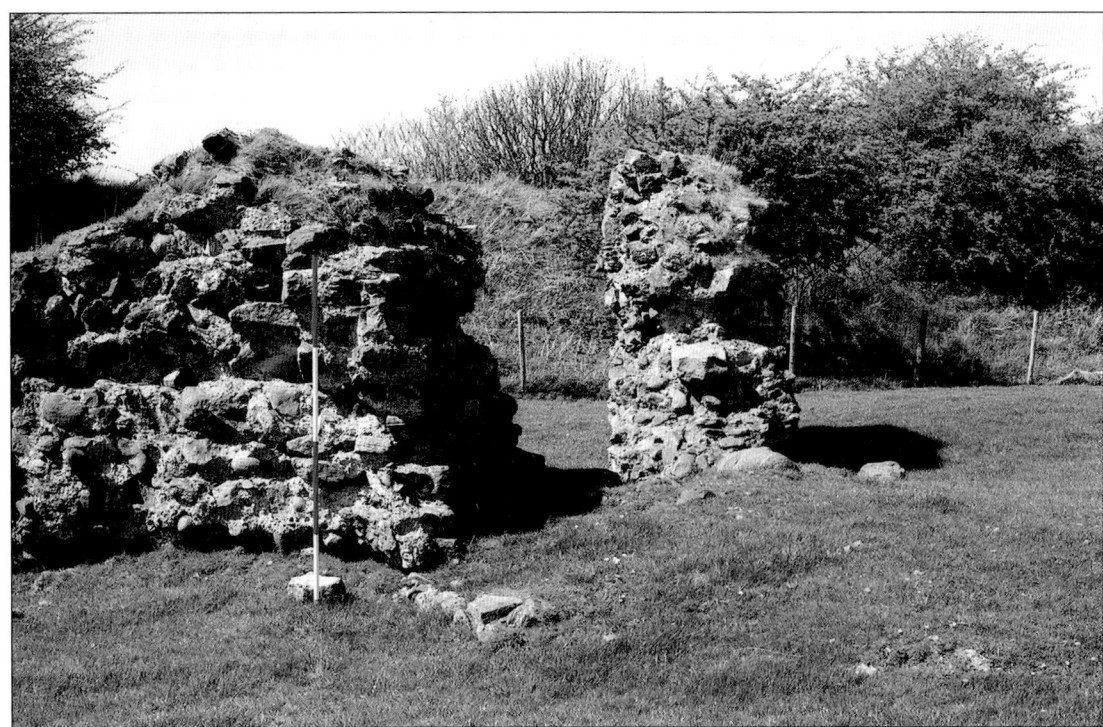

Figure 5.7: The robbed-out remains of the corner tower at Burrow Walls. The facing stones still in situ against what survives of the curving inner face of the tower (to the right of the ranging pole) have been taken to indicate the presence of a "newel stair"

the walls are yet standing, by which it appears to have been only one of these old towns, which we do frequently see in the north, and which sometimes bear the name of Burgh or Brugh. I saw no appearance of a ditch, no remains of other buildings about it, or near it; and in short nothing that looked like a Roman station or town. If it has ever been a Roman fort of any kind, I think it must only have been one of those small exploratory *castella*, which some observe to have been placed along the coast" (Horsley 1732, 483). As well as leaving open the possibility that the Burrow Walls are indeed Roman, Horsley explicitly identifies the ruins as appropriate for those of a *castella* or fortlet. Horsley is not the only student of Roman military works to have made this link. In his seminal paper on Roman deployment along what is now the Cumbrian coast, Collingwood argued that two phases of construction were visible in the surviving masonry. While the latter could be Norman, he saw no reason why the earlier should not be Roman. In making this conclusion, Collingwood was, though, influenced by the need to establish a provenance for a group of five altars discovered at the site in 1852 (Collingwood 1929, 157–159).

Bellhouse's 1955 discovery of a conventional Roman fort directly underlying the Burrow Walls resolved the question of the altars' source. As Blake observed, one apparent knock-on effect of this was that "the discovery of such a fort removes the possibility of giving the [standing masonry] a direct Roman context" (Blake 1956a, 40).

Indeed the quantity of 4th-century pottery recovered from the underlying fort appears to offer very little room for the Burrow Walls ruin to fit chronologically between the fort phase and the end of Roman Britain. Gillam noted that "only two vessels [from the fort] were recognisably earlier than the 4th century in date...The high proportion of such late pieces...is very striking" (Gillam 1956, 40). Nevertheless, the fort plan deduced by Bellhouse is clearly earlier in character, while the presence of inscribed altars would not be in keeping with a late foundation as the epigraphic habit in the north had essentially ceased by this period (Roach 2013, 115). In reality, the nature of late 4th-century activity at the fort site remains little understood. The observation that much of the pottery dating to this period was deposited in ditches cut directly inside the earlier fort rampart highlights that these defences did not endure in their original form (Gillam 1956, 40). On this basis it is not impossible that late 4th-century activity was focused on the installation represented by the Burrow Walls masonry, although this is only one of many possible readings of the evidence.

Blake described the upstanding masonry as consisting "largely of core material, rough stones set in hard mortar; many of the stones are slanting, as in herringbone work..." (Blake 1956a, 40). Ferguson was also moved to comment that "the plan is Norman, yet the work has not been carried out in the Norman manner, but in the Roman" (Ferguson 1900, 52). It is clear from inspection of the surviving

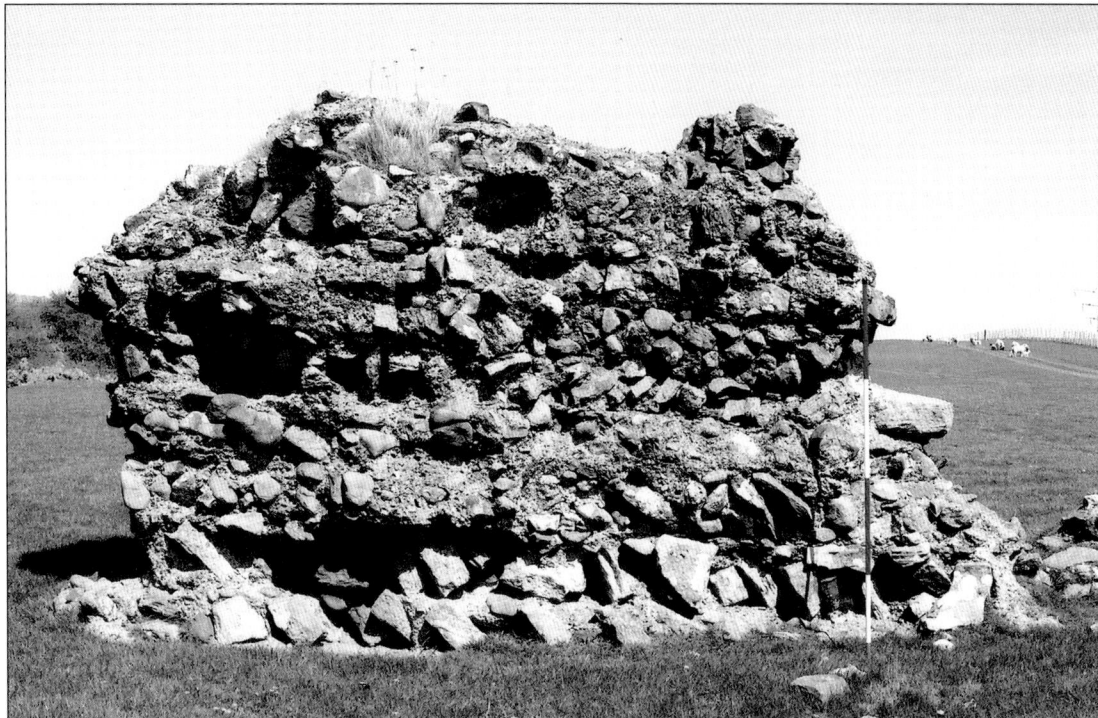

Figure 5.8: The northern length of extant masonry at Burrow Walls, seen from the south. As well as areas of herringbone work, stretches of two, or perhaps three, possible levelling courses are visible

fabric of Burrow Walls that its resemblance to the curtain at Hen Waliau and Caer Cybi extends beyond stretches of herringbone work. The mortar also seems similar in character, and traces of what appear to be two, or perhaps three, horizontal levelling layers are visible in the northern length of masonry (Fig. 5.8). Parallels with the Welsh fortlets are not restricted to construction technique, as what little survives of Burrow Walls is closely comparable in plan to Caer Gybi. Although these similarities could be wholly coincidental, they are sufficiently marked that it seems premature to exclude the possibility of a Roman origin for at least some of the extant masonry. Just how indicative of a "newel stair" the curving wall face within the corner tower is, the present author is not competent to say (Fig. 5.7). Yet even if this is conclusive evidence of a later feature, two of the towers at Caer Gybi were completely rebuilt in the medieval period (Burnham and Davies 2010, 217). This later adaptation of Caer Gybi is a reminder that durable fortifications can have a longstanding utility, and it could be speculated that Orme's 12th-century mansion or fortalice was built within the shell of a late Roman fortlet at Burrow Walls.

If the origin of the Burrow Walls ruin does lie in the late Roman period, it helps to provide a context for Caer Gybi and Hen Waliu. Rather than an anomaly focused on Anglesey, it would cast these installations as part of a wider initiative using state-of-the-art fortifications to secure the western seaboard. As well as displaying a different template to the Yorkshire stations, the execution of these west-coast installations avoids features that would undermine defensive integrity. In particular, the presence of bastions suitable for enfilading fire arguably represents a more refined design. The possibility that an additional fortlet existed at Burrow Walls must also raise the question of whether further installations once stood along the west coast. The apparent absence of defensive ditches at these sites would make them hard to detect once their masonry had been robbed out, and it is conceivable that these installations were originally deployed in greater numbers than we currently appreciate.

Late fortlets on the Carlisle – York road

If the design of the Caer Gybi, Burrow Walls, and, possibly, Hen Waliau ramparts surpasses that of the Yorkshire stations, some late installations constructed along the road network belong at the other end of the spectrum. Although various sites described as *burgi* have been claimed in Britain (see Bidwell and Hodgson 2009, 161–164), the following discussion will focus on installations erected along the trans-Pennine highway connecting Carlisle and York (Fig. 5.9). The most impressive new fortifications were constructed at Wreay Hall and Barrock Fell, 10 km and 11 km south of Carlisle respectively. Barrock Fell was equipped with a rampart of rough masonry set in hard white mortar (Collingwood 1931, 113), while Wreay Hall probably also had a stone curtain (Annis 2001, 107). Enclosing *c.* 13.4 × 15.8 m and 16.5 × 16.5 m respectively, these installations were built to far more modest dimensions than their coastal counterparts. Neither fortlet was equipped with projecting bastions, although they were provided with ditches. Both installations were carefully situated in the landscape and enjoyed sweeping views, with Barrock Fell well placed to overlook the approaches to the road from both the Lake District and the River Petteril valley. These fortlets may have acted as satellites for a late garrison in Old Penrith fort. Late Roman pottery from Barrock Fell and Wreay Hall indicates that construction occurred after *c.* AD 360 (Bidwell and Hodgson 2009, 70–71), placing them in the general chronological range of the Yorkshire stations. The meagre dating evidence available for the west-coast fortlets allows no firmer statement than that it is plausible they were also broadly contemporary.

Although Barrock Fell and Wreay Hall are the only known examples of stone fortlets built along the Carlisle–York highway in the 4th century, a third example of a masonry fortlet occurs at Maiden Castle (Fig. 5.9). Far larger than Barrock Fell and Wreay Hall, Maiden Castle dominates the western approach to the important Pennine pass at Stainmore. This fortlet, though, was built much earlier, probably in the 2nd century, and either remained occupied into, or was re-occupied during, the 4th century (Collingwood 1915). Late installations were also established on the eastern approach to the Stainmore Pass at Bowes Moor and Rey Cross, but unlike the 4th-century fortifications considered so far, they were constructed of turf and timber rather than stone. As well as highlighting that masonry was not uniformly employed for 4th-century ramparts, this choice of material could imply that less-robust fortifications were judged equal to the threat, that the length or deployment was considered likely to be short, that the installations needed to be erected swiftly, or perhaps all three.

Excavations within the turf-and-timber enclosure at Bowes Moor dated it to the third quarter of the 4th century and assigned it "a short life" (Fig. 5.9; Annis 2001, 111). The discovery of a *manica* – armguard – fragment within the installation makes a military context likely (Bishop 2001, 170). Bowes Moor only enclosed a 10 × 6.5 m area within its turf rampart, and was interpreted as a tower by its excavators, despite the absence of any postholes to support such a structure (Annis 2001, 99; 105). They reconstructed a timber tower perched on a set of padstones, which Ottaway has likened to the distinctive postpads found within the central towers in the Yorkshire fortlets (Ottaway 2013, 298). The Bowes Moor padstones appear to be large, unworked rocks, however, making them far cruder than the socketed stones manufactured for the Yorkshire fortlets. Although using padstones is an acknowledged feature of late Roman buildings (R. Collins *pers. com.*), it must be questioned whether this approach would be an effective means of erecting a structurally stable tower (Bidwell and Hodgson 2009, 58).

The excavators' interpretation of Bowes Moor was probably influenced by the existence of a tower cordon across the Stainmore Pass. Although datable finds from these sites remain elusive, excavation has revealed that in at least two cases they contained substantial postholes (Annis 2001, 99), and it is probable that the Stainmore tower cordon was constructed far earlier in the Roman period. Equally, while the size of Bowes Moor would certainly make it appropriate for a tower site, it is only roughly half the size of the fortlets at Barrock Fell and Wreay Hall and could have held a limited garrison rather than an elevated viewing platform. The absence of any other structural traces within Bowes Moor need not indicate that a tower is the only conceivable internal building. The scarcity of discernible internal buildings is a recurrent problem among newly constructed 4th-century fortlets in Britain. Apart from a barrack block inferred from a line of hearths at Goldsborough (Hodgson 1997, 65), the only certain examples are the central stone towers within the Yorkshire fortlets. These seem more likely to be a component of the fortlets' defensive architecture than garrison accommodation. Although identifying internal buildings within earlier fortlets is not always straightforward, the contrast between the effort expended on defences and internal living quarters is particularly pronounced during the 4th century.

Further activity on the eastern approach to the Stainmore Pass is attested by limited excavation inside an earlier marching camp at Rey Cross, which revealed 4th-century pottery. There is no indication that a late turf or masonry rampart was inserted within the former camp, but the pottery was associated with a haphazard set of stakeholes, c. 0.05 m – 0.15 m in diameter. Robinson concluded that "this later occupation could also have been by the Roman army on the march, but is more likely to have been by a smaller group over a more extended period, perhaps manning a signal tower built inside the camp. It may be significant that the pottery here is of similar date and form to that excavated at the Bowes Moor tower site" (Robinson 2001, 80). As at Bowes Moor, this activity is compatible with the presence of a detachment of soldiers and there is no reason why it should be associated with a tower in particular. That late fortlets could be inserted into earlier fortifications appears to be demonstrated at Elslack, which lies in a Pennine pass to the south of Stainmore. LiDAR survey of a late-3rd-century fort indicates that a fortlet was subsequently constructed in its north corner (Toller 2014, 10). What is known of the fortlet's plan is, though, reminiscent of 1st- and 2nd- century designs, making clarification of its relationship with the fort desirable.

Claiming that Bowes Moor and Rey Cross represent

5. Fourth-century fortlets in Britain: sophisticated systems or desperate measures?

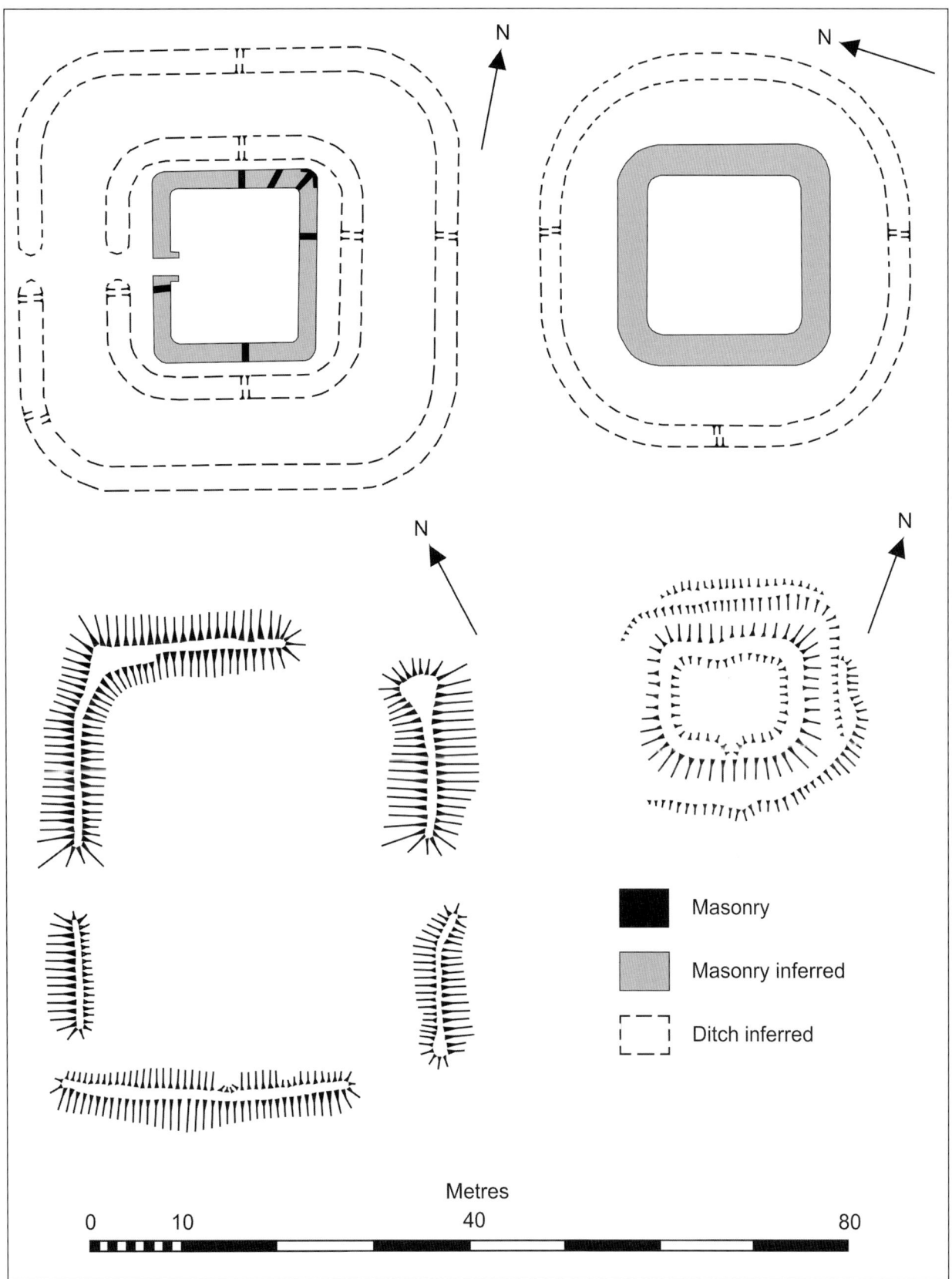

Figure 5.9: The late Roman installations on the Carlisle–York Highway. Clockwise from top left: Barrock Fell, Wreay Hall, Bowes Moor, Maiden Castle. After: Collingwood 1931; Bellhouse 1953; Vyner et al. 2001

installations that can be described as fortlets in the 1st- to 3rd-century meaning of the term would be disingenuous, as the former is so small, while the latter produced no evidence for late defences more substantial than stakes. Both sites are, though, most plausibly interpreted as small, lightly defended posts intended for use by modest detachments of soldiers. Given their vulnerability, it is unlikely that they operated in isolation. Instead they probably acted in conjunction with the forts at Bowes and Brougham, both of which have yielded late 4th-century pottery (Bidwell and Hodgson 2009, 55; 65), and the fortlet at Maiden Castle to provide additional security on the Stainmore Pass. This 4th-century iteration of a smaller-structure cordon could be seen as a parallel for the earlier tower chain erected along this stretch of road, probably in the 1st or 2nd century. If so, it suggests that local security had regressed to a level not seen since much earlier in the Roman period.

One possible explanation for the variety of materials used to construct fortifications along the Carlisle-York road is that this amounts to the difference between installations intended for long- and short-term occupation. If so, one obvious historical context for the latter would be the need to restore stability in the aftermath of the AD 367 "Barbarian conspiracy" (R. Collins *pers. com.*). A temporary measure to ensure the safety of traffic using this critical component of the communication system would certainly make sense following an episode of acute disruption. Regardless of the precise explanation for the turf and timber installations on the eastern approach to the Stainmore Pass, the general picture of 4th-century fortifications along this road that are of second-rate quality, or worse, when compared to many of their coastal counterparts seems clear. Whether such variable quality was also reflected in the calibre of the soldiers garrisoning these sites remains an open question.

Cardurnock

An example of a 4th-century coastal fortlet with a turf rampart appears to exist on the Cardurnock peninsula. This stretch of coast extends beyond the western terminus of Hadrian's Wall near Bowness-on-Solway, as far as the mouth of a sea inlet at Moricambe. A sequence of milefortlets and towers, mirroring the milecastle and turret cordon on Hadrian's Wall, was constructed both on the Cardurnock peninsula and to the south of Moricambe in the 2nd century AD. Unlike the milecastles, the milefortlets proved to be of fleeting utility to the frontier system. Only a handful of them were reoccupied following the return from the Antonine Wall, and all appear to have been abandoned by the end of the 2nd century (Turnbull 1998, 104–105).

One installation on the Cumbrian coast has produced evidence of being recommissioned after around 150 years of obsolescence. The milefortlet that lay on the northern lip of Moricambe, number "5" in the sequence, is believed to form the terminus of the Cardurnock group. It was the first milefortlet to be fully excavated, and numerous aspects of its execution have subsequently proven to diverge from the standard template for these installations. Milefortlet 5 is also exceptional for producing pottery dating to the second half of the 4th century, despite having been abandoned throughout the preceding century. Although the associated occupation layers had been lost to the plough, the excavators associated this pottery with a refacing of the turf rampart, and an enigmatic 4 m-long stone platform erected against one side of it. This refurbishment was linked to the aftermath of the AD 367 "Barbarian Conspiracy" (Simpson and Hodgson 1947, 124). If correct, milefortlet 5 might provide a parallel for the turf and timber installations established on the Carlisle–York highway, and in particular the opportunistic reuse of existing earthworks at Rey Cross.

Whatever the precise context for the renewed interest in the northern lip of Moricambe, the apparent failure to erect a more sophisticated or robust installation here is suggestive of a shift in the military significance of this stretch of shore. It was subjected to unprecedented surveillance for a coastline in the Hadrianic period, but by the 4th century was – judging by the relative expenditure of resources on installations – a backwater compared to the North Yorkshire coast, the area around Anglesey, and quite possibly the wider Liverpool Bay area. On the west coast it is tempting to read this as the consequence of a change in the prevailing direction of approach by coastal raiding parties from north–south in the 2nd century, to east–west in the 4th century.

Discussion

Despite the distinction between forts and fortlets becoming increasingly blurred elsewhere in the Roman empire during the late period, it seemingly remains possible to distinguish between these types in Britain. The late installations with masonry ramparts known on the north Yorkshire coast, around Anglesey, and directly south of Carlisle can all be identified as fortlets. A case can also be made for adding the extant masonry at Burrow Walls to that list. Whether the seemingly more transient turf and possibly even stake-built defences found on the eastern approach to the Stainmore Pass and the Cardurnock peninsula should also be classed as fortlets is less clear-cut. Both Bowes Moor and Rey Cross are small compared to earlier fortlets, and what little is currently known of the latter's structure could fairly be described as flimsy. Milefortlet 5 on Cardurnock is more conventional, so long as the excavators' belief that the earlier defences were reused is sound. Whether ramparts that needed little more than cosmetic refacing to be made viable would be left unattended for over a century in a sensitive frontier zone is an open question, though. It is possible that the late pottery at milefortlet 5 was associated with a slighter structure, which was subsequently lost to the plough. Either way, these late turf fortifications appear to be more satisfactorily described as abnormally small fortlets than towers, although this may simply expose the limitations of our terminology.

The design of the late fortlets discussed here can be broken down into three broad categories: sophisticated masonry ramparts with bastions and, in North Yorkshire, an internal tower, simple masonry ramparts without bastions or interval towers, and turf and timber fortifications. If Boyle's contention that Hen Waliau was not equipped with bastions is correct, and this remains uncertain, then all three of these types can be found on the 4th-century British coastline. Only the latter two designs are known to occur among fortlets founded on the road network. As such, present evidence suggests that the most advanced 4th-century fortlets were constructed exclusively on the coast. It could be argued that coastal fortlets needed bastions, or perhaps in Yorkshire towers (Wilson 1991, 146), in order to mount artillery, as projectile weapons would be the only way for soldiers to engage enemy vessels directly from a fortlet. Late 3rd- and early 4th-century forts with bastions were built inland at Horncastle and Caistor (Lincolnshire), however, demonstrating that these features had a military utility inland in Britain. This makes it more likely that the absence of bastions from the later fortlets at Barrock Fell and Wreay Hall stems from a deliberate decision not to provide them.

Although the distinction between fortlets operating in coastal and inland areas does not fully correlate with the level of sophistication of the defensive architecture, there is a clear disparity between these two contexts. Significant variation between individual installations is a trait of fortlets, but such a marked distinction between the scale of defences of installations operating in coastal and inland areas is not discernible in preceding centuries. In Germany, fortlets on the Rhine and Danube are far more likely to be equipped with corner towers than their counterparts on the road or land *limes*, presumably because missile troops were necessary to control passage along the river channel (Symonds 2007, 46). Such a provision is not paralleled among early coastal fortlets in Britain. Although the 1st-century fortlets on the Exmoor coast at Old Burrow and Martinhoe both feature an unusual second outer rampart and ditch, this additional defensive feature also occurs at fortlets set inland from the coast at Stoke Hill and Ide, near Exeter (see Fox and Ravenhill 1966; Fox and Ravenhill 1959; Griffith 1984). In the 2nd century the most heavily defended fortlets in Britain were built along highways running through southern Scotland, which were critical for supplying the Antonine Wall. In essence, the pattern in preceding centuries among freestanding fortlets in Britain is for installations displaying elaborate defences to occur in areas where the threat is likely to have been judged most severe. As such, the proliferation of late fortlets equipped with advanced defences on the coast indicates that the low-level threats their garrisons were best suited to counter, such as raiding, were most acute in those areas.

All known examples of late stone fortlets on the coast occur in areas where such installations had never previously been necessary. The 1st-century fortlets on the Exmoor coast, and the 2nd-century fortlets on the western coastal flanks of Hadrian's Wall and the Antonine Wall all faced land occupied by hostile groups that was clearly visible across the water. Such enemy territory cannot be seen from the Yorkshire or Welsh fortlets, although Ireland is visible from the Holyhead Mountain tower, and so the need for these installations could be a consequence of the raiders' increased maritime prowess. It is also possible that the existence of stone, turf, and timber fortifications in the late period, if not simply a reflection of the available resources, reveals a distinction between installations planned for long-term and short-term use. The presence of pottery dating to the AD 360s in turf-and-timber installations at Bowes Moor, Rey Cross, and milefortlet 5, would fit with these being intended as short-term measures to restore stability after the "Barbarian Conspiracy". The extensive use of stone in the coastal fortlets may reflect a more open-ended commitment. Building durable installations could acknowledge the army's inability to tackle the raiders at their source.

The striking structural similarities between Caer Gybi and Hen Waliau seem best explained by these installations fulfilling both a complementary and comparable function. Founding fortlets at these sites would have ensured that both the east and west shipping passages around Anglesey were directly supervised. If the fortlet garrisons were to intervene before any raiders landed, and also protect supply ships from piracy, they must have had a naval capability. The locations of Hen Waliau, Caer Gybi, and Burrow Walls all indicate a desire to be immediate to natural harbours or moorings. Indeed, it could conceivably be the need to secure the garrison's craft that resulted in Hen Waliau being erected within 150 m of the fort at Caernarfon. Regardless of whether Hen Waliau was equipped with projecting towers, the character of its perimeter wall clearly matches that of a rampart. Although the purpose of the upstanding masonry at Burrow Walls remains opaque, a strong tradition has built up in favour of the ruins being medieval. Yet similarities in both plan and construction technique with the Anglesey installations suggest that the possibility of a late Roman origin has been dismissed too quickly. If the Burrow Walls ruin does prove to be Roman, it raises the question of whether there was once a west-coast fortlet cordon to rival that in North Yorkshire.

Bibliography

Annis, R. (2001) The Stainmore "Signal Stations" or Tower Chain. In B. Vyner, P. Robinson, R. Annis and J. Pickin (eds) *Stainmore, the Archaeology of a North Pennine Pass*, 98–111. Tees Archaeology Monograph Series 1, London, English Heritage.

Bellhouse, R. L. (1953) A Roman Post at Wreay Hall, near Carlisle. *Transactions of the Cumberland and Westmorland Antiquarian and Archaeological society* NS 53, 49–51.

Bellhouse, R. L. (1956) The Roman fort at Burrow Walls, Workington. *Transactions of the Cumberland and Westmorland Antiquarian and Archaeological society* NS 56, 30–45.

Bidwell, P. and Hodgson, N. (2009) *The Roman Army in Northern England*. Newcastle upon Tyne, Arbeia Society.

Bishop, M. (2001) A Fragment of Laminated Armguard from the Bowes Moor Tower Site. In B. Vyner, P. Robinson, R. Annis and J. Pickin (eds) *Stainmore, the Archaeology of a North Pennine Pass*, 169–170. Tees Archaeology Monograph Series 1, London, English Heritage.

Blake, B. (1956a) The Medieval Occupation. *Transactions of the Cumberland and Westmorland Antiquarian and Archaeological Society* NS 56, 40–42.

Blake, B. (1956b) The physical geography of the site. *Transactions of the Cumberland and Westmorland Antiquarian and Archaeological society* NS 56, 42–43.

Boyle, S. D. (1991) Excavations at Hen Waliau, Caernarfon, 1952–1985. *Bulletin of the Board of Celtic Studies* 38, 191–212.

Breeze, D. J. (2006) *J. Collingwood Bruce's Handbook to the Roman Wall*. Newcastle upon Tyne, Society of Antiquaries of Newcastle upon Tyne.

Burnham, B. C. and Davies, J. L. (2010) *Roman Frontiers in Wales and the Marches*. Aberystwyth, Royal Commission on the Ancient and Historical Monuments of Wales.

Casey, P., Davies, J. L. and Evans, J. (1993) *Excavations at Segontium (Caernarfon) Roman fort, 1975–9*. CBA Research Report 90, London, CBA.

Collingwood, R. G. (1915) Roman remains from Maiden Castle on Stainmoor. *Transactions of the Cumberland and Westmorland Antiquarian and Archaeological Society* NS 15, 192–193.

Collingwood, R. G. (1929) Roman signal-stations on the Cumberland Coast. *Transactions of the Cumberland and Westmorland Antiquarian and Archaeological society* NS 29, 138–165.

Collingwood, R. G. (1931) A Roman fortlet on Barrock Fell, near Low Hasket. *Transactions of the Cumberland and Westmorland Antiquarian and Archaeological society* NS 31, 111–118.

Collingwood, R. G. and Richmond, I. (1969) *Archaeology of Roman Britain*. London, Meuthen.

Crew, P. (1981a) Holyhead Mountain SH 2185 8295. *Archaeology in Wales* 21, 35–36.

Crew, P. (1981b) Pen Bryn Yr Eglwys SH 2930 9243. *Archaeology in Wales* 21, 66.

Dickinson, W. (1879–1880) Burrow Walls near Workington. *Transactions of the Cumberland and Westmorland Antiquarian and Archaeological society* 5, 22–24.

Ferguson, C. (1900) Excursions and Proceedings, *Transactions of the Cumberland and Westmorland Antiquarian and Archaeological society* 16, 47–55.

Fox, A. and Ravenhill, W. (1959) The Stoke Hill Roman signal station. *Report and transactions of the Devonshire Association* 91, 71–82.

Fox, A. and Ravenhill, W. (1966) Early Roman outposts on the north Devon coast, Old Burrow and Martinhoe. *Proceedings of the Devon Archaeological Exploration society* 24, 3–39.

Frere, S. and St Joseph, J. (1983) *Roman Britain from the air*. Cambridge, Cambridge University Press.

Gillam, J. (1956) The Roman pottery, *Transactions of the Cumberland and Westmorland Antiquarian and Archaeological society* NS 56, 38–40.

Griffith, F. (1984) Roman military sites in Devon: Some recent discoveries. *Devon Archaeological Proceedings* 42, 11–32.

Griffiths, W. (1954) Excavations at Caer Gybi, Holyhead, 1952. *Archaeologia Cambrensis* 103, 113–116.

Hind, J. G. F. (2005) The watchtowers and fortlets on the north Yorkshire coast (Turres et Castra). *Yorkshire Archaeological Journal* 77, 17–24.

Hodgson, N. (1997) Relationships between Roman river frontiers and artificial frontiers. In W. Groenman-van Waateringe, B. van Beek, W. Willems and S. Wynia (eds) *Roman Frontier Studies 1995*, 61–66. Oxford, Oxbow.

Horsley, J. (1732) *Britannia Romana, or, The Roman antiquities of Britain*. London.

Jackson, W. (1892) *Papers and pedigrees mainly relating to Cumberland and Westmorland*. vol. 1 Kendal, T. Wilson.

Johnston, D. (1977) The Gallic evidence: the Channel Islands. In D. Johnston (ed.) *The Saxon Shore*, 31–34. CBA research report 18, London, CBA.

Livens, R. (1974) Litus Hibernicum. In D. Pippidi (ed.) *Actes du IX congrès international D'Études sur les Frontières Romaines*, 333–339. Koln, Bohlau Verlag.

Mackensen, M. (1987) *Frühkaiserzeitliche Kleinkastelle bei Nersingen und Burlafingen an den Oberen Donau*. München, C.H. Beck'sche.

Mattingly, D. (2007) *An Imperial Possession: Britain in the Roman Empire*. London, Penguin.

Maxfield, V. (1996) The eastern Eyptian desert forts and the army in the principate. In D. M. Bailey (ed.) *Archaeological Research in Roman Egypt: The Proceedings of the Seventeenth Classical Colloquium of The Department of Greek and Roman Antiquities, British Museum, held on 1–4 December, 1993*, 9–19. JRA Supplementary Series 19, Ann Arbor, Journal of Roman Archaeology.

Monaghan, J. (2011) The Nunnery: Alderney's Roman fort? *Current Archaeology* 261, 28–33.

Ottaway, P. (2013) *Roman Yorkshire: people, culture and landscape*. Pickering, Blackthorn Press.

Pearson, A. (2002) *The Roman shore forts: coastal defences of southern Britain*. Stroud, Tempus.

Pennant, T. (1810) *Tours in Wales*. London.

Roach, L. (2013) From the Severans to Constantius Chlorus: the lost century, in R. Collins and M. F. A. Symonds (eds) *Breaking down boundaries: Hadrian's Wall in the 21st century*, 105–121. JRA supplementary series 93, Rhode Island, Journal of Roman Archaeology.

Robinson, P. (2001) The Rey Cross camp. In B. Vyner, P. Robinson, R. Annis and J. Pickin (eds) *Stainmore, the archaeology of a*

North Pennine Pass, 76–86. Tees Archaeology monograph series 1, London, English Heritage.

Simpson, F. G. and Hodgson, K. S. (1947) The coastal milefortlet at Cardurnock. *Transactions of the Cumberland and Westmorland Antiquarian and Archaeological society* NS 47, 78–125.

Symonds, M. F. A. (2007) Built for purpose: early fortlet use in Britain and Germany. *Hadrianic Society Bulletin* NS 2, 39–47.

Toller, H. (2014) Current research into Roman roads in Yorkshire based on Lidar evidence. *Forum: the journal of Council for British Archaeology Yorkshire* 3, 7–11.

Turnbull, P. (1998) Excavations at milefortlet 21. *Transactions of the Cumberland and Westmorland Antiquarian and Archaeological society* NS 98, 61–106.

Vyner, B., Robinson, P., Annis, R. and Pickin, J. (2001) *Stainmore, the archaeology of a North Pennine Pass*, 98–111. Tees Archaeology monograph series1, London, English Heritage.

Walker, J. (1989) The function of Castleshaw fortlet. In J. Walker (ed.) *Castleshaw: The Archaeology of a Roman Fortlet*, 79–108. Manchester, Greater Manchester Archaeological Unit.

Wheeler, M. (1924) *Segontium and the Roman occupation of Wales* Cardiff: Honourable Society of Cynmodorion.

Wilson, P. (1991) Aspects of the Yorkshire Signal Stations. In V. Maxfield and M. Dobson (eds) *Roman Frontier Studies 1989*, 142–147. Exeter. Exeter University Press.

6

THE LATE ROMAN COASTAL FORT OF OUDENBURG (BELGIUM): SPATIAL AND FUNCTIONAL TRANSFORMATIONS WITHIN THE FORT WALLS

Sofie Vanhoutte

In contrast to the most of the late Saxon Shore forts along the British side of the Channel, no remains of the Roman military installation survive above ground at Oudenburg in *Belgica Secunda*. Its use as a stone quarry during the Carolingian and high medieval periods, and the later development of this location into the core of a medieval settlement and city, led to the partial destruction of the Roman remains and a build-up of soil over the surviving remains, while little is known about the internal ground plans of the British Saxon Shore forts (see Pearson 2002, 139–140), excavations in the centre of Oudenburg in the first decade of the 21st century have yielded insight into the spatial and functional organisation of the fort, as well as its remarkable evolution and transformation over the course of its occupation history. The first fort at Oudenburg was erected in the late 2nd century AD, but it is the evidence for activity in the 4th century that makes the archaeological data unique.

The fort site and its excavation history

Nowadays Oudenburg is a relatively small town, located about 8 km from the Flemish coastline, between Ostend and Bruges (Fig. 6.1). During the Roman period, the site was an elevated sandy ridge providing a strategic vantage over the coastal plain (Fig. 6.2), which at that time consisted of mud flats and marshes, cut by natural gullies. The combination of this topographical position, the rectangular layout of the late Roman stone fort, and several finds suggest that in the 4th century AD this was the site of a Continental element of the *Litus Saxonicum*, and that its garrison worked closely with the Saxon Shore forts in southern *Britannia*. According to J. Mertens, who led the excavations at Oudenburg in the 1950s, 1960s, and 1970s (Fig. 6.3), various elements suggest that the site can probably be identified with the *Portus Aepaticus* listed in the *Notitia Dignitatum* (Mertens and Van Impe 1971, 36; Mertens 1987a and b; Brulet 2006d, 58–59), a conclusion that was preempted by Gysseling (1944). Nevertheless, several scholars reject this hypothesis (*e.g.* Will 1973; Leman 2004; Seillier 2010).

The existence of a Roman fort at Oudenburg was proved by Professor Mertens' excavations in the 1950s. Its presence had, though, long been assumed on the basis of toponymic, topographic, and historic sources in conjunction with the many Roman finds reported from the site since the 17th century (see Bauwens-Lesenne 1963, 91–94). In 1956–1957, the contours of the stone fort and its northwestern corner tower were located, while the northern tower of the western gate was traced in 1960 (Mertens 1962; 1977). Complementary research was conducted in 1970, which provided sections across the western defences of the fort (Fig. 6.3). The 1960 and 1970 trenches yielded insights into the chronology of the consecutive defensive ditches (Mertens 1978; Mertens 1979, 460–463; see also Mertens 1987a and b). When the city cemetery was taken out of use in 1976–1977, Mertens and his team seized the opportunity to search for remains of the fort internal buildings. Mertens' research revealed a complex stratigraphy that had built up over the course of an extended military occupation stretching from the end of the 2nd century until the beginning of the 5th century AD. The excavations were undertaken in rather small trenches sunk in the northwest and northern portion of the fort, which revealed a sequence of three successive forts built on top of each other: two of earth and timber, and one of stone (see Mertens 1977; 1979; 1987a and b).

The 1960s excavations of two late Roman military cemeteries more than 400 m to the west of the *castellum*

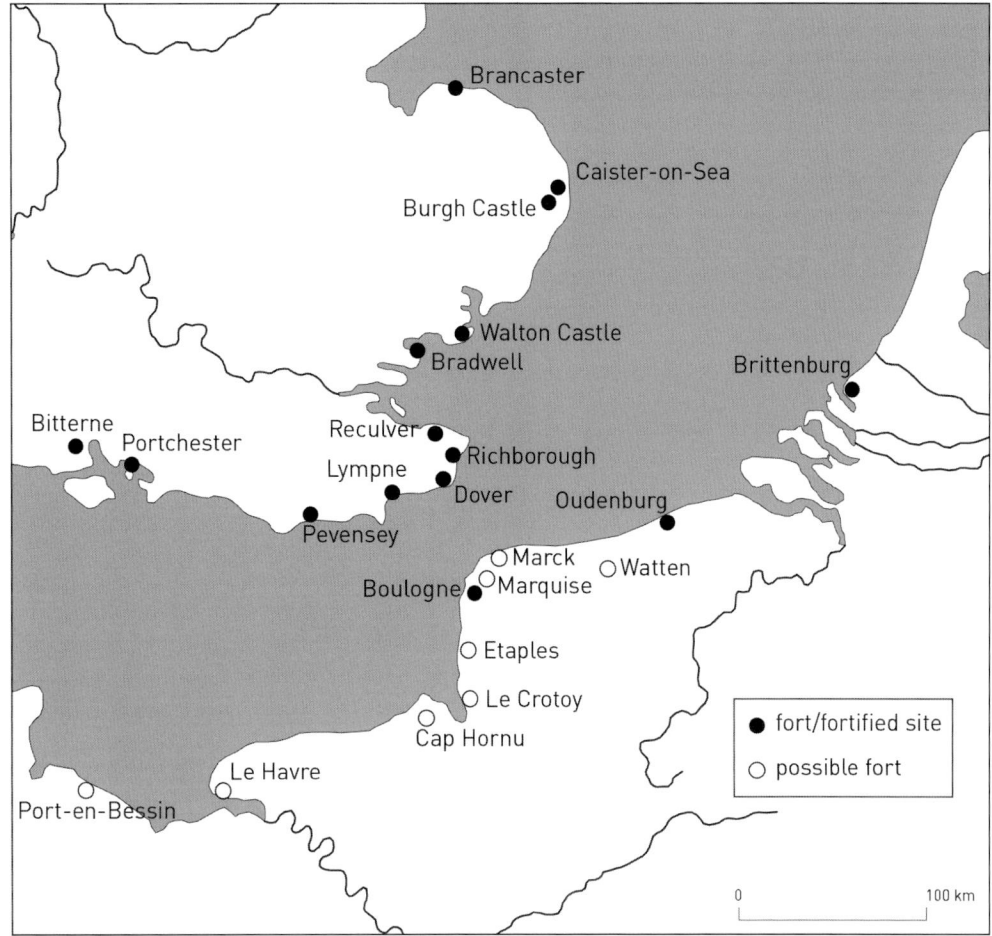

Figure 6.1: The location of Oudenburg fort, along with other military installations of the Litus Saxonicum

(Fig. 6.2) revealed burials of 4th-century fort inhabitants furnished with rich grave goods (Mertens 1977; Mertens and Van Impe 1971). Only three graves from the southern cemetery (cemetery A) were detected and excavated in 1962. They contained ceramic vessels belonging to the first half of the 4th century (Mertens 1977, 60). One of the graves yielded a face-pot of Much Hadham ware (UK) (Hollevoet 2004), demonstrating the unit's close connection with Britain.

The northern cemetery (B) was separated from cemetery A by a 60 m-wide strip that, according to Mertens, was devoid of archaeological material. Systematic and near-complete excavation of cemetery B in 1963–1964 and 1968 yielded 216 graves ranging in date from the second half of the 4th century through to the first decade of the 5th century (Mertens 1977, 59–62; Mertens and Van Impe 1971). The deceased were buried fully clothed, either wearing ornaments or with dress objects placed at their feet, in large wooden coffins. Accessories such as buckles, belt fittings, and crossbow brooches illustrate the military character of the graveyard. The high number of crossbow brooches (32 examples), the later type "Zwiebelknopf"-*fibula*, a well-known military symbol, points to the presence of several high ranking soldiers. The almost total absence of weapons distinguishes the Oudenburg cemetery from late Roman graveyards of *laeti* such as Eprave, Furfooz, Abbeville, or Vermand (see Böhme 1974). The Oudenburg soldiers must have belonged to a regular Roman army unit, perhaps *limitanei*, and not to auxiliary units or *laeti* groups (Mertens 1977, 62; Mertens 1987).

The cemetery does not seem to have been exclusively for soldiers, as a number of women and children also appear to have been buried there. Of the 138 skeletons that could be osteologically studied, 12 belonged to children under the age of 16. Of the 133 furnished burials, 21 produced assemblages that were feminine in character, while the sex of nine further graves was inconclusive (Mertens 1977, 61–62). Two female graves contained *tutulus* or cone-shaped brooches, a Germanic or Germanic-inspired brooch type worn in pairs by women (Swift 2000, 90). The bronze bracelets from the women's graves also reveal influences from *Germania Libera*, alongside connections with *Pannonia*, *Raetia*, and

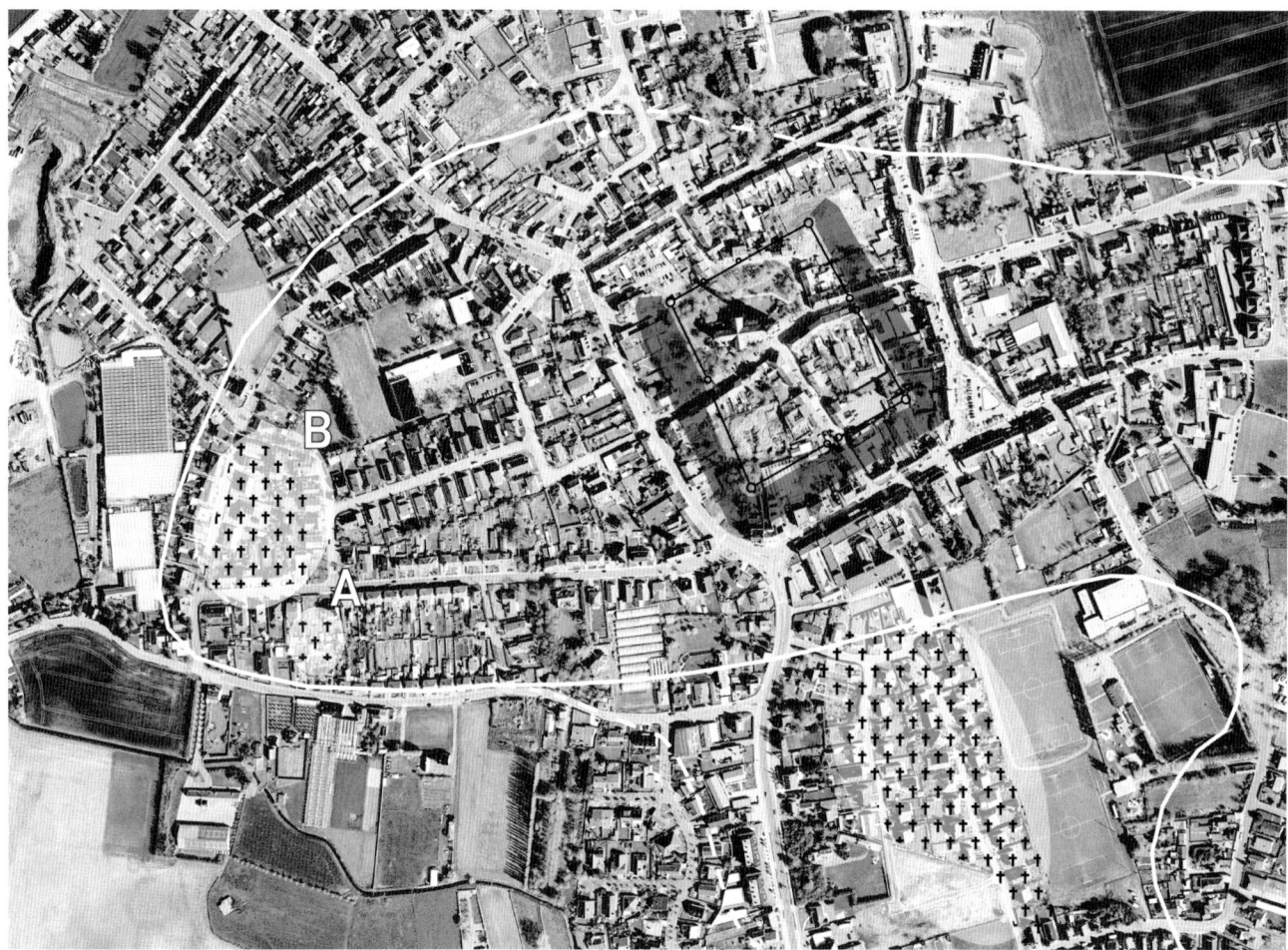

Figure 6.2: An aerial view of Oudenburg showing the location of the stone fort on the sandy ridge in the city center, the late Roman military graveyards to the west, and the civil cemetery to the south

Britannia, thus indicating either their region of origin or the places where their husband-soldiers were previously stationed (Sas 2004). This relationship with the material culture of Free Germany and the fact that it was initially not Roman practice to be buried wearing clothes and other accessories, both provide arguments to suggest that at least a large number of these soldiers were Germanic troops that had been recruited into the Roman army and brought their families with them (see Swift 2000, 90–92). Identical bracelets at Oudenburg and Portchester suggest that troops from the fort at Portchester or its hinterland may have been sent to Oudenburg with their families. Alternatively, the troops from Oudenburg were at least able to obtain much of their jewellery from there (Swift 2000, 99–100; Sas 2004, 369).

The 216 graves comprising the northern cemetery appeared to be clustered around the ruins of a presumed bath house, which was a relic of an older civil settlement (see Creus 1975). In the second half of the 1st century AD, long before the Roman army had chosen this location, a civil settlement developed on the site (Mertens and Van Impe 1971; Mertens 1987). Excavations and survey have shown that during its 2nd-century heyday this non-military presence must have covered most of the sandy ridge (Hollevoet 1987). From the late 2nd century onwards – that is the period when the fort was installed – this civil settlement developed into an extra-mural village, which was abandoned around AD 270. A cremation cemetery found to the south of the fort was connected to this civil presence (see Hollevoet 1992 and 1993) (Fig. 6.2).

Recent research on the fort site

No further excavations were carried out within the fort between the era of the Mertens' campaigns and 2001, when the construction of a supermarket prompted new archaeological research. This work continued until 2005,

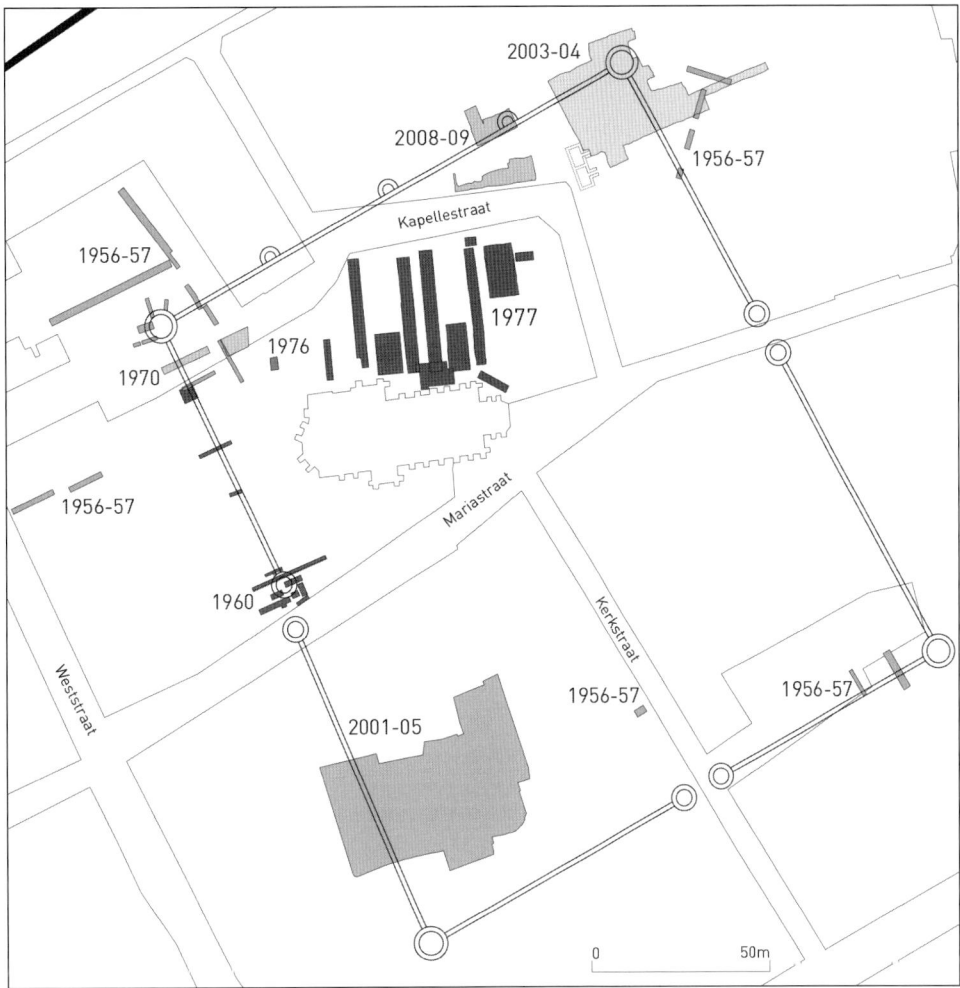

Figure 6.3: The city center of Oudenburg showing the location of the different excavation campaigns on the fort area

and occurred in the southwest corner of the fort precinct (see Vanhoutte 2007) (Fig. 6.3). Although this site only covers 5% of the total area within the fort walls, it provided a unique opportunity to carry out systematic research over an area of almost 18 are (0.18 ha). In 2003, another rescue excavation was conducted in the northeastern corner, which appeared to have largely been disturbed by medieval structures. Archaeological work to the west of this area followed in the spring of 2009, prior to the building of a block of flats. The findings here corresponded to the stratigraphy observed in the excavations at the southwest corner, and yielded new data concerning the stone fort defences (see Vanhoutte *et al.* 2014).

The fort sequence that was determined from numismatic and ceramic data within Roman occupation levels a metre or more thick was rather more complex than the stratified sequence that was presented following the research of the 1960s and 1970s. The recent archaeological research resulted in a refined chronology for the occupation of the *castellum*, including five main fort periods, running from the late 2nd century AD until the very beginning of the 5th century. They represent three earth and timber *castella* and two stone forts (Vanhoutte 2007; Vanhoutte 2009b). These Roman levels lay beneath a medieval accumulation of so-called "dark earth".

Studying occupation within the fort revealed that phase after phase brought change to the spatial and functional organisation of its interior. Over the course of its long occupation history, the southwest corner of the fort was obviously used for various purposes. Although the three 3rd-century phases could imply ongoing occupation, there was no such continuity in the fort. This is clearly attested by the surface being levelled prior to each phase of occupation, an act often preceded by a thorough clearance of the area, and followed by radical changes in layout. Although the late 2nd- to later 3rd-century levels all display elements typical of fort layouts, the internal organisation of the 4th-century stone fort presents a rather different picture. An explanation for the "non-military" appearance of the later Roman levels will be provided in the following reconstruction of the fort's occupation history.

The earth and timber forts

The first earth and timber fort was erected in the late 2nd century AD, probably as part of a system of coastal defence that appears to have been initiated with the construction of a *castellum* at Maldegem, after invasions by the Chauci in AD 172–174 (see Dhaeze 2011a, 170–176). The erection of a stone *castellum* at Aardenburg (Aardenburg II) was approximately contemporary with the first fort at Oudenburg (van Dierendonck and Vos 2013, 325–326). Since most 2nd- and 3rd-century forts received stone defences (Johnson 1987; Brulet 2006c, 167), the Oudenburg *castellum* must have originally been intended as a temporary measure installed during a period of troubles and threats.

The course of the earliest defensive ditch can be traced on Mertens' excavation maps, 108 m to the north where the ditch probably bends to the east. This defines a primary fort that appears to be smaller than its successors. The earliest level revealed several wooden constructions, associated pits, drainage gullies, and parts of floor levels that lay within course of the defensive ditch and an earthen rampart. Traces of the civil settlement that, at its peak in the 2nd century, probably spread over most of the sandy ridge are not stratigraphically distinguishable from the military traces. However, several wooden constructions, which are laid out parallel to the defensive ditch, can certainly be attributed to the military phase. Two of them are most likely to be interpreted as a *contubernium*. In one, the division partitioning the space into an *arma* and *papilio* is still preserved.

A new earth and timber fort was built in the second quarter of the 3rd century AD, for which a new defensive ditch was dug. A large timber-framed courtyard building measuring 32 × 23 m dominated the southwest corner of this fort. The small rooms and corridors were furnished with painted-plaster walls, and boasted mortar and stone floors. A collapsed wall from the southern corridor allows the decorative scheme to be reconstructed (study by L. Laken, see Vanhoutte, Laken, and Mazereel 2011), and also provides a height of 3.8 m, revealing a building of monumental character. The building shows many similarities in dimensions and layout with a stone courtyard building in Housesteads (see Charlesworth 1976; Johnson 1987, 184, 186 and Abb. 121) and Wallsend (Hodgson 2003, 129–133) on Hadrian's Wall, both of which are identified as *valetudinaria* or military hospitals. At Oudenburg, vestiges of a small structure could be distinguished in the courtyard along the axis of the building. In terms of both location and dimensions it resembles the *sacellum* in the legionary *valetudinarium* at Novae (Bulgaria) (Cf. Dyczek 1997, 202). The identification of the structure at Novae as a *sacellum* for the healing gods (Dyczek 1997, 203) supports the interpretation of the Oudenburg building as a *valetudinarium*.

Around the middle of the 3rd century AD, when a third temporary fort was built with new timber fortifications, the courtyard building was superseded by detached timber residential units with central fireplaces. Different phases can be distinguished, and the buildings underwent renovations that extended to changed orientations. A new style of barrack blocks consisting of detached units or "chalets" is also known in *Britannia*, where it appears in the first half of the 3rd century (Hodgson and Bidwell 2004, 148–149). Some of the Oudenburg timber units housed craft activities. Localised burning deposits mark the end of this period, which can be dated prior to *c.* AD 260.

The later 3rd-century stone fort

Around AD 260, during the reign of Postumus, the first stone fort at Oudenburg was erected on the same spot as its timber predecessors. This was obviously intended as a permanent army base. Occupied until *c.* 275 / 280 (Vanhoutte, Dhaeze, and De Clercq 2009), this fourth *castellum* was subject to a significant, long-term occupation. Due to its use as a medieval quarry, a robber trench containing some stone rubble was all that remained of the fort's masonry rampart. This allowed a rectangular fort plan to be reconstructed, with its west rampart changing course at the west gate. The defences extend for the following distances: *c.* 147 m on the north side, *c.* 162.5 m on the south side, *c.* 183 m on the west side and *c.* 182.5 m on the east side, resulting in a total area of *c.* 2.8 ha, or *c.* 2.72 ha within the defences.

During this fourth fort period, the southwestern corner was dedicated to industrial activity and dominated by various workshops, as well as open-air hearths and ovens. The finds point to bronze and iron objects being manufactured there. The production of simple spiral brooches is proven by evidence that the various steps in the manufacturing process all occurred there (Vanhoutte 2009a). On the basis of several unbent and therefore unfinished bracelets, these too were crafted on site. Burnt layers full of charred grains of spelt, in conjunction with nearby heaps of charred beans and peas, and numerous quern finds suggest that food processing and consumption occurred nearby. This space was also occupied by a central well, and, in the corner, a large waste-pit *c.* 10 m in diameter. A larger building lying on the northern edge of this workshop area probably marks the edge of the residential area.

Both the construction and occupation of this later-3rd-century permanent army base can be linked to the changing fortunes of the Gallic Empire (Vanhoutte, Dhaeze, and De Clercq 2009; Vanhoutte *et al.* 2009). While the instigation of this stone fort is most likely to be related to the actions of Postumus in the 260s against the Franks, the fort continued

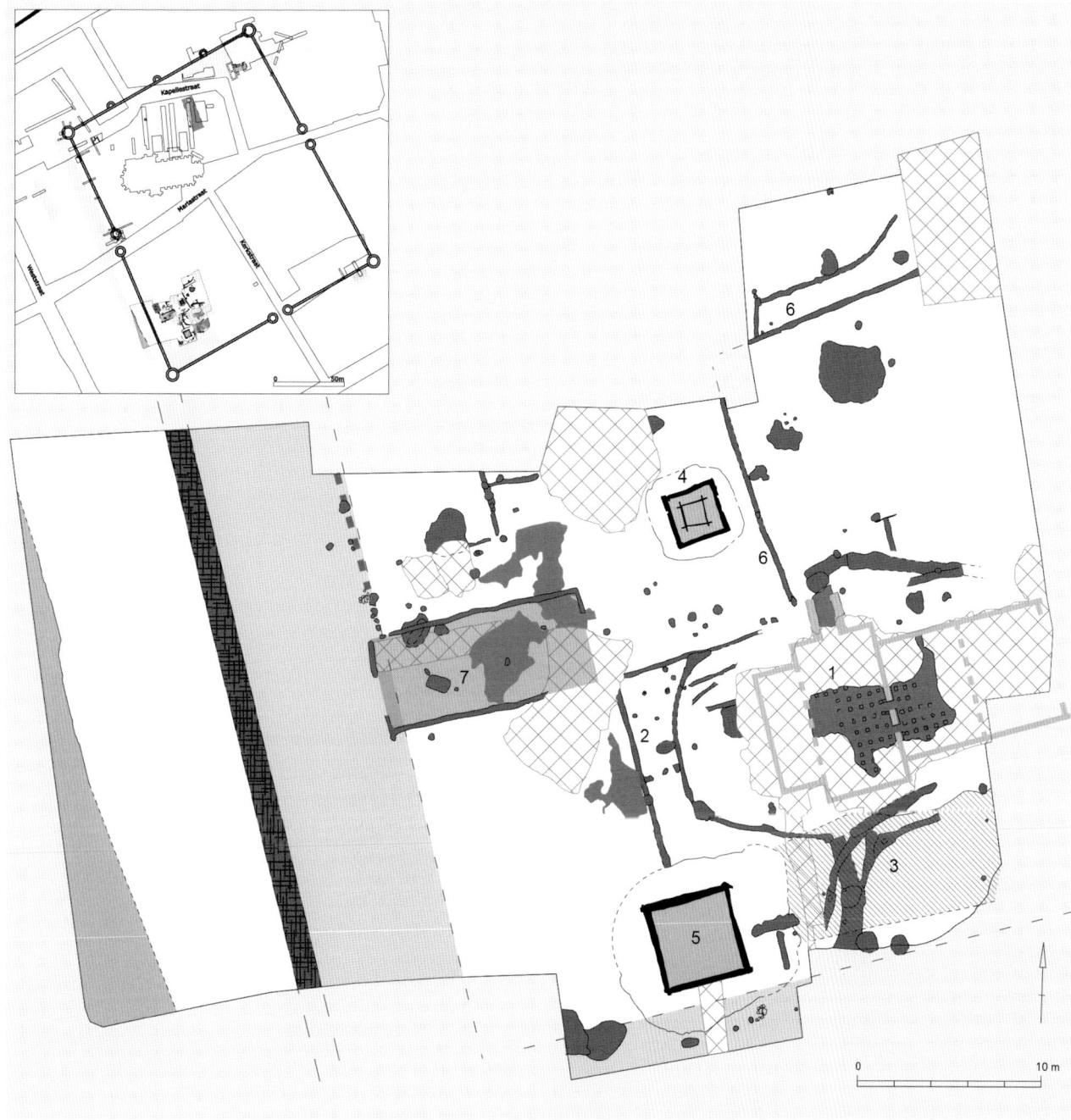

Figure 6.4: A simplified excavation plan of the fifth fort period

to play an important role in the Gallic Empire under his successors. The final occupation layers contain imitation coins of Tetricus I and II (271–274). It seems likely that the end of this fourth *castellum* is associated with the Germanic invasions of northwestern Gaul at the end of the third quarter of the 3rd century (De Boone 1954, 42–45; Thoen 1978, 196–201; Brulet 2006b, 43).

The 4th-century stone fort

The stone *castellum* was renovated and reoccupied in the second quarter of the 4th century. It was this 4th-century occupation that featured intriguing changes and remarkable evolutions to the fort layout (Fig. 6.4).

The historic context

The reoccupation of the stone fort is most likely to have been a consequence of the consolidation policy of Constantine I (306–337). His reign brought a period of regeneration and prosperity. Constantine I succeeded in restoring Roman authority along the northwestern border of the Roman empire after decades of chaos (see Engemann 2007), not only by consolidating the border with a system of defense in depth, but also by prosecuting offensive actions (De Boone 1954, 73).

A dendrochronological date of AD 379–380 from the latest well within this sequence indicates that the final phase of occupation occurred within the reign of Gratian (367–383), son of Valentinian I (364–375). This subphase of the fifth fort period may already have started under Valentinian I. J. Mertens assumed, based on the dating of the grave goods in cemetery B, that the *castellum* was renovated and garrisoned with new troops during Valentinian I's reign (Mertens and Van Impe 1971, 34). He implemented important troop movements in *c.* AD 369, a necessary reaction to the invasions by Frankish tribes (Hoffmann 1970, 342–344, 350–351). In the 4th century, the predominantly military sites in the region became isolated posts, as Frankish immigrants tightened their control of the countryside, with or without the blessing of Roman authorities (van Enckevort and Thijssen 2002, 83; Brulet 2006a). This Frankish presence is attested in Flanders, at sites such as Donk and Neerharen-Rekem, for example (see Van Ossel 1992). Valentinian I pursued an offensive policy against the Germans, and in this regard he followed in the footsteps of his predecessor Julian, who had turned the tide in the northwest of the Roman Empire after a series of severe Frankish invasions around the middle of the 4th century (van Es 1981, 51; Oldenstein 2006, 47).

In AD 368–369, Valentinian I initiated an ambitious building program that involved erecting or – more often – renovating *limes* fortifications along the Rhine and the Danube (Brulet 1990, 338; van Enckevort and Thijssen 2002, 83; Oldenstein 2006, 48). Presumably, the occupation of the fort at Oudenburg may be seen in light of these activities. The *castellum* of Oudenburg possibly had a similar occupation history in the 4th century as the fort at Cuijk, which underwent an occupation during the reign of Constantine I and rebuilding in stone under Valentinian I (see van Enckevort and Thijssen 2002, 81–83).

Following the reorganisation of the border by Valentinian, the province continued to be protected for at least another generation. Under the reign of Gratian (367–383), order and peace were maintained. At the end of his successor's reign, the usurper Magnus Maximus (383–388), new civil wars weakened the border and Germanic invasions took place once again (van Es 1981[2], 53). As no finds that can be dated to later than the beginning of the 5th-century have yet been found at Oudenburg, the fort was probably abandoned as part of the total withdrawal of Roman authority from the north west *c.* AD 410.

The 4th-century defences at Oudenburg fort

Excavations in 2009 at the Kapellestraat site on the northern side of the fort added a previously unknown aspect to our knowledge of its rampart architecture, namely the presence of intermediate towers (see Vanhoutte *et al.*, 2014). The dimensions of the robber trench that extracted the masonry from the intermediate tower allow us to estimate that this feature was 5.6 m wide, and projected 3.6 m beyond the stone curtain. These dimensions are quite similar to those known from the Saxon Shore forts in southeast England. The second generation of these forts, built after *c.* AD 260, were systematically equipped with similar intermediate towers (see Pearson 2002). Since only the robber trench and debris layer from the Oudenburg intermediate tower have survived, it is not possible to determine how the tower was attached to or integrated into the stone rampart. This intermediate tower probably only projected beyond rather than within the rampart.

There is no hard evidence regarding whether the tower and rampart belong to the same building phase, as the date of the intermediate tower remains unknown. It was not, of course, built earlier than *c.* AD 260, when the stone rampart was erected at the beginning of the fourth fort period. Whether these intermediate towers were contemporary with the later 3rd-century fort, which was constructed at a time when projecting half-round and U-shaped intermediate towers make their appearance (Johnson 1983, 38; Brulet 2006c, 171) or added in the 4th century, cannot be concluded. When the layout of the Oudenburg *castellum* is considered in its entirety, the question of whether the stone fabric was the product of two building phases arises. After all, the entrance and corner towers at Oudenburg were round, while the intermediate towers were projecting U-shaped structures. The intermediate tower distinguishes itself in terms of dimensions, form, and concept, from the circular corner and gate towers, which project from both the interior and exterior of the fortification wall (see Mertens 1962; 1977), following the fashion of the civil and military architecture from the High Empire in Gallia Belgica (Johnson 1989, 39; Dhaeze 2011b, 56; Dhaeze 2012, 81; van Dierendonck and Vos 2013).

This results in the hypothesis that the intermediate tower was not part of the initial stone fort, but was a later addition during the second sub-phase of the fourth fort period or, more likely, during the renovation in the fifth fort period in the 4th century. By extrapolating from the known tower, three intermediate towers can be anticipated along the northern side of the fort, leaving no space for an elaborate northern gateway. There are currently no indications that intermediate towers were installed along the other sides of the fort. During the late Roman period, the marine influence increased and it is thought that a branch of a tidal gully reached the north side of the fort. This direct contact with a tidal channel, and therefore the sea, probably explains why the northern rampart received extra protection from intermediate towers rather than an elaborate gateway.

The intramural layout during the 4th century AD

Very few late Roman forts have been sufficiently excavated to allow a detailed appreciation of their ground plan. The best understood examples in the western empire are Alzey and Altrip (Germany), but even here the picture is incomplete and several buildings remain unidentified. No ground plan of a late Roman Saxon Shore fort in Britain has yet been established (Pearson 2002, 139). As for Oudenburg, the early 21st-century excavations yielded detailed information about a small area in the corner of the fort. Although the extent of the excavations was limited, the 4th-century transformations are clear and new insights can be drawn from the structures that were discovered.

During the 4th century, the southwestern corner of the Oudenburg fort was dominated by a bath house (1) positioned along the metalled *intervallum* road (3) (Fig. 6.5). This road was eventually cut by a large basin (5). Long fences (6) and a simple timber building (7) can also be attributed to this later phase. A so-called "double well" (4) in the north of this area provides an insight into the chronology of the features (Vanhoutte *et al.* 2009). The well (Fig. 6.6) consisted of an outer framework of *c.* 3 × 3 m surrounding an inner wooden well measuring 1.4 × 1.4 m. Dendrochronological dating of the beams comprising the outer framework of the well, however, yielded a felling date of *c.* AD 266. Intentionally made holes with a regular inner spacing indicate that they had originally been used in earlier structures. At the internal base of the outer framework, a wooden frame was laid after AD 319–322 as either an element in the construction process or for clearing out the pit during its use in the second quarter of the 4th century. The felling date of AD 379–380 for the boards of the inner framework sets a *terminus post quem* for the construction of the inner well and also establishes the beginning of the final occupation phase at Oudenburg fort. This allows the chronology of these features to be reconstructed, with the outer well – more accurately a tank for receiving rain water – functioning during the second quarter of the 4th century. The structure was subsequently abandoned and only reactivated following the construction of an inner well during the last quarter of the 4th century AD.

The two phases compressed within the fifth fort period are also discernible in the coin assemblage and the Argonne roller-stamp Samian found on site. Moreover, these two occupation periods can be linked with the two military cemeteries found to the west of the fort. Graveyard B can

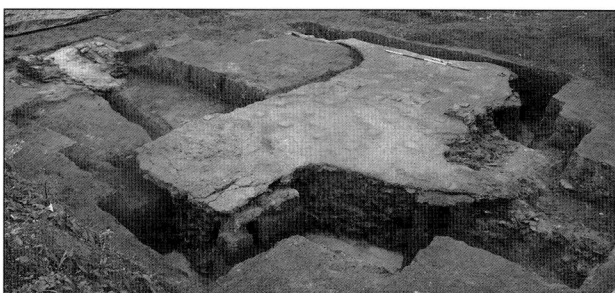

Figure 6.5: A view of the hypocaust floor from the fifth fort period, looking from west to east, with the stoke hole to the left

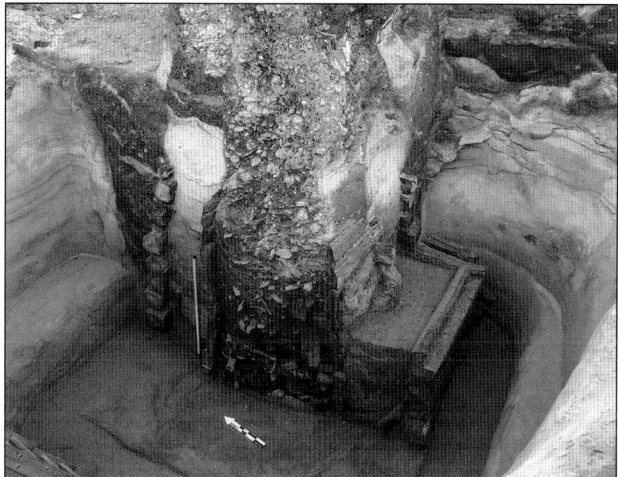

Figure 6.6: A section through the double well of the 4th century AD

be dated from the second half of the 4th century until the beginning of the 5th century, while the graves in cemetery A are slightly earlier (Mertens and Van Impe 1971; Hollevoet 2004). Whether the second sub-phase represents renewed occupation following an interruption cannot be concluded with certainty.

At the beginning of phase 5A, which starts in the second quarter of the 4th century, a row-type bath house dominated the area of the fort's southwest corner (Fig. 6.5, Fig. 6.8). Due to medieval stone-robbing, only part of a hypocaust floor, which covered an area of 7.75 × 5 m, and the end of its stoke hole survived *in situ*. On the basis of the location of the stoke hole and a central partition in the preserved portion of floor, the *caldarium*, *tepidarium*, and *frigidarium* (which lay outside the excavation area) can be identified. Based on the location of the robber trenches, the layout of the bath house can be hypothetically reconstructed. It had a maximum width of *c.* 6.5 m to / locally extended to 8.5 m. Since the hypocaust floor is situated on the same level as the surrounding ground surface, the bath house must have had a raised floor, requiring the presence of steps. On the

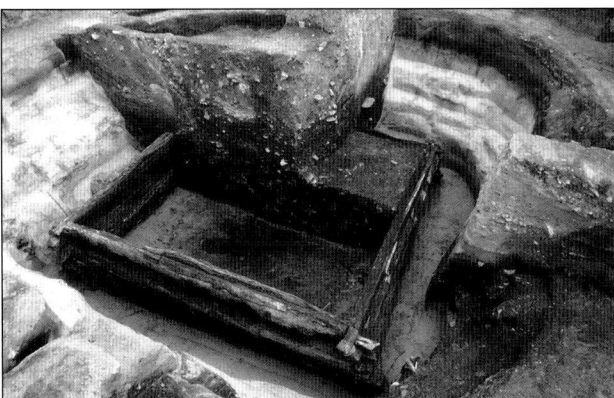

Figure 6.7: The large wooden water-basin, 4.5 m square, from the second half of the 4th century AD

west side of the bath house, the wooden fences (2) appear to be related to the construction phase of the bath house.

The presence of an intramural bath house is not an exceptional phenomenon in the late Roman period. While bath houses associated with middle-Imperial Roman military sites tend to be situated *extra muros*, the *thermae* often moved inside the fort walls during the late Roman period. The Saxon Shore forts of Richborough (Cunliffe 1968; Pearson 2002, 143, 145; Wilmott 2012, 15), Lympne (Cunliffe 1980, 257; Pearson 2002, 143, 145), and Reculver (Wilmott 2012, 20–23) all yielded small bath suites within the fort perimeter. Little is known about the internal buildings at Portchester, but *tegulae* and *imbrices*, as well as hypocaust and box flue tiles were present in significant quantities, suggesting not only structures with tiled roofs, but at least one building equipped with a heating system (Cunliffe 1975, 71–72). At Dover, the 2nd-century bath house built outside the *Classis Britannica* fort was incorporated within the Saxon Shore fort (Pearson 2002, 146).

The bath house at Oudenburg has been thoroughly demolished; almost all the walls and floors were removed during the Middle Ages. While exploring the robber trenches, however, a remarkable stone rubble and mortar foundation platform over 1 m thick came to light (Fig. 6.5). Since the medieval robber trenches continued to precisely the depth at which this foundation occurred, the digging was obviously intended to extract the building fabric. Although the fort rampart was built directly on top of sandy soil without any extra foundations, the bath building was apparently judged in need of a major stability measure. Perhaps this was a consequence of previous disturbances to the building plot on this site. Although little remains of the bath house, building material collected from the demolition trenches allow a fragmented glimpse of its architecture, which featured *tubuli*, calc-sinter from the baths, and plaster fragments displaying the remains of wall paintings. These plaster fragments display two different mortars and decorative motifs, indicating that the interior of the bath house was refurbished. It is therefore most likely that the bath house had a second phase, later in the 4th century AD.

The duration of the bath house's use cannot be determined from the archaeological evidence since the medieval robber trenches destroyed the stratigraphic relationships. The wooden water tank (Fig. 6.7) to the southwest of the bath building can be dated to the second half of the 4th century. Whether the bath house was still in use at that time is not certain, but it can be supposed. Similar reservoirs were excavated in the earlier forts of Valkenburg (NL), Wiesbaden, and Oberstimm (G). The water-basin at Oberstimm, which measured 3.25 × 3.25 m and was dated to *c.* AD 40–70, was found in the inner court of a *fabrica* complex (Schönberger 1978, 35). Based on these findings, the water tanks at Valkenburg and Wiesbaden were also interpreted within the context of workshops (see Schönberger 1979). Johnson mentions that tanks were used in 1st and 2nd century to collect rain water (Johnson 1987, 230). Such facilities are also found in the 3rd century AD, as in the inner court of the *principia* at the *castellum* of Echzell (Baatz 2006).

It is most likely that the Oudenburg basin was also used to collect rain and supplied water. Although a stratigraphic relationship cannot be proven, the vicinity of the bath house suggests that this enormous water-basin served as a reservoir to supply the baths, a function that was probably initially fulfilled by the outer framework of the "double well".

Stratigraphic analysis reveals that the final demolition of the bath house took place after the so-called "dark earth" had covered the Roman site. Obviously, the ruins were still visible at that time, projecting above the accumulated "dark earth". The robber trenches yielded high medieval ceramics, dating the last phase of demolition to the 11th–12th centuries. Since the ruins of the bath complex were still visible until this date, allowing the medieval diggers to extract the fabric, this structure must have been standing until the end of the fort occupation at Oudenburg. However, surrounding features, such as the fences (6) and the simple timber building with a footprint of *c.* 12 × 5.5 m standing nearby (7), call into question whether the bath house was operational until the very end of the fort occupation at the beginning of the 5th century. It seems more likely that the bath house went out of use in the late 4th century AD and was left in a derelict state. This was not an isolated phenomenon; after the middle of the 4th century, other examples of bath houses are known to be abandoned (Brulet 2006c, 179). It seems that the function fulfilled by the Oudenburg bath building remained important until the second half of the 4th century, but its continued use is debatable after that. However, the thorough medieval removal of the floor level has eliminated any traces of whether the complex was adapted to a new role.

Detailed research on the "double well" (Fig. 6.6) provides

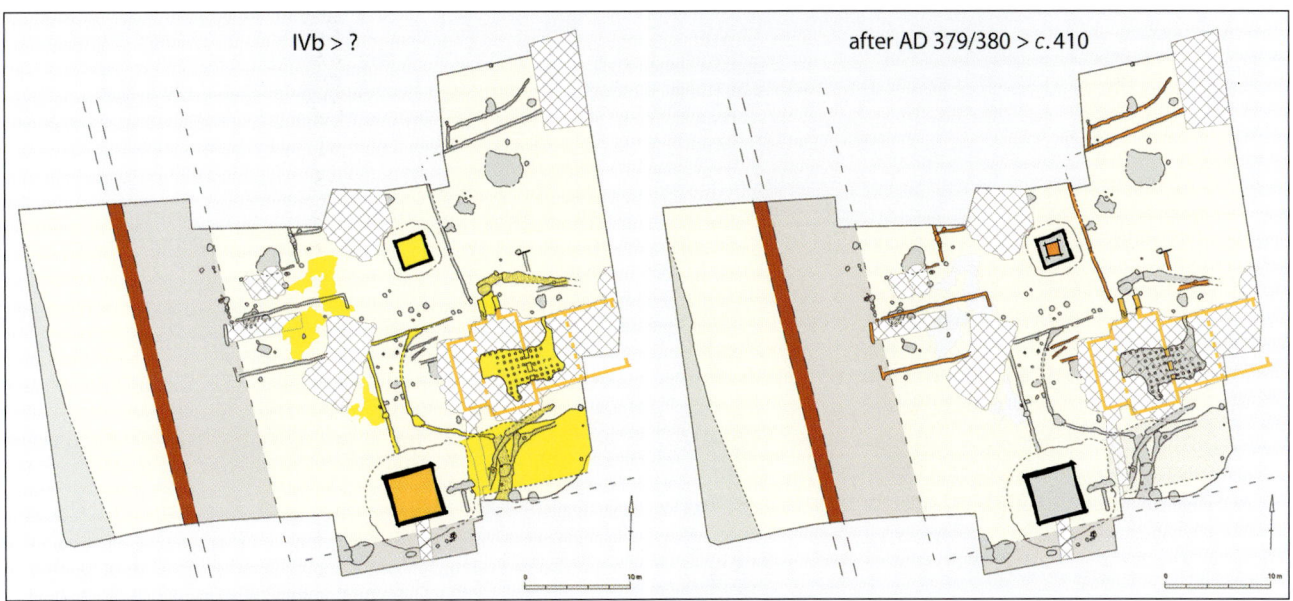

Figure 6.8: An excavation plan of the fifth fort period. To the left: features to be attributed to the second quarter of the 4th century onwards. To the right: features datable after AD 379–380

further insight into the occupation history of the 4th century and the interpretation of the features surrounding the bath house (Vanhoutte *et al.* 2009). The construction of the inner well proved to be an engineering masterpiece. The lowest portion of the shaft sandwiched between the wooden frameworks revealed a sequence of pure clay, sand and moss layers, with the well-preserved moss lining the joints between the boards comprising the inner well. Combining the thick layer of clay between the two well linings at the bottom of the shaft with further clay on the outside of the inner frame seems to indicate that water coming from both beneath and the sides needed to be stopped, although the well itself was open at the bottom. There must have been a specific reason for the use of moss and it seems to have been used as a filtering system. Mineralogical analysis of a yellow crust that developed on clay samples taken from between the timber frameworks suggests this as well. This deposite was identified as yarosite, which indicates an abundance of iron and sulphur, possibly as a result of the metal production in this area during period four. This could have had a significant effect on ground water. Presumably this matrix of alternating sand, clay, and moss layers served as a filter to improve the quality of the water seeping into the pit from its sides, while the water rising up from underneath was judged to be pure.

A number of ritual deposits were discovered at the bottom of the well, including the skull of a brown bear and peculiar finds such as a human femur and parts or all of two non-butchered pigs, two dogs, a juvenile roe deer, a sheep, and a cat. The sediments that filled up the well during its final phase of use and immediately after its abandonment appear to have come from heavily polluted areas, displaying traces of dung and midden materials on which nitrophilous pioneer and ruderal plant species grew. Black rat, house mice, black vulture, and raven remains were present within these rubbish deposits: all animals that live off offal and carrion.

The results of scientific analysis suggest that this area was filthy, perhaps partially derelict, and dedicated to animal husbandry, with livestock that grazed outside the fort being stabled in this area. These data offer an explanation for several structures found on the site (Fig. 6.8). The fences formed an enclosure, and probably made use of the bath house ruins to help partition the area, while the structure erected along its western wall can be identified as a stable. The scale of the fences suggests paddocks, perhaps for horses, dividing this area into a series of yards. The discovery of several rein holders and harnass fittings in this area may confirm this inference.

"Non-traditional" use of the fort

The most striking aspect of the late Roman Saxon Shore forts is the less intensive use of space within the defences (Pearson 2002, 140, 144), a phenomenon also detected in some Gaulish forts (Brulet 2006c, 174). This also seems to be the case at Oudenburg.

The reason for this probably lies in the late Roman reorganization of the army, and in particular in the reduction in unit size (Coello 1996, 60–62). The late Roman forts were mostly reused and refurbished forts from earlier periods, resulting in internal spaces that were excessive for late Roman units. The later Roman "chalet" barracks along Hadrian's Wall certainly indicate a reduction in auxiliary unit strength. This decline in the number of soldiers within forts must have had severe economic repercussions, which may have meant that the military *vici* were no longer viable. Along Hadrian's Wall all of the military *vici* seem to have been wholly or largely abandoned in the later 3rd or early 4th century AD (Bidwell and Hodgson 2009, 33–34). At Vindolanda, Housesteads, and Wallsend, the abandonment of the military *vici* can even be dated more specifically to *c.* 270 (Hodgson 2003, 17). The spare space in late Roman forts coupled with the abandonment and disappearance of the military *vici* can be presented as reasons why the Oudenburg bath building was moved within the perimeter in the late Roman period. It has traditionally been assumed that families moved into the forts at this time, but analysis of structures and finds from Wallsend, South Shields, and Vindolanda does not support this thesis (Hodgson and Bidwell 2004, 153–154). Recent studies of artefact distributions at the fort of South Shields (Hodgson 2014) and of Vindolanda (Birley 2013) indicate an increased presence of women and children does not occur until the (later) 4th century.

The 21st-century Oudenburg excavations did yield substantial archaeological evidence for the presence of women and children within the fort walls (Vanhoutte and Verbrugge (in press)). The five principal fort levels between the late 2nd century and the beginning of the 5th century offer a unique chronological framework for the study of gender-related items and the implications for the evolution of the fort community. This reveals that although finds associated with females and children within the fort walls are initially sparse, they become more numerous from the later 3rd century onwards (*c.* 260–275/280), and increase significantly during the 4th century. The assemblage comprises dozens of hair pins, bracelets, beads, spindle whorls, and women's and children's shoes. The manufacturing of bracelets with fairly small diameter in the workshop area during the later 3rd century can be added to this list. The military *vicus* outside Oudenburg fort seems to have been abandoned *c.* AD 270, while the Germanic invasions in this area peaked in 268–275/276 (Thoen 1978, 196–201). Moreover, the landscape around Oudenburg underwent significant changes at this time: the marine influence increased, while the sandy ridge on which the fort lay diminished and occupation along the coastline became more difficult. A distinct civilian presence on the sandy ridge at Oudenburg seems to have ended, a pattern that was probably replicated along the whole Flemish coastline. The late Roman military graveyards clearly testify that at least some soldiers were accompanied by their families. Given that only an area amounting to 5% of the fort interior was sampled, a significant quantity of female- and child-related finds was found, especially among the late Roman phases. By this period it may be assumed that the fort housed both the military and (part of the) civil community. Together with the evidence for bracelet production within the fort walls, this may imply that the late Roman fort at Oudenburg should be seen as a fortified town where the soldiers lived side by side with their families.

A similar increase in female- and child-related finds has been noted at Portchester. Both infant burials and finds associated with females indicate that women were living within the fort walls from AD 300 onwards. It has been suggested that a mixed civilian and military community took over the fort (Cunliffe 1975, 427). Changes in internal organisation at the late 4th-century *castrum* of Arras (F) also correspond with an influx of female jewellery and thus, with the shifting composition of the fort community (Jacques 2007, 79).

The abandonment of the *vicus* at Oudenburg and the general desertion of the Flemish coastline in the late Roman period were probably caused by several factors: the collapse of the *vicus* economy; the increased pressure from the sea; and the constant threat of the Germanic invasions. This latter risk must have influenced the relocation of the soldiers' families into the protected area within the fort. These new data from the Oudenburg fort appear to offer supplementary evidence supporting the notion that the late Roman fort in general was more of a fortified settlement than a purely military installation.

If we can assume that the bath house was not relocated to another place within the fort, can we also conclude that by the end of the 4th century bathing was no longer an important part of military life? There are certainly further examples of bath houses in Gaul that seem to have gone out of use after the middle of the 4th century (Brulet 2006c, 179). The differences in the style of occupation in the excavated area suggest that the resident army unit changed. Thanks to the military cemetery excavated 400 m to the west of the fort, the inhabitants of the latest fort period are known. As discussed above, at least part of this unit seems to have Germanic roots. These soldiers were probably no longer imbued with Roman culture and had their own dress and traditions. Did these differences also extend to what could be characterised as a much lower standard of cleanliness? The dumping of dung heaps and organic waste such as offal in this corner of the fort during the final phase of occupation does seem to substantiate this possibility. Activities that were formerly excluded from the fort interior for hygiene reasons were no longer excluded. Daily bathing in the bath house, a typical Roman practice, presumably also no longer formed an "official" part of military life.

The combination of finds and scientific analyses provides a compelling explanation for the "non-military" look of the late Roman fort at Oudenburg. Its apparent evolution into a compound housing a mixed military and civil community, coupled with the Germanic roots of its garrison, must have had a marked impact on the appearance of the fort precinct.

Bibliography

Baatz, D. (2006) Echzell. Hesse, Allemagne. In M. Reddé, R. Brulet, R. Fellmann, J. K. Haalebos and S. von Schnurbein (eds) *L'architecture de la Gaule romaine 1: Les fortifications militaires*, 270–272. Documents d'archéologie française 100, Bordeaux, MSH-Ausonius.

Bauwens-Lesenne, M. (1963) Oudenburg. In M. Bauwens-Lesenne *Bibliografisch repertorium der oudheidkundige vondsten in West-Vlaanderen (vanaf de vroegste tijden tot aan de Noormannen)*, 91–94. Oudheidkundige repertoria IV, Brussel, Nationaal Centrum voor Oudheidkundige Navorsingen in Belgie.

Bidwell, P. T. and Hodgson, N. (2009) *The Roman Army in Northern England*. Newcastle-upon-Tyne, Arbeia Society.

Birley, A. (2013) The fort wall: a great divide? In R. Collins and M. Symonds (eds) *Breaking Down Boundaries. Hadrian's Wall in the 21st Century*, 85–104. JRA supplementary series 93, Rhode Island, Journal of Roman Archaeology.

Böhme, H. W. (1974) *Germanische grabfunde des 4. bis 5. Jahrhunderts zwischen unterer Elbe und Loire. Studien zur chronologie und Bevölkerungsgeschichte*, Münchner Beiträge zur ur- und frühgeschichte 19, München, Beck.

Brulet, R. (1990) *La Gaule septentrionale au Bas-Empire. Occupation du sol et défense du territoire dans l'arrière-pays du Limes aux IVe et Ve siècles. Nordgallien in der Spätantike*, Trierer Zeitschrift. Beiheft 11, Trier, Selbstverlag des Rheinischen Landesmuseums Trier.

Brulet, R. (2006a) De Dioclétien à Valentinien Ier. In M. Reddé, R. Brulet, R. Fellmann, J. K. Haalebos and S. von Schnurbein (eds), *L'architecture de la Gaule Romaine 1: Les fortifications militaires*, 44–47. Documents d'Archéologie Française 100, Bordeaux, MSH-Ausonius.

Brulet, R. (2006b) Du milieu du IIIe s. à Dioclétien. In M. Reddé, R. Brulet, R. Fellmann, J. K. Haalebos and S. von Schnurbein (eds) *L'architecture de la Gaule romaine 1: Les fortifications militaires*, 42–44. Documents d'Archéologie Française 100, Bordeaux, MSH-Ausonius.

Brulet, R. (2006c) L'architecture militaire romaine en Gaule pendant l'Antiquité tardive. In M. Reddé, R. Brulet, R. Fellmann, J. K. Haalebos and S. von Schnurbein (eds) *L'architecture de la Gaule romaine 1: Les fortifications militaires*, 155–179. Documents d'archéologie Française 100, Bordeaux, MSH-Ausonius.

Brulet, R. (2006d) L'organisation territoriale de la défense des Gauls pendant l'Antiquité tardive. In M. Reddé, R. Brulet, R. Fellmann, J. K. Haalebos and S. von Schnurbein (eds) *L'architecture de la Gaule romaine 1: Les fortifications militaires*, 50–66. Documents d'archéologie Française 100, Bordeaux, MSH-Ausonius.

Charlesworth, D. (1976) The Hospital, Housesteads. *Archaeologia Aeliana* 5th series, 4, 17–30.

Coello, T. (1996) *Unit Sizes in the Late Roman Army*. BAR International Series 645, Oxford, BAR.

Creus, I. (1975) *De Gallo-Romeinse nederzetting onder het laat-Romeins grafveld van Oudenburg*. Archaeologia Belgica 179, Brussel, Nationale Dienst voor Opgravingen.

Cunliffe, B. W. (1968) *Fifth Report of the Excavations of the Roman Fort at Richborough, Kent*. Reports of the research committee of the Society of Antiquaries of London 23, Oxford, Oxford University Press.

Cunliffe, B. W. (1975) *Excavations at Portchester Castle. Volume I: Roman*. Reports of the Research Committee of the Society of Antiquaries of London 32, London: Society of Antiquaries of London.

Cunliffe, B. W. (1980) Excavations at the Roman Fort at Lympne. *Britannia* 11, 227–288.

De Boone, W. J. (1954) *De Franken van hun eerste optreden tot de dood van Childerik*. Amsterdam, Proefschrift-Groningen.

Dhaeze, W. (2011a) *De Romeinse kustverdediging langs de Noordzee en het Kanaal van 120 tot 410 na Chr. Een onderzoek naar de rol van de militaire sites in de kustverdediging en drie casestudies over de militaire versterkingen van Maldegem-Vake, Aardenburg en Boulogne-sur-Mer*, unpublished doctoral thesis, Universiteit Gent.

Dhaeze, W. (2011b) Een schakel in de 2de-eeuwse kustverdediging: het *castellum* te Aardenburg. In B. Hillewaert, Y. Hollevoet and M. Ryckaert (eds), *Op het raakvlak van twee landschappen. De vroegste geschiedenis van Brugge*, 55–56. Brugge, Van de Wiele.

Dhaeze, W. (2012) Het *castellum* Aardenburg: een schakel in de 2de- en 3de-eeuwse kustverdediging. In W. De Clercq *Over vlees en bloed. Menapische boeren en soldaten aan de rand van het Romeinse Rijk*, 80–82. Publicaties van het Provinciaal-Archeologisch Museum Velzeke. Gewone reeks, 5, Be Stichting Kunstboek.

Dyczek P. (1997) The valetudinarium at Novae – new components. In W. Groenman-van Waateringe, B. L. van Beek, W. J. H. Willems and S. L. Wynia (eds), *Roman Frontier Studies 1995. Proceedings of the XVIth International Congress of Roman Frontier Studies*, 199–204. Oxford, Oxbow.

Engemann, J. (2007) Konstantins Sicherung der Grenzen des Römischen Reiches. In A. Demandt and J. Engemann (eds), *Imperator Caesar Flavius Konstantin. Constantinus der Grosse. Ausstellungskatalog*, 155–159. Mainz, von Zabern.

Gysseling, M. (1944) De Romeinse Kustverdediging in Belgica Secunda volgens de Notitia Dignitatum. *Feestbundel H.J. van de Wijer: den jubilaris aangeboden ter gelegenheid van zijn vijfentwintigjarig hoogleeraarschap aan de R.K. Universiteit te Leuven 1919–1943*, 287–301. Louvain, Instituut voor vlaamsche toponymie.

Hodgson, N. (2003) *The Roman Fort at Wallsend (Segedunum). Excavations in 1997–8*. Newcastle upon Tyne, Tyne and Wear Museums.

Hodgson, N. (2014) The accommodation of Soldiers' wives in Roman fort barracks – on Hadrian's Wall and beyond. In R. Collins and F. McIntosh (eds) *Life in the Limes. Studies of the People and Objects of the Roman Frontiers Presented to Lindsay Allason-Jones on the Occasion of her Birthday and Retirement*, 18–28. Oxford, Oxbow.

Hodgson, N. and Bidwell, P. T. (2004) Auxiliary barracks in a new light: recent discoveries on Hadrian's Wall. *Britannia* 35, 121–157.

Hoffmann, D. (1970) *Das spätrömische Bewegungsheer und die Notitia dignitatum*. Epigraphische Studien 7, Düsseldorf, Rheinland-Verlag.

Hollevoet, Y. (1987) Prospectie in Oudenburg. In H. Thoen

(ed.) *De Romeinen langs de Vlaamse kust*, 48–50. Brussels, Gemeentekrediet van België.

Hollevoet, Y. (1992) Speuren onder het sportveld. Romeinse en middeleeuwse sporen ten zuiden van de Stedebeek te Oudenburg (prov. West-Vlaanderen). Interimverslag 1990–1992. *Archeologie in Vlaanderen* 2, 195–207.

Hollevoet, Y. (1993) Ver(r)assingen in een verkaveling. Romeins grafveld te Oudenburg (prov. West-Vlaanderen). Interimverslag. *Archeologie in Vlaanderen* 3, 207–216.

Hollevoet, Y. (2004) Le site militaire d'Oudenburg et la Bretagne insulaire durant l'Antiquité tardive; quelques éléments inédits. In F. Vermeulen, K. Sas and W. Dhaeze (eds) *Archaeology in confrontation. Aspects of Roman military presence in the Northwest. Studies in honour of prof. em. Hugo Thoen*, 335–342. Archaeological Reports Ghent University 2, Gent, Academia Press.

Jacques, A. (2007) Arras-Nemetacum, chef-lieu de cité des Atrébates. Bilan des recherches 1984–2002. In R. Hanoune (ed.), *Les villes romaines du Nord de la Gaule. Vingt ans de recherches nouvelles. Actes du XXVe colloque international de HALMA-IPEL UMR CNRS 8164*, 63–82. Revue du Nord. Hors série. Collection Art et Archéologie 10, Villeneuve d'Ascq, Université Charles-de-Gaulle-Lille.

Johnson, A. (1987) *Römische Kastelle des 1. und 2. Jahrhunderts n. Chr. in Britannien und in den germanischen Provinzen des Römerreiches* (übersetzt von G. Schulte-Holtey, bearbeitet von D. Baatz), Kulturgeschichte der Antiken Welt 37, Mainz am Rhein, Philipp von Zabern.

Johnson, S. (1983) *Late Roman Fortifications*, London, Batsford.

Johnson, S. (1989) The architecture of the Saxon Shore forts. In V. A. Maxfield (ed.) *The Saxon Shore. A Handbook*, 30–44. Exeter Studies in History 25, Exeter, University of Exeter.

Leman, P. (2004) À propos de quelques lieux de la Notitia Dignitatum. Etat de la recherche et suggestions. In F. Vermeulen, K. Sas and W. Dhaeze, (eds) *Archaeology in Confrontation. Aspects of Roman Military Presence in the Northwest. Studies in honour of Prof. Em. Hugo Thoen*, 213–215. Archaeological Reports Ghent University 2, Gent, Academia Press.

Mertens, J. (1962) Oudenburg et le Litus Saxonicum en Belgique. *Helinium* II, 51–62.

Mertens, J. (1977) Oudenburg and the northern sector of the continental Litus Saxonicum. In D. E. Johnston (ed.) *The Saxon Shore*, 51–62. CBA Research Report 18, London, CBA.

Mertens, J. (1978) *Het laat-Romeins castellum te Oudenburg*, Archaeologia Belgica 206, Conspectus MCMLXXVII, 73–76.

Mertens, J. (1980) Recherches récentes sur le limes en Gaule Belgique. In W. S. Hanson and L. F. J. Keppie (eds) *Roman frontier studies 1979: Papers presented to the 12th International Congress of Roman Frontier Studies*, 423–470. BAR International Series 71 (i), Oxford, BAR.

Mertens, J. (1987a) De Romeinse legerbasis te Oudenburg. In H. Thoen (ed.) *De Romeinen langs de Vlaamse kust*, 81–90. Brussels, Gemeentekrediet van België.

Mertens, J. (1987b) Oudenburg. *Romeinse legerbasis aan de Noordzeekust, (tweede aangevulde uitgave verzorgd door R. Crabbé)*. Archaeologicum Belgii Speculum IV, Brussel.

Mertens J. and Van Impe, L. (1971) *Het laat-Romeins grafveld van Oudenburg*. Archaeologica Belgica 135, Brussel.

Oldenstein, J. (2006) De Valentien Ier à la fin de l'Empire romain occidental. In M. Reddé, R. Brulet, R. Fellmann, J. K. Haalebos and S. von Schnurbein (eds) *L'architecture de la Gaule romaine 1: Les fortifications militaires*, 47–50. Documents d'archéologie Française 100, Bordeaux, MSH-Ausonius.

Pearson, A. (2002) *The Roman Shore Forts. Coastal Defences of Southern Britain*, Stroud, Tempus.

Sas, K. (2004) "Military" bracelets in Oudenburg: troop movements, origins and relations in the Litus Saxonicum in the 4th century AD. In F. Vermeulen, K. Sas and W. Dhaeze (eds) *Archaeology in Confrontation. Aspects of Roman Military Presence in the Northwest. Studies in honour of Prof. Em. Hugo Thoen*, 343–378. Archaeological Reports Ghent University 2, Gent, Academia Press.

Schönberger, H. (1978) *Kastell Oberstimm. Die Grabungen von 1968 bis 1971*. Limesforschungen 18, Berlin, Mann.

Schönberger, H. (1979) Valkenburg Z.H.: Praetorium oder Fabrica? *Germania* 57, 135–141.

Seillier, C. L. (2010) Rupture et continuité dans le Boulonnais et le Ponthieu entre le Bas-Empire et le haut Moyen Age. In B. Béthouart, S. Lebecq and L. Verslype L. (eds) *Quentovic. Environnement, archéologie, histoire. Actes du colloque international de Montreuil-sur-Mer, Etaples et Le Touquet et de la journée d'études de Lille sur les origines de Montreuil-sur-Mer (11–13 mai 2006 et 1er décembre 2006)*, 125–146. Lille, Éditions du Conseil scientifique de l'Université Lille.

Swift, E. (2000) *The End of the Western Roman Empire. An Archaeological Investigation*. Stroud, Tempus.

Thoen, H. (1978) *De Belgische kustvlakte in de Romeinse tijd. Bijdrage tot de studie van de landelijke bewoningsgeschiedenis*. Verhandelingen van de Koninklijke Academie voor Wetenschappen, Letteren en Schone kunsten van België. Klasse der Letteren XL, 88, Bruxelles, AWLSK.

van Dierendonck, R. M. and Vos, W. K. (2013) *De Romeinse agglomeratie Aardenburg: onderzoek naar de ontwikkeling, structuur en datering van de Romeinse castella en hun omgeving, opgegraven in de periode 1955-heden*. Hazenburg Archeologische Serie 3, Middelburg, Hazenberg Archeologie.

van Enckevort, H. and Thyssen, J. (2002) *Cuijk. Een regionaal centrum in de Romeinse tijd*. Archeologische Berichten Nijmegen 5, Utrecht, Matrijs.

van Es, W. A. (1981) *De Romeinen in Nederland*. Haarlem.

Vanhoutte, S. (2007) Het Romeinse castellum van Oudenburg (prov. West-Vlaanderen) herontdekt: de archeologische campagne van augustus 2001 tot april 2005 ter hoogte van de zuidwesthoek. Interim-rapport. *Relicta. Archeologie, Monumenten- en Landschapsonderzoek in Vlaanderen* 3, 199–236.

Vanhoutte, S. (2009a) Brooch production at the Roman fort of Oudenburg (Belgium) in the later 3rd century A.D. In H. van Enckevort (ed.) *Roman Material Culture. Studies in honour of Jan Thijssen*, 41–52. Zwolle, Stichting Promotie Archeologie.

Vanhoutte, S. (2009b) The Saxon Shore fort at Oudenburg (Belgium): new excavation results. In Á. Morillo, N. Hanel and E. Martín (eds) *Limes XX. XX congreso internacional de estudios sobre la frontera romana*, 1383–1392. Anejos de Gladius 13, Madrid, Consejo Superior de Investigaciones Científicas.

Vanhoutte, S., Bastiaens, J., De Clercq, W., Deforce, K., Ervynck, A., Fret, M., Haneca, K., Lentacker, A., Stieperaere, H., Van Neer, W., Cosyns, P., Degryse, P., Dhaeze, W.,

Dijkman, W., Lyne, M., Rogers, P., van Driel-Murray, C., van Heesch, J. and Wild, J. P. (2009) De dubbele waterput uit het laat-Romeinse *castellum* van Oudenburg (prov. West-Vlaanderen): tafonomie, chronologie en interpretatie. *Relicta. Archeologie, Monumenten- en Landschapsonderzoek in Vlaanderen* 5, 9–142.

Vanhoutte, S., Dhaeze, W. and De Clercq, W. (2009) The pottery consumption *c*. AD 260–70 at the Roman coastal defence fort, Oudenburg, northern Gaul, *Journal of Roman Pottery Studies* 14, 95–141.

Vanhoutte, S., Dhaeze, W., Ervynck, A., Lentacker, A., van Heesch, J. and Stroobants, F. (2014) Archeologisch onderzoek aan de noordzijde van het Romeinse *castellum* van Oudenburg: nieuwe inzichten in de *lay-out*, het verdedigingssysteem en de bewoningsgeschiedenis van het fort. *Relicta. Archeologie, Monumenten- en Landschapsonderzoek in Vlaanderen* 11, 163–269.

Vanhoutte, S. and Laken, L., m.m.v. Mazereel, S. (2011) *Post-excavation* onderzoek van het Romeinse *castellum* van Oudenburg: De muurschilderingen. *Romeinendag – Journée d'Archéologie Romaine* 2011, 137–146.

Vanhoutte, S. and Verbrugge, A. (in press) Women and children at the Saxon Shore fort at Oudenburg (Belgium). In P. Bidwell *et al.* (eds) *Limes XXI Roman Frontier Studies; Proceedings of the International Conference. University of Newcastle upon Tyne (16–23 August 2009)*. Oxford, BAR.

Van Ossel, P. (1992) *Etablissements ruraux de l'Antiquité tardive dans le nord de la Gaule*. 51e supplement à Gallia, Paris.

Will, E. (1973) Compte rendu de J. Mertens and L. Van Impe 1971, Het Laat-Romeins grafveld van Oudenburg, Archaeologia Belgica 135, Bruxelles. *Revue du Nord* 216, 71–72.

Wilmott, T. (2012) *Richborough and Reculver*. London, English Heritage Guidebooks.

7

THE LEGIONARY FORTRESS OF VINDOBONA (VIENNA, AUSTRIA): CHANGE IN FUNCTION AND DESIGN IN THE LATE ROMAN PERIOD

Martin Mosser

Introduction

Traces of the Roman settlement of Vindobona in present day Vienna are rare. They are most likely to be found in the historic core of the city, which is today dominated by buildings and architecture of the Habsburg monarchy. The streetplan and building plots still reflect their ancient origin, although most Roman remains have only survived underground at a depth of up to 4 m.

Vindobona was recorded by Jordanes in the 6th century AD as one of the Pannonian cities ceded to the Ostrogoths after Attila's death in 454 (Iord. Get. 264), suggesting the settlement was still known, but probably no longer existed. The burden of taxes, acts of war, captivity and enslavement in the late Roman provinces of Pannonia from the end of the 4th century and later led to various waves of emigration of the inhabitants of the still fortified Vindobona (Bratož 2011, 589–608). The archaeological record from the central area of settlement indicates abandonment around 430 AD.

Preconditions

What marked the beginning of the late antique town? When *legio XIII gemina* arrived in Vindobona around AD 98, after leaving the provincial capital at Poetovio (Ptuj, Slovenia), the *ala I Flavia Augusta Britannica mil. c. R.* had already been in garrison for a couple of years (Kronberger 2005, 28–30; Mosser 2005, 128–134, 143–149). The erection of the legionary fortress effectively upgraded the settlement in conjunction with an extensive building program along the middle Danube *limes*, which was accelerated by the emperor Trajan on the eve of the Dacian wars. This program included building activities inside the existing fortresses of Carnuntum and Aquincum (Budapest), as well as the construction of new bases at Brigetio and Vindobona. Both the new and old garrisons were provided with stone fortifications (Mráv and Harl 2008, 50–54).

The most recent excavations inside the legionary fortress of Vindobona (Vienna, Judenplatz 1995 to 1998; Am Hof 2007 to 2009) brought to light numerous insights into the chronology, social changes, building types, and reconstruction of Roman Vienna (Fig 7.1, nos 1–4; Table 7.1). The results have been especially revealing regarding the barrack blocks, a newly discovered *fabrica* building and the situation along the western *intervallum* (Jandl and Mosser 2008; Mosser 2010; Mosser *et al.* 2010).

Before starting excavations at Judenplatz (1995–1998; Fig. 7.1 no 4) and Am Hof (2007–2009; Fig. 7.1, nos 1–3) the scientific community assumed that stone buildings had

Table 7.1: Construction periods of the legionary fortress in Vindobona. Source: Mosser et al. 2010

Period	Date (AD)
1	98–114
2	114–180/200
3	180/200–280/320
4	280/320–350/360
5	360/375–390/410
6	390/410–420/440

7. The legionary fortress of Vindobona

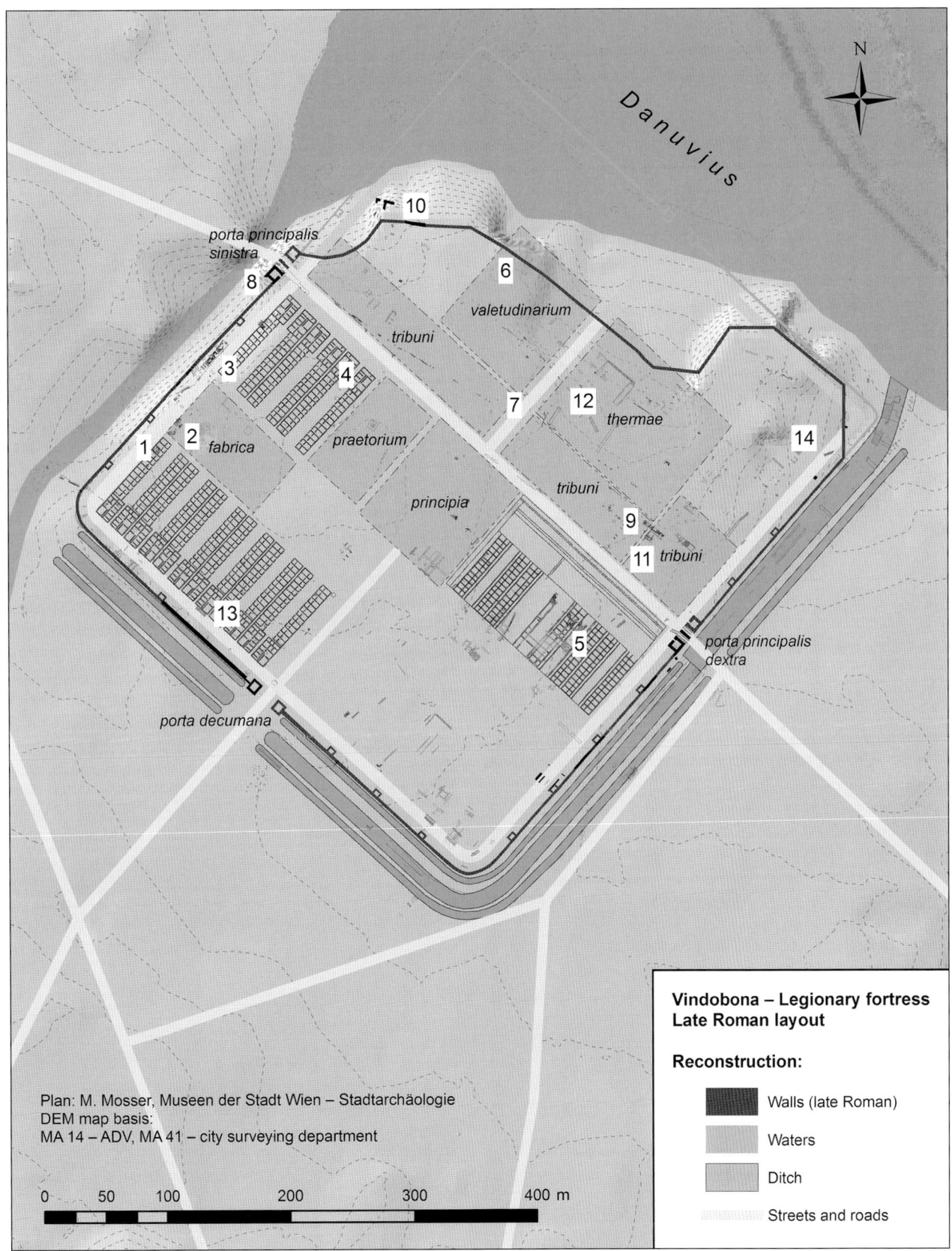

Figure 7.1: Vindobona – the Late Roman legionary fortress with sites numbered. Image credit: M. Mosser, Museen der Stadt Wien – Stadtarchäologie; DEM map basis: MA 14 – ADV, MA 41 – city surveying department

been constructed inside the Vindobona fortress from the beginning, as masonry foundations had been demonstrated for the first cohort barracks in 1982/83 (Fig. 7.1, no 5; Harl 1986; Mosser 2007). Stone was probably also used for important buildings such as the *principia*, the bath, the tribune's houses, and the *fabrica*. But the 1990s excavations proved that timber or adobe barracks provided accommodation for the ordinary legionary soldiers (*cohortes quingenariae*) until the end of the 2nd century AD, when they were replaced by clay brick buildings on stone plinths with a height of 0.8–1 m (Jandl and Mosser 2008, 15–20; Mosser *et al.* 2010, 47–48).

The remnants of these first- and second-period structures do not display the cohesive ground plan typical of legionary barracks. Only more or less disconnected trenches and postholes, marginal remains of stamped clay floors, and a few fireplaces could be assigned to buildings of these periods. Both unit history and some small finds from the first period conditionally relate to *legio XIII gemina* and *legio XIIII gemina Martia victrix* being in residence from AD 98 to 114. The arrival of *legio X gemina* in AD 114 (Mosser 2005, 139–140) triggered the rebuilding of the timber or adobe accommodation. Structures from this second period have a similar appearance to the remains of the first period, although a number of rubbish pits contained considerable quantities of ceramics, bronze and iron objects that are best dated to the end of the 2nd century, after the Marcomannic Wars (Mosser *et al.* 2010a, 95–97). There was no evidence of a destruction horizon attributable to these wars, but a tile bearing the stamp of *legio II Italica* that was located in a layer between the second and third period could indicate the presence of this legion, perhaps while *vexillationes* of *legio X gemina* were absent. The important role of *legio X gemina* in the Marcomannic Wars can be seen in its presence at the headquarters of the Roman army at Burgstall near Mušov in the years between AD 172 and 180, an event well recorded by tile stamps (Komoróczy 2009, 119–125).

The third-period barrack buildings were erected, at the latest, towards the beginning of the Severan era. These structures rested on stone plinths and were comparatively spacious. Each *contubernium* covered about 36 m², an area that is comparable with the very large examples in the Lambaesis fortress (Mackensen 2008, 300–301). Except for some supplemental building and refurbishment, these barracks were very long-lasting and endured for about 200 years, surviving the 3rd-century crisis and also a possible mid-4th-century earthquake (see below). Three of the four gate towers, the *porta principalis dextra* and *sinistra*, and *porta decumana*, also display a similarly robust construction. Their square foundations are aligned on or partly project from the line of the fortress wall (Mosser 2011b, 167–169; 171–172; 176), and might have been constructed during the first period at the end of the 1st century AD (Bechert 1971, 222–234). They survived without any detectable changes, such as a conversion to U-shaped towers common elsewhere, until the late Roman period (Gugl and Kastler 2007, 466–467).

A military settlement (*canabae legionis*) grew up around the rectangular fortress (occupied by 4000–6000 soldiers), which, together with an associated civil town a "leuga"-distance away, a legionary brickyard, an aqueduct, stone quarries and a Danube river port, resulted in a typical 2nd-century legionary base with appropriate infrastructure. Until the mid-3rd century AD, there were no dramatic changes in society, architecture, or infrastructure that could be verified in the archaeological or epigraphic record.

When considering late Roman Vindobona, the serious question of to what extent written sources, documented history, epigraphy, and the archaeological record can be reconciled should be kept in mind (*e.g.* Witschel 2011). Evidence for the late Roman periods is quite poor due to the selective and fragmentary character of the few professionally performed excavations within the fortress. In many cases indirect conclusions are necessary to supply appropriate bases of discussion.

The "Acaunus altar" (Fig. 7. 2)

An altar dedicated to Jupiter, Neptune, Salacaea, the nymphs and the river deity Acaunus (CIL III 14359, 27) was found in 1899 at the confluence of the Wien-river (ancient name "Acaunus"?) and the Danube, on the eastern side of the *canabae legionis*. It was recently republished and newly interpreted by Geza Alföldy (2011). The inscription reads:

[I(ovi)] O(ptimo) M(aximo), Neptuno [Aug(usto)],
[S]alaceâe (!), Nimph[is (!), Flu]-
[v]io Acâuno, diṣ [deab]-
[us]q(ue) omnib(us) v[exill(arii) leg(ionis)]
5 [VI]II Aug(ustae) suḅ c[ura M(arci)?]
A[u]re[l(ii)] Secun[dini (centurionis)]
[p]r(aepositi) traḷati (!) a ḷe[g(ione) X g(emina) VII]
[p(ia)] V[II] f(ideli) in leg(ionem) I[I Italicam]
[[[Gallienam VII p(iam) VII f(idelem)]]]
10 Aurel(io) Monṭa[no]
[v(ices)] a(gente) leg(ati) ḷeg(ionis) s(upra) s(criptae) [et -circ. 3- Sa]-
ṭ[u]rṇ[i]n[o et - - -]
[e]ṭ Aurel(io) [- - - et - - -]
[.]NAVMA(?)[- - - 77 (i. e. centurionibus) et - - - opt(ione)]
15 eq(uitum) f[ec(erunt) Mariniano et]
Paterno co(n)[s(ulibus) - - -]
(vac.) Maias. (vac.)

According to Alföldy the donators were soldiers of a detachment of *legio VIII Augusta*, integrated into the *legio X gemina* of Vindobona. The motive for the erection of the monument was the transfer of this vexillation from Vindobona to Lauriacum, in Noricum, in AD 268. Before

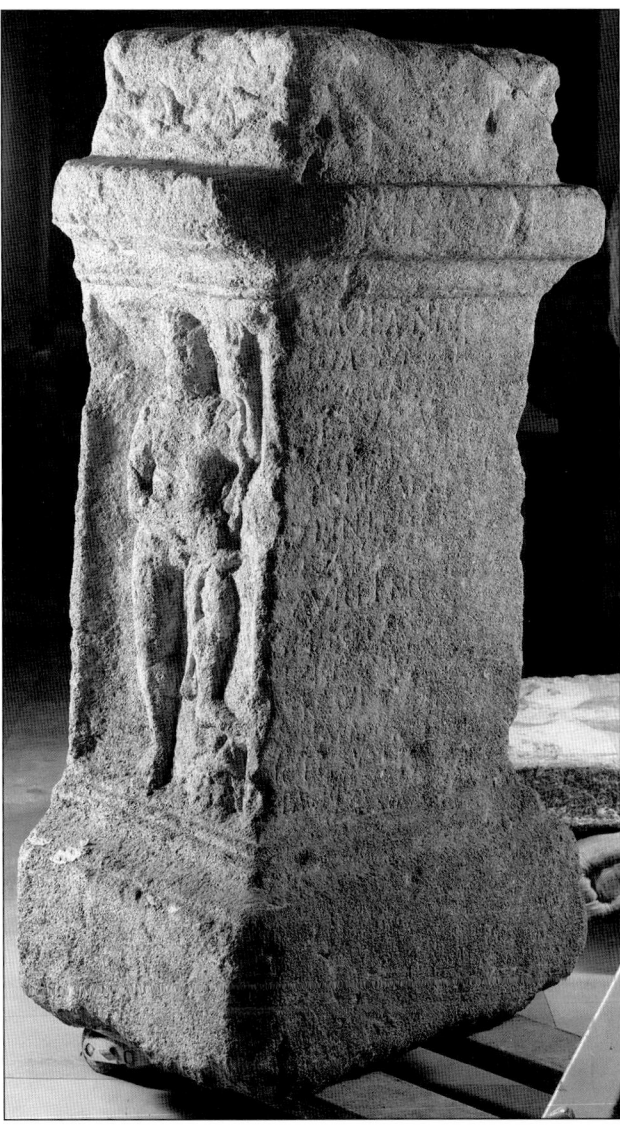

Figure 7.2: The altar from Vindobona dedicated to Jupiter, Neptune, Salacaea, the nymphs and the river deity Acaunus, erected by the vexillatio of legio VIII Augusta. Image credit: Wien Museum, Inv. Nr. MV 631

necessarily lead to a restructuring of the interior space and architecture of the fortresses, as we can see in Vindobona. One typical 3rd-century aspect that is observable in the barracks of Vindobona was the installation of corridors inside the vestibules (*armae*) of the *contubernia* (Kastler 2002; Hodgson 2003, 115–118; Gugl and Kastler 2007, 85–92). Such legionary accommodations can be verified in Vindobona in period 4, that is from the end of the 3rd century AD (Mosser *et al* 2010, 48).

A Danube flood

The so called "Acaunus" altar inscription may contain more information than just the dislocation of legionary vexillations. The dedication to Neptune and other water deities may point to a local incident and subsequent reconstruction activities. In collaboration with geologists, it was possible to prove that the northern part of the original, rectangular fortress was swept away by a Danube flood in the Late Roman period (Grupe and Jawecki 2004, 21–23; Gietl *et al.* 2004, 45–48). A street, perhaps the new course of the *via sagularis*, constructed in the 3rd century over demolished parts of the *valetudinarium* (Fig. 7.1, no 6) could be indirectly associated with the flood (Krenn *et al.* 2006, 74). A recent, quite small investigation revealed the sewer on the western side of *via praetoria* (Fig. 7.1, no 7), which originally ran to the northern edge of the fortress. Its innundation with soil during the second half of the 3rd century could be proved (Mosser *et al.* 2012). Although we cannot be certain, a correlation between the natural disaster and the abandoned sewer can be assumed. The early 20th-century excavation archive relating to the *porta principalis sinistra* may imply further evidence for the flood (Mosser 2011b, 167–168). There were remains of two fortification walls added to the southern foundation of that gate tower (Fig. 7.1, no 8). Both appeared originally to run parallel in a southerly direction along the brook that defined the western limits of the fortress. But having two contemporary and parallel fortification walls does not seem to be plausible. A possible explanation could be that when the brook flooded it destroyed the outer wall, necessitating the erection of a new wall, which was slightly offset from the course of its predecessor. While the exact date of these (one or more) natural disasters is yet to be determined, the shape of the fortress changed fundamentally in their aftermath. The fortified area was reduced from 22.5 ha to about 20 ha, while the northern stretch of defences facing the Danube adopted an irregular course, mirroring the sinuous riverbank of late Roman Vindobona. Evidently the fortifications along the northern edge of the fortress were rebuilt after the flood, enclosing an area appropriate for the diminished strength of the late Roman garrison (Fig. 7.1, no 10; Mosser *et al.* 2010a, 16).

this, the vexillation of *legio VIII Augusta* was sent from Argentorate (Strassbourg) to Illyricum to supress the usurpers Regalianus and Ingenuus in 260, before engaging in the *bellum Serdicense* against Macrianus in 261 in the northern Balkan region. After the cessation of the war, the detachment was transferred from Sirmium to Vindobona (Alföldy 2011, 16–18). This monument therefore highlights the situation in legionary fortresses along the Danube *limes* in the second half of the 3rd century: vexillations of several legions were detached to countless theatres of war and, depending on their location, were temporarily based at different bases, which were not always fully occupied (Witschel 2011, 32–33). This did not, though,

Continuity and change in function and design (period 4 to 5)

During the late Roman period the function of the barrack buildings gradually changed from military accommodation to small workshops (*e.g.* Bidwell 1991, 11), which included facilities for glass production and metal working, as well as a possible bone manufactory, and also a pottery kiln, possibly for producing lamps. The evidence for the insertion of workshops within the former legionary barracks (period 4 to 5) is concurrent with the installation of channelled hypocausts in certain rooms, which seem to be accommodation for (civilian?) craftsmen. Traces of this transformation could be seen in parts of two barracks investigated during the Judenplatz excavations (Mosser *et al.* 2010a, 48–49) .

These developments have to be seen in context with the reduction of the size of the legions during the reign of Diocletian or Constantine (Coello 1996, 14–17). This further eroded the space needed to accommodate the garrison, 5 ha maximum (Tomlin 2000, 169), within a fortresses originally planned to house up to 6000 men. The free space was gradually filled by the civilian population that previously living outside the fortress in the *canabae legionis* (Gugl and Kastler 2007, 470–471). Examining the Late Roman graveyards inside the former *canabae legionis* reveals a similar picture; the cemeteries spread over the site of the former *canabae legionis* in the last decades of the 3rd century, with burials continuing until the second half of the 4th century (Fig. 7.5). During this period both the settlement outside the fortress and the civil town were abandoned (Kronberger 2005, 207; Mosser 2011a, 476).

Some small, scattered rural settlements or *villae rusticae* outside the core zone, which in some cases are only attested by the associated graveyards, might have survived until the late Roman period (Kenner 1897, 145–149; Adler-Wölfl 2003). It may be hypothesized that their residents sheltered from the common crises and external threats of the 4th century inside the fortified *castrum* (Bratož 2011, 594).

Evidence that a civilian population resided inside the Late Roman fortress includes female jewellery, such as bracelets and hairpins, as well as the (displaced) bones of infants (Bidwell 1991, 12–15) within the confines of the barracks and the *fabrica* (Mosser 2011a, 489). Not all parts of the fortress seem to have been affected by these changes. A barrack block *contubernium* discovered in the southwest of the fortress in 2007 (Am Hof, Fig. 7.1, no 1) seems to have been continuously occupied by legionary (?) soldiers until at least the end of the 4th century AD (Jandl and Mosser 2008, 18–19).

Fabrica (Fig. 7.1, no 2)

As well as the *papilio* of a *contubernium*, the 2007 excavations (Am Hof) brought to light the south-western corner of a stone building lying north of the barrack. The masonry walls enclosed four rooms, which were identified as the western part of a previously unknown *fabrica* of the legionary fortress (Jandl and Mosser 2008, 23–28). This interpretation relies on a sequence of numerous furnaces dating from the 1st century until the 4th century. Mostly levelled, some still survived in a good state of preservation. The first period furnaces appeared as carved double-pits. Above the hotplates lay a fill containing slag and cinder, which lead to the conclusion that these furnaces were designed for metal working. Material discovered within the lowest levels of the furnace-pits can be dated to the Flavian or Trajanic period, associating them with the period when the legionary fortress was erected (Jandl and Mosser 2008, 25). In the northern portion of the excavated *fabrica* area there was a levelled feature containing raw material for producing blue paint ("Egypt blue"), pottery with a surface that displayed traces of paint production, and an accumulation of coins from the end of the 3rd century AD. These were taken as indications that a Late Roman painter's workshop was established inside the *fabrica* building. Together with the metal working, it shows the multifunctional character of the *fabrica*. Despite the transformation from a metalworker's to a painter's workshop within a small area of the *fabrica*, it seems that the building as a whole retained its function until the end of the Roman settlement.

Intervallum (Fig. 7.1, no 3, Fig. 7.3)

Until recently knowledge of the *intervallum* between the *via sagularis* and the fortress rampart was based on very sparse evidence. The width of the fortress wall was seen in 1902 (Kenner 1904, 117–124, Mosser 2011b) while a fallen portion was found in 1953 (Neumann 1967, 12–15, 21–23), and again in the vicinity of the excavations of 2008/09. These excavations, undertaken in Vienna's fire brigade station, covered an area of 180 m² along the western fortification wall, but did not provide an opportunity to uncover the wall itself. The campaign identified a clear sequence of four phases of construction in the area of the rampart.

The first phase included the installation of a sewer along the *via sagularis*. This feature was also seen in 1953, to the south of the recently discovered channel, which makes the total known length of the sewer 60 m. For the first time, the remains of the rampart were encountered, consisting of ochre- and brown-coloured irregular-sized clay bricks, which alternated with thin timber and stone layers (see also Crummy 1988, 29–31). The rampart was approximately 5 m wide. A sequence of four round baking ovens was found in front of the rampart along the *via sagularis* (Hoffmann 2002, 895–896). In the following phase (during the 2nd or at the latest the 3rd century AD) these ovens were cut by the insertion of big (more than 1.00 m deep) post-pits, which can be interpreted as a wooden structure instead of the wall-walk along the fortification wall.

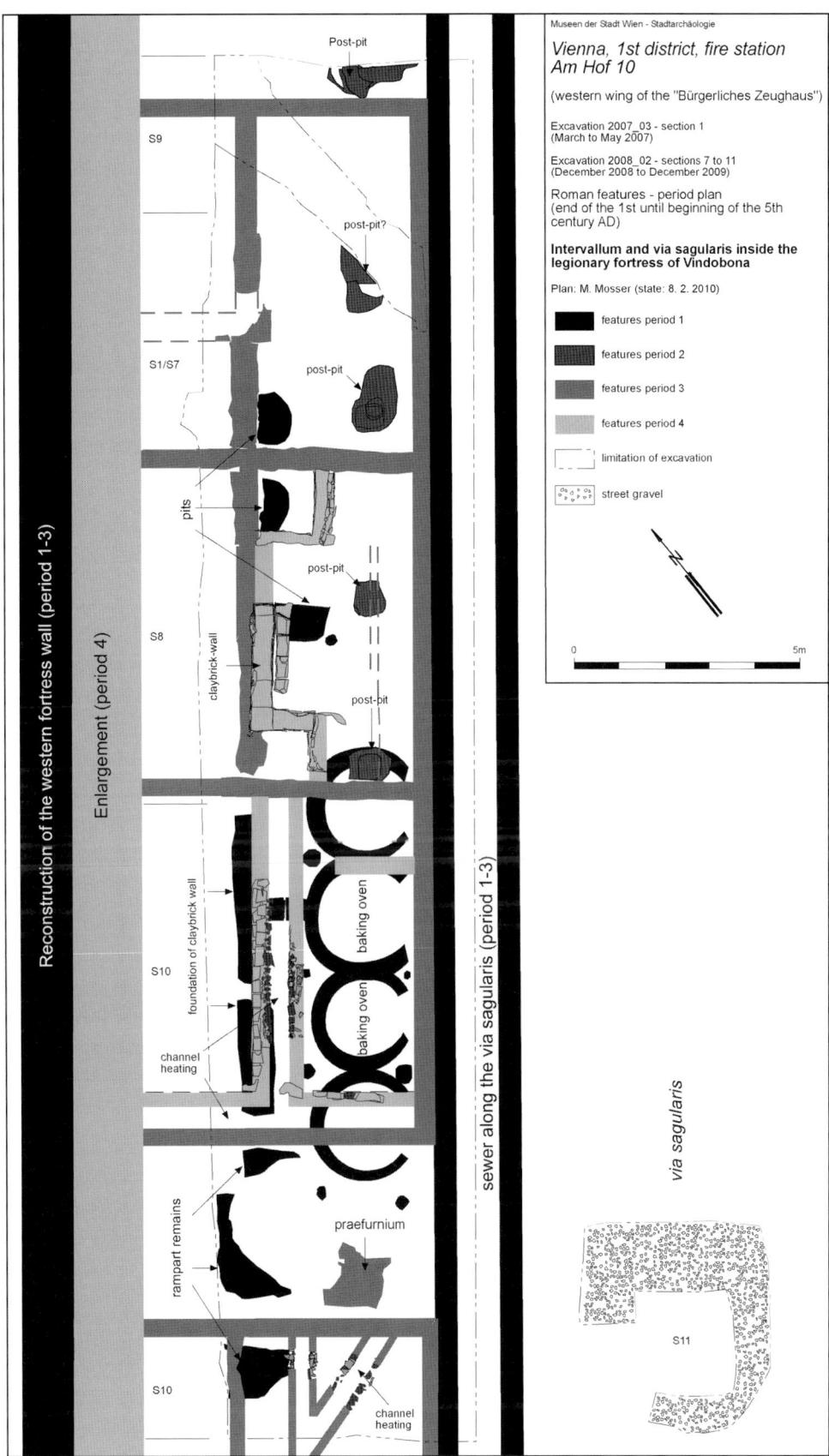

Figure 7.3: A period plan of the western intervallum and via sagularis of the Vindobona legionary fortress. Image credit: M. Mosser

In the Late Roman period two phases of elongated buildings, partly furnished with channel hypocausts, were constructed directly against the fortress wall (Hoffmann 2002, 896–898). But there is a substantial break between those late Roman phases equivalent (?) to period 4 and 5 (see above). The central axis of the building had moved eastwards, while the northern part of the elongated building appears to have been demolished, while the side walls of the sewer were pulled out and backfilled. These measures may have been in connection with an enlargement of the fortress wall, with its width being increased by up to 3 m, possibly under Valentinian I (Mosser 2010; 2011a, 484).

Seismic event?

The evidence for an earthquake occurring in the mid-4th century in Carnuntum has been extensively discussed by scholars (Kandler 1989; Decker *et al.* 2006; Gugl and Kastler 2007, 457–461; Gugl 2011, 512–513). Characteristic destruction layers comprising collapsed walls and roof tiles in conjunction with seismological data are the arguments in favour of this natural disaster. Although the destruction horizon inside the Vindobona barracks cannot be definitively assigned to the same period, in the following period 5 the barrack blocks display partially renovated stone plinths with added broken tiles and repairs using clay bricks set in mortar. This means that parts of the Vindobona barracks were destroyed before period 5, that is in the mid-4th century AD, with sufficient force to damage their foundations. In contrast to Carnuntum, the destruction material was cleaned up and the barracks were reinstated upon the same foundations (Mosser *et al.* 2010a, 212).

Tile production

The wide distribution of late Roman tiles in the Pannonian provinces (Pannonia I, Valeria) produced by the *legio X gemina* reflects the economic significance of the legionary brickyard in Vindobona. Evidently those bricks and tiles were utilized for Valentinian's fortification construction program along the middle Danube *limes* during the AD 370s (Mráv 2005; Mosser 2011a, 491–493). The same type of brick stamps have also been found spread throughout the Vindobona settlement area (about 80 late Roman stamps out of more than 3000 total from Vindobona, Fig. 7.5), although most of the newly erected walls added to existing structures within the fortress and dating to period 4 and 5 consist of reused stone and brick rubble. Unbroken *tegulae* were often placed on stone foundations, prior to clay brick walls being laid on top of them (period 5). So we can observe a dense agglomeration of buildings inside the thickened fortification wall over the course of the 4th century, but tile production was obviously not increasing to cater for these construction projects.

Tribune's houses and thermae

Excavations from 1948–1949 and 1959–1961 at Hoher Markt brought to light several well-preserved Roman building walls, which could be identified – on the basis of their position within the fortress – as the remains of two of the six tribune's houses (Fig. 7.1, no 9) north of *via principalis* (Neumann 1967, 27–46). Initially interpreted as 2nd and 3rd century structures, the remains are still visible in the Roman Museum of Vienna (Kronberger 2013), and will be digitally recorded as part of an ongoing project (Mosser *et al.* 2010b, 57–59). Preliminary results lead to the conclusion that the rooms with pillar hypocausts and very thick mortar floors enclosed by mixed masonry walls, which dominate the exhibition room in the basement floor of the Roman Museum, are Valentinianic in origin (period 5). These structures, from which the main components could be viewed as a private bathroom within a high-ranking officer's house, were built upon the Trajanic foundations, as well as collapsed rubble from older walls. The fabric of the masonry, incorporating reused bricks, tiles, and various types of stone material, coupled with the possibility that the underlying rubble was a product of the supposed earthquake, could suggest that dating.

Because of the changes to military organisation from the end of the 3rd century onwards it is impossible to determine who lived in the houses that were originally occupied by the legionary tribunes (*e.g.* Zienkiewicz 1993). As mentioned above, a high-ranking military or civil officer is to be expected, though. A similar situation has to be assumed for the legionary *thermae* of the 2nd and 3rd centuries, which was connected to the tribune's houses in the north. There is very little archaeological evidence from the *thermae* (Neumann 1967, 58–64), but its footprint is more-or-less known. A modification of the legionary bath building, which was a common occurance in late Roman fortresses (Witschel 2011, 32–33) – as we know it explicitly from Aquincum (Budapest), where the complex was transformed as the headquarters for the dux of Valeria (Zsidi 2011, 555) – could be expected in some way for Vindobona too.

Notitia Dignitatum *and* classis Histrica

The *Notitia Dignitatum* mentions a new force alongside the well-known *legio X gemina*, the *classis Histrica*, which had been transferred from neighbouring Carnuntum, to the new naval base at Vindobona (*ND occ.* 34, 28). Further parts of *legio X gemina*, together with sections of the 14th legion, originally stationed in Carnuntum, were listed as *liburnarii* in Arrabona (Fig. 7.4). Even without any additional written, epigraphic, or archaeological evidences for the *classis Histrica*, and despite the problems associated with dating the *Notitia* (Dietz 2011, 64–65), this reference could indicate Vindobona's continuing importance in the second half of

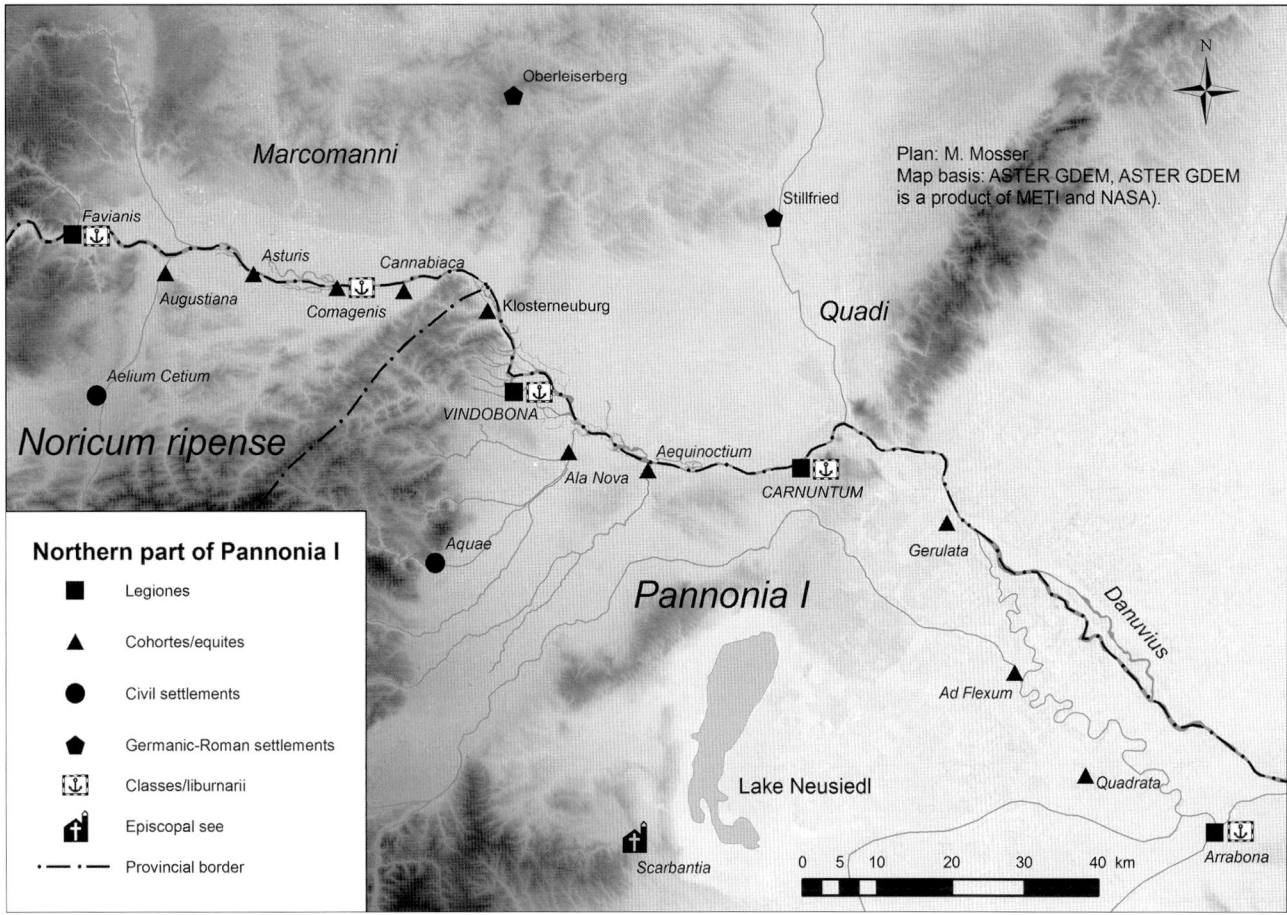

Figure 7.4: A map showing the northern portion of Pannonia I and the eastern part of Noricum ripense, with the most important settlements marked. Image credit: M. Mosser; map basis: ASTER GDEM, ASTER GDEM is a product of METI and NASA

the 4th century. There is evidence for military structures in Carnuntum decaying during the last third of the 4th century (Gugl and Kastler 2007, 482–490; Gugl 2011, 511), a development that is not mirrored in Vindobona, as we have seen. Tower-like structures erected quickly after the flood destruction discussed above, were found at the beginning of the 20th century at the foot of the late Roman fortress plateau (Fig. 7.1, no 10). Perhaps these could be connected with the *classis Histrica* naval base (Mosser *et al.* 2010a, 16; Mosser 2011b, 177–178).

When summing up the developments from the end of the 3rd century onwards we can focus on the following phenomena: the results of the excavations described above confirm that during the 4th century AD the military fortress was transformed into a strongly fortified town with a civil population and military troops (Dietz and Fischer 1996, 199–200). The main reason for this transformation process lies in the constant assaults, in particular by German tribes, which started in the mid-4th century (Amm. Marc. 17, 12). During this period Vindobona represented a very strong fortified town, and although only the area of the former legionary fortress was populated, the result was a very dense settlement surrounded by a 3 m-wide fortification wall. At present, we cannot separate civil areas within this Late Roman town from those occupied by the military. A further, occasional phenomenon of late Roman architecture in Noricum and Pannonia is the construction of large fortified annexes and enclosures connected to the original fortress, but which contain few or no internal buildings. This development has been identified at Favianis (Mautern) and Aquincum (Groh and Sedlmayer 2002, 561; Zsidi 2011, 552–554). These are interpreted as shelters for refugees, grazing areas for cattle, or military camps, but it should be kept in mind that the late Roman crises would have created massive quantities of prisoners of war and slaves, which could have been quartered in these areas. Such annex-fortifications are also comparable with the late Roman inland forts of Pannonia (Heinrich-Tamáska 2011), but such a feature is not currently known at Vindobona.

Large cemetery areas lay outside the walls of late Roman Vindobona (Fig. 7.5), containing tile graves, stone-slab coffins, and simple earth graves (Kronberger 2005).

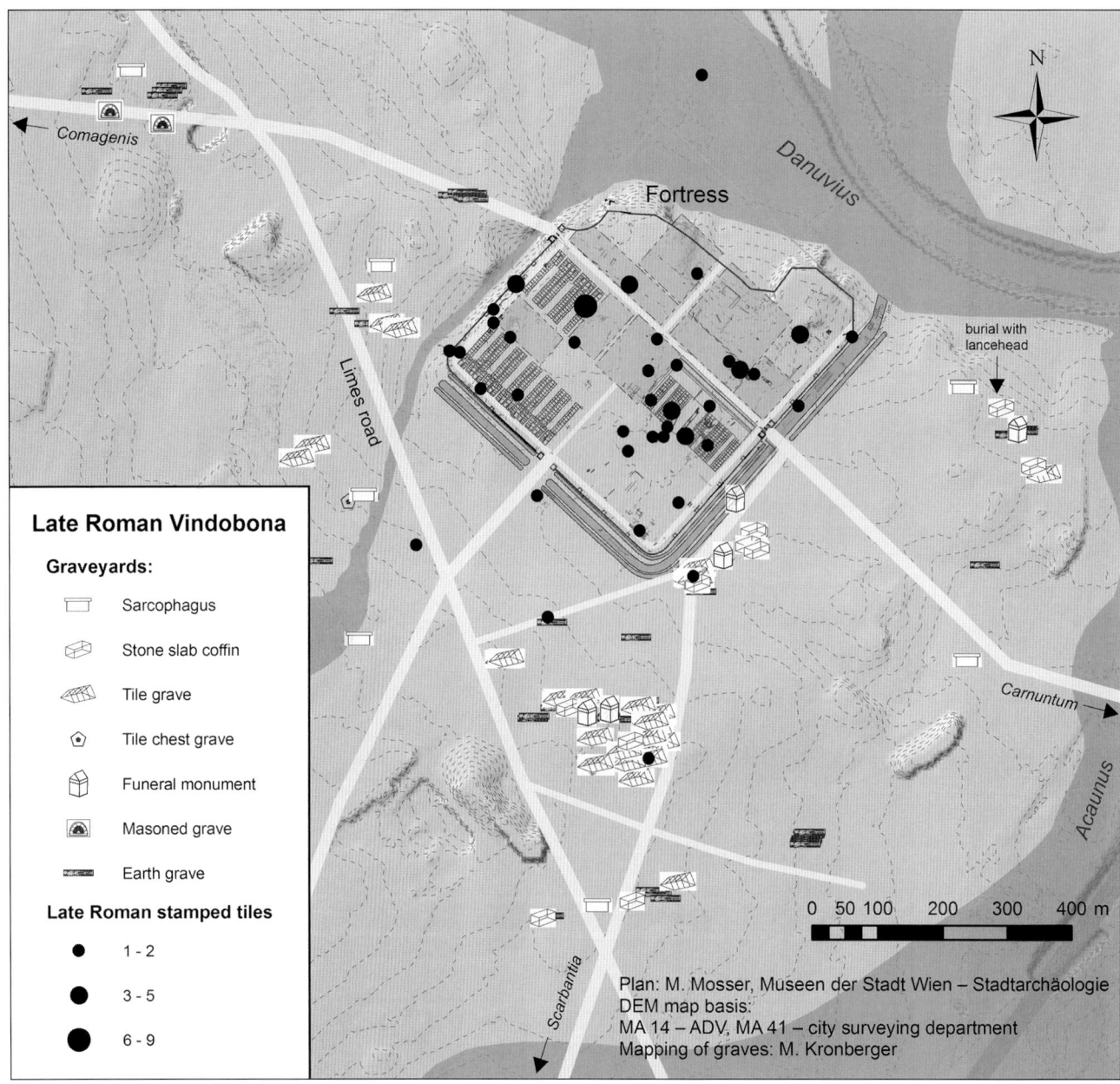

Figure 7.5: Late Roman Vindobona. A plan showing the late Roman graves and stamped tiles sites. Image credit: M. Mosser, Museen der Stadt Wien – Stadtarchäologie; DEM map basis: MA 14 – ADV, MA 41 – city surveying department, mapping of graves: M. Kronberger

Extramural infrastructure remained intact, confirmed by the continued existance of the legionary brickyard and presumably also the stone quarries to the west of the settlement (Neumann 1968, 78–83).

In this new urban environment a portion of the inhabitants were of Germanic origin, and a gradual acculturation of Roman and Germanic culture is apparent in the pottery and small finds (Kronberger 2005, 162–164; Pollak 1992, 125–126; 156 Tab. 13; Jandl and Mosser 2008, 18–19, 21, figs 18, 29). To take one example of the culture of 4th-century Vindobona, a stone-slab coffin in a cemetery to the east of the legionary fortress (Fig. 7.5, today's Fleischmarkt) contained the two skeletons of a 50- to 60-year-old man and woman. The burial was furnished with typical late Roman pottery and a lancehead (Kronberger 2005, 259–261). A grave furnished with weapons was not conceivable for contemporary Roman culture, so the presence of a lance within the coffin should point to a Germanic origin for the deceased or a highly competitive local society (Kronberger 2005, 184–185).

Final settlements (period 6)

The end of the prosperous, diverse Late Roman society is visible in the archaeological record as decay and debris levels after period 5. Collapsed mud-brick walls and layers of broken roof tiles can be dated, at the earliest, to the end of the 4th century AD. Following that Vindobona was temporarily abandoned before being repopulated. The intervening settlements (period 6A–C) were limited in extent and are only found in certain repaired areas of the former barracks. These reduced residential areas, sometimes encroaching on the former fortress streets, can feature partial adobe walls resting upon drystone foundations, mortar floors, and channel hypocausts. Craft areas and ovens have been found inside the rooms (Mosser *et al.* 2010a, 238–240). The situation inside the main fortress buildings (*principia, praetorium, thermae, valetudinarium,* etc.) is uncertain during period 6, so we cannot prove the existence of any ongoing administration, supply, markets, or other commercial or military activities.

The phenomenon of the reduced settlements ignoring the original layout and architecture of the fortification area is repeated along the whole Danube *limes* (*e.g.* Gomolka-Fuchs 2007, 212; Gugl 2011, 520–524; Konrad 2011, 383–385). It seems plausible to associate the origin of these obviously non-military structured settlements with the migrations of the Huns to the west from 375/376 onwards, and the ensuing migration of east-Germanic groups, who became *foederati* in the Danube provinces of the Roman Empire (Bierbrauer 2007). High taxes, civil wars, raids, and plundering, especially around AD 400 may have led to the downfall of Roman military organisation in at least certain bases in northern Pannonia (Bratož 2011, 590–604). The date at which Vindobona lost its military role cannot be proved, but the discovery of a hoard or a place to melt down scrap metal in the north-eastern part of the fortress yielded more than 500 coins terminating with issues dating to 408 (Fig. 7.1, no 14; Mosser 2011a, 496–497); this hoard may relate to the problems of the early 5th century.

Tombstones as reused material in the late Roman fortress wall?

St. Stephen's cathedral in central Vienna is situated close to the south-eastern ditch of the former Roman fortress. The find spots of six funeral *steles* that were used in the church and subsequently incorporated into demolished buildings around the cathedral (Fig. 7.6) remain a bit of mystery. Their inscriptions date from the 1st to the early 3rd century (Kronberger 2005, 275–277), a period when we should expect an intact urban settlement (*canabae legionis*) around the fortress, rather than a cemetery. This suggests that the stones were imported from a cemetery outside the settlement (Kronberger 2005, 198–201). One obvious reason for transporting tombstones from the graveyards to the centre would be the desire to reuse them as building material after they lost their memorial value at the end of the 3rd century, at the earliest.

The findspots suggest that the fortress wall was the first destination of the stones, and we know that similar material was used in the town wall of Gorsium-Herculia in Valeria in the 4th century (Hajnóczy and Mezós 1999, 87). The precise dating of this activity at Vindobona is unclear, but either the aftermath of the assumed mid-4th-century earthquake or the thickening of the rampart during the reign of Valentinian I in the AD 370s, offer two plausible possibilities. We cannot, though, exclude short-term renovation measures during the final decades of Roman Vindobona. The reorganisation of the Pannonian *limes* by the *magister militum* Generidus in 409 (Zos. 5, 46, 2; Soproni 1985, 103–105), when the town would have been provisionally restored, offers another possible context for the reuse of the gravestones. After the fortress area was resettled in the high medieval period, the rampart was used anew and demolished around 1200 AD. Afterwards its broken-up fabric was employed to build the cathedral and surrounding precincts (Mosser 2002, 102–105).

Written sources on the emigration from northern Pannonia

For a better understanding of the admittedly limited archaeological evidence for the last Roman period in Vienna, it might be helpful to summarize the written sources concerning the decades from the end of the 4th century to the beginning of the 5th in Pannonia. The compilation made by Rajko Bratož (2011), mainly drawing on the ancient authors Hieronymus, Claudianus, Zosimus, and Ambrosius as well as the Codex Theodosianus and Constitutio Sirmondiana, may serve as a starting point to assess the situation in northern Pannonia.

Following the battle of Adrianople in 378 the Goths, other east-Germanic groups, and Huns expropriated and exploited as *foederati* large sections of the Pannonian population. Meanwhile Probus, the *praefectus Illirici* (AD 368–375, 383–387), was responsible for a merciless fiscal policy. This ongoing threat, which served as a stimulus for a first depopulation of Pannonia, had lasted for 20 years before Stilicho defeated the insurgent *foederati* in 399 (Bratož 2011, 590–594). In contrast to Carnuntum (see also Amm. 30, 5, 2), these difficult conditions are not reflected in the archaeological record at Vindobona (period 5). A polyethnic group that invaded Pannonia and northern Italy under the leadership of Radagaisus in AD 405 / 406 was soon repulsed, but brought further danger for the provincials. When Alaric, king of the Visigoths, moved to Italy in 408, Athaulf followed him one year later to assist his brother-in-law at the head of the federate Goths and Huns (Zos. 5, 37, 1–2 and 5, 45, 5–6). Until

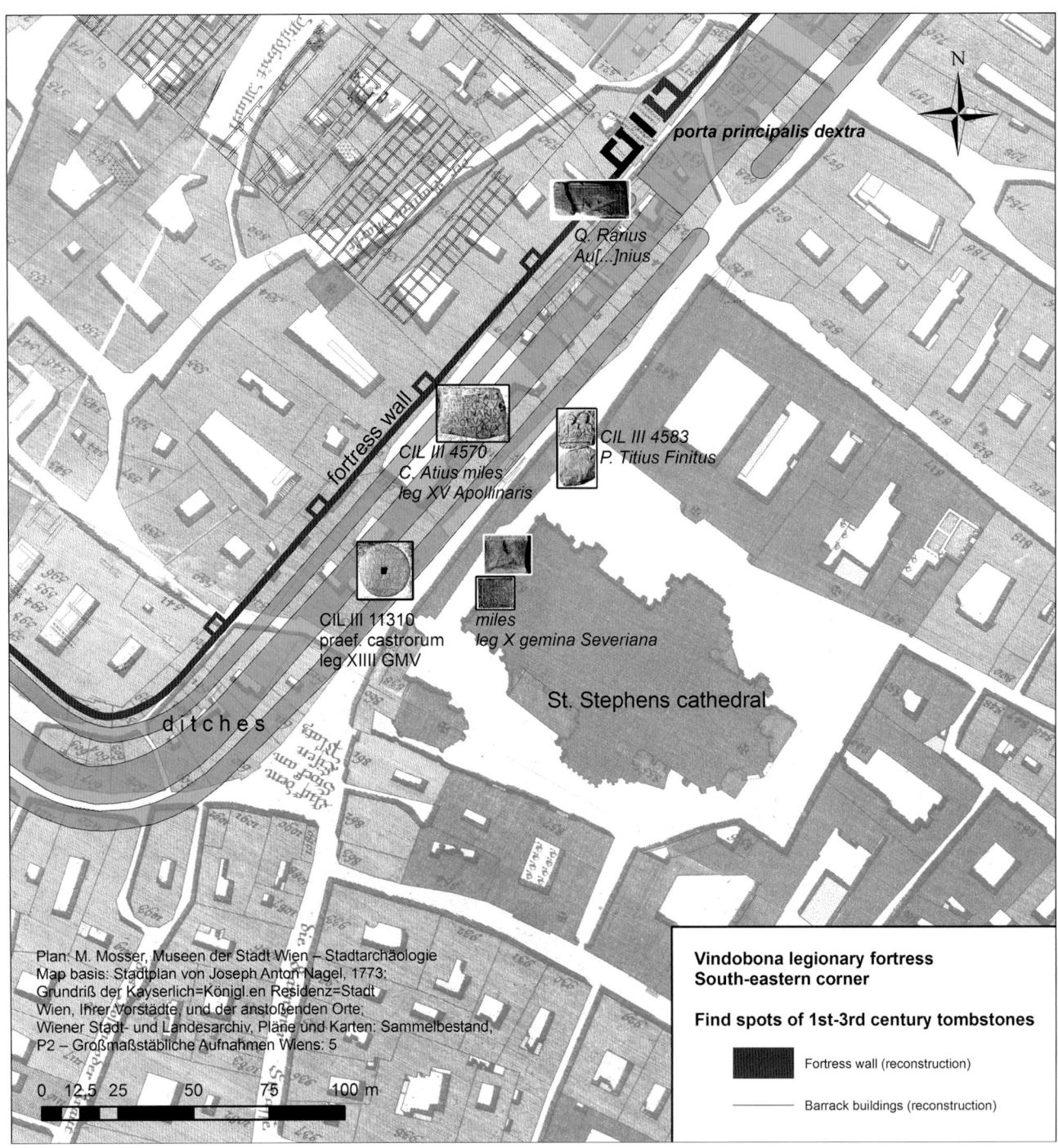

Figure 7.6: Vindobona. The south-eastern stretch of the fortress wall showing the find spots of 1st- to 3rd-century tombstones. Image credit: M. Mosser; map basis: Stadtplan von Joseph Anton Nagel, 1773: Grundriß der Kayserlich=Königl.en Residenz=Stadt Wien, Ihrer Vorstädte, und der anstoßenden Orte; Wiener Stadt- und Landesarchiv, Pläne und Karten: Sammelbestand, P2 – Großmaßstäbliche Aufnahmen Wiens: 5

then we could presume that group resided alongside the local Roman population within Vindobona's fortifications. The acculturated inhabitants would have ensured the maintenance of military administration and public order with the still existing *legio X gemina* and *classis Histrica*. As such, it is not unlikely that the documented emigration of Goths and Huns in 409 may have included some of the Roman population from Vindobona as well.

Captivity and enslavement was widespread at the beginning of the 5th century. The church organization in southern Pannonia and northern Italy was highly developed, and Bishops attempted to curtail the enslavement of thousands of prisoners of war and to organize the return of refugees to their regions of residence (Bratož 2011, 599). The slave trade may have been a profitable commercial sector, especially along the Pannonian Danube (Drexhage 1982, 343–344) and possibly also in Vindobona. Furthermore, the church did not acquire much influence in northern parts of Pannonia (Fig. 7.4), where the only known episcopal see was in Scarbantia (Bratož 2011, 600). Archaeology has not provided any evidence for either an early Christian church or any Christian artefacts in Vindobona, although early Christianity should be anticipated to some extent (Mosser 2011a, 490). One exception is a gravestone that was obviously erected for a Christian woman in a graveyard inside the fortress. The gravestone was found in the area of the former tribune's houses and its inscription reads (Fig. 7.1, no 11, Hoher Markt) (Année Épigr. 1956, 9): *[S?]abini(a)e [---] / Marcio con(iugi) san(c)/t(a)e o(biit) or(a) V n[o]n dig/na mori s[i p]ossu/nt fata mov[e]ri.* The burial of a Roman woman in a populated area is only conceivable in period 6 at the beginning of the 5th century, when the fortified settlement was sparsely occupied.

One well-attested group of northern Pannonian people that became quite significant and famous during the 5th and 6th centuries were the predatory collectives consisting of deserted Roman soldiers and members of various social and ethnic groups (Alans, Vandals, Quads, and Suebi). The ancient sources called them *hostes Pannonii* (Hier. *Epist.* 123, 16) or *Scamarae* who destabilized the Danube region and the western provinces of Gallia and Spain (Bratož 2011, 602–603). It can be reasonably assumed that parts of the community in Vindobona joined these groups. Consequently, Vindobona became increasingly depopulated over the course of the first half of the 5th century. The present state of research indicates that the definite end of the settlement within the old fortress occurred during the 430s AD, when the Huns finally seized control of the province of Pannonia. This was determined on the basis of ceramic evidence from 5th-century deposits, which is analogous to that from the 5th-century graveyards in nearby Mautem (Soproni 1985, 80–81; 105–106; Pollak 1992, 126).

The fortress during the dark ages

The intramural area of Vindobona has provided no evidence of settlement activity from the mid-5th century through until at least the 9th century (Hofer 2013, 324–325). During the Migration period and the Dark Ages this was a landscape of ruins. But the site did not fall into oblivion and certain semi-nomadic groups have left their mark (Mosser 2011a, 498–499). Four earth graves inserted into the former legionary bath (Fig. 7.1, no 12) date to the end of the 5th century and can be seen in the context of the Heruls and Lombards whose territory extended to the Vienna Basin until the middle of the 6th century (Neumann 1967, 57–58). Those Lombards might have lived 2 km west of the former legionary settlement in the 6th century, where a further cemetery was unearthed in 1897 / 1898 (Tobias *et al.* 2010). A glass bead pendant of Merovingian origin provides an isolated find from the area of the former barracks that can also be dated to the 6th century (Tarcsay 2006).

Recent discoveries associated with the Avars' culture are very well documented by large graveyards in the outskirts of Vienna (Daim 1981, 188–196; Tobias *et al.* 2010, 301–303). An Avar harness fitting dating to the 8th century was found in the so-called "dark earth" between the Roman and medieval layers in the southern part of the fortress (Fig. 7.1, no 13; Mosser 2013a). Finally, a skeleton of a woman interred without burial gifts in the area of the former tribune's houses (Fig. 7.1, no 9) was radiocarbon dated to AD 770–1000 (Mosser 2013b), the period between the Avar occupation and the earliest traces of high medieval settlement in Vienna. It was only in the 12th century that the old fortress wall briefly regained its fortifying function.

Bibliography

Adler-Wölfl, K. (2003) *Die römische Siedlung von Wien - Unterlaa (Grabungen 1974 – 1999).* Unpublished thesis. University of Vienna

Alföldy, G. (2011) Eine umstrittene Altarinschrift aus Vindobona. *Tyche* 26, 1–22.

Bechert, T. (1971) Römische Lagertore und ihre Bauinschriften. *Bonner Jahrbücher* 171, 201–287.

Bidwell, P. T. (1991) Later Roman barracks in Britain. In V. A. Maxfield and M. J. Dobson (eds) *Roman Frontier Studies 1989. Proceedings of the XVth International Congress of Roman Frontier Studies,* 9–15. Canterbury, University of Exeter Press.

Bierbrauer, V. (2007) Ostgermanen im mittleren und unteren Donauraum. Die hunnische Herrschaft. *Attila und die Hunnen,* 97–103. Ausstellungskatalog Speyer, Stuttgart, Theiss.

Bratož, R. (2011) Die Auswanderung der Bevölkerung aus den pannonischen Provinzen während des 5. und 6. Jahrhunderts. In M. Konrad and Ch. Witschel (ed.) *Römische Legionslager in den Rhein- und Donauprovinzen – Nuclei spätantik-frühmittelalterlichen Lebens?* 589–614. München, Bayerische Akademie der Wissenschaften.

Coello, T. (1996) *Unit Sizes in the Late Roman Army.* Oxford, Oxbow.

Crummy, P. (1988) Colchester (Camulodunum / Colonia Victriciensis). In G. Webster (ed.) *Fortress into City. The Consolidation of Roman Britain First Century AD,* 24–47. London, Batsford.

Daim, F. (1981) Archäologische Zeugnisse zur Geschichte des Wiener Raums im Frühmittelalter. *Wiener Geschichtsblätter* 36, 175–197.

Decker, K. and Gangl, G. and Kandler, M. (2006) The earthquake of Carnuntum in the fourth century A.D. – archeological results, seismologic scenario and seismotectonic implications for the Vienna Basin fault, Austria. *Journal of Seismology* 10, 479–495.

Dietz, K. (2011) Zur Verteidigung der Nordgrenze des römischen Reiches in der Spätantike aus althistorischer Sicht. In M. Konrad and Ch. Witschel (eds) *Römische Legionslager in den Rhein- und Donauprovinzen – Nuclei spätantik-frühmittelalterlichen Lebens?* 63–77. München, Bayerische Akademie der Wissenschaften.

Dietz, K. and Fischer, T. (1996) *Die Römer in Regensburg*. Regensburg, Pustet.

Drexhage, H.-J. (1982) Die "Expositio totius mundi et gentium". Eine Handelsgeographie aus dem 4. Jh. n. Chr. *Savaria* 16, 341–346.

Gietl, R., Kronberger, M. and Mosser, M. (2004) Rekonstruktion des antiken Geländes in der Wiener Innenstadt. *Fundort Wien* 7, 32–53.

Gomolka-Fuchs, G. (2007) Spätrömische Limeskastelle an der mittleren und unteren Donau im Licht des ostgermanischen und reiternomadischen Fundstoffs. *Attila und die Hunnen*, 209–218. Ausstellungskatalog Speyer, Stuttgart, Theiss.

Groh, St. and Sedlmayer, H. (2002) *Forschungen im Kastell Mautern-Favianis. Die Grabungen der Jahre 1996 und 1997*. Wien, Verlag der Österreichischen Akademie der Wissenschaften.

Grupe, S. and Jawecki, Ch. (2004) Geomorphodynamik der Wiener Innenstadt. *Fundort Wien* 7, 14–30.

Gugl, Ch. (2011) Carnuntum und sein Legionslager in Spätantike und Frühmittelalter. Von der Carnutensis scutaria zur frühmittelalterlichen Siedlung des 9./10. Jahrhunderts. In M. Konrad and Ch. Witschel (eds) *Römische Legionslager in den Rhein- und Donauprovinzen – Nuclei spätantik-frühmittelalterlichen Lebens?* 505–532. München, Bayerische Akademie der Wissenschaften.

Gugl, Ch. and Kastler, R. (2007) *Legionslager Carnuntum. Ausgrabungen 1968–1977*. Wien, Verlag der Österreichische Akademie der Wissenschaften.

Hajnóczy, G. and Mezós, T. (1999) *Pannonia Hungarica Antiqua*. Budapest, Archaeolingua.

Harl, O. (1986) Kasernen und Sonderbauten der 1. Kohorte im Legionslager Vindobona. In *Studien zu den Militärgrenzen Roms III. 13. Internationaler Limeskongress, Aalen 1983*, 322–327. Forschungen und Berichte zur Vor- und Frühgeschichte in Baden-Württemberg 20, Stuttgart, Theiss.

Heinrich-Tamáska, O. (2011) Pannonische Innenbefestigungen und die Kontinuitätsfrage: Forschungsstand und –perspektiven. In M. Konrad and Ch. Witschel (eds) *Römische Legionslager in den Rhein- und Donauprovinzen – Nuclei spätantik-frühmittelalterlichen Lebens?* 571–588. München, Bayerische Akademie der Wissenschaften.

Hodgson, N. (2003) *The Roman Fort at Wallsend (Segedunum). Excavations in 1997–8*. Newcastle, Tyne and Wear Museums.

Hofer, N. (ed.) (2013) *Archäologie und Bauforschung im Wiener Stephansdom. Quellen zur Baugeschichte des Doms bis zum Ende des 13. Jahrhunderts*. Wien, Wiener Dom-Verlag.

Hoffmann, B. (2002) The rampart buildings of Roman legionary fortresses. In P. Freeman *et al.* (eds) *Limes XVIII. Proceedings of the XVIIIth International Congress of Roman Frontier Studies, Amman, Jordan 2000*, 895–899. Oxford, Oxbow.

Jandl, M. and Mosser, M. (2008) Befunde im Legionslager Vindobona. Teil IV: Vallum, fabrica und Kasernen in der westlichen retentura – Vorbericht zu den Grabungen Am Hof im Jahr 2007. *Fundort Wien* 11, 4–34.

Kandler, M. (1989) Eine Erdbebenkatastrophe in Carnuntum? *Acta archaeologica Academiae Scientiarum Hungaricae* 41, 313–336.

Kastler, R. (2002) Legionslager an der Wende zur Spätantike – Ein Überblick zu Carnuntum und vergleichbaren kaiserzeitlichen Standlagern des Rhein-Donau-Raumes in einer Periode des Umbruchs. In P. Freeman *et al.* (eds) *Limes XVIII. Proceedings of the XVIIIth International Congress of Roman Frontier Studies, Amman, Jordan 2000*, 605–624. Oxford, Oxbow.

Kenner, F. (1897) Die archäologischen Funde aus römischer Zeit. *Geschichte der Stadt Wien* 1, 42–159. Wien, Holzhausen.

Kenner, F. (1904) Römische Funde in Wien aus den Jahren 1901 bis 1903. *Jahrbuch der k. k. Zentralkommission* Neue Folge 2, 1. Teil, 103–170.

Komoróczy, B. (2009) Marcomannia. Der Militärschlag gegen die Markomannen und Quaden – ein archäologischer Survey. *2000 Jahre Varusschlacht. Konflikt*. Ausstellungskatalog Kalkriese, 114–125. Stuttgart, Theiss.

Konrad, M. (2011) Castra Regina – Das Lager der Legio III Italica in Regensburg. Kontinuitätsformen im Legionslager, in den canabae legionis und im Umland. In M. Konrad and Ch. Witschel (eds) *Römische Legionslager in den Rhein- und Donauprovinzen – Nuclei spätantik-frühmittelalterlichen Lebens?* 371–407. München, Bayerische Akademie der Wissenschaften.

Krenn, M. and Mitchell, P. and Wagner, J. (2006) 1. Bezirk, Salvatorgasse 12. *Fundberichte aus Österreich* 45, 74.

Kronberger, M. (2005) *Siedlungschronologische Forschungen zu den canabae legionis von Vindobona. Die Gräberfelder*. Wien, Phoibos.

Kronberger, M. (2013) A Roman Museum for Vienna. In N. Mills (ed.) *Presenting the Romans. Interpreting the Frontiers of the Roman Empire World Heritage Site*, 85–91. Woodbridge, The Boydel Press.

Mackensen, M. (2008) Mannschaftsunterkünfte und Organisation einer severischen Legionsvexillation im tripolitanischen Kastell Gholaia/Bu Njem (Libyen). *Germania* 86/1, 271–306.

Mosser, M. (2002) C. Atius und die legio XV Apollinaris in Vindobona. *Fundort Wien* 5, 102–126.

Mosser, M. (2005) Die römischen Truppen in Vindobona. *Fundort Wien* 8, 126–153.

Mosser, M. (2007) *Die Kasernen der ersten Kohorte im Legionslager Vindobona*. Unpublished PhD thesis, University of Vienna.

Mosser, M. (2010) Befunde im Legionslager Vindobona. Teil V: Das Intervallum an der westlichen Lagermauer – Vorbericht zu den Grabungen Am Hof in den Jahren 2008/09. *Fundort Wien* 13, 50–74.

Mosser, M. (2011a) Das Legionslager Vindobona – Wien zwischen Spätantike und Frühmittelalter. In M. Konrad and Ch. Witschel (ed.) *Römische Legionslager in den Rhein- und Donauprovinzen – Nuclei spätantik-frühmittelalterlichen Lebens?* 475–504. München, Bayerische Akademie der Wissenschaften.

Mosser, M. (2011b) Befunde im Legionslager Vindobona. Teil VI: Die Lagermauer – Profildokumentation auf der Parzelle Wien 1, Kramergasse 13. *Fundort Wien* 14, 164–185.

Mosser, M. (2013a) Wien 1, Bognergasse/Seitzergasse/Am Hof/ Heidenschuß/Naglergasse. *Fundort Wien* 16.

Mosser, M. (2013b) Wien 1, Hoher Markt/Lichtensteg/Bauernmarkt. *Fundort Wien* 16.

Mosser, M., Adler-Wölfl, K., Binder, M., Chinelli, R., Chmelar, W., Czeika, S., Dembski, G., Grupe, S., Gschwantler, K., Hejl, E., Jäger-Wersonig, S., Jawecki, Ch., Kieweg-Vetters, G., Litschauer, C., Öllerer, Ch., Sakl-Oberthaler, S., Tarcsay, K. and Wedenig, R. (2010a) *Die römischen Kasernen im Legionslager Vindobona. Die Ausgrabungen am Judenplatz in Wien in den Jahren 1995–1998*. Wien, Phoibos.

Mosser, M., Kronberger, M. and Pregesbauer, M. (2010b) 3D-Laserscanning in two Sites of ancient Vindobona. *Vindobona – Aquincum. Herausforderungen und Ergebnisse in der Stadtarchäologie*, 55–60. Budapest, Budapest Történeti Múzeum.

Mosser, M., Adler-Wölfl, K., Czeika, S., Gaisbauer, I., Radbauer, S. and Sedlmayer, H. (2012) Befunde im Legionslager Vindobona. Teil VII: Der Abwasserkanal der via praetoria – Wien 1, Wipplingerstraße 6 (Altes Rathaus). *Fundort Wien* 15, 74–118.

Mráv, Zs. (2005) Quadian Policy of Valentinian I. and the never-finished late Roman Fortress at Göd-Bócsaújtelep. In Zs. Visy (ed.), *Limes XIX. Proceedings of the XIXth International Congress of Roman Frontier Studies, Pécs, September 2003*, 773–784. Pécs, University of Pécs.

Mráv, Zs. and Harl, O. (2008) Die trajanische Bauinschrift der porta principalis dextra im Legionslager Vindobona – Zur Entstehung des Legionslagers Vindobona. *Fundort Wien* 11, 36–55.

Neumann, A. (1967) *Forschungen in Vindobona 1948 bis 1967 I. Teil, Lager und Lagerterritorium.* Graz – Wien – Köln, Böhlau.

Neumann, A. (1968) *Forschungen in Vindobona 1948 bis 1967 II. Teil, Zivilstadt und Landbezirk.* Graz – Wien – Köln, Böhlau.

Pollak, M. (1992) Ein spätantiker Fundkomplex vom Wildpretmarkt in Wien. *Beiträge zur Mittelalterarchäologie in Österreich* 8, 117–157.

Soproni, S. (1985) *Die letzten Jahrzehnte des pannonischen Limes.* München, Beck.

Tarcsay, K. (2006) Ein merowingerzeitlicher Glasperlenanhänger mit Rosettendekor aus Wien 1, Judenplatz. *Fundort Wien* 9, 132–139.

Tobias, B., Wiltschke-Schrotta, K. and Binder, M. (2010) Das langobardenzeitliche Gräberfeld von Wien-Mariahilfer Gürtel. *Jahrbuch des Römisch-Germanischen Zentralmuseums Mainz* 57, 279–337.

Tomlin, R. S. O. (2000) The Legions in the Late Empire. In R. J. Brewer (ed.) *Roman Fortresses and their Legions*, 159–182. London, Society of Antiquaries.

Witschel, Ch. (2011) Die Provinz Germania Superior im 3. Jahrhundert – ereignisgeschichtlicher Rahmen, quellenkritische Anmerkungen und die Entwicklung des Städtewesens. *Das römische Reich im Umbruch. Auswirkungen auf die Städte in der zweiten Hälfte des 3. Jahrhunderts. Kolloquium Bern/Augst, 23–64*. Montagnac, Editions Monique Mergoil.

Zienkiewicz, J. D. (1993) Excavations in the scamnum tribunorum at Caerleon: The legionary museum site 1983–5. *Britannia* 24, 27–140.

Zsidi P. (2011) Vom spätantiken Aquincum zum mittelalterlichen Vetus Buda (Altofen). In M. Konrad and Ch. Witschel (eds) *Römische Legionslager in den Rhein- und Donauprovinzen – Nuclei spätantik-frühmittelalterlichen Lebens?* 549–569. München, Bayerische Akademie der Wissenschaften.

8

THE DWINDLING LEGION: ARCHITECTURAL AND ADMINISTRATIVE CHANGES IN NOVAE (MOESIA INFERIOR) ON THE THRESHOLD OF LATE ANTIQUITY

Martin Lemke

Introduction

The Roman fortress at Novae (Fig. 8.1), garrisoned by the *legio I Italica*, was one of the few strongholds in Moesia and Thracia that did not fall during the first Gothic raids of the mid-3rd century (Derda *et al.* 2008; Sarnowski 2009; 2012; Biernacki 1995–2008). However, later invasions and the structural changes that the years of crisis heralded, affected both the province and the empire, and so would not have passed unnoticed at Novae (Poulter 2007; Gerov 1977; Konrad, Witschel 2011). Indeed, irreversible change had come to the *limes* in Lower Moesia. Due to the depopulation of the wider landscape, as well as changes in defensive strategy, larger settlements were fortified, and civilians also started using the free space that had become available within military installations following the reduction in garrison strength.

The principal tendency towards diminished garrisons within the old fortresses and civilians moving into army buildings in late antiquity (Liebeschuetz 2007, 101–102) is confirmed by changes in both the architecture and artefacts at Novae. Over 50 years of fieldwork have resulted in thorough descriptions of the evolution of entire *scamna* over time. In this first summary since a comparative study by A. Poulter in 1994, the available information from three large structures – the *principia*, *valetudinarium*, and *thermae* – will be summed up and accompanied by a description of changes taking place in less ostentatious areas of the premises, i.e. the barracks, and the defensive perimeter. When considered alongside the available historical information this should allow us to draw some conclusions about how Novae functioned and defended itself on the threshold of late antiquity.

For methodological clarity, the structural changes underway at Novae from the 3rd century onwards will be presented in accordance with the designated fieldwork zones established in the 1960s, when the excavation team divided the entire fortress into an eastern (Bulgarian) and western (Polish) part, with a number of subdivisions, called Sectors (see Dyczek 2008 for the excavation history). Essentially these can be broken down into the headquarters building (*principia*) and the Trajanic baths (Sector 11), the army hospital and adjacent buildings in the *scamnum tribunorum* (Sector 4), and the recently implemented Sector 12 to the east of the *principia*. The fortification walls will also be examined, with a specific focus on the 3rd-century extension of the defended perimeter to the east ("Novae II").

History

Novae became a major hotspot when the Goths attacked the province of lower Moesia in AD 249. Their leader Kniva had split his army into two parts, and the western portion crossed the Danube at Novae. There is ample stratigraphic evidence for destruction inflicted during a battle outside the fortress walls (Kolendo 2008, 128–130; Vladkova 2003, 221). Novae also played a major role later on in the conflict in 250 / 251, as it was one of the few places where the Romans managed to hold their ground. Emperor Decius gathered his forces there for an (unsuccessful) counterattack, which ultimately cost him his life at Abrittus in 251 (Radoslavova, Dzanev, Nikolov 2011). In the years following the battle, Rome was initially able to drive the invaders back, but not for long. Towards the end of the 3rd century, Novae was at least partially damaged during Gothic invasions (Milcheva, Gencheva 1996, 191). It was only after the province of Dacia had been abandoned in AD 272, during Aurelian's reign, and military reforms were carried out by Diocletian and Constantine that border security was reestablished

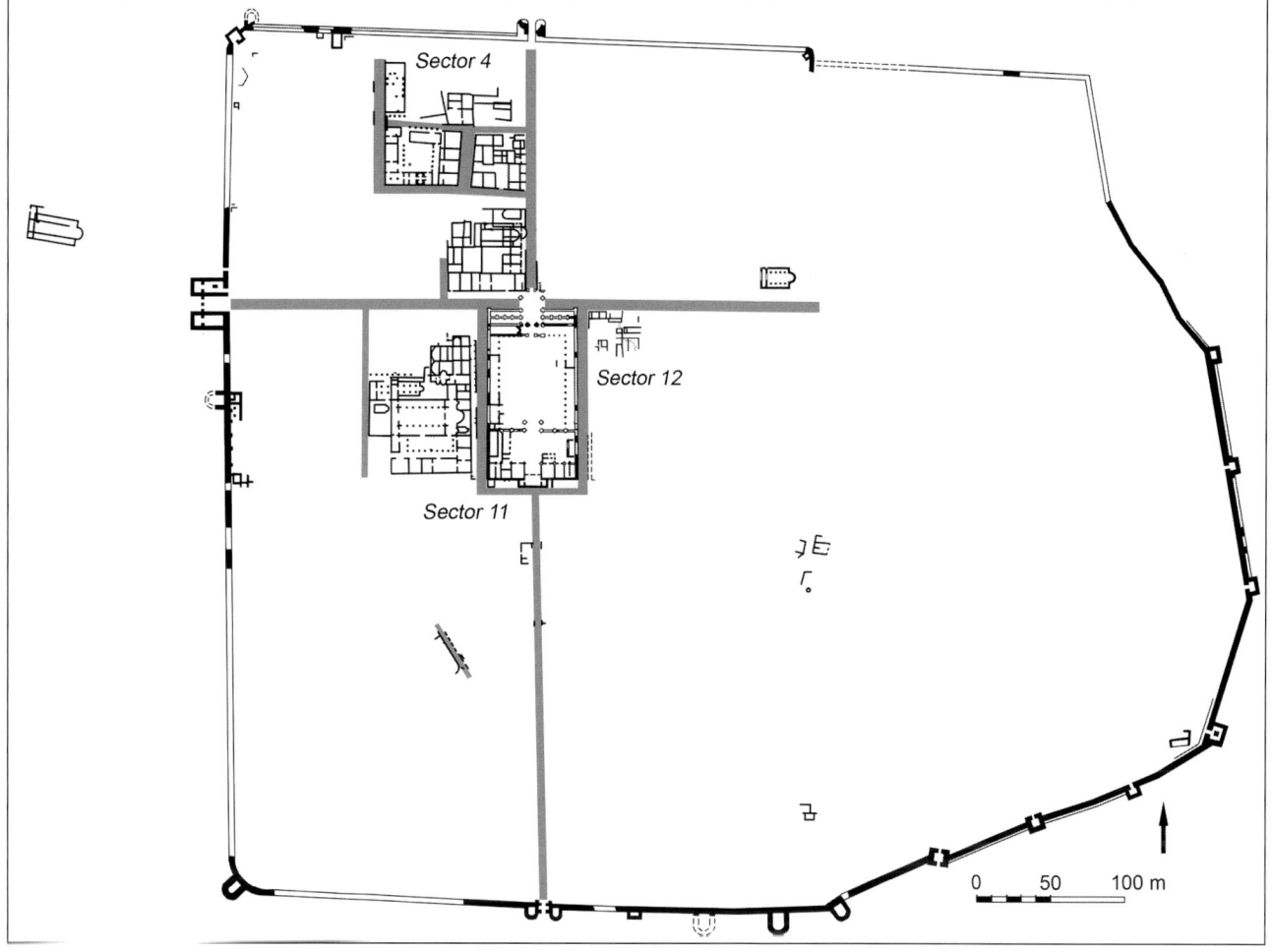

Figure 8.1: Novae in late antiquity. Image credit: courtesy of L. Kovalevskaya and T. Sarnowski

(Sarnowski 1988, 121–125; Poulter 2007, 29). The region then experienced a second "golden age" between 332 and 376 (Liebeschuetz 2007, 102).

The 4th century also brought numerous encounters with the Goths, which reached their catastrophic climax at the Battle of Adrianople in 378, when Valens became the second emperor to lose his life defending the Balkan route to Constantinople. On that occasion, the Goths seem to have bypassed the *limes* defences using ships (Poulter 2007, 37). In the early 5th century, Rome regained control of the Lower Danube provinces, although the price for this included accepting Gothic settlers (Prostko-Prostyński 2008, 141) south of the Danube and a reorganization of the supply chains (Poulter 2007, 38–39; see below). The Hunnic invasions after AD 447 proved a disaster for the Balkan provinces in general (Liebeschuetz 2007, 104) and Novae in particular: the *principia* was burned down and never repaired (Poulter 2007, 40). It also has been argued, though, that Attila's troops never reached Novae (Prostko-Prostyński 2008, 138; cf. Vagalinski 2012 for the difficulties arising from the attempt to reconcile the archaeological record with historic events). In any case, it was half a century before Roman control could be reasserted to some extent in the early 6th century (Poulter 2007).

Principia

The headquarters building (Fig. 8.2; Sarnowski 1979; 1989; 1992; 1999; 2012) was modified on a number of occasions during the 3rd and early 4th centuries, but there is no doubt it was still serving its original purpose during that period. Still, there is at least one notable shift towards a civilian influence during that timeframe, which not only offers an interesting clue regarding the role of the *principia*, but also the progressive reorganization of the Roman army. In the 2nd and 3rd centuries, certain votive statues were set up in the headquarters courtyard (*forum militare*), dedicated by the first centurions (*primipili*) of the legion (Sarnowski 2005, 226; 2013, 138), who, among other duties, were

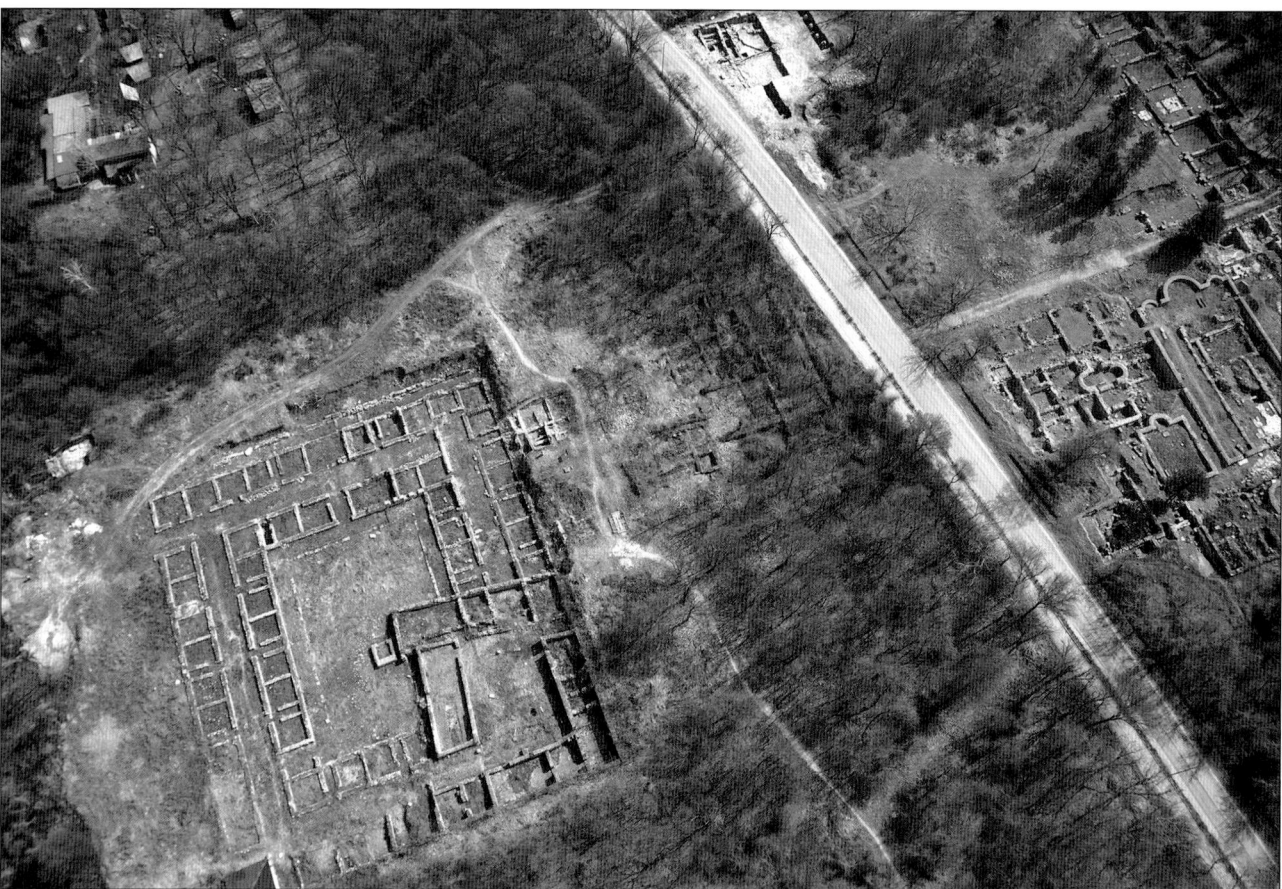

Figure 8.2: Novae: the military hospital with the courtyard house visible on the left and the principia and surrounding area to the right. Sector 12 lies at the top. Image credit: courtesy of M. Pisz

responsible for provisioning logistics within the fortress (Roth 1999, 274). In *c.* AD 300, the *primipilarii*, who were civil functionaries responsible for organizing supplies, assumed this responsibility (Sarnowski 1999; 2013). They came from the Cyclades, Hellespont, and Phoenicia (Lajtar 2013; Sarnowski 2013). By then the Roman army relied to a significant degree on a central provisioning system (Sarnowski 2005). Nine such bases from the early 4th to the early 5th century were erected by individuals from Novae. Hence it can be assumed that from roughly the second half of the 4th century through to the middle of the 5th century, the building complex with its courtyard fulfilled both its original, yet somewhat reduced, role as the headquarters of the remaining garrison of the *legio I Italica*, and also served as a meeting place and town centre (*forum civile*) for the civilian inhabitants (Sarnowski 2013; cf. Poulter 1994, 146). Hundreds of small pieces of worked bronze were found in a destruction layer dating to the 5th century. These fragments were concentrated in the treasuries, although they also occurred in other rooms in the rear wing of the headquarters building. Most of those pieces derived from statues of emperors supposedly erased from history by means of *damnatio memoriae*, although others came from statues of gods and goddesses. T. Sarnowski argues these fragments might hint that scrap metal was being stored under the care of the standards of the legion (Sarnowski 1985).

In the late 5th and 6th centuries, the rooms in the southern part of the headquarters no longer served their original role. By then, the area was filled with small, crude rectangular buildings that exploited the existing walls of the *principia*, and were obviously the handiwork of civil inhabitants. At that time the *principia* basilica no longer had a roof, while a destruction layer from the mid-5th century suggests this might be the consequence of a complex confluence of disasters, including an earthquake and a Hun raid (T. Sarnowski, pers. comm.). The courtyard statues had been destroyed and chunks of limestone from their bases were apparently burned for secondary use here. Other fragments of worked limestone were found in loess pits, reused in the pavement of the early Christian cathedral to the east of the former *principia*, serving as raised doorsteps in the rear row of rooms, and immured in the west boundary wall of the former principia complex, once it had been rebuilt after a 6th-century earthquake (Sarnowski 2013; 2012; 1999).

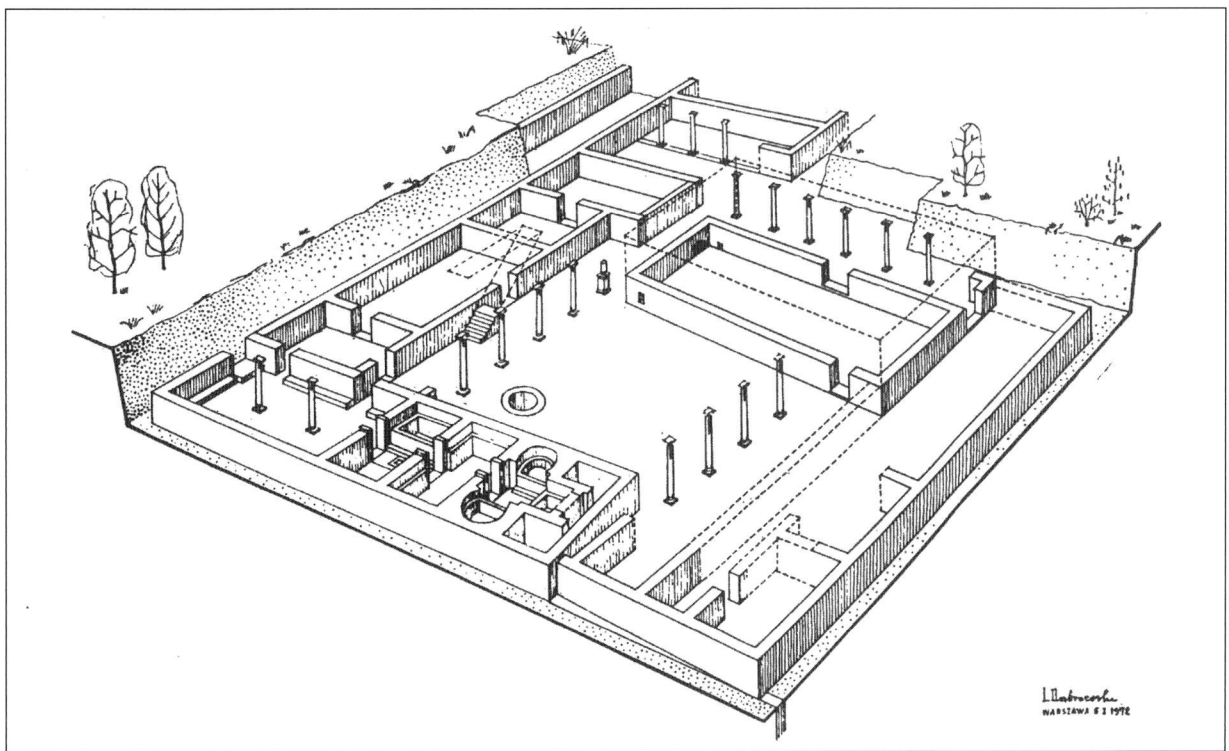

Figure 8.3: The courtyard house in Sector 4, courtesy of L. Dąbrowski. After: Dyczek 2008

The courtyard of the former *principia*, where the statues of emperors had once stood, was also diminished. Stripped of its former splendor, the courtyard seems to have served, together with the roofless shell of the *basilica principorum*, as a market square in the 5th and 6th centuries AD. Poulter, however, also suggests the less romantic use of the area as "a convenient rubbish tip" (Poulter 1994, 145). After the Hunnic raids in the AD 440s, the religious and administrative centre was eventually moved slightly westwards, to the site of the former legionary baths. A large basilica, marking the rising influence of Christianity at Novae, was erected here (Sarnowski 1999; Biernacki 2005).

Valetudinarium

After the military hospital fell out of use, probably *c*. 238 (Dyczek 2011, 25), the area now designated Sector 4 was apparently abandoned for some time as a result of a settlement hiatus following the Gothic raids (Dyczek 2008, 44–55; Dyczek 2011, 25). The same applies to a house south of the hospital, which was part of the *scamnum tribunorum*. This structure was heavily damaged in the second half of the 3rd century and only partially in use at the beginning of the 4th (Milcheva, Gencheva 1996, 191). Civilian settlers returned here towards the end of the 3rd century, in the years following AD 270, when systematic changes to the overall layout of the area were taking place (Dyczek 2005, 232). The settlers established a new street grid that divided the formerly square plot roughly into quarters. One street was aligned north–south, the other east–west. The latter street is now referred to as the *via inscriptionum* (Dyczek 1998) as its surface incorporated parts of funerary steles and structural elements from a nearby necropolis, which had probably been desecrated during a Gothic raid (Dyczek 2005, 233). This urban street grid has a rather amateuristic touch: some of the walls of the former hospital were reused as foundations, but in other cases the walls were displaced by about half a meter from the former layout. This did not help stability and the spaces between old and new walls were filled with rubble. Apparently, measurement problems were the cause of the discrepancies, a clear hint that the highly irregular insula had not been built *manu military*. It has even been suggested that "it is hard to imagine such incompetent army architects and builders" (Dyczek 2005, 234).

Various buildings displaying rather primitive architecture were also erected at this time. Not all of them have been fully investigated, but a glass workshop and a *horreum* are identifiable among them. A residence of *villa urbana* type was constructed over the southeastern part of the hospital ruins. Above the former officer's house in the *scamnum tribunorum*, a large public building was founded at the beginning of the 4th century (Milcheva, Gencheva 1996, 192). The walls of the *valetudinarium* were either demolished or partly reused as foundations for new mud-brick buildings. In the southeast corner of the former *valetudinarium* a sequence of rooms was built around a courtyard. One of these rooms boasted a hypocaust heating system, while a network of sewage channels plumbed the rooms into the existing fortress system. Workshops for craftsmen were located in the northern part of the building. There is evidence for the processing of different raw materials in separate rooms: horn and bone in one, a glass workshop equipped with two kilns in another.

The vestiges of the courtyard house (Fig. 8.3; a.k.a. "Building with porticoes") remain visible, and are the reason why the underlying southwestern quarter of the *valetudinarium* has not been excavated. This villa remained in use until the 6th century and was partly constructed using reused stones from the legionary buildings. The rooms were arranged around a courtyard with two porticoes and a well – both features that can still be seen on site. The building was modified towards the middle of the 4th century, when a new paved yard was built on a higher level, with a portico lining its eastern and western sides. The rooms in the eastern wing were subdivided by partition walls. The bathhouse in the southern wing may also have been accessible from the street to the west. Elongated and very narrow, yet complete, the bathhouse is a remarkable feature that takes up an area of about 150 m² (Press 1973, 286). At ground level the eastern side of the villa contained workshops, while the western side provided various kitchen amenities and storage rooms. The living quarters would have lain on the first floor. The building was repaired and modified several times until its final destruction during the mid-5th-century Hunnic raids.

Sector 12

In 2011 a new sector at Novae was excavated to the east of the *principia* and to the south of the *via principalis*. As of 2013, ca 900 m² of this plot has been investigated. According to standard Roman fortress layout, legionary barracks should have been located here, possibly those housing the first cohort, or perhaps the houses of the *immunes* (Lemke 2013a; 2012, 195). Although the function of the principate-period building is yet to be established, we can see traces of civilian life appearing towards the end of the 3rd century, similar to most other parts of the fortress. In this case, a glass kiln and numerous finds of slag are proof of a further glass workshop here. A small water basin can also be connected to this civilian phase.

Near the current southern edge of the fieldwork area another late antique portico was found (Fig. 8.4). Five bases for columns were unearthed, set on square slabs of stone. Considering the size and proportions of the reused elements, this portico was built of material gathered from the ruins of the *principia*, but the exact date of its construction is not known yet. Whatever the purpose, its execution can be perceived as another example of rather inferior civilian craftsmanship, albeit with an ambitious scheme. Out of the five bases discovered, only three are of almost, but not exactly the same proportions, the fourth base is altogether different and the fifth is in reality an unfinished capital turned upside down. Likewise, the underlying plinths all have different dimensions. Judging by style and diameter, these elements must originally have been part of three different architectural compositions (although these could all have been within the *principia*). The foundations beneath three of the bases also employ recycled legionary architecture, but in all five cases the result is so thin and weak that it is impossible to envisage them supporting a portico with large columns. The outcome is in a way monumental, but since traces of both solid substructures and an equally large building to which the portico might have belonged are lacking, one should assume that there were no columns standing on top, much less a roof, and the portico was either never finished or had a rather flat-ornamental character (Lemke 2013a).

Fortifications and *canabae*

As a result of the local geography, Novae could be most easily attacked from the west. It is thus hardly surprising that this western wall was equipped with an arsenal of throwing stones near the towers in late antiquity (Lemke 2013b, 362–364) – a defensive measure that was not exclusive to professional soldiers. Still, the civilian buildings outside the fortress defences were easy pickings for attackers. Over the course of the 1st–3rd centuries, the civil settlement around Novae had grown to considerable proportions. The *canabae* stretched westward and southward to cover an area of about 70–80 ha (Sarnowski 2012, 79; Tomas 2013). At some point after the Gothic invasion of 250/251, towards the end of the 3rd century or the beginning of the 4th (Poulter 1994, 145), the fortress rampart at Novae was equipped with a kilometer-long extension (Chichikova 1974, 229; Dimitrov, Chichikova, Dimitrova, Najdenova 1967).

This new wall connected with the north-east and south-east corners of the fortress to enclose a 12 ha area lying directly to the east. About 650 m of its length has been explored archaeologically. Subsequently, the former eastern curtain wall was perceived to be obsolete and dismantled. The only inscription attesting that Novae achieved the status of a *municipium* was found within this "annex", strengthening the theory that it was indeed the *canabae* and not the *vicus*, which was promoted and fortified (Gerov 1977, 300; Poulter 2007, 32). In spite of the rather large area of the *canabae*, it remains somewhat unclear why preference was given to building a new wall and removing the old one, as the interior of the fortress itself was not intensively

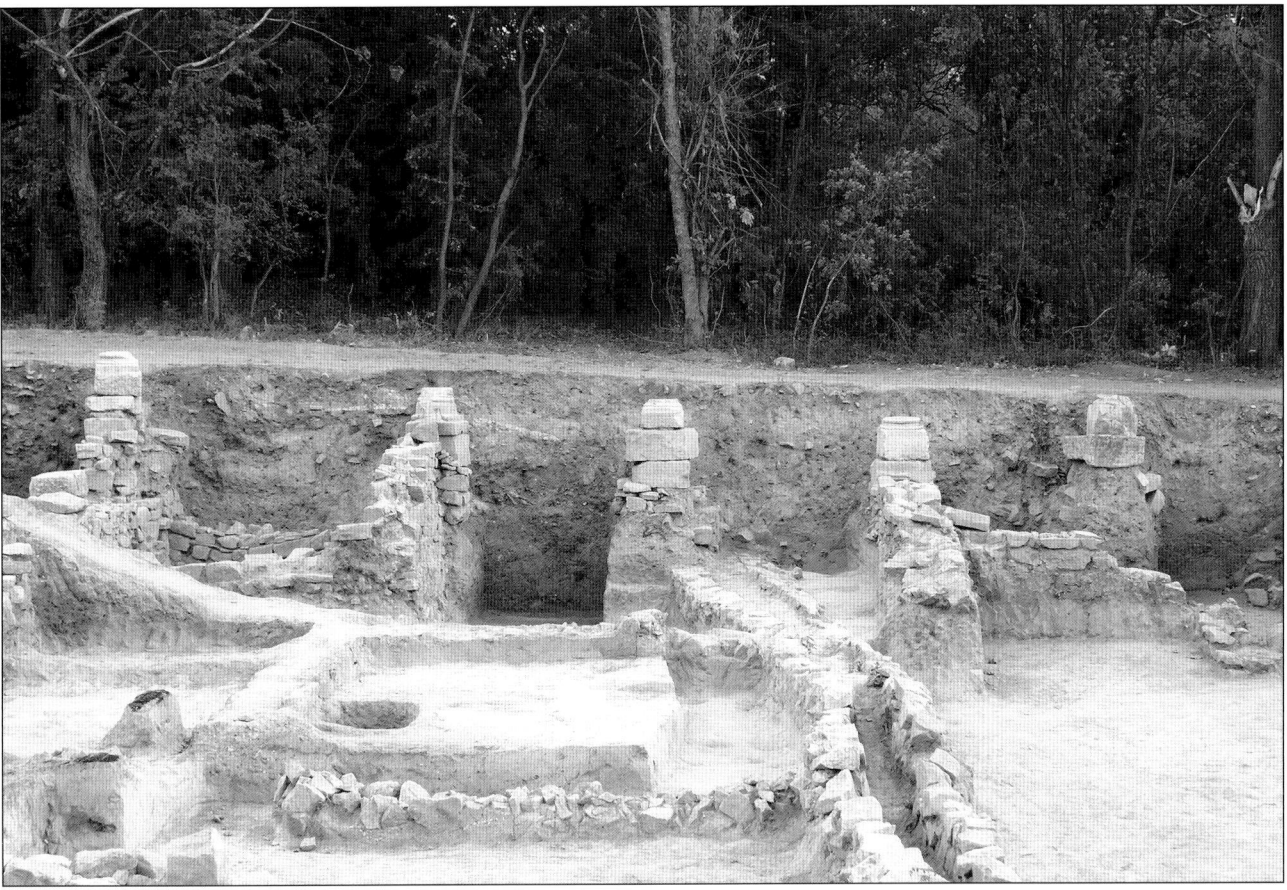

Figure 8.4: Late antique portico looking towards the south, Sector 12

occupied at the time and so could have provided shelter (Poulter 1994, 145).

The excavations in the 1960s revealed six rectangular towers lining the new wall, while a gate-tower provided access to the town from the southeast. The new wall follows a somewhat irregular course along a natural ridge formed by the local river valley. The wall was made largely of stones taken from the dismantled east fortress wall. These new defences were modified several times; they were reinforced and thickened to a width of 3 m, while two additional towers were also erected, probably after the destruction of 378 (Chichikova 1974, 228–229). In the first half of the 4th century, work was underway on the gates, corners and walls of the original fortress, which were now equipped with U-shaped towers. The last known modifications were carried out in the reign of Justinian I, when the western gate received two large rectangular towers (Sarnowski 2012, 94–96).

Summary and conclusions

Late Roman Novae was arguably more of a fortified town than a military base. The fortress was, though, still fulfilling its original purpose when traces of destruction were removed and several buildings rebuilt in the early 4th century (Milcheva, Gencheva 1996, 191). Several buildings from the principate remained in good order throughout most of that century, such as the *principia*. The baths and hospital were no longer is commission, though, just like a number of barracks in the *retentura* (Poulter 2007, 31). Traces of the tendency for civilians to flee from open territory to fortified sites can also be observed at 4th-century Novae. The fortified area was expanded to encompass *c.* 30 ha, significantly more than 18 ha contained within the old fortress. Changes to the fortress fabric seem to be in accordance with patterns observed elsewhere across the Empire, where it was decided to dismantle large buildings such as the *valetudinarium* and *principia*, or adapt them to serve new functions (Poulter 1994, 143 citing the legionary fortress Caerleon/Isca in *Britannia*). The central streets of the town were narrower now, and the sidewalks had been removed.

Changes in administration are highlighted by the erection of statues by civilian *primipilarii*, who are providing long distance logistical support for the army, especially from the Hellespont region (Sarnowski 2005; 2013). This task was predominantly the domain of army professionals during the principate. One large Greek inscription among this corpus (Łajtar 2013; Lemke 2012, 199) records, for the first time at Novae, the name of the place itself in a context where the *legio I Italica* is also mentioned. It stated that two dignitaries from Ilion and Alexandria in the province of Hellespont founded a monument for the "glorious town of Novesians" (Łajtar 2013, 100–104). Similar dedications were found in the colony at Oescus (Sarnowski 1999, 61), in the western part of the province. The civil *primipilarii* apparently followed the tradition of their military namesakes, the *primipili* of the principate, by erecting a statue or comparable dedication in the headquarters of the legion where they worked after finishing their one-year duty, the *pastus militum*, (Sarnowski 2013). The *pastus militum* seems to have already existed during the Tetrarchy, although it had a different name and was part of a reorganization of the Roman army's supply chains.

It has been established that the *primipilarii* were employed by provincial governors as civilian officials responsible for supplying the troops on the *limes*. Their task, referred to as *pastus primipili* in legal sources, or *pastus militum* on inscriptions, (Łajtar 2013, 105), was originally attested at the start of the 3rd century as the responsibility of the *primi pili* in the army. However, as part of the aforementioned administrative reforms, this responsibility was transferred to the *primipilarii*. They did not collect *annona*, though: civic magistrates were in charge of that. The duty of the *primipilarii* was to transport supplies from the province where they were collected (which was also their home province) to the location where the given legion was stationed, although it is not clear yet, who financed the procedure (Łajtar 2013, 105; Sarnowski 2013; 2005). Supplying the legions of Lower Moesia from distant provinces of the Mediterranean seems to have been a consequence of the devastations wrought by the Goths, and the ensuing logistical complications (Sarnowski 2013, 144; Poulter 2007, 37–38). Relying on privateers to supply the army allowed those forces engaged in the logistic process to be returned to the fighting pool. In a time when manpower was being constantly reduced this would have been a successful means of making more soldiers available for guarding the frontier.

Clearly, the changes visible in the layout of the fortress reflect modifications to the late Roman legion itself, which include a drastic reduction in unit strength (Poulter 1994, 141–147). Between the reigns of Aurelian and Constantine, the Roman army was thoroughly reorganized (Campbell 2008, 120–130; Strobel 2007; Poulter 2007, 29). At Novae, this can also be seen in the brick stamps made by small new units (Sarnowski 2007; Speidel 1992). The Tetrarchic building programme acknowledged this dramatic reduction in the number of soldiers stationed in legionary bases (Poulter 2007, 31). It seems likely that either the *legio I Italica* was reduced in size in the 4th century or the practise of sending detachments away from their home base had become more marked than ever before (Poulter 2007, 32–33). Many events in the history of Novae are still unclear and will probably remain so. The *limitanei* garrison at Novae in around 400–450 AD may well have been *legio I Italica* (Sarnowski 1999, 63), but after the Hunnic invasions, there are no further hints about its identity or even its presence. Either way, the grandeur of a legion once famed as *Alexandri Magni phalanga* (Suet. Nero 19, 2) had faded slowly but surely ever since the principate ended.

Bibliography

Biernacki, A. (ed.) *Novae. Studies and Materials*, I–III, Poznań 1995–2008.

Biernacki, A. (2005) A city of Christians: Novae in the 5th and 6th C AD. *Archaeologia Bulgarica* 9, 53–74.

Campbell, B. (2008) The army. In A. K. Bowman, P. Garnsey and A. Cameron (eds) *The Crisis of Empire, AD 193–337, The Cambridge Ancient History*, 110–130. Second Edition, Vol. 12, Cambridge, Cambridge University Press.

Chichikova, M. (1974) Les fouilles de Novae, Moesia Inferior, Secteur Est. Campagnes 1960–1968. In E. Birley, B. Dobson and M. Jarrett (eds) *Roman Frontier Studies. The International Limes Congress 1969*, 226–234. Cardiff, University of Wales Press.

Ciołek, R. and Dyczek, P. (2011) *Novae: Legionary Fortress and Late Antique Town, vol. II: Coins from Sector IV*. Warsaw, University of Warsaw.

Derda, T., Dyczek, P. and Kolendo, J. (eds) (2000) *Novae: Legionary Fortress and Late Antique Town, vol. I: A Companion to the Study of Novae*. Warsaw, University of Warsaw.

Dimitrov, D., Chichikova, M., Dimitrova, A. and Najdenova, V. (1967) Wykopaliska archeologiczne we wschodnim sektorze Novae w 1965 roku., *Archeologia (PL)* 18, 115–131.

Dyczek, P. (1998) *Via inscriptionum* at Novae. *Novensia* 10, 17–29.

Dyczek, P. (2005) The site of the valetudinarium in Novae in the third century AD: remodeling the architecture. In M. Mirković (ed.) *Römische Städte und Festungen an der Donau. Akten der regionalen Konferenz, Beograd, 16–19 Oktober 2003*, 231–238, Beograd, Filozofski Fakultet.

Dyczek, P. (2008) Archaeological excavations at Novae. A history of research with special consideration of Sector IV (Legionary Baths, valetudinarium, late architecture). In T. Derda, P. Dyczek and J. Kolendo (eds) *Novae: Legionary Fortress and Late Antique Town, vol. I: A Companion on the Study of Novae*, 31–70. Warsaw, University of Warsaw.

Dyczek, P. (2011) Settlement and architectural changes in sector IV. In R. Ciołek and P. Dyczek (eds) *Legionary Fortress and Late Antique Town, vol. II: Coins from Sector IV*, 1–44. Warsaw, University of Warsaw.

Gerov, B. (1977) Zum Problem der Entstehung der römischen Städte am Unteren Donaulimes. *Klio* 59, 299–309.

Kolendo, J. (2008) Novae during the Goth raid of AD 250/1 (Iordanes, *Getica* 101–103). In T. Derda, P. Dyczek and J. Kolendo (eds) *Novae: Legionary Fortress and Late Antique*

Town, vol. I: A Companion on the Study of Novae, 117–131. Warsaw, University of Warsaw.

Konrad, M. and Witschel, C. (eds) (2011) *Römische Legionslager in den Rhein- und Donauprovinzen- Nuclei spätantikfrühmittelalterlichen Lebens? Abhandlungen der Philosophischhistorische Klasse. Neue Folge, 138.* München, Verlag der Bayerischen Akademie der Wissenschaften.

Lemke, M. (2012) Fieldwork at Novae 2011, *Światowit* IX (L) /A (2011), 195–200.

Lemke, M. (2013a) Fieldwork at Novae 2012, *Światowit* X (LI) /A (2011), 151–156.

Lemke, M. (2013b) Stone Projectiles discovered in the *castra legionis* Novae near Svishtov (BG). In I Radman-Liaja and M. Ilkić (eds) *Proceedings of ROMEC 17 (Zagreb 2010) Weapons and military equipment in a funerary context,* 357–364. Zagreb, Arheoloski muzej u Zagrebu.

Liebeschuetz, W. (2007) The lower Danube region under pressure from Valens to Heraclius. In A. Poulter (ed.) *The Transition to Late Antiquity on the Danube and Beyond,* 101–134. Oxford, Oxford University Press.

Łajtar, A. (2013) A newly discovered inscription from Novae (Moesia Inferior) connected with pastus militum. *Tyche* 28, 97–111.

Milcheva, A. and Gencheva, E. (1996) Die Architektur des römischen Militärlagers und der frühbyzantinischen Stadt Novae (Erkundungen 1980–94). In P. Petrović (ed.) *Roman Limes on the Middle and Lower Danube,* 187–193. Cahiers des Portes de Fer, Monographies 2, Belgrade, Archaeological Institute.

Poulter, A. (1994) Novae in the 4th century AD: city or fortress? A problem with a British perspective. In G. Susini (ed.) *Limes,* 139–148. Bologna, Pàtron.

Poulter A. (ed.) (2007) *The Transition to Late Antiquity on the Danube and Beyond.* Proceedings of the British Academy 141, Oxford, Oxford University Press.

Press, L. (1973) The Building with the Porticoes in Novae. *Archaeologia Polona* 14, 279–295.

Prostko-Prostyński, J. (2008) Attila and Novae. In T. Derda, P. Dyczek and J. Kolendo (eds) *Novae: Legionary Fortress and Late Antique Town, vol. I: A Companion on the Study of Novae,* 137–138. Warsaw, University of Warsaw.

Radoslavova, G., Dzanev, G., and Nikolov, N. (2011) The Battle at Abritus in AD 251: Written Sources, Archaeological and Numismatic Data. *Archaeologia Bulgarica* 15.3, 23–49.

Roth, J. (1999) *The Logistics of the Roman Army at War (264 B.C.–A.D. 235).* Leiden, Brill.

Sarnowski, T. (1979) La destruction des principia à Novae vers 316/317 de notre ère. Révolte militaire ou invasion gothique? *Archeologia* 30, 149–163.

Sarnowski, T. (1985) Bronzefunde aus dem Stabsgebäude in Novae und Altmetalldepots in den römischen Kastellen und Legionslagern. *Germania* 63, 521–540.

Sarnowski, T. (1988) *Wojsko rzymskie w Mezji Dolnej i na północnym wybrzeżu Morza Czarnego.* Novensia 3, Warszawa.

Sarnowski, T. (1989) The headquarters building of the Legionary fortress at Novae (Lower Moesia). In V. Maxfield and M. Dobson (eds) *Roman Frontier Studies 1989, Proceedings of the XVth International Congress of Roman Frontier Studies,* 303–307. Exeter, University of Exeter Press.

Sarnowski, T. (1992) Das Fahnenheiligtum des Legionslagers Novae. In A. Lipska, E. Niezgoda and M. Ząbecka (eds) *Studia Aegaea et Balcanica in honorem Lodovicae Press,* 221–233. Warszawa, no publisher known.

Sarnowski, T. (1999) Die Principia von Novae im späten 4. und frühen 5. Jh. In G. v. Bülow, and A. Milčeva (eds) *Der Limes an der unteren Donau von Diokletian bis Heraklios, Vorträge der internationalen Konferenz Svištov, Bulgarien (1.–5. September 1998),* 57–64, Sofia, Nous.

Sarnowski, T. (2005) Drei spätkaiserzeitliche Statuenbasen aus Novae in Niedermösien. In M. Mirković (ed.) *Römische Städte und Festungen an der Donau. Akten der regionalen Konferenz,* 223–230. Belgrade.

Sarnowski, T. (2007) Novae in the *Notitia Dignitatum. Archeologia* 58, 25–29.

Sarnowski, T. (2007) The name of Novae in Lower Moesia. *Archeologia* 58, 15–23.

Sarnowski, T. (ed.) (2012) *Novae. An Archaeological Guide.* Warszawa, Instytut Archeologii Uniwersttetu Warszawskiego.

Sarnowski, T. (2013) *Accepta pariatoria* und *pastus militum*: Eine neue Statuenbasis mit zwei Inschriften aus Novae. *Tyche* 28, 135–146.

Speidel, M. (1992) Spätrömische Legionskohorten in Novae, *Roman Army Studies, vol. II,* 400–402, Mavors 8, Stuttgart, F. Steiner.

Strobel, K. (2007) Strategy and army structure between Septimius Severus and Constantine the Great. In P. Erdkamp (ed.) *A Companion to the Roman Army,* 267–285. Oxford, Blackwell.

Tomas, A. (2013) Canabae legionis I Italicae: state of research on civil settlements accompanying the legionary camp in Novae (Lower Moesia) compared to relevant Lower Danubian sites. *Światowit* L/A, 2011–2012, 155–168.

Vagalinski, L. (2012) The problem of destruction by warfare in Late Antiquity: archaeological evidence from the Danube Limes. In L. Vagalinski, N. Sharankov and S. Torbatov (eds) *The Lower Danube Roman Limes (1st–6th c. AD),* 311–326. Sofia, NIAM-BAS.

Vladkova, P. (2003) The portico building extra muros in Novae, investigations and problems, *Novensia* 14, 221–229.

SEVERAN *CASTRA*, TETRARCHIC *QUADRIBURGIA*, JUSTINIAN *COENOBIA*, AND GHASSANID *DIYARAT*: PATTERNS OF TRANSFORMATION OF *LIMES ARABICUS* FORTS DURING LATE ANTIQUITY

Ignacio Arce

Introduction

The aim of this paper is to analyze the physical transformations and changes of use within relevant Roman military installations on the *limes Arabicus,* between the 4th century AD and the 7th century. The transformations identified in these structures during this *"longue durée"* period illustrate and correspond to three key transitional periods that determine the history of the Levant from the apex of Roman domination in *Oriens*, until the advent of Islam. They are also key to understanding this historical shift. In accordance with the aim of this volume, to foreground the military architecture of the *limites* during late antiquity, we will focus on the first two transitional phases of the four historical periods, and the three related shifts that can be identified in the military installations. The last shift, coinciding with the advent of Islam and the transformation of these former Roman forts into Umayyad *qusur* is only presented briefly, as it exceeds the scope of this volume. Nonetheless, reference is made to it as an essential aspect of this diachronic analysis, and the final output of the processes is described and analyzed.

The hypotheses and conclusions presented here are based on recent excavations and research conducted at several sites in Jordan and Syria. They focus on the patterns of change identified in the first two transitional periods, which correspond to the transformation of *Severan* forts into *quadriburgia* during the Tetrarchic period, and the vicissitudes of these structures and their associated *vici* in the aftermath of the claimed withdrawal of regular Roman soldiers from the forts comprising the southern section of the *limes Arabicus* following a change in strategy in the 5th century AD. In many cases the former forts were adapted into monastic and / or palatial venues by the Ghassanid *phylarchs*, a change linked to the new strategic defense of this *limes* stretch and the socio-political events that accompanied this new *status quo*.

Analysis of the changes made to these structures, including subsequent monastic conversion, has brought other closely related issues into discussion, such as the development of new architectural types derived from this pattern of transformation. The repertoire of defensive architecture, whether a modified *quadriburgia* or fortified shrine, exceeded the defensive needs of the new monastic communities themselves, but played a key logistic role in the defense of the *limitrophe* – that is the area proximal to the frontiers – during the 6th century at a territorial scale.

Finally, we will briefly assess the reuse of these former Roman structures during the Umayyad period. This will focus on functional criteria to illustrate their reuse as venues to carry out an agenda of political clientelism and religious proselytism, similar to that conducted at the same sites a century earlier by the Ghassanids. We will also discuss the influence exerted by this late Roman military architecture on the development of residential and palatial architecture of the rising Arab elites in Arabia during the 4th and 5th centuries. It is they who, under the Umayyads, inherited full political control of the region. This dimension poses interesting questions about when and how the influence exerted by Roman military architecture on Early Islamic (Umayyad) palatial architecture began.

The research presented here makes use of archaeological evidence produced by surveys and excavations carried out in the last decade by the author and other colleagues working on the *limes Arabicus*, including Ulbert and Konrad's

Limesprojekt; Parker's *Central Limes Arabicus Project*; and Arce in north Jordan. Although the increasing number of sites explored in the last two decades has contributed to a new perspective, the relatively small number of fully-excavated sites means that the conclusions presented here should be viewed as a hypothesis and a guide for future research.

This contribution combines and summarizes the results of research published in at least three different papers, which in sum constitutes a theoretical paradigm for interpreting the *limes Arabicus* throughout late antiquity (Arce 2012), the building techniques that were employed (Arce 2010), and the pattern of transformation and change that the structures presented here underwent (Arce 2009a; 2009b; and 2009c).

I. The Setting of the *limes Orientalis*: Continuity and Change

The *limes Orientalis*, which ran from the Black Sea to the Red Sea, was divided into two principal sectors: the northern section or *limes Armenicus*, which stretched from the Black Sea to the Euphrates, and the *limes Arabicus*, which ran between the Euphrates and the Red Sea at Aila (Fig. 9.1). These two sections display very different characteristics and were a product of divergent historical evolution.

The northern areas of *Oriens* entered the Roman sphere in 64 BC, when Pompey the Great, annexed Syria as a Roman province and transformed the other regional states into clients of Rome (creating a *de facto limes Armenicus*). The southernmost section, the *limes Arabicus*, was not established until 170 years later, when the Nabatean kingdom was annexed in AD 106 to become *Provincia Arabia*.

The stretch of the *limes Orientalis* where the two great superpowers, Rome and Persia, were contiguous was quite short and corresponded mainly to Armenia and the stretch of the Euphrates River from Armenia to the north of the Syrian desert – that is the *limes Armenicus* and the northernmost section of the *limes Arabicus*. In the desert areas, the frontier apparently remained comparatively static, while in the north, continued struggle for the control of Armenia led to a more fluid situation. Originally, from the initial stages of Roman conquest until annexation in 64 BC, the control of the *limes Armenicus* had been the role of client kings. Continuity in the north has been attested by the German missions, which have detected that contrary to both previous thinking, and what occurred on the rest of the *limes Arabicus*, the regular Roman army was not replaced by new forces in the 5th century. This factor may also be reflected in the planning of the *vici* that grew up around Roman forts on both sections of the *limes*. In the south they seem to follow a quite irregular "organic" pattern, as at Umm al-Jimal, Umm ar-Rassas/Kastron Mefa'a, Khirbet es-Samra, for instance; in the north, however, soundings conducted within the walled *vici* at Tetrapyrgium and Cholle revealed a regular and orthogonal *Hippodamian* layout (Konrad 2008, 434, figs. 5a & 8b).

Another key difference is that in the northern section of the *limes Arabicus*, the Roman fortifications would have been the very first permanent settlements created (*ex-nihilo*) (Konrad 2008, 434). In the southern section, however, we can see that in many cases the Roman forts would have re-occupied strategic positions where Nabatean stations or forts previously existed (in some cases even structures from the Iron Age period – Ammonite, Moabite, and Edomite forts – were occupied). This further extends the "*longue durée*" process back to previous epochs, necessitating that additional transitional periods are acknowledged in our analysis (five stages and four shifts, at least).

According to the picture emerging from these data, Roman legions in the region of the Euphrates were initially garrisoned in positions near potential invasion routes for Persian armies. In later periods, auxiliary units and new installations were built near the Euphrates, projecting Roman force beyond the natural defensive line offered by the river.

In the northern section of the *limes Arabicus*, between Palmyra and the Euphrates, the strategic and logistic system established *ex-nihilo* by the Romans from the 1st century AD onwards was refortified in the 3rd and 4th centuries after the Persian wars and the peace of Nisbis. This sector seems to have been effective and remained in use until AD 540, when the Sassanians under Chosrau I invaded and plundered Syria. The impact of the ensuing devastation was exacerbated by a plague that desolated the region. The border works consisted of a chain of forts, with three main legionary fortresses at Sura (on the Euphrates), Oresa, and Palmyra, linked by a *via militaris* known as the *Strata Diocletiana*, along its southern length at least.

German archaeologists insist that there is a dearth of evidence for the abandonment of fortifications in this northern sector during the 5th and 6th centuries; furthermore there are "even good reasons to postulate that at the most important sites official troops carried out service until the 7th century AD" (Konrad 2008, 434). This assertion of continuity of fort and *vici* occupation could be explained by the *limitanei* also acting as permanent settlers, responsible for their own maintenance, and all needs not supplied by the governmental *annona*. The shift of strategic defense would have changed the responsibilities of these populations, but would not have been enough reason for them to leave their homes and towns. It is evident, though, that most of the small forts (such as Tetrapyrgium) were eventually transformed into monasteries, similar to the examples encountered to the south, where they played a key logistic role in the Ghassanid mobile troops' defensive scheme.

Another factor that explains this divergence is that the chain of forts in the northern sector linked by the *strata Diocletiana* was not established along the natural border

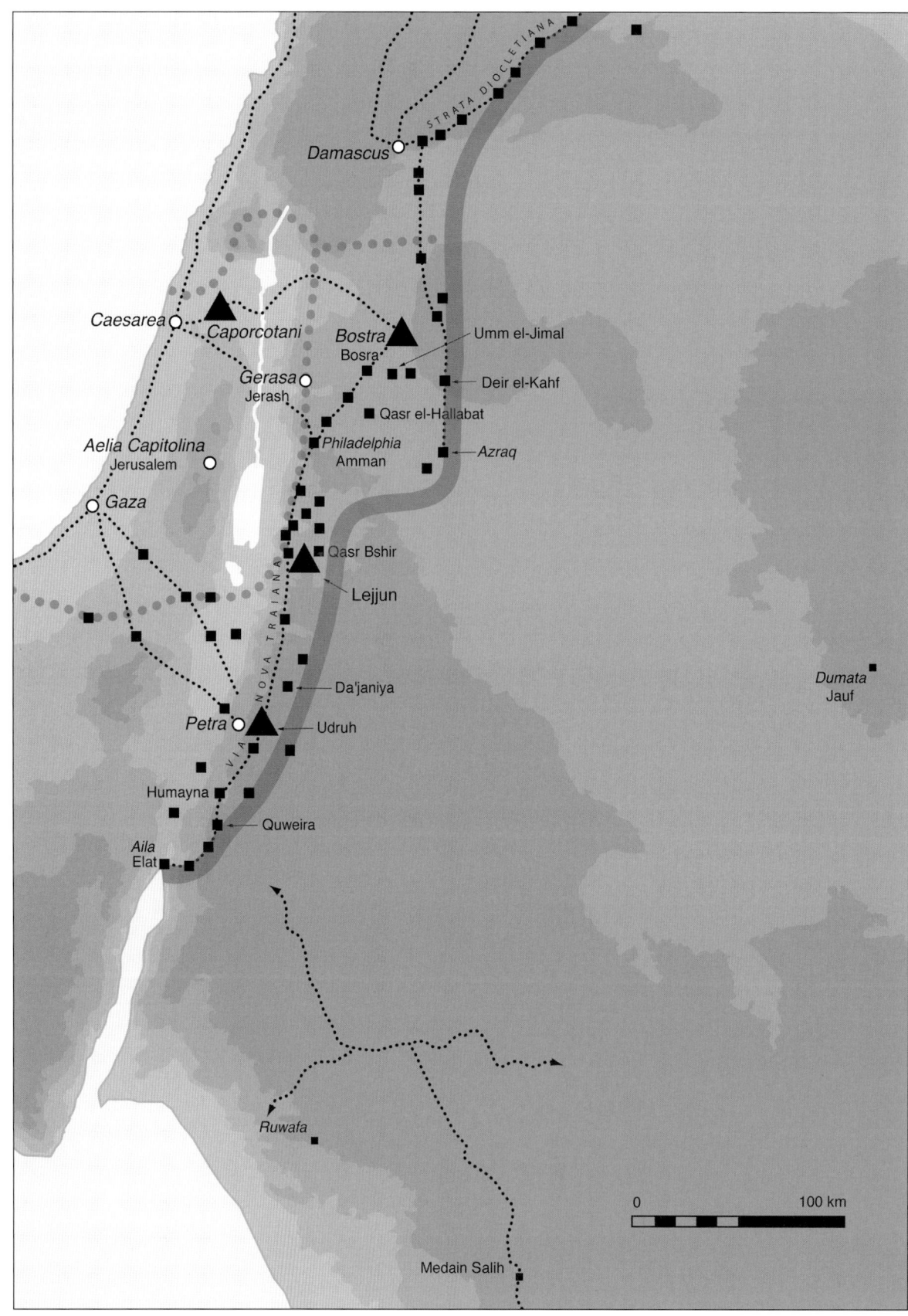

Figure 9.1: Map of the Limes Arabicus showing the location of some of the key sites in the region. Source: Culture 2000 Project

between the desert and the sown, defined by the 200mm rain isojet (as occurs in the south). Instead they were built further to the east, away from cultivable land, and in the only places where water was available, means that these forts along the *Strata Diocletiana* were not only the primary settlements in those places, but also the only ones until the end of the Umayyad period (Konrad 2008, 435).

This situation on the southern section of the *limes Arabicus*, established after the annexation of the Nabatean kingdom in the 2nd century AD, was different. This featured vast tracts of desert that acted as a natural buffer zone, creating an apparently ideal "*no-man's-land*". This "desert", though, was not a depopulated area, and thus not a true "*no-man's-land*"; the Arab population inhabiting its fringes had a strong semi-nomadic pastoralist cultural tradition, and they had mastered the art of caravan-trading across the desert. These travel and trading capabilities gave rise in some cases to wealthy and prosperous kingdoms, such as the Nabatean one, or to emporium-cities like Palmyra. Such wealthy states would eventually be annexed by Rome as part of their attempt to wrest control of the trade with Persia, and beyond, and *Arabia Felix*, which until then was controlled by the Palmyreans and the Nabateans respectively.

Many tribes of "Saracens", however, lived a more traditional pastoralist lifestyle, combining animal husbandry and trade with pillage in difficult times. This created a complex symbiosis with settled urban and peasant populations who lived in neighboring areas, blessed with either water brought by irrigation systems or by minimum annual precipitation of 200mm. A secondary use of the *limes Arabicus*, therefore, was to protect settled populations living in major cities, towns, and, overwhelmingly, agricultural villages within these deeply Hellenized provinces, from raids in moments of crisis or famine by the tribes that lived in the *limitrophe*, the area proximal to the frontier (Ammianus 14, 4, 1; 23, 3, 8). This depicts a deeply divided society, with two groups living side-by-side, but not mingling, and observing two very different lifestyles. The result is two contiguous Cultural Landscapes, a situation that deserves more in-depth analysis, as we will see.

Clear attempts to settle elements of those pastoral groups had already been carried out by the Nabatean Kings. Indeed, this socio-cultural and territorial framework had apparently forced the Nabateans, who controlled the deserted fringes of the former kingdom of Edom, to establish a network of stations to secure their trade routes against looters, and settle populations in key locations. These sites were later reused by the Romans, when they established their new military infrastructure (like Hawara, Avdat, etc). This process of sedentarization could be reflected by the contrasting descriptions of the Nabateans given in the 1st century AD by Strabo (16.4.26), and in the 4th century AD by Hieronymos of Kardia (Diodorus 19.94.2–10; see also Olesson 2001, 571). These testify to the Nabateans shifting from nomadic pastoralism to sedentarism. Hawara provides an early example of this apparently induced process.

The Limes Arabicus *and the* Double Frontier *Interpretation Model*

The peculiar situation described above derives from the fact that the stretch of land where the *limes Arabicus* stood was not only the political border between two mighty empires, but also the area where a socio-political and cultural "internal border" had existed for centuries, if not millennia, between settled populations or "*Fellahin*" living in towns and villages devoted to agriculture, and the semi-nomadic pastoralists inhabiting the semi-deserted steppe known as the "*Badiya*" (this term relates to "bdw", *bedu*, Bedouin). This is a border area between the desert and the sown, which corresponds with the *limitrophe*, where nomadic groups would have interacted with settled populations living in cultivated areas since prehistory. New Arab tribes also regularly migrated towards this area from Yemen and the Hijaz, joining groups that had inhabited these steppe zones from the 6th millennium BC. The interaction of these new waves of Arab tribes, especially the migrations that occurred from the 4th century AD onwards, with the "dual" society that they found in the Levant, which was already "split" between *fellahin* and *bedouin*, and the patterns of social relationship they developed, are essential to understanding the late antique socio-political and military contexts during the last phases of Roman / Byzantine activity in the region. While the Arab tribers were new to the area, it should be remembered that efforts to control various groups of *bedouin* had been made by *fellahin* since the prehistoric era, and that even when the practice of sedentarization was successful it was not irreversible.

The existence of this "double and superimposed frontier" is also key to understanding the final stages of the defensive strategies and ultimate collapse of both the *limes* and this portion of the Roman Empire itself. An interpretational model explaining the range of consequences of this frontier is provided here, which can be labeled the *Double Frontier Model* (Arce 2012). It derives from (and allows) a "*longue duree*" diachronic interpretation of the evolution of these societies throughout Antiquity and down to the modern period. This paradigm recognises the continuity of the social division defined by this "socio-cultural frontier", between peasants and pastoralists, between urbanites and semi-nomads, and their respective *cultural landscapes,* which coincides geographically with the political and military frontier, i.e.: the *limes Arabicus*. This "socio-cultural frontier" still exists today in Jordanian society; as such, this interpretative model is valid for understanding the dynamics of the evolution of society and major political events in the region in recent times.

This model explains four aspects of the region in late antiquity: the effects of the change of Byzantine defensive strategy, the adaptation and re-occupation of abandoned forts as monasteries and palatial venues by the Ghassanids or Jafnids, the later reoccupation of the same sites by the Umayyads, and the proliferation of fortified monasteries along the *limitrophe* as defensive and logistic bastions of the new political and religious agenda of the Ghassanids.

The evolution of the southern section of the limes Arabicus

After the annexation of the Nabatean kingdom, the need for defensive and logistic infrastructure within this territory was addressed by the construction of both the *Via Nova Traiana* (between AD 111 and 114), running from Bosra to Aila (Aqaba), and a series of military installations to the east, which constituted the southern stretch of the *limes Arabicus*. As in the northern stretch, the defensive strategy relied not on a continuous *vallum*, but on forts and legionary fortresses that were visually linked – in many occasions via small intermediate watchtowers – and usually connected by roads. These forts and fortresses were strategically located at important crossroads or beside water sources, and hosted garrisons ranging from small detachments through to complete legions, which were mobilized according to the scale of the menace.

The main difference to the northern stretch is that the southern defensive chain occupies the eastern edge of the area suitable for farming. This arrangement was well suited to protect the agricultural zone to the west, as well as to project force into the desert to the east (Parker 2006, 114). The border works were intended to defend the settled territories to the west of the *limes* from both Persian attacks and raids by pastoralists who periodically ravaged the villages and towns under direct Roman control. Reuse of pre-existing roads, such as the King's Highway that became the *Via Nova Traiana*, and many forts and structures from the Iron Age and Nabatean period, which were incorporated in this chain of military structures, provide proof of the existence of a border (or borders) in this region for centuries before the arrival of Rome. As we have seen, these fortifications were not just a product of political expediency, but overwhelmingly motivated by the peculiar socio-economic and environmental context of the region.

Building activity remained vigorously under Septimius Severus, when a road was built to Azraq in AD 208/210 and additional military structures were added to the *limes Arabicus*. We can demonstrate that a major effort was made during this period to control and block access through the wadi Sirhan, which acted as the main conduit linking Iraq and the Persian Gulf to *Provincia Arabia* and Syria. The ensuing network of forts and roads established between the *Via Nova* and Azraq form the core of the analysis presented here. Most of the structures created during the 2nd and 3rd centuries AD were carefully built using *opus quadratum* masonry (in limestone or basalt), combining precise jointing with intermediate-size ashlars (Arce 2010). In most cases, the forts were small- to medium-sized square installations without towers, as exemplified by Hallabat and Deir el-Kahf.

The 3rd century AD brought major political changes and significant instability for *Oriens*. The new Sassanian kingdom that defeated and succeeded the Parthian one in AD 224 heralded a renewed Persian threat for Rome. The disastrous wars against Shapur I led to the sacking of Antioch in 253, the destruction of many cities and forts, and, in AD 260, the defeat and capture of Emperor Valerian. In the aftermath Odenathus of Palmyra sought revenge, taking over the defense of the region on Rome's behalf. This initiative soon degenerated into Zenobia's attempt to carve out a Palmyrean Empire of her own, an ambition that Aurelian brought to an end.

By the end of the century Diocletian's Tetrarchy was providing much needed stability and security, especially in the Levant. Diocletian bolstered the frontier defenses and introduced major political and administrative reforms, partitioning *Provincia Arabia* and transferring its southern portion to *Provincia Palestina*. Later in the 4th century AD the area to the south of Wadi Hasa was split off to become *Palestina Tertia*, perhaps creating the *limes Palestina* (Parker 1986, 6). Awareness of the increasing threat posed by Persian armies resulted in the *limes Arabicus* receiving attention throughout the Tetrarchic period, even after the victory of co-emperor Galerius over the Sassanians in AD 297. This prompted the rapid construction of several new military installations, particularly legionary fortresses and *quadriburgia* housing cavalry units, and the refurbishment of several forts built in preceding centuries. The rough building techniques employed, especially among the new *quadriburgia* founded at this time, bear witness to both the pressing need and the speed of construction (Arce 2010).

The Saracen threat grew during the 4th century, as increased cooperation between tribes led to the establishment of confederations, and rulers who were more than tribal chiefs. Indeed, during the reign of Valens (364–378), Mavia, "Queen of the Saracens", attacked the *limes* and the lands of Palestine and Arabia. This created a new scenario in which the chance – and need – to negotiate alliances between Rome and these "confederations of tribes" by means of a policy of clientelism commenced. It represents a transitional moment when these groups started to play a new political and military role in the region.

The 4th and 5th centuries AD saw the incorporation of Arab tribes into the armies of both rival empires, as well as a shift towards a new mode of warfare, in which heavy armored cavalry gave way to light cavalry units capable of greater mobility. The increasing use by the Persians of mobile Arab troops from the *Lakhmid* tribes based at

Hira (near present-day Kufa) therefore posed a new risk to the Roman provinces of *Oriens* from the 4th century AD onwards (Arce 2010, 2012). To counter this threat, the existing Roman strategy of static defense was radically transformed. The regular soldiers garrisoning the *limes* forts were withdrawn, and a *foedus* with Christian Arab tribes, firstly with the Tanoukh, later the Salih, and finally with the Ghassanid / Jafnids (Shahid 2002), was established.

Consequences of the new frontier defence strategy under Justinian

The military reorganization of the frontiers of the Byzantine Empire conducted primarily under Justinian had a direct impact on the *limes Orientalis*. It involved the diocese of *Oriens*, and the Armenian provinces of the diocese of *Pontus*. The *limes Orientalis* was divided into two major sectors, Armenian and Arab. The first, running from the Black Sea to the Euphrates, was put under the control of Sittas as *magister militum per Armeniam*. In the southern sector – the *limes Arabicus* – Justinian placed as many tribes as possible under the command of Arethas ibn Jabala, who ruled over the Arabs, bestowing on him the dignity of king (Shahid 2002, 21). In each case the intention was to unify the command of all the territories and military forces of the respective circumscriptions under a single officer in order to optimize resources and guarantee maximum efficiency against increasing military threats.

Justinian's shift in the defensive strategies of the *limes Orientalis* in the 6th century also resulted in the dismissal of the *limitanei*, following the assignment of Christian Arab tribes to the defense of the *limes*. The mobile character of the new army did not rely on garrisons and forts, but on strategically-located, seasonal encampments (*hira* or *hirta*). In some cases, these were the same places where the Romans had built their installations, which were in many instances transformed into monasteries and palatial venues, thus playing a complex role as a focus for religious proselytism and political propaganda concurrent with providing logistic support for the defensive strategic system. But this also meant a subversion in the social structure of the region, as those groups that had previously been seen as a potential threat were now empowered and entrusted with the defence of the frontier.

The mistrust of the urban and settled populations of the countryside of Arabia, Syria and Palestine, towards these new defenders was deep-rooted, and they did not welcome this change to the *status quo*. In addition, the Ghassanids started to develop an exclusive political and religious agenda, according to their new role as "*archiphylarchs* of all the Arabs" and patrons of the Monophysite Church. This policy eventually became a source of conflict with Byzantium. The Ghassanids / Jafnids were aware of this, and used the abandoned forts as not only logistic bases for their mobile army, but also theatres for this policy of political clientelism and religious proselytism among the other tribes of the region, which were growing in power and influence. Ultimately this led to open conflict, the suspension of the *foedus*, and even attacks against the areas the Ghassanids were supposed to defend.

II. Physical transformation and change of use of Roman Forts in the area to the west of Azraq Oasis

Detailed case studies of forts presented here illustrate the changes effected to their fabric over time, and the implications of these for Roman defensive strategy. Identifying the nature of these transformations is essential to understanding the changes in the *limes Arabicus* and the underlying defensive strategy throughout the period of study.

Qasr el-Azraq is the key fort in our area and a special case of transformation. At this site, an old-fashioned "playing-card" shaped fort (typical of the Principate) was replaced by a *quadriburgium* covering 70 × 70 m. This was equipped with intermediate towers and built ex-novo (Kennedy 2000, fig. 7.2). No element from the previous fort was reused in the new construction, as occurred at other sites discussed below. The new fort was more compact than its predecessor, but probably housed a garrison of equal size due to the paramount strategic importance of the site at the mouth of *wadi* Sirhan.

Qasr al-Hallabat

Qasr Hallabat is situated on a hill with commanding views. It controls the surrounding terrain and in particular a road that runs eastwards and links Hallabat with Azraq, from where the so-called "*Strata Severiana*" leads towards Deir el-Kahf and Imthan in the north. This branch road runs from Khirbet el-Khaw, and before that Zarqa (and/or from Khirbet es-Samra), where it joins with the *Via Nova Traiana*.

The complete excavation and analysis of Qasr al-Hallabat (Arce 2008) has allowed a thorough understanding of the pattern of transformation presented in this paper (Fig. 9.2). It provides a template for a series of similar forts, which underwent comparable evolution in terms of both physical transformation and change of use. These include Deir el-Kahf, Khirbet el-Khaw, and probably Umm al-Jimal and Khirbet es-Samra (discussed below).

According to this model, the first Roman forts, originally built without turrets in the Severan period, were enlarged during the Tertrarchic period and transformed into *quadriburgia* (see Fig 9.3). After their abandonment, most of these *quadriburgia* became monasteries, and a church was founded within the walled precinct. In some cases, as at Hallabat, a palace was established, with reception halls

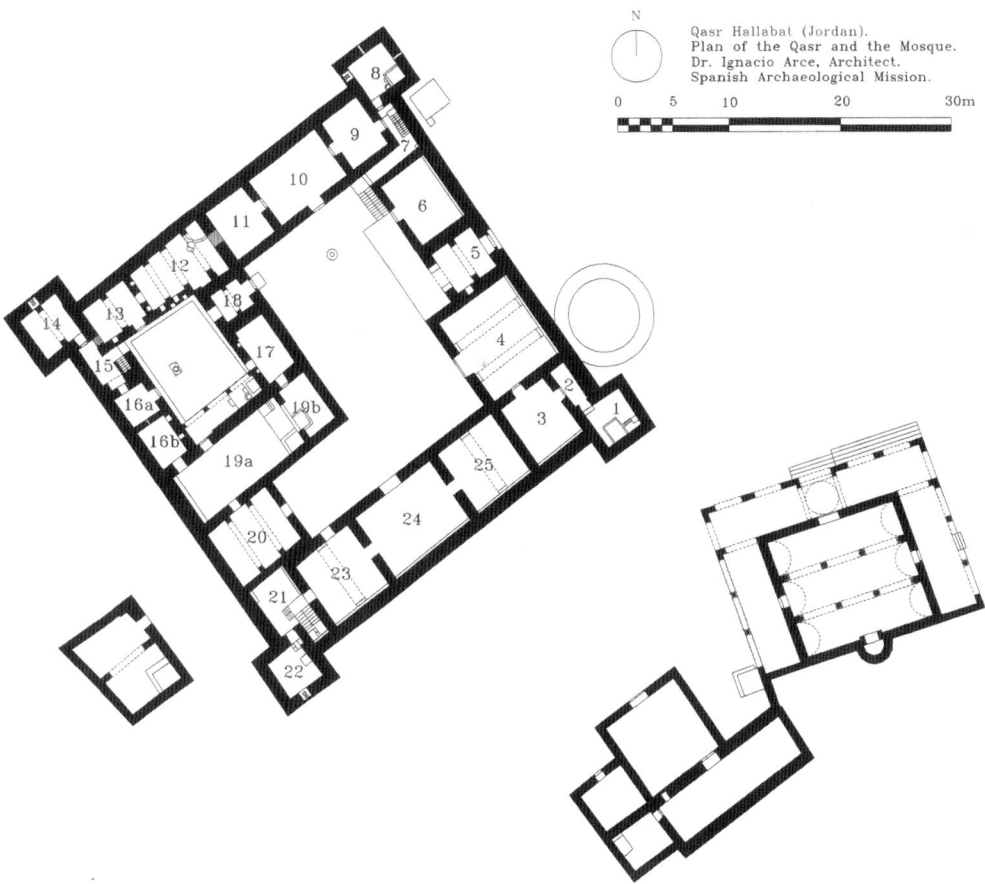

Figure 9.2: A plan of Qasr al-Hallabat. Source: Arce 2008

suitable for the clientele policy of the Ghassanid *phylarchs*. In many cases the *vici* became the nuclei of agricultural settlements that fed the forts and later the monasteries; in some instances, the *vici* were the origin of important new urban developments, as at Umm al-Jimal, Kh. es-Samra, Kh. el-Khaw, and Umm ar-Rassas.

At Hallabat, the earliest, Severan, fort measured 17.5 × 17.5 m (equating to rooms 12 to 18 on the plan), and was probably founded atop a Nabatean station or settlement, as indicated by several inscriptions found in the area, including a tombstone. The Tetrarchic enlargement incorporated the Severan fort by extending it from two sides to create a *quadriburgium* covering 38 × 38 m. This featured projecting towers, including one inserted in the corner of the original fort. Following its abandonment in the 5th century, Hallabat was badly damaged by an earthquake in 551. The site was then occupied by the Ghassanids. They rebuilt the fort following the pre-existing Tetrarchic *quadriburgium* plan, in some cases from the foundations, utilizing a distinctive building technique, but also transforming it into a palace and monastery.

The monastery at Hallabat was inserted within the former Severan fort (rooms 12 to 18), and the *katholicon*, or chapel of the monastery, was located in an early extension (room 19) of the first fort. The palatial component of the compound was established within the perimeter of the Tetrarchic installation. Both monastic and palatial components were connected through room 20, which acted as a kind of filter between these areas. A door with a very low lintel, similar to the "door of humility" at the Nativity church and other sanctuaries, allowed access to the church from room 20. In the 7th century, after the monastery had been abandoned, perhaps due to Persian invasion; the Umayyads transformed it into a fortified palace (*qasr*).

Deir el-Kahf

Deir el-Kahf is located on the "*Strata Severiana*" that runs from Imthan southwards to Azraq. The site occupies the crossroads of the "*Strata Severiana*" and the *via militaris* that originates from the *Via Nova Traiana* at Qasr el-Ba'ij. This secondary branch road, which continues eastwards to Deir el-Qinn, belongs to a network of roads and forts linking a series of forward positions designed to project power deep into the desert, and control access towards the core of *Provincia Arabia* and Palestine from Wadi Sirhan.

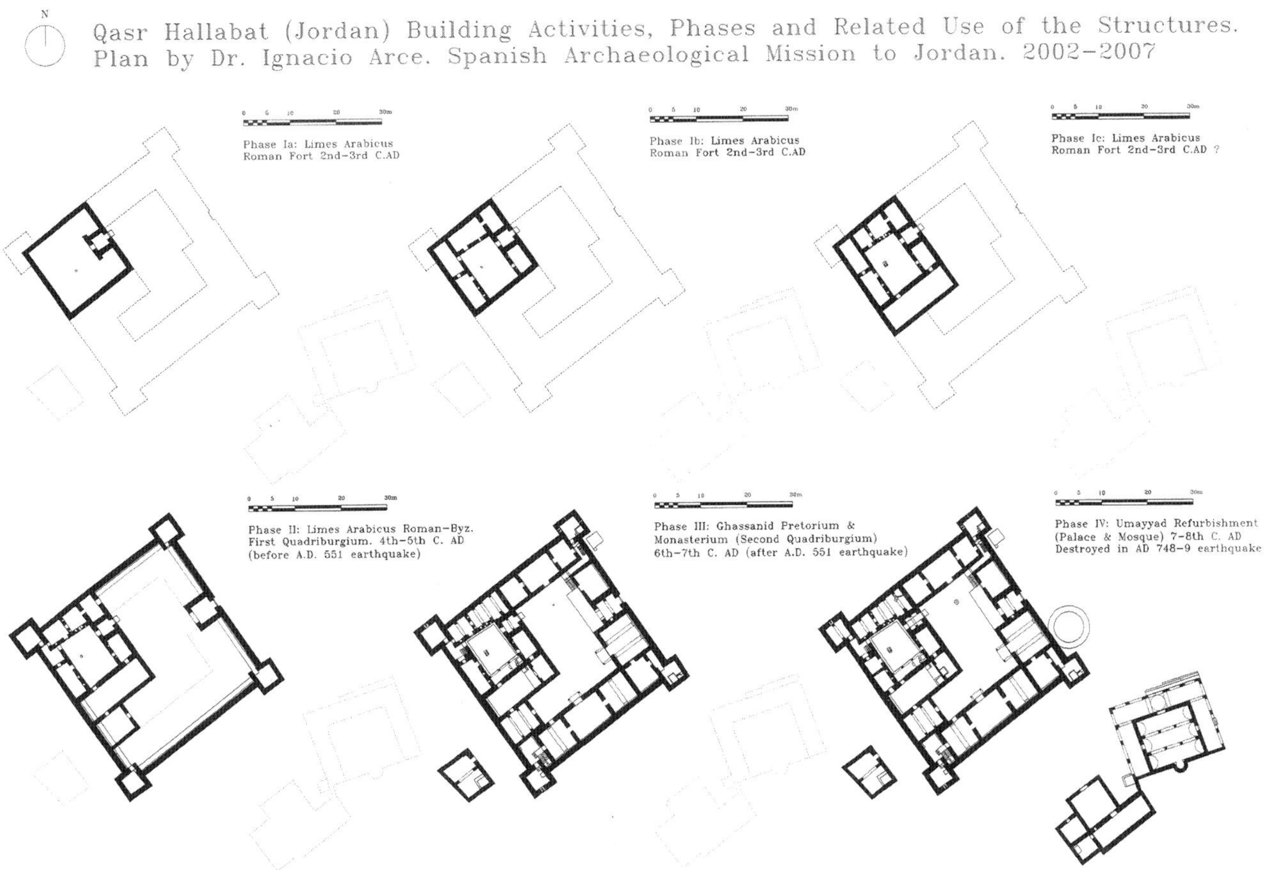

Figure 9.3: Qasr al-Hallabat Sequence of the evolution of the complex from Severan to Umayyad periods

Excavation and stratigraphic analysis of the different structures and building phases (and of their relative building techniques) conducted at Deir el-Kahf, have provided information about its origin and evolution (Fig. 9.4; Arce In Press; 2010). Deir el-Kahf undergoes almost exactly the same process of physical transformation and change of use from the 3rd century through to the 8th century AD as Hallabat. Even the formal configuration and phases of transformation of these structures are very similar. Deviations from the standard plan expected from the *quadriburgium* type at Deir El-Kahf, including an intermediate tower and a pair of towers flanking the entrance being missing, while an additional tower projected from the installation's south-east corner (Fig. 9.4) prompted the research. Excavation confirmed that a standard transformation pattern of Severan forts into Tetrarchic *quadriburgia* should be observable at many sites in the area between the *Via Nova Traiana* and the "*Strata Diocletiana*". At Deir el-Kahf, four phases were identifiable.

First Phase: A square fort covering *c.* 28 × 28 m, with no towers and finely built basalt walls 0.9 m thick and displaying thin, tight joints, was built in the Severan period, in conjunction with the construction of a new road between Azraq and Imthan.

Second Phase: In the Tetrarchic period, the fort was incorporated within a larger installation that extended to the north and west. Where the walls of the first fort were embedded in the new perimeter wall, the upper courses were dismantled, while the remainder was thickened internally to a width of 1.65 m. The upper courses were then reinstated. Roughly hewn blocks of basalt were employed in this phase, together, in places, with blocks recycled from the previous fort. A protruding joint of lime mortar, similar to that found at Hallabat and Bshir, was used for the jointing. This effort was expended on transforming the original square fort into a *quadriburgium* with intermediate towers and a footprint of *c.* 60 × 60 m. This enlargement generated the irregularities identified in plan.

Third Phase: In the mid-6th century the fort was abandoned by the Roman army. It was reused by a monastic community that occupied a portion of it, and built a chapel to service their ritual needs. It is uncertain what happened to the remainder of the fort buildings, but their use as stores or as temporary encampment and logistic base of Ghassanid *foederati* troops can be hypothesized.

Fourth Phase: The monastery was abandoned prior to the compound being re-used in the Umayyad period. The

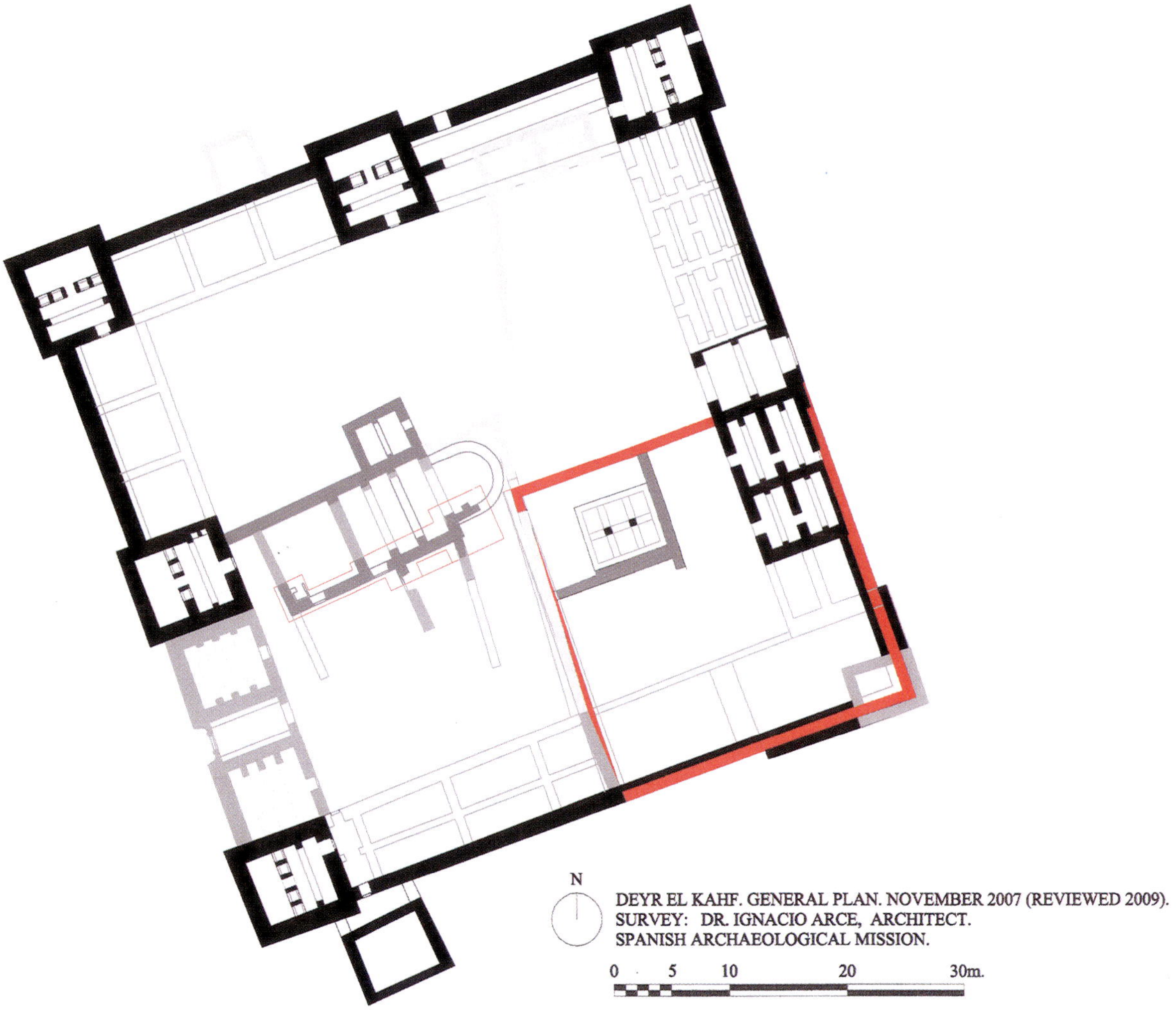

Figure 9.4: Deir el Kahf, plan. Source: Arce In Press b; Arce 2010

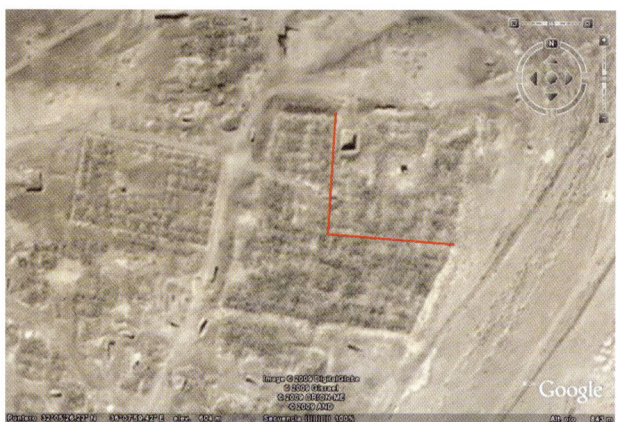

Figure 9.5: Khirbet el-Khaw. A satellite image (Google Earth) with the superimposed line outlining the hypothesized original Severan fort that was embedded within the Tetrarchic quadriburgium. Note the shap of the plateau on which it was built (visible in the lower-right corner), which forced the new extension to adopt a distorted plan.

site's new role is unclear, but it probably served as part of an agricultural estate. Lime kilns and basins found within the remains of the church could correspond to its final use as an industrial or agricultural building. Alternatively, if the lime kilns and other infrastructure were only temporary installations for the purpose of refurbishment, then the final use remains uncertain. Extensive field systems in the hinterland and the remains of an unexcavated *vicus* also mirror developments identified at other sites.

Khirbet el-Khaw

Located on the road which links Hallabat to the now completely destroyed fortress at Zarqa (located beside the *Via Nova Traiana* itself), Khirbet el-Khaw represents the third case of this very characteristic type series. It remains quite well preserved due to its location within the perimeter of a Jordanian Army camp.

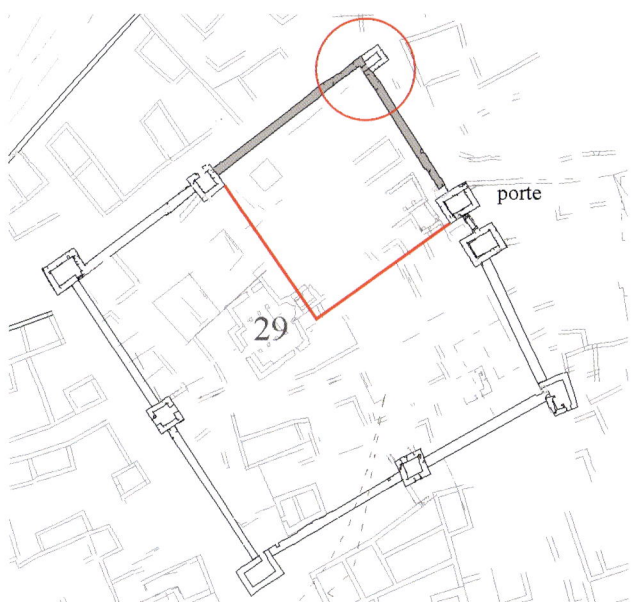

Figure 9.6: Khirbet es-Samra. A plan of the fort. Source: Desreumaux and Humbert 2003, Fig.1

Despite the impossibility of surveying or excavating the site, aerial and satellite imagery have enabled us to determine that this fort follows the same pattern of transformation as the previous ones (Fig. 9.5). The satellite photos clearly reveal an original square fort with a central courtyard, but no towers, embedded in the NE corner of the *quadriburgium*.

This first fort, presumed to be Severan on the basis of morphological similarities to Hallabat and Deir el-Kahf, measures approximately 57 × 57 m and is located at the edge of a rocky outcrop. This forces its Tetrarchic successor to adopt quite a distorted plan. As a consequence of the terrain the new installation's west wall does not align with the pre-existing one, instead it is rotated towards south-west. On the other hand, the extension of the north wall westwards is perfectly aligned with the pre-existing one. The south wall of the extension is roughly parallel to that of the first fort, while the new west wall is also tilted according to the orientation (towards the cardinal points) of the original fort. The ensuing *quadriburgium* has a quite irregular trapezoidal shaped plan, with sides 90 m in length, excepting the

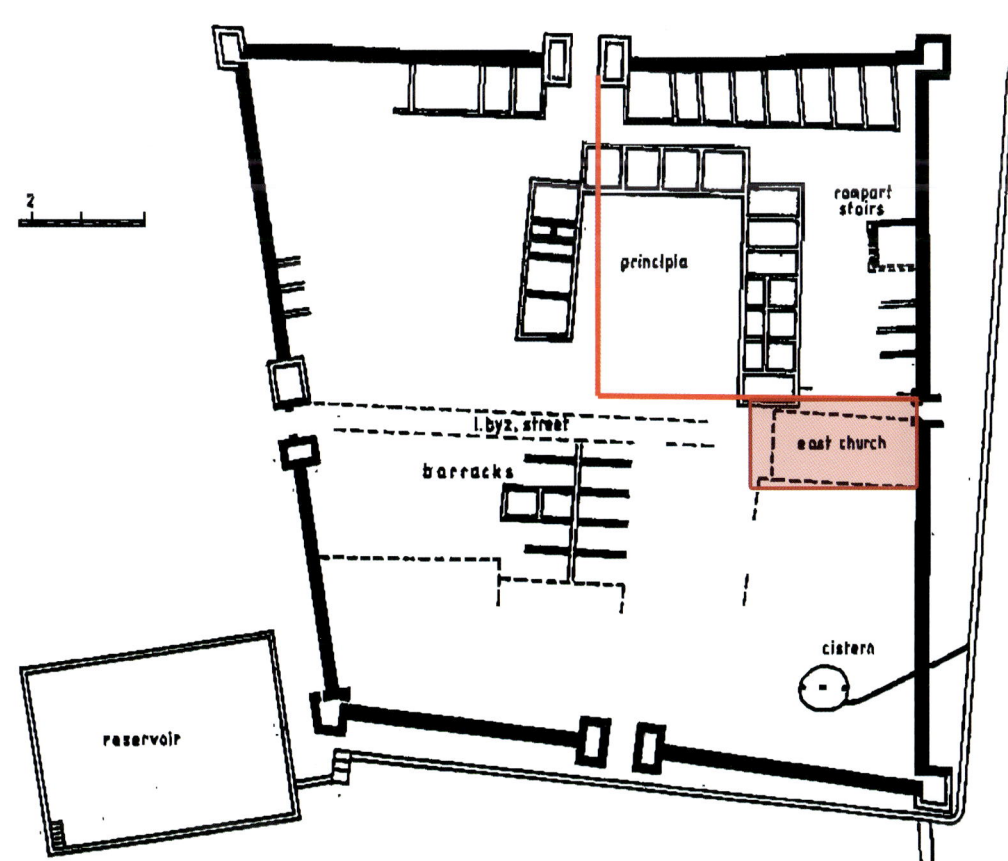

Figure 9.7: Umm al-Jimal. The castellum showing the outline of the hypothesized first fort and the location of the church ("East" Church) built within the walls. After de Vries 1993, Fig. 4

irregular east side, which is 57 + 47 m long. An entrance, flanked by two towers, is identifiable in the centre of the west wall. It faces another building, later in date, located to the west. Surrounding these two main buildings are several buildings belonging to the *vicus*, which do not follow any apparent grid system.

Khirbet es-Samra

The fourth candidate to become part of this series of *quadriburgia*, created by extending earlier Severan forts is Khirbet es-Samra. Located on the *Via Nova Traiana* almost midway between Philadelphia (Amman, 37 km south-southwest) and Bosra (48 km northeast), the *quadriburgium* measures approximately 60 × 65 m, and is surrounded by a partly walled town displaying an irregular layout similar to that at Umm al-Jimal. Once again, the lack of regularity of some *quadriburgium* walls, and other singularities in the plan suggest it originated as a square fort that was subsequently enlarged (Fig. 9.6).

The hypothetical first square fort, covering *c.* 28 × 28 m, lies in the north-east quarter of the Tetrarchic *quadriburgium*. The two stretches of curtain wall that meet here are orthogonal and free-standing, and not embedded into previous structures. The other stretches of curtain wall are less regular and incorporate previous structures within them (Gérard Thebault, pers. comm.). In addition, the north-east corner tower (encircled in Fig. 9.6) is much smaller than the others, and seems to have been added to a pre-existing structure represented by the two orthogonal curtain walls that join there and which may date to the 3rd century (G. Thebault, pers. comm.). The remaining three corner towers are larger, similar in size and plan, and seem to be bonded into the curtain walls, as part the Tetrarchic fort. An inscription from the fort (Gatier 1998, 381, no 64) was found reused in a church in the village of Kh.es-Samra. Dating to AD 367–375, this names the emperors Valentinian, Valens, and Gratian, who are also referred to in the (re)built military structures at Umm al-Jimal (*burgus* in 371) and Deir el-Kahf (*castellum* 367–375), which bear very similar dates (Kennedy 2000, 98).

In a later phase, a church (no. 29 in fig. 9.6) was erected inside the *quadriburgium* in the location where the *principia* would have been expected. Once again, this mirrors the pattern of transformation observed at Hallabat and Deir el-Kahf, especially as the dimensions of Khirbet es-Samra are almost identical to those of Deir el-Kahf.

Excavation carried out by the French Mission suggested building activity as early as the 2nd to 3rd centuries AD (Gérard Thebault, pers. comm.). The earlier fort's gate was replaced with a new one when the installation was extended in the 4th century AD (Kennedy 2000, 98; Gérard Thebault, pers. comm.). This gate was blocked in the 6th century, when the fort lost its military role and the church was constructed within. This dating and sequence corresponds precisely with those verified at Hallabat and Deir el-Kahf. Humbert considers it very likely that this church would have been part of a monastic complex built within the abandoned fort, and that in a later Umayyad phase the church was refurbished as an industrial workshop, when channels were cut into the choir floor (Desreumaux and Humbert 2003, 29–30). Industrial reuse of a church is paralleled at Deir el-Kahf.

Umm al-Jimal

The fifth case-study is the fort at Umm al-Jimal. It is located on the road that links the *Via Nova Traiana* with the "*Strata Severiana*", which runs from Qasr el Ba'ij until Deir el-Kahf. The installation at Umm al-Jimal was not identified until 1981 (De Vries 1993) and has only been partly excavated (Fig. 9.7). The irregularities in its plan provide the first indication that it underwent a similar process of transformation to that confirmed at Deir el Kahf, and suspected at Khirbet el-Khaw and Khirbet es Samra. The curtain at Umm al-Jimal forms an awkward trapezoid with sides between 95 m and 112 m long, of which only the north and east walls are orthogonal.

Following the model rehearsed above, the north-east corner of the *quadriburgium* – that is the only right-angled one – would have originally been built in Severan period, creating a square, primary fort occupying 42 × 42 m, which would have been enlarged under the tetrarchs. The exposed masonry in the north-east corner displays a very fine dressing and jointing, in contrast with the other areas exposed. This accords with the characterization of the respective building techniques used in these different and successive phases at other sites.

The suggested phasing is also supported by the irregularity of the east door, which is the only one without flanking towers. The orthogonal layout of the north and east walls of the *quadriburgium* would correspond to the aligned extension of the orthogonal walls of the pre-existing fort. The irregular layout of the south and west walls seems to be determined by pre-existing features in the local landscape, for example, a former quarry transformed into a cistern, with a channel feeding water into it (Arce 2014). The south and west walls are aligned with these pre-existing hydraulic elements.

After its abandonment by the army, Umm al-Jimal underwent changes in a sequence that, according to the accounts of the excavators, fits the pattern seen in the other case studies: a church and an "extensive domestic complex", maybe a monastery, was built in "the southeast quadrant, in which much of the fort masonry was reused" (Fig. 9.7; De Vries 1993, 435).

The wall surrounding the *vicus* / town was apparently built abutting against the south-east and north-east corner towers of the fort. An inscription of Marcus Aurelius and

Commodus (PES III. A.3: 131–132, N°232), which is now lost, was found near the town's west gate. Its proximity prompted Butler to assume that the inscription came from this entrance, and accordingly he dubbed it the "Commodus gate". The fact that this wall seems to be later than the fort, casts doubt on both the dating of this gateway and the origin of this inscription. Kennedy (2000, 82) suggests that the gate might have "belonged originally to some earlier structure", such as a 2nd-century fort. More likely is that the door was coeval to the late antique town wall, and the inscribed stone was simply reused as *spolia* in its construction, as occurred in many other places. The *burgus* inscription of AD 371 (PES III.A.3:131–132 no 233), for instance, was reused as a lintel in the 5th–6th century cathedral. It would not be surprising that an inscription from two centuries earlier, like the "Commodus" one, was reused in a secondary context. The risk of associating reused inscriptions with the actual construction history of a structure is real (see Arce 2008; 2009a; 2009b for the case of Hallabat and the Anastasius Edict inscription). The irregular "organic" urban planning of the *vicus* or town, consisting of clusters of houses enclosing shared, private courtyards, contrasts with the orthogonal *Hippodamian* layout of the *vici* from the Northern Syrian *limes*, such as those at Cholle and Tetrapyrgium (Konrad 2008, 434, figs. 5a and 8b), but is consistent with those found in our area of study.

Qasr el-Ba'ij

The *Via Nova Traiana* passes just 1 km west of Qasr el-Ba'ij. From here a linking road would have run east–west to connect the *Via Nova Traiana* with the *Strata Severiana*. This branch road would have run through Umm al-Quttein and Umm el-Jimal, until it reached Deir el-Kahf, where it joined the *Strata Severiana*. In all these sites we have found structures with the same sequence of transformation and change of use, except at Umm el-Quttein where the original structure, of which nothing remains, would be expected to exhibit a different typology and dimensions, and probably a Nabatean origin.

Gregory (1995–1997, 261–265) has already suggested that the fort of Qasr el-Ba'ij displays two building phases, a possibility rejected by Butler (PES II.A.2, 80–83; PES III.A.2, 42–44). The first fort would be a square structure without towers measuring about 15 × 15 m in size (Fig. 9.8), similar dimensions to those observed at Hallabat. It would have been surrounded on three of its sides by a new *quadriburgium* covering 38 × 38 m in plan, which makes it an identical size to the one at Hallabat. Qasr el-Ba'ij is, though, apparently devoid of corner towers projecting from the external line of the walls. As with most of the case studies presented here, it would have been transformed into a monastery with the inclusion of a church within its perimeter. Others structures (including a chapel) would have

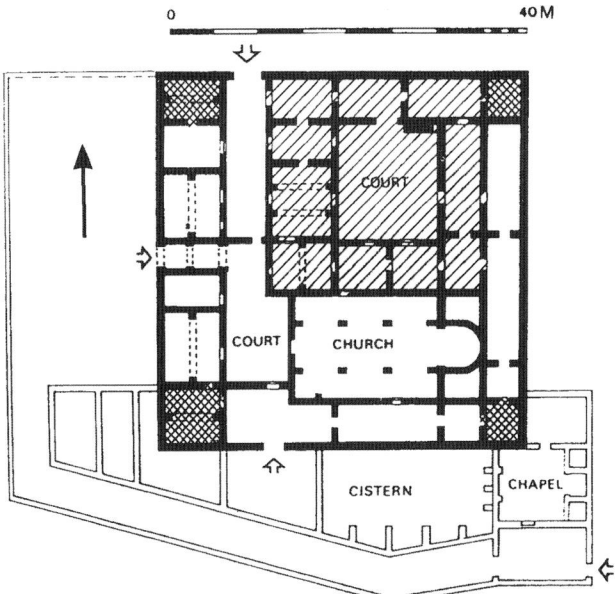

Figure 9.8: Qasr el-Ba'ij. Source: Gregory 1995-97, 3, Fig. 1.1a

been added afterwards in the extramural area. Regrettably the lack of excavation prevents confirmation of some of these suppositions. On the basis of the information gathered we can, though, elicit some relevant data, conclusions, and hypotheses that can be used as a basis for the continuation of our research.

Dimensions of the forts before and after enlargement

The forts created through this recurrent process of enlargement can be divided into three groups according to their size, with a modular sequence or dimensional series according to the dimensions of the original fort.

Firstly, small forts without towers, measuring *c.* 15 × 15 m or 17.5 × 17.5m, ultimately formed the nucleus of small to medium *quadriburgia* with an average footprint of 38 × 38 m, which were devoid of intermediate towers (Ba'ij and Hallabat). Secondly, medium-size forts without towers and measuring on average 28 × 28 m square, were enlarged into medium-size *quadriburgia* that were equipped with intermediate towers and had an average footprint of 60 × 60 m (Deir el-Kahf and Kh. es-Samra). Thirdly, medium to large size forts of 42 × 42 m or 57 × 57 m, most probably without corner towers, were transformed into large forts of *c.* 100 × 100 m. These feature intermediate towers and entrances flanked by a pair of towers (Umm al-Jimal and Kh. el-Khaw).

In general the largest sites present overt irregularities in plan, probably derived from the difficulties associated with reconciling such a substantial extension of the original existing fort with topographic irregularities or other pre-

Table 9.1: Small square forts without towers, which generate small to medium size quadriburgia

Enlarged Forts				Single-phase Forts		
	Site	Original dimensions	Enlarged dimensions		Site	Dimensions
Small square forts, no towers	Qasr el-Ba'ij	15 × 15 m	38 × 38 m	**Small**	Upper Zoar	18 × 18 m
	Qasr el-Hallabat	17.5 × 17.5 m	38 × 38 m		En Boqeq	20 × 20 m
Medium sized forts, no towers, enlarged with intermediate towers	Kh. Es-Samra	28 × 28 m or 30 × 30 m	60 × 65 m	**Small-Medium**	Bir Madkhur	32 × 34 m
					Mezad Tamar	38 × 38 m
	Deir el-Kahf	28 × 28 m	60 × 60 m		Gharandal	37 × 37 m
					Thuraiya	37.5 × 34.5 m
Medium & large forts without corner towers enlarged with intermediate towers	Khirbet el Khaw	57 × 57 m	94 × 104 m		Quweira	32.5 × 31.5 m (internal)
	Umm al-Jimal	42 × 42 m	95 × 112 m		Yotvata	39.7 × 39.4 m
					Khirbet ez-Zona	30 × 30 m or 40 × 42 m
				Medium-Large	Upper Muhattat el-Hajj (Karakun)	50 × 50 m
					Lower Muhattat el-Hajj	56 × 46 m
					Avdat (Citadel fort)	60 × 40 m
				Large	Azraq	79 × 72 m
					Dajaniya	100 × 100 m
					Avdat (low fort)	100 × 100 m

existing structures, such as water courses. These last forts are related somehow to the ones at Avdat and Dajaniya, which boast the same dimensions, but were clearly built in a single phase. We include for the sake of comparison with our series of "enlarged" forts, a list of *quadriburgia* that were the product of a single building phase. The former category attempts to emulate the standard dimensions of the latter.

Hypothesis on the reasons for this recurrent pattern of distribution in the Severan period and transformation / enlargement in the Tetrarchic period

All of the Severan forts enlarged in the Tetrarchic period are located on roads running east–west, which link the *Via Nova Traiana* with the *"Strata Severiana"* that runs from Azraq north towards Imthan through Deir el-Kahf (Fig. 9.1). This road has been hypothesized to be a southerly extension of the *Strata Diocletiana,* although the numerous Severan milestones found nearby provided a date and name for the road (Kennedy 2000, 64). Thus, the *"Strata Severiana"* predates the *Strata Diocletiana,* a conclusion supported by the dates of the primary forts erected along its course.

All of the known examples lie in the southern section of the *limes Arabicus,* within an area corresponding to the former Nabatean kingdom, and more precisely the region of the southern Hauran, where the route following the wadi Sirhan starts.

It is clear that this Severan network of roads and forts, which was probably based on a pre-existing network of Nabatean stations or forts, was effectively protecting passage to the Levant through wadi Sirhan from any potential threat, be it Saracens raiders or Persian armies.

It seems that most of the Severan structures built in the area between the two main Roman military roads were transformed into *quadriburgia* during the Tetrarchic period. This process of enlargement follows a standard pattern, and is explained by the need to cope with the renewed threats from across the desert. The *quadriburgia* were primarily intended to reinforce this pre-existing network of forts and secondary roads, which had proved very effective during the 3rd century, to further protect access from Wadi Sirhan through Azraq. The first secondary road ran from Zarqa and/or Kh. Es-Samra to Kh. El-Khaw, then Hallabat, before reaching Azraq where the *"Strata Severiana"* commenced. The next secondary road would also have run east–west, but lay further to the north, linking the *Via Nova Traiana* (from Qasr al-Ba'ij) with the "*Strata Severiana*" at Deir el-Kahf, passing through Umm el-Quttein and Umm al-Jimal, and eventually Deir el-Qinn.

Due to the importance of Wadi Sirhan as a major thoroughfare in Antiquity, access had to be firmly controlled. This area was also a communications hub, from which major roads provided access to the north, including Palmyra via the *Strata Diocletiana*, as well as to the area of the Decapolis and the coast, and to the south on the *Via Nova Traiana* to *Palestina Tertia* and then Egypt. This clearly illustrates the region's prime strategic value, and the importance of ensuring that its defenses did not fail.

In conjunction with the Tetrarchic expansion of the Severan forts, the entire region witnessed a major campaign of fort construction along the *limes Arabicus* from Aila on the Red Sea to Sura on the Euphrates. The *Via Diocletiana* was constructed to link the chain of forts forming the northern section of the *limes* (which as we have seen had been built *ex-nihilo*), which were in turn reinforced or rebuilt *a fundamentis*, or in some cases even built *ex-novo*.

In the southernmost section of the *limes Arabicus* (*Palestina Tertia*) the major intervention involves the construction of two legionary fortresses (Betthorus/Lejjun and Adroa/Udruh), which are related to this strategic defensive scheme. These were located on the *Via Nova*, allowing them to block any access southwards towards Aqaba, and the corridor to Egypt and the Mediterranean coast. This latter runs across the north Negev from Petra to Gaza, and the forts along it at Mampsis / Kurnub, Nessana / Nitzana and Oboda / Avdat were also reinforced.

Comparable enlargement has not been identified on the northern section of the *limes Arabicus*. Only at Resafa-Sergiopolis can we identify a case that appears somewhat similar, even though its origins, size, and the outcome of the transformation all differ. At Resafa, the original 1st-century Roman fort became a large walled city under Justinian as a result of its role as the main pilgrimage destination in the region. It owed this pre-eminence to its connection to the burial location of St. Sergius, an important local martyr discussed below (Konrad 2008, Fig.7a). At Sura I, on the Euphrates, the walled town annexed to the Roman fort was built in a way that resembles the manner in which the Severan forts were enlarged in Tetrarchic period (Konrad 2008, Fig. 2).

The transformation into monasteries as consequence of the changes in the defensive strategy of the limes Arabicus

The other feature common to all the cases studied is their apparent transformation into monasteries – in some cases with associated palatine venues – in the 6th century. This development is closely linked to changes in the defensive strategy of the *limes Arabicus* under Anastasius and Justinian.

As we have seen, analysis of the structures from Hallabat and Deir el-Kahf, and similar sites in the surrounding area, reveals the existence of a recurrent pattern of transformation of forts from the 3rd century through to the 8th. The enlargement of the Severan forts in the Tetrarchic period was prompted by the increasing threat posed by the Sassanian army. These forts were eventually abandoned, following the dismissal of the *limitanei* troops by Justinian, when the Ghassanids were charged with protecting the *limes*. These Arab Christian *foederati* transformed most of those abandoned forts into monasteries and palatial venues in line with their religious and political agendas. These changes were part of an overall rethinking of defensive strategy, replacing a static defensive system of forts and permanent garrisons with more mobile and autonomous army units.

These phases correspond to three main phases of the *limes Arabicus*. The first phase corresponds to the incorporation of *Oriens* into the Roman Empire in the first centuries AD. This phase witnessed the construction of the *Via Nova Traiana*, the "*Via Severiana*", and the first military structures associated with the *limes Arabicus*, which was designed to protect the region from the threat posed by the Persian army and the raids of the nomad pastoralists.

The second phase corresponds to the overhaul of this eastern *limes* and its defensive system by Diocletian in the Tetrarchic period. This is characterized by the rapid construction of numerous *quadriburgia*, intended mainly to host auxiliary cavalry units, and the refurbishment and expansion of structures erected during the first phase. The haste in their construction, in response to the increasing Persian threat, is reflected in the cruder building techniques and materials used in this period, such as roughly hewn blocks, in contrast with the finely squared ad dressed masonry of previous phases.

The third phase covers the period from the overhaul of the defenses by Justinian through to the demise of the *limes* under Heraclius. In this third phase, the Ghassanids were entrusted with the task of defending the *limes Arabicus*. During this phase the forts' role changed dramatically. They lost their previous military character and were transformed into monasteries, watch-posts, and even palaces, but retained their strategic significance due to their locations at crossroads and water sources. They acted as meeting points for the local pastoral population and travelers, merchants, and pilgrims. As they offered shelter and sustenance they were ideal places for performing both political clientele persuasion and religious proselytism. Such practices and locations were useful for the itinerant Ghassanids phylarchs, as attested in the works of Hamza al-Isfahani (Shahid 2002). This period also corresponds with the implementation of Justinian's ambitions for westward expansion and reunification of the Mediterranean. Such an agenda implied a will to achieve a stable truce and conciliation with the Sassanians in the East, something that materialized in the "endless peace" of 532 with

Khusraw I. This change of priorities took place after years of conflict with the Sassanians, as well as natural disasters including poor harvests, plagues, disease, and several earthquakes which marked the first half of the 6th century.

We can conclude that from the 6th century through to the 8th century many military structures on the *limes Arabicus* underwent a process of transformation and re-use that capitalized on their strategic location, which followed a recurrent pattern. The final aim in all cases, despite the different approaches, was to achieve effective control of the territory and the population that inhabited the *limitrophe* (Arce 2008; 2009a; 2009b). The setting where the Ghassanids deployed their palatine protocol and their patronage of the monastic institution, happened in many cases to be the same locations where the clientele policy carried out by the Umayyads with the Bedouin population of the *Badiya* would take place years later.

III. Roman Forts from the *limes Arabicus* transformed into Monasteries

The second major shift in the transformation of the forts of the *limes Arabicus* into monastic communities and palatine venues took place after their abandonment by the regular Roman army. This process has been confirmed at: Hallabat, Deir el-Kahf, Tetrapyrgium, Qasr el-Ba'ij, Khirbet es-Samra, Fudain-Mafraq, and Qasr el Hayr el-Gharbi.

The *basileia* (kingship) and the *archiphylarchia* conferred on Arethas in AD 529 as a result of the renewed *foedus* represented a major change in the political and military role played by the Ghassanid kings. This shift would determine future events, and illuminates the architectural changes that occurred at our sites. The previous *foedus* of AD 502 established by Anastasius with Jabala (Arethas' father), was more modest in political terms than the consecration of Arethas as "king" in the treaty of AD 529. This new eminence had important architectural implications, as the new "king" of the federate Arabs needed a sufficiently magnificent backdrop for his performance. The result was the palatial venue identified at Resafa (Al-Mundhir *pretorium*) and Hallabat. On the other hand, we know that the "building fever" of the Ghassanids (Shahid 2002) was linked to the promotion of Christian Monophysitism and the construction of monasteries, which could concurrently offer logistic support to their mobile army.

Monasteries as defensive elements

According to this scheme, monasteries played a key role as a defensive element of the *limitrophe*, once the *limitanei* of the regular Roman Army were replaced by the Ghassanid *foederati*. These fortified monasteries (and their towers) would act as vanguard watch posts that could alert nearby military stations and face an attack, acting as a *vigilarium* of the Roman Army would have done in the past.

Monasteries as socio-economic elements

The monasteries would have played an active role in socio-economic affairs that exceeded mere religious issues (Hull 2008). This would have made them a key element in the development and control of the peripheral areas where they were established. Hull's research, however, points out the difference between the isolated character of the monasteries of the Hauran or Jordan, and those of the Limestone Massif in northern Syria. He notes how striking it is that in the latter case many monasteries are located very close to areas of secular settlement. This image of "isolated monasticism" in our area of study does not, though, correspond to reality; instead it recalls the denounced *cliché* of the *limitrophe* as a deserted no-man's-land. Many of the monasteries in our study area acted as foci for sedentarization in the *limes*, with the development of associated settlements and related agricultural activities following in the footsteps of the pre-existing *vici* or even earlier Nabatean settlements.

Monasteries as pilgrimage stations

In the area of the northern section of the *limes Arabicus* close to the Euphrates, the transformation of forts into monasteries was strongly influenced by pilgrimage. This was due to the fact that the area of Sura-Tetrapyrgium-Resafa was the setting for the martyrdom and burial of St. Sergius, the soldier-saint, who became the devotional focus for all the populations living in the area, especially the Monophysite Ghassanids and the other Arab Christian tribes. We cannot underestimate the economic importance, together with the religious one, of this fact, and the possibility that the forts along the *Strata Diocletiana* could have been kept occupied by the *limitanei* to offer protection to pilgrims travelling these otherwise deserted and dangerous roads. We have to consider that from the 5th or 6th centuries until the 13th century a pilgrimage to the tomb of Saint Sergius at Resafa-Sergiopolis could have had a similar role and relevance among the population of this region to that played centuries later by the pilgrimage to the tomb of Saint-Jacques at Santiago de Compostela.

We can see also the influence of this culture of pilgrimage throughout the region, with an extension of the cult for relics, which was reinforced by the massacre of the Martyrs of Najran in Northern Yemen in the 6th century, when Christianity first took root in South Arabia. In many cases, these monasteries reinforced their importance as instruments of proselytism for conversion, with the added value offered by relics that became increasingly important from the 5th century onwards. The chance to attract pilgrims and become either a pilgrimage destination, or station, informed transformations at some of these former Roman forts. Resafa-

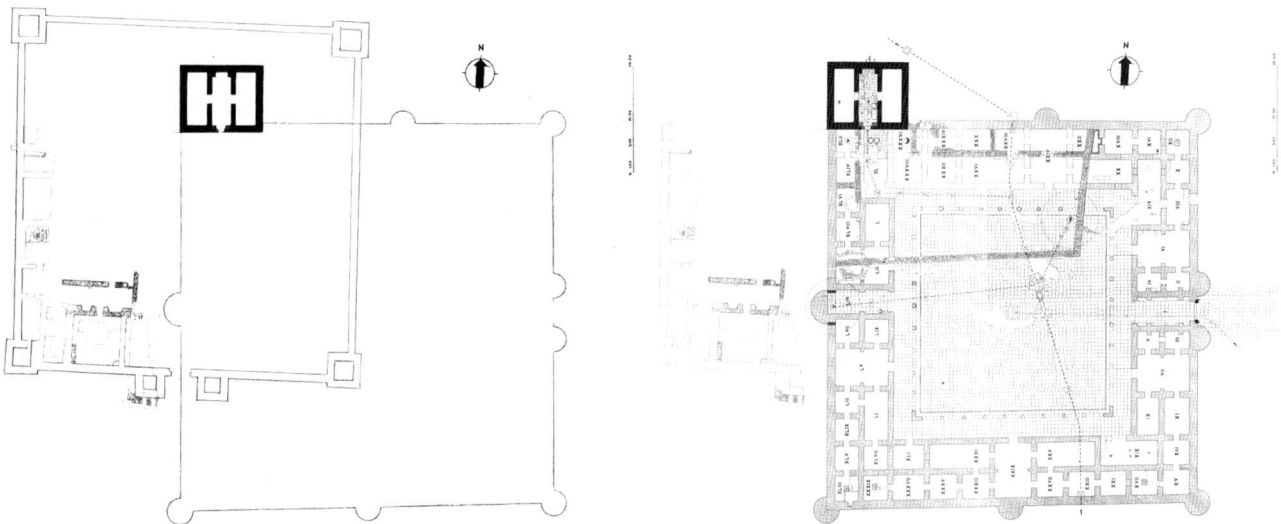

Figure 9.9: Qasr al-Hayr al Gharbi (Hauliaram). (a) Plan of the hypothetical quadriburgium, which would have been transformed into a monastery. Its security would have been reinforced by the addition of a 6th-century tower. (b) This tower would have been the only pre-existing structure reused by the Umayyads, who embedded it into the corner of the qasr built ex-novo, but not ex-nihilo by Caliph Hisham abd el-Malik. Source: drawn by the Author on the basis of the pre-Umayyad remains recorded by Schlumberger

Sergiopolis itself is the archetype of this transformation. Thus, most monasteries (and afterwards ordinary churches) competed for the possession of relics that guaranteed an influx of pilgrims, augmenting both the relevance of the community, and economic revenue. In addition, St Sergius was a Roman soldier who served at the Roman forts of Sura and Tetrapyrgium, and was martyred and buried in another one at Resafa. As such, any abandoned Roman fort would have been an ideal venue to establish a monastic community, especially given their privileged locations.

Fortified towers: A characteristic feature of late antique monastic settlements of the 5th and 6th centuries in the limitrophe

The role of monasteries, especially in the 6th century, as key logistic elements of the new defensive strategy, gave rise to the recurrent use of fortified towers. It could be argued that in some cases this proliferation of defensive elements was motivated by a local desire for self-defense against Saracen attacks, but it seems clear that a co-ordinated operation on a wider territorial scale, a strategy, was involved. The addition of fortified towers to pre-existing compounds can be detected at several sites:

Qasr al-Hayr al-Gharbi

In some cases the need to reinforce the existing defenses would lead to the addition of fortified towers. In many cases, as we have seen, the defences belonged to former Roman forts, which were in bad shape due to the poor quality of the building techniques employed, especially in the northern section where they were built with mud-bricks. This is well illustrated by the late antique compound at Qasr al-Hayr al-Gharbi in Syria (Fig. 9.9).

Excavators of the site in the 1930 produced a plan of the Umayyad palace (Schlumberger 1986), which incorporated a pre-existing tower built of well-dressed and finely jointed masonry that bears a dedicational inscription to the Ghassanid phylarch al-Harith ben Jabala-Arethas, who visited and funded it (Chabot 1907–1933, I, 233, II, 155). The plan also showed what seemed to be the remains of a *quadriburgium* that had been partially built over by the subsequent Umayyad palace. Surprisingly, no mention of this earlier, comparatively crudely constructed structure is made in the excavation report.

It is not clear what the stratigraphic relationship between this pre-Umayyad *quadriburgium* and the tower with the Ghassanid inscription is. Some typological characteristics, however, suggest that the tower was added to the pre-existing *quadriburgium* in the 6th century as part of a monastic complex. According to our interpretation of the sequence, after the *quadriburgium* was abandoned by the Roman army, it was refurbished and used as a monastery patronized by the Ghassanid *Phylarchs*. Adding the tower at this time would have reinforced the defences of the complex. After the site was annexed by the Umayyads, a new *qasr* was built, which incorporated the old tower due to the quality of its construction. The remainder of the fort was abandoned. This sequence of transformation and change of use is quite similar to the one identified at Hallabat, Deir el-Kahf, and Fudayn-Mafraq. The only difference is that in

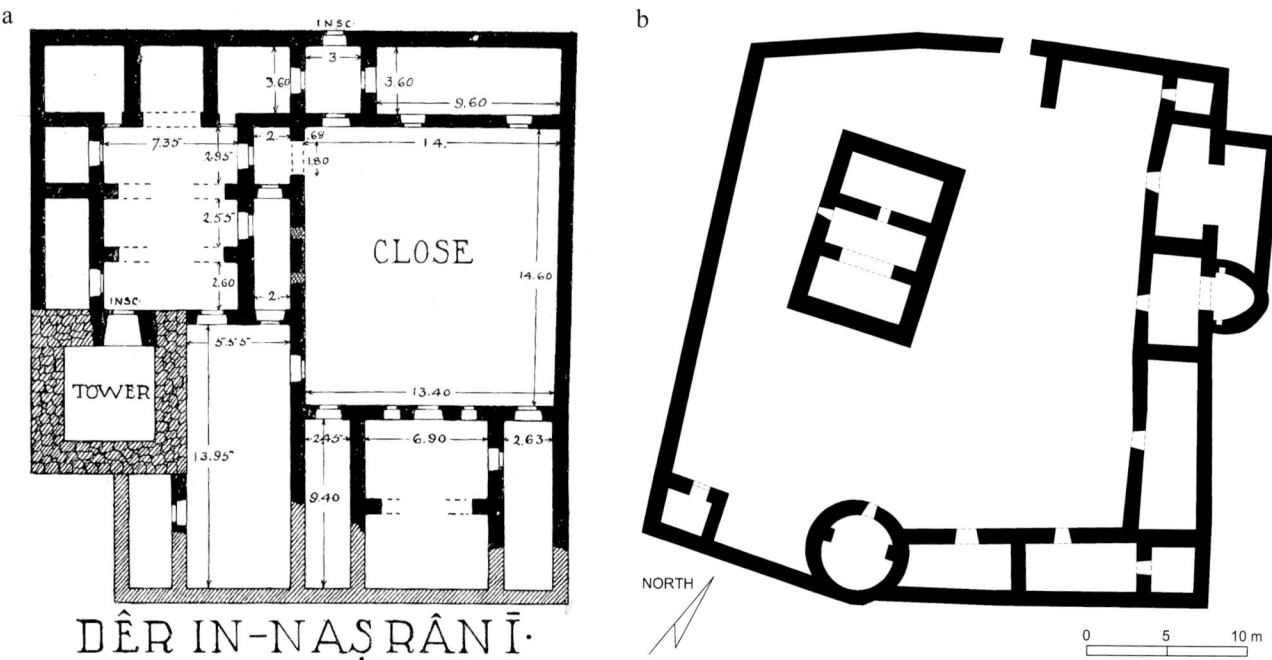

Figure 9.10: (a) Deir an-Nasrani; (b) Qasr Burqu. Source: Butler 1913

this case, the Roman fort was not reused in the Umayyad period, because of its poor state of preservation. According to our hypothesis, the original Roman fort would have had dimensions of 44 × 44 m, similar to those of the new Umayyad *qasr* (48 × 48 m)

The reuse of previous defensive towers as part of new monastic developments can be proposed at the following sites.

Deir an-Nasrani

The case of Deir an-Nasrani in the Hauran is a very peculiar one, as this monastic compound is built against and around a Nabatean tower perched atop an extinct volcano (Fig. 9.10). Recently a walled enclosure displaying a very irregular plan and ultra-semicircular towers was discovered at the foot of the mountain (although it has not been archaeologically verified on the field).

This structure might be a temporary Roman camp, related to the expedition of Septimius Severus against Saracen nomads in the beginning of his reign (SHA Sev. 9.9; 18.1). The monastery built around the Nabatean tower crowning the extinct volcano would belong to the 5th or 6th century, as the square apse is characteristic of the Monophisite / Jacobite Churches of this period.

Qasr Burqu

Another example of a monastic compound with a fortified tower built during late antiquity is provided by Qasr Burqu (Fig. 9.11). Burqu represents a special case, as this was not originally a Roman fort. It is most probably the result of an adaptation of a tower built by the Ghassanids to protect a permanent lake.

The location, over 200 km east of the *limes*, eliminates the possibility of it being part of the group of structures erected between the 2th and 4th centuries as part of the frontier system. The building technique used in the construction of the tower is identical to that dating to the second half of the 6th century at Qasr al-Hallabat. This offers a *terminus post-quem* for the complex, while the presence of an inscription naming the Umayyad Caliph Walid I in the monastic compound provides a clear *terminus ante quem* for the complex. Thus the tower and the monastic complex were probably built near-contemporaneously during the 6th century. This chronology, and the dual function of the compound as a monastic complex and a key logistic-defensive structure protecting a vital water source, recalls the aforementioned reuse of abandoned Roman forts by the Ghassanids as monasteries supporting logistical elements for their mobile army.

IV. The Birth of a New Building Type?

The sites and buildings under investigation in this section pose an interesting question. Does the recurrent sequence of transformation of former Roman military sites give rise to a new architectural type? The new phenomenon under consideration can be characterized as a fortified precinct

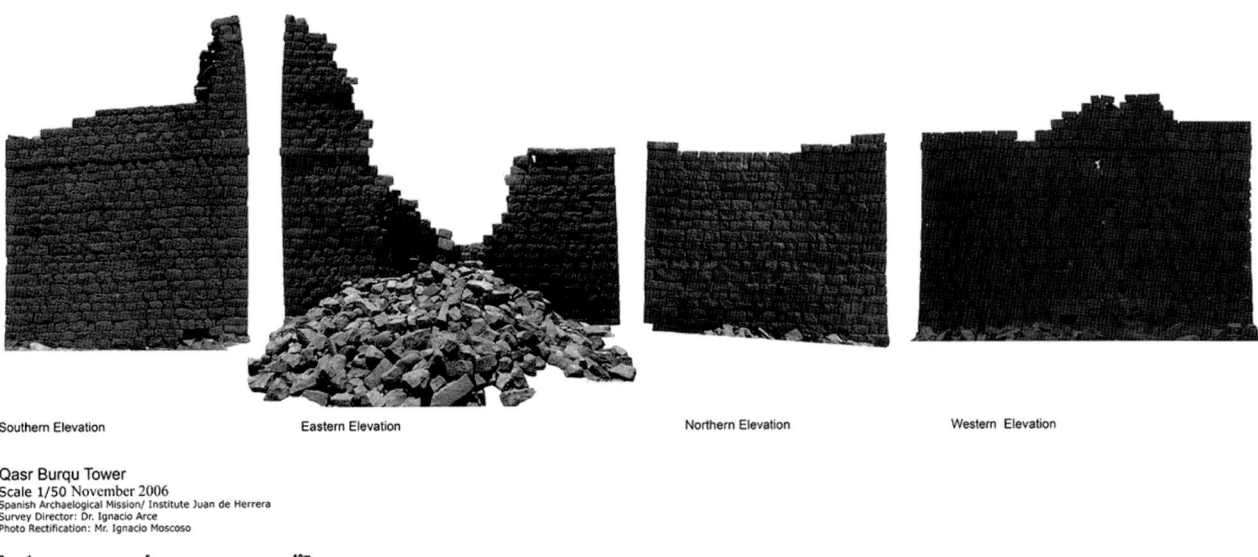

Figure 9.11: Qasr Burqu. Ortho-rectified elevations of the tower, which show a building technique that is identical to the one encountered in the Ghassanid-period remains at Hallabat

containing a civic or monastic complex with a basilica hall or church and / or a palace. Although complexes demonstrably occur at former Roman *quadriburgia* sites, they are also attested within other late antique compounds that may not have Roman military origins.

Among this latter group are the following sites: the fortified church and monastery of St. Mary Theotokos on Mount Gerizim at Nablus, the *castrum-lavra* of S. Catherine in the Sinai, the complexes of Khirbat al-Kerak besides Lake Tiberias, which was recently identified as Sinabbra by D. Whitcomb, the *Kastrum* of Androna /el-Anderin, and the so-called "barracks" at Qasr Ibn-Wardan. Some of these offer stratified sequences of partial and / or complete structures where a similar sequence of transformation and change of use can be identified. Former Roman military structures were abandoned and reused as monastic or palatial venues in the 6th and 7th century, as at Kh. al-Kerak (Fig. 9.14). In other cases, such as St. Catherine (Fig. 9.13), documents testify to a combined role as monastery and *castrum*, complete with garrison. Elsewhere the sequence is unclear, for example at Mt. Gerizim. The lack of modern stratigraphic analysis of these structures and their deposits prohibits clear conclusions.

This pattern should not be confused with the construction of churches within the walled *temenos* precinct of former pagan temples in major urban centers, including Damascus, Baalbek and, apparently, Palmyra. In these cases, the final aim was not to establish monastic compounds, but to build Christian temples, usually a cathedral, on top of previous pagan shrines as part of a process of religious conversion and cultural assimilation. The church of St Mary on Mt. Gerizim is the only example within our study area that may be related eventually to this type of activity (Fig. 9.12).

The complex on Mount Gerizim consists of an octagonal church within a fortified walled precinct with corner towers and a doorway measuring 70 × 54 m. This design evokes that of a Tetrarchic *quadriburgium* (*SWP Vol. 2* pp. 188–189). According to Procopius of Cesarea, construction of the church started under Zeno in AD 484, which triggered the Samaritan revolt in 529 (*SWP Vol. 2* pp. 188–189). Justinian may have been responsible for the external fortifications that resemble a *quadriburgium*.

The existence of a later circuit of fortified walls expanding and abutting against the "*quadriburgium*" that surrounds the church, together with the different building techniques identified, raises some doubts about the real sequence of construction of the complex. The roughly dressed masonry used in the "*quadriburgium*" contrasts with the finely dressed and neatly jointed masonry used in the church (Magen 1993; 2008). It also, though, contrasts with the techniques used in the later extension surrounding the monastery. Thus the first enclosure was enlarged with a new wall enclosing the monastery to the north, reaching final dimensions of 100 × 83 m. This circuit has been neither ascribed nor dated, but it effectively doubled the extension of the previous "*quadriburgium*" precinct.

It is possible that these new walls, enclosing both the earlier and enlarged monastery and church, and abutting against the "*quadriburgium*", might have been the work patronized by Justinian and mentioned by Procopius.

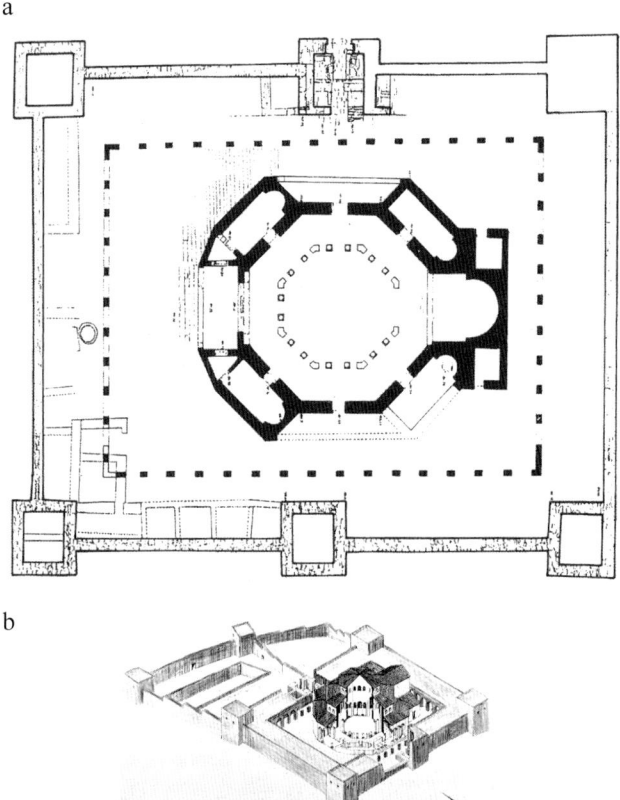

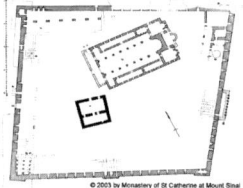

Figure 9.13: Castrum-Lavra of St. Catherine in Sinai

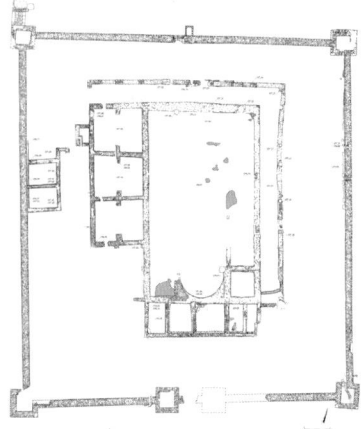

Figure 9.14: Khirbet al-Kerak, identified as Sinnabra. Source: Whitcomb 2002

Figure 9.12: Monastery of St. Mary, Mt. Gerizim, Neapolis-Nablus (Palestine). (a) a plan of the complex; (b) an axonometric view of the church with the first (pre-existing?) circuit of fortifications, and the later precinct, added abutting on the north side of the earlier one

This establishes a new hypothetical sequence: firstly, a "*quadriburgium*" was built in the Tetrarchic period on Mount Gerizim; later, in the 5th century, when the fort was abandoned, a church was built by Zeno within the former defences. Finally, under the auspices of Justinian the enlarged monastery was enclosed within a larger walled circuit abutting the pre-existing walls.

An alternative hypothesis would cast the *quadriburgium* as Justinian's work, in the aftermath of the Samaritan revolt, and this was the archetype for a new type of monastery and *quadriburgium*-style structure hybrid (like S. Catherine in Sinai). Such an intervention would have been inspired by the recurrent reuse of abandoned *quadriburgia* as monasteries in the 5th and 6th centuries.

The complex of St Catherine in Sinai provides an interesting example of a *castrum* built to host a garrison to defend the monastery, following a direct request to Justinian from the brethren for protection against the Saracens (Fig. 9.13). There are clear references to verify this account (Monferrer Sala 1999). The *castrum* (85 × 76 m) enclosed the Chapel of the Burning Bush, also known as St Helen's Chapel, and a pre-existing defensive tower, probably built in the 4th or 5th century. The plan of the defensive wall, although partly destroyed and rebuilt (the south and west walls are the original ones from the 6th century) seems to adopt a sort of distorted *quadriburgium* plan, with slightly projecting towers in the north-west and probably north-east corners. In the south-east and south-west corners the so-called towers appear as mere buttresses with almost no projection.

The site of Khirbet al-Kerak is located on the southwest shore of the Lake of Galilee (Fig. 9.14). Excavations carried out in the 1950s by P. L. O. Guy, and later B. Maisler, discovered structures identified as "a Roman fort of the 2nd century, a Byzantine bath of the 6th century, and within the fort, a large synagogue" that was actually a basilical building oriented southward (Maisler, B and Stekelis, M., The Excavations at Beth Yerah (Khirbet el-Kerak) in IEJ 2 – 1952 165, 218). The interpretation and dating of these structures is controversial; the identification of the basilical structure as a synagogue has been completely discarded (Reich 1993). Further excavations uncovered a Byzantine church of three phases to the north of the fort. An inscription on a mosaic belonging to the final phase of the church provided a *terminus ante quem* of AD 528–529 (Whitcomb 2002, 1). On this basis Whitcomb advanced the hypothesis of a Ghassanid palace that was later reused by the Umayyad caliphs as one of their palaces (*qusur*); this hypothesis is reinforced by the identification of the

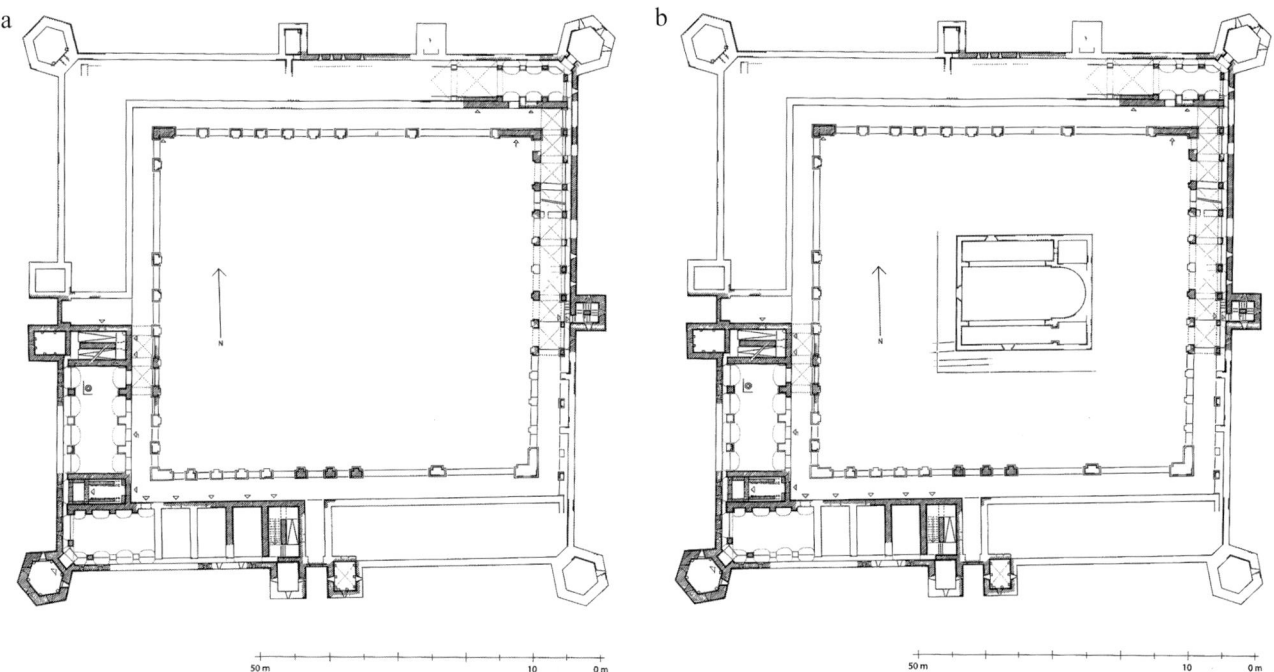

Figure 9.15: Kastron at Al-Andarin / Androna before (a) and after (b) the addition of the basilical church, which constitutes part of the installation's transformation into a monastic complex

complex as Sinnabra or Sinn al-Nabra, the wintering site of Umayyads caliphs Mu'awiya and 'Abd el-Malik (Whitcomb 2002, 4). Thus, it can reasonably be proposed that a basilica-structure of palatial and religious function (similar to the al-Mundhir *praetorium* at Resafa) was built or refurbished in an abandoned Roman fort; the addition of an extra-mural bath at the entrance suggests the later transformation of the complex into an Umayyad *qasr*.

The *kastron* at Al-Andarin/Androna, which according to an inscription was built in AD 558–559 by a private citizen called Thomas, was designed as a defensive structure comprising a walled perimeter with two storeys of chambers surrounding an inner porticoed court (Fig. 9.15). A church lay at the centre (Strube 2003, 31–76; 2008, 57, Fig. 4; Mundell Mango 2002, 303–310), but this was not part of the original configuration. This is attested by a different masonry technique and a further inscription (Prentice 1922, nos. 916–917). The discovery of mural paintings featuring religious motifs in a room that was originally used for communal purposes suggests that the whole building was used as a fortified monastery. The difference here is that the fortified structure was not originally built by the Roman army, but funded by civil members of the local community.

The so-called "barracks" is a poorly understood structure in the complex of Qasr Ibn Wardan (Fig. 9.16). It was dubbed the "barracks" due to its appearance in plan, although it has not been thoroughly excavated. The remains of a probable basilica structure or church can be found in the centre of the courtyard of a rectangular walled precinct. The dearth of

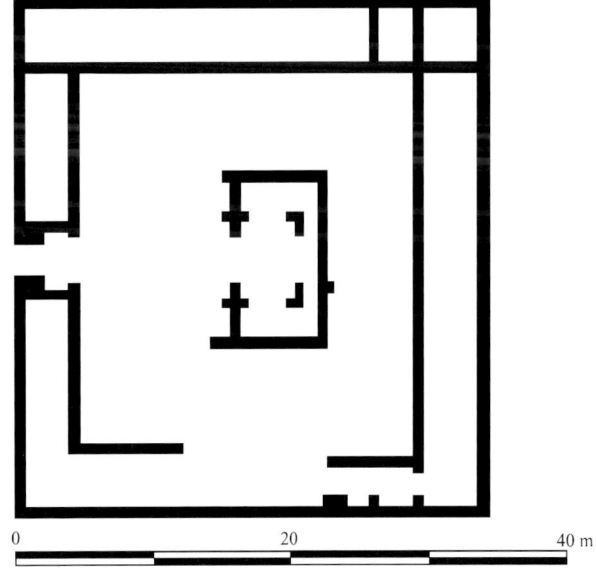

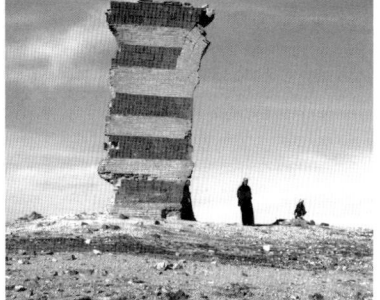

Figure 9.16: Qasr Ibn-Wardan. The so-called 6th-century "Barracks"

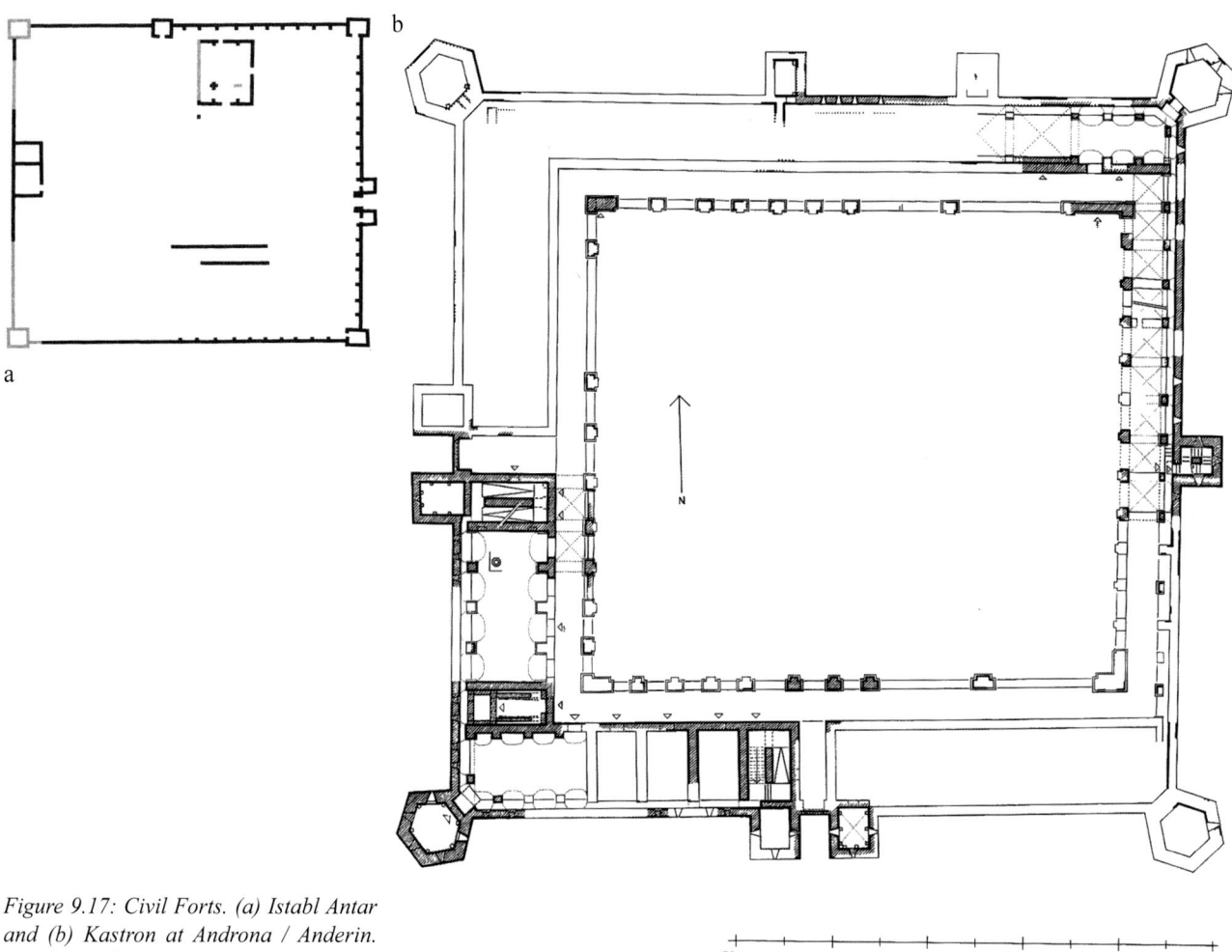

Figure 9.17: Civil Forts. (a) Istabl Antar and (b) Kastron at Androna / Anderin. Source: Butler 1913

excavation means that all interpretation is conjectural, but this seems to be another potential candidate to belong to the series of fortified / military structures that were transformed into monastic compounds with the addition of a church in the central courtyard.

V. Influence of Late Roman Forts on other building types

This process of adoption and adaptation of military architectural types for civic (fortified) residential consumption can also be found in Istabl Antar, an unexcavated fortified villa near Andarin in northern Syria. This site is dated to the second half of the 6th century by a lintel inscription of 577 (Butler 1920, 63–64; Prentic 1922, 60–61, no 947). Similarly to the structure at Andarin / Androna, prior to the addition of the central church, Istabl Antar resembles a *quadriburgium*, defining a formal type that endured into the Umayyad period (Fig. 9.17). The "fort" at Dumeyr in Syria, is dated to the 6th century and was probably patronized by the Ghassanids (Lenoir 1999). It is reminiscent of the Diocletianic palace at Split, and the walled precinct of the *misr* of Aqaba (a walled city built ex-novo by the Umayyads), which was clearly influenced by the nearby Tetrarchic legionary fortresses of Lejjun and Udruh (Whitcomb 2005, Fig. 5).

This discussion leads us to another important issue that arises from this study: the influence exerted by Roman and Persian military architecture on the development of fortified residences in Arabia from the 2nd and 3rd century onwards (Northedge 2008 provided further examples of the sites discussed here). This represents an alternative and indirect source of architectural inspiration with models and types adopted and adapted to the local needs of the elites of Arabia. It may, in turn, have influenced the later design of the Umayyad *qusur* before their conquest of the Roman provinces of Syria, Arabia, and Palestine and subsequent reuse of Roman structures. Significantly, this possibility is relevant to current debates in Islamic archaeology about the origins of the Umayyad *qusur*, making these

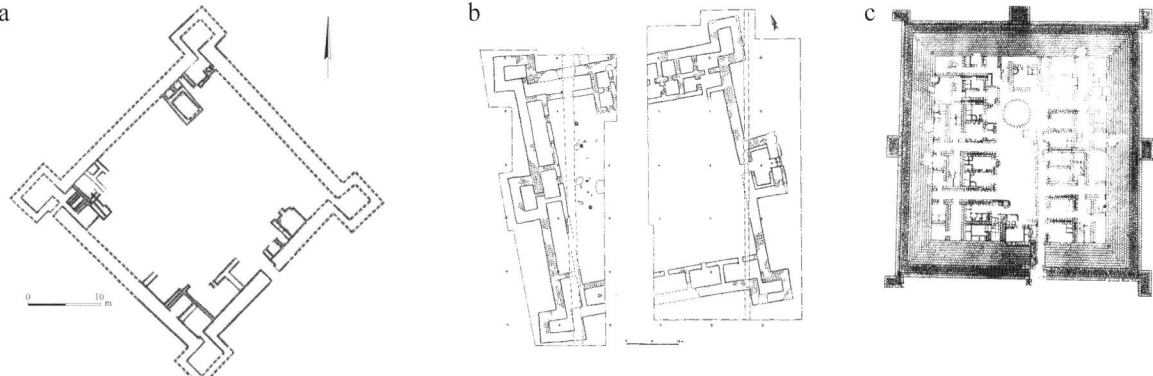

Figure 9.18: Roman forts might have served as inspiration for Arab fortified residences: (a) Yotvata (Negev), a Roman Quadriburgium of the 3rd to 4th century AD; (b) Mleiha (Sharja UAE) an Arab fort of the 3rd to 4th century AD; (c) Qaryat al-Faw (Saudi Arabia) a fortified residence that was transformed into a fortified market in the 3rd to 4th century AD. Source: Northedge 2008, fig. 8; fig.10

sites fundamental to crossing a *limes academicus* between Classical and Islamic Archaeology.

The key question is what was the origin of the influences that inspired structures like those of Qaryat al-Faw and Qasr Radm in Saudi Arabia, or the one at Mleiha at Sharja, in the UAE (Fig. 9.18). All of these evoke the Roman *quadribugium* style with square or oblong corner towers, which can also be related to Parthian examples, such as that of Gobekly-Tepe. The example from Ed-Dur at Umm al-Qawaiwayn, in the UAE (Northedge 2008, Fig. 11) prefigures the standard Umayyad type with rounded towers. This could be the result of early Persian influence through the Sassanian presence in South Arabia, instead of, or simultaneously to, that exerted from contact between the Roman and Sassanian armies in Mesopotamia.

The date and characteristics of these structures, all apparently abandoned by the 4th century, supports the hypothesis that the early adoption of Roman models for the construction of the first fortified palaces (the "proto-*qusur*") of these Arabian elites could have created a specific architectural type. This would have already been familiar to the Umayyads while they were living in Arabia, and could have been used as a template for their very first *qusur* in *Bilad es-Sham* (Great Syria). The adoption of the so-called Syrian *bayt*, which characterizes the standard Umayyad *qasr* in the Levant, may have been a later modification that took place once the Syrian form was established. The round towers, in contrast, were already known in areas of Arabia under Persian influence, as the example from Ed-Dur at Umm al-Qawaiwayn testifies (Northedge 2000, Fig.11). This influence was due to the presence of Sassanian forts in the south and east of the Arabian peninsula and the Gulf area (such as the one at al-Mushaqqar), which would have been an alternative source of technical transmission of Partho-Sassanian military architecture models. These worked in conjunction with direct influence from Roman military architecture in northern Syria.

An intermediate model developed in the 6th century AD, in Bilad es-Sham, is represented by the *qasr* at Khirbet el-Bayda, and the "fort" or building "D" in the Northern group of pre-Umayyad buildings at Jabal Says (both in the Hauran, in southern Syria), which could have an antecedent, or parallel, at Ed-Dur in the UAE (Fig. 9.19a). It is remarkable how the round corner towers in the forts at Jabal Says and ed-Dur are located, not exactly on the corners, but at the end of each wall (see Fig.19a and c), thereby creating a sort of "swastika" arrangement (both lack intermediate towers). At Khirbet el-Bayda, however, the towers are placed precisely at the corners of the building, and present semi-circular intermediate towers corresponding to those in the "canonical" Umayyad palaces. Kh. el-Bayda still lacks the "Syrian *bayt*" arrangement of rooms in its lay-out, and instead has the same layout as the 6th-century palatial halls of Hallabat, where single rooms flank the main reception halls.

The hypotheses and conclusions presented above draw on recent excavations and research in Jordan and Syria, in particular, and highlight a recurrent pattern of Severan forts being transformed into Tetrarchic *quadriburgia*. Subsequent abandonment by the *limitanei* in the 5th and 6th centuries was followed by reappropriation and adaptation of these sites by Ghassanid forces and then the Umayyad elite. The Tetrarchic modification of the sites can be seen as part of the expansion and modification of the *limes Arabicus* under Diocletian, which was continued by his successors. A shift in defensive strategy in the 5th and 6th centuries resulted in the replacement of the static *limitanei* with more mobile *foederati* troops of the Ghassanid *phylarchs*. Though the Ghassanids continued to use Roman *limes* fortifications, the role of these sites was tailored to the political and religious agendas of the *phylarchs*. As a consequence the forts became palatial residences for peripatetic leaders and monastic centres that served both the religious needs of the local territory and provided the necessary logistic apparatus

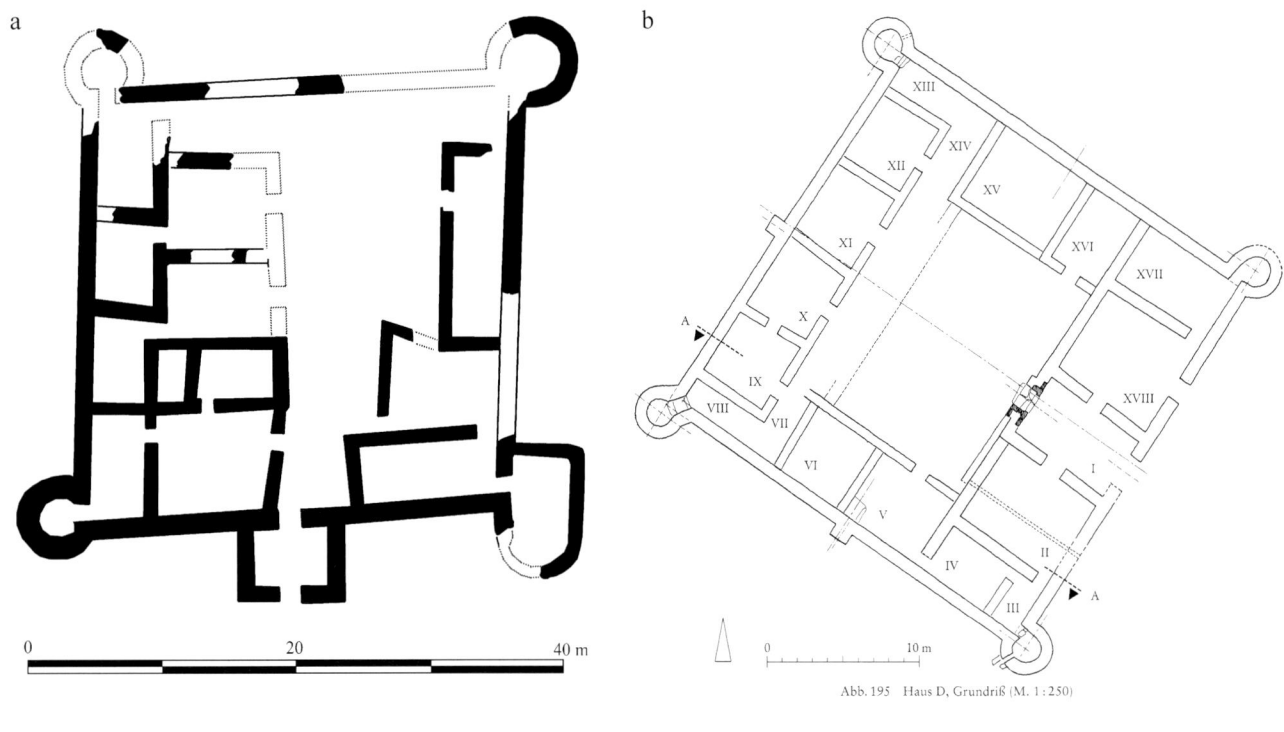
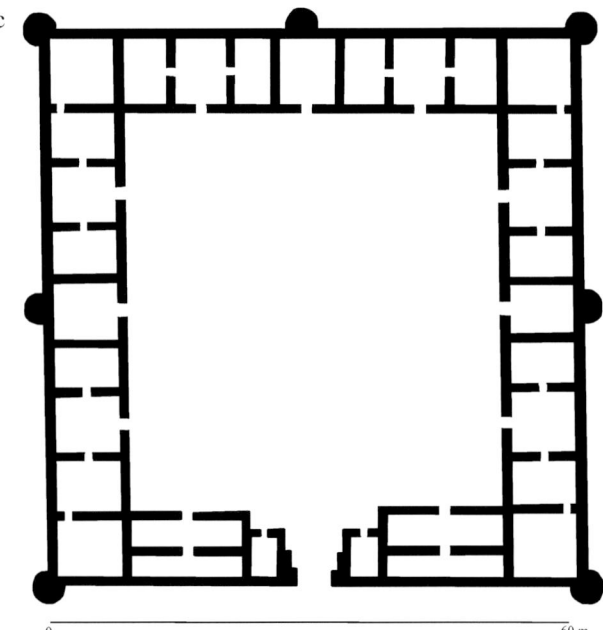

Figure 9.19: (a) Ed-Dur Fort (chantier F) (UAE); (b) Jabal Says 6th-century pre-Umayyad (Ghassanid?) fort; (c) Kh. el-Bayda (Hauran, Syria). Source: Lecomte 1993 in Northedge 2008; Brisch 1965; Gaube 1974

to support the Ghassanid troops. The success and utility of these sites under the Ghassanid *phylarchs* proved influential, and the template these sites provided continued to inspire settlement in the Early Islamic period.

Bibliography

Arce, I. (2006a) Qasr Hallabat (Jordan) revisited: reassessment of the material evidence. In H. Kennedy (ed.) *Muslim Military Architecture in Greater Syria*, 26–44. Leiden, Brill.

Arce, I. (2006b) Umayyad building techniques and the merging of Roman-Byzantine and Partho-Sasanian traditions: continuity and change. In I. Jacobs, A. Sarantis and E. Zanini (eds) *Technology in Transition: AD 300–650, Late Antique Archaeology 4.1*, 491–537. Leiden, Brill

Arce, I. (2008) Hallabat: Castellum, Coenobium, Praetoriun, Qasr. The construction of a Palatine architecture under the Umayyads (I). In K. Bartl and A. Moaz (eds) *Residences, Castles, Settlements – Transformation Processes from Late Antiquity to Early Islamic Times, (Proceedings of the Colloquium on Late Antiquity and Early Islamic Archaeology in Bilad al-Sham Damascus, November 2006)*, 153–182. Orient Archäologie, Band 24, Damascus, DAI German Archaeological Institute.

Arce, I. (2009a) Qasr al-Hallabat (Jordan): transformation of a *Limes Arabicus* fort into a monastic and Palatine complex. In A. Morillo, N. Hanel and E. Martín (eds) *Limes XX, (Proceedings of the 20th International Congress of Roman Frontier Studies, held at León, Spain, Sept 2006. Consejo Superior de Investigaciones Científicas. Instituto Histórico Hoffmeyer. Instituto de Arqueología de Mérida*, 155–180. Madrid Anejos de *Gladius*13 (vol. II).

Arce, I. (2009b) Coenobium, Palatium and Hira: The Ghassanid complex at Hallabat. In F. Al-Khraysheh (ed.) *Studies in the History and Archaeology of Jordan X (Proceedings of the 10th International Conference ICHAJ – Washington, May 2007)*, 937–966. Amman, Department of Antiquities.

Arce, I. (2010) Qasr Hallabat, Qasr Bshir and Deir el Kahf. Building techniques, architectural typology and change of use of three *Quadriburgia* from the *Limes Arabicus*. Interpretation and significance. In S. Camporeale, H. Dessales, and A. Pizzo (eds) *Arqueología de la Construcción II. Los procesos constructivos en el mundo romano: Italia y las provincias orientales (Proceedings of the workshop "Archeologia della Costruzione II: I cantieri edili dell'Italia e delle provincie Romane orientali" held at the Certosa di Pontignano in Siena 13–15 November 2008)*, 455–481. Madrid, Anejos de Archivo Español de Arqueología (AEspA).

Arce, I. (2012) Romans, Ghassanids and Umayyads. The transformation of the Limes Arabicus: From coercive and deterrent diplomacy towards religious proselytism and political clientelism. In G. Vannini and M. Nucciotti (eds) *Limina/Limites: Archaeologies, histories, islands and borders in the Mediterranean (365–1556) 1: Proceedings of the International Conference "La Transgiordania nei secoli XII–XIII e le frontiere del Mediterraneo medievale" (Atti del Convegno di Firenze -Palazzo Vecchio-Palazzo Strozzi, 5–8 novembre 2008)*, 53–72. BAR International Series S2386, Oxford, Archaeopress.

Arce, I. (2014) Late Antique and Umayyad quarries in the Near East: a model of optimization of resources. In S. Camporeale, H. Dessales and A. Pizzo (eds) *Arqueología de la Construcción IV: Le Cave nel Mondo Antico*, 359–388. Madrid, Anejos de Archivo Español de Arqueología (AEspA) LXIV.

Arce, I. (in press) Transformation patterns of Roman forts in the *Limes Arabicus* from Severan to Tetrarchic and Justinean periods. The case of *Deir el-Kahf* (Jordan). In P. Bidwell *et al.* (eds) *Limes XXI Roman Frontier Studies; Proceedings of the International Conference. University of Newcastle upon Tyne (16–23 August 2009)*. Oxford, BAR.

Breeze, D. J. (2011) *The Frontiers of Imperial Rome*. Barnsley, Pen and Sword.

Brisch, K. (1963–1965) Das Omayyadische Schloss in Usais (I & 2). In Vorläufiger Bericht über die mit Mitteln der Forschungsgemeinschaft unternommenen Grabung (Frühjahr 1962 & 1963). *Mitteilungen des Deutschen Archäologischen Instituts, Abteilung Kairo 19*, 141–187 and *Mitteilungen des Deutschen Archäologischen Instituts, Abteilung Kairo 20*, 138–177

Butler, H. C. (1913) *Publication of the Princeton University Archaeological Expedition to Syria in 1904–5 and 1909*. Div. II. Section A, Leiden, Brill.

Chabot, J. B. (1907–1933) Documenta ad Origenes Monophysitarum Illustrandas. 2 Vols. *Corpus Scriptorum Christianorum Orientalorum, Sriptores Syri*, 2nd series, vol. 37, Paris, Imprimerie de la République.

Desreumaux, A and Humbert, J. B. (1990) Huit Campaignes de fouilles au Khirbet es-Samra (1981–1989), *Revue Biblique* 97, 252–269.

Desreumaux, A. and Humbert, J. B. (eds) (1998) *Fouilles de Khirbet es-Samra, Jordanie. Vol. 1*. Paris, Brepols.

Desreumaux, A. and Humbert, J. B. (2003) Les Vestiges chreétiens de Khirbet es-Samra en Jordanie. In N. Duval (ed.) *Les Églises de Jordanie et Leurs Mosaïques*, 23–34. Beirut, IFAPO.

Gatier, P. L. (1998) Les inscriptions greques et latines de Samra et de Rihab. In A. Desreumaux and J. B. Humbert (eds) *Fouilles de Khirbet es-Samra, Jordanie. Vol. 1*, 359–430. Paris, Brepols.

Gaube, H. (1974) *Ein Arabische Palast in Südsyrien; Hirbet el-Baida*. Beirut, Beiruter Texte und Studien 16.

Gregory, S. (1995–1997) *Roman Military Architecture on the Eastern Frontier*, 3 vols, Amsterdam, Adolf M. Hakkert.

Helms, S. (1990) *Early Islamic Architecture of the Desert: A Bedouin Station in Eastern Jordan*. Edinburgh, Edinburgh University Press.

Hull, D. (2008) A spatial and morphological analysis of monastic sites in the northern limestone massif, Syria. *Levant* 40, 89–113.

Kennedy, D. (2000) *The Roman Army in Jordan*. London, CBRL.

Konrad, M. (2008) Roman military fortifications along the eastern desert frontier. In K. Bartl and A. Moaz (eds) *Residences, Castles, Settlements – Transformation Processes from Late Antiquity to Early Islamic Times, (Proceedings of the Colloquium on Late Antiquity and Early Islamic Archaeology in Bilad al-Sham Damascus, November 2006)*, 413–418. Orient Archäologie, Band 24, Damascus, DAI German Archaeological Institute.

Lenoir, M. (1999) Dumayr, faux camp romain, vraie residence palatiale. *Syria* 76, 227–236.

Littman, E. (1913) Greek and Latin inscriptions Syria. *Publication of the Princeton University Archaeological Expedition to Syria in 1904–5 and 1909 (PPUAES)*. Leiden, Div.III. Section A.

Magen, Y. (1993) *The Church of Mary Theotokos on Mt. Gerizim, Ancient Churches Revealed.* Yoram Tsafrir (ed.) Jerusalem, Israel Exploration Society.

Magen, Y. Misgav, H. and Tsfania, L. (2008) *Mount Gerizim Excavations Vol II – A Temple City*. Judea and Samaria Publications 8, Jerusalem, Israel Antiquities Authority.

Monferrer Sala, J. (1999) Documento fundacional en árabe del monasterio de Santa Catalina en el Monte Sinai. *Anaquel de estudios árabes, Nº 10*, 79–96. Madrid, Editorial de la Universidad Complutense.

Northedge, A. (2008) The Umayyad desert castles and pre-Islamic Arabia. In K. Bartl and A. Moaz (eds) *Residences, Castles, Settlements – Transformation Processes from Late Antiquity to Early Islamic Times, (Proceedings of the Colloquium on Late Antiquity and Early Islamic Archaeology in Bilad al-Sham Damascus, November 2006)*, 243–259. Orient Archäologie, Band 24, Damascus, DAI German Archaeological Institute.

Olesson, J. P. (2001) King, Emperor, Priest and Caliph: cultural change at Hawara (ancient al-Humayma) in the first millennium AD. *Studies in the History and Archaeology of Jordan* 7, 569–580.

Palestinian Exploration Fund (1875) *The Palestinian Exploration Fund Quarterly Statement*, 180–189.

Parker, S. T. (1986) *Romans and Saracens. A History of the Roman Frontier*. Winona Lake, American Schools of Oriental Research.

Parker, S. T. (2006) *The Roman Frontier in Central Jordan. Final Report on the Limes Arabicus Project, 1980–1989*. Washington DC, Dumbarton Oaks.

Plontke-Lüning, A. (2006) *Three Unknown Roman Fortresses in Southern Hauran*. www.hauran-monuments.eu (ed.: Marcell Restle) http://www.hauran-monuments.eu/Roman_fort.html

Prentice, W. K. (1922) Greek and Latin inscriptions, Section B, N. Syria. *Syria. Publications of the Princeton University Archaeological Expedition to Syria 1904–1905 and 1909*. Leiden, Brill.

Reich, R. (1993) The Beth Yerah "synagogue" reconsidered. *Atiqot* 22, 139–144.

Sartre, M. (1985) *Inscriptions de la Jordanie, 4: Petra et la Nabatène*. Paris.

Shahid I. (2002) *Byzantium and the Arabs in the Sixth Century, Vol. 2, Part 1: Toponymy, Monuments, Historical Geography and Frontier Studies*. Washington DC, Dumbarton Oaks.

Strube, C. (2003) Androna/Al-Andarin. Vorbericht über die Grabungskampagnen der Jahre 1997–2001. *Archäologischer Anzeiger*. 25–115.

Strube, C. (2008) Al-Andarin/Androna: site and setting. In K. Bartl and A. Moaz (eds) *Residences, Castles, Settlements – Transformation Processes from Late Antiquity to Early Islamic Times, (Proceedings of the Colloquium on Late Antiquity and Early Islamic Archaeology in Bilad al-Sham Damascus, November 2006)*, 57–71. Orient Archäologie, Band 24, Damascus, DAI German Archaeological Institute.

De Vries, B. (1993) The Umm al-Jimal Project (1981–1992) *Annual of the Department of Antiquities* 27, 433–460.

Whitcomb, D. (2002) Khirbet al-Kerak identified with Sinnabra. *Usur al-Wusta, The Bulletin of the Middle East Medievalist* 14, 1–6.

Whitcomb, D. (2006) The walls of Islamic Ayla: defense or symbol? In H. Kennedy (ed.) *Muslim Military Architecture in Greater Syria*, 61–74. Leiden, Brill.

10

CASTRA OR *CENTENARIA*? INTERPRETING THE LATER FORTS OF THE NORTH AFRICAN FRONTIER

Alan Rushworth

Introduction

The military fortifications associated with the late Roman frontier in Africa can present a bewildering picture. Forts displaying many of the typical features of late Roman castramentation, such as projecting towers and ranges of rooms set against the back of the enceinte, are certainly well-represented, particularly in Numidia and western Tripolitania (Fig. 10.1). These sites can, however, vary greatly in size. Forts with square or near square proportions, covering *c.* 0.35–0.75 ha, are fairly typical (Fig. 10.2). Examples include the well-known sites of Bourada and Oued Naima (*Centenarium Aqua Viva*). Many others are much smaller, such as *Aquae Herculis* and most of the equivalent Tripolitanian sites, while Zebaret et Tir, which covers 2.19 ha, is as large as some forts of the Principate. Moreover, while a number of these sites are labeled *centenaria*, this term is also born by much smaller courtyard tower fortlets like Gasr Duib and Ksar Tarcine (*Centenarium Tibubuci*) and even by private fortified dwellings in the Tripolitanian Jebel and pre-desert and the Mauretanian hill-country.

To further confuse matters, the *Notitia Dignitatum* – the list of significant office holders (*dignitates*) in both halves of the empire – when it comes to detail the three military commands covering the African diocese (*ND Occ.* XXV, XXX and XXXI) does not incorporate the usual list of individual regimental commands and associated forts of the kind set out in the chapters relating to equivalent frontier commands in Britain, the Danube ducates or even neighbouring Mauretania Tingitana, for example (*ND Occ.* XXVI). Instead it gives a list of territorial sector or district commands (*limites*), each under their respective *praepositus*. Their titles suggest many of these *praepositi* were quartered at sites first garrisoned during the 2nd and 3rd centuries, when the African frontier zone took on its definitive form.

How are we to make sense of all this? For all its apparent difficulties the *Notitia* does provide a broad framework within which to work. If the location of some of the military districts still remains stubbornly obscure, the headquarters of many others can be pinpointed and analysed, enabling some conclusions to be reached regarding the role of those *limites*. The evidence regarding the identification of these sites will not be dealt with here, but detailed analysis can be found in Rushworth (1992, 100–117).

It would be characteristic of a system of territorial commands, such as that recorded by the *Notitia*, for the military posts within a given area to form a definite site hierarchy dependent on the headquarters at the centre of the command. This section will attempt to show how this is reflected in the archaeological record.

Site hierarchy: I, the *limes* headquarters

Location and Classification

The most important sites, those which formed the headquarters and principal base of each *limes*, are perhaps the most enigmatic elements of the region's late Roman military infrastructure. Those which can be identified fall into two main categories.

The first group consists of those derived from regimental or legionary detachment forts established during the Principate. These are particularly common in Tripolitania and Numidia, notable examples being *Gemellae*, *Tillibari*, *Bezereos* and probably *Tentheos* and *Talalati*. Gheriat-el Garbia (*Myd...*), the large, legionary vexillation fort on the Saharan desert margin of Tripolitania, may also fall into this category if it can be equated with the seat of the

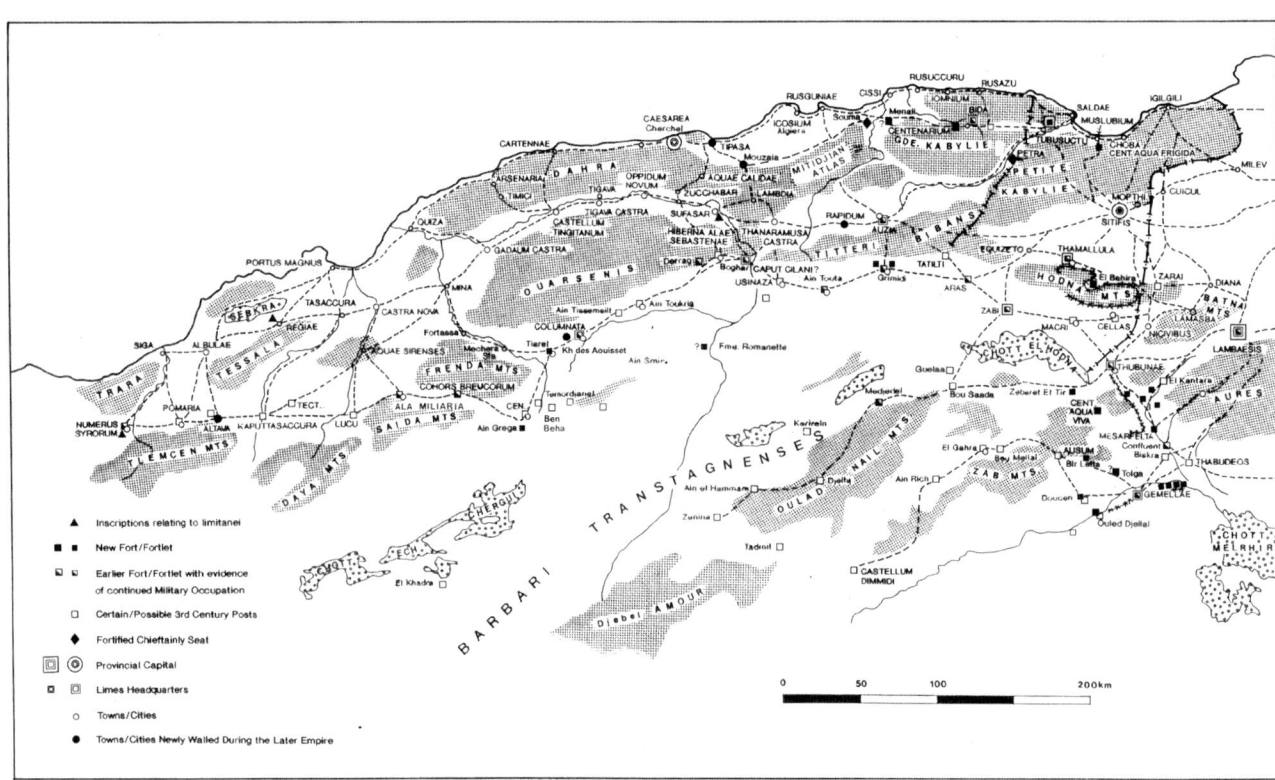

Fig. 10.1: Map showing the location and hierarchy of late Roman military sites in Mauretania Caesariensis, Sitifensis and eastern Numidia

praepositus limitis Madensis and the base of the *milites munifices*, both listed in the chapter of the *dux Tripolitanae* (*ND Occ.* XXXI, 22 and 30), as suggested by Mackensen following recent fieldwork there (Mackensen 2012; Haensch and Mackensen 2011).

In the second category are the *limes*-centres which were located in cities, such as *Turris Tammaleni* in Tripolitania or *Badias* and *Tubunae* in Numidia. The latter type was most common in the two Mauretanias. Fortification work on city walls is not considered in detail in this study, however, though it may have some relevance to the location of *limes* headquarters and for field army deployment. An overview of urban fortification in ancient North Africa has been provided by Daniels (1983). Regional examples of late imperial work attested by epigraphy include: the rebuilding of the *municipium Rapidense* by the governor Ulpius Apollonius between 293–305 (CIL VIII 20836 = ILS 638); the dedication of new gates and towers at *Tipasa* in 305–307 (AE 1966, 600); the construction of *muru et porta nova et turres* at *Altava* in 349 (AE 1935, 86); and the *nova moenia* built at El Hadjeb near Mouzaia in accordance with the *iussa cuncta comitum* (CIL VIII 9282). The *portas ac valvas factas* at Kherba of the Aouisset in 346 may also derive from a small urban site (AE 1955, 139).

In fact there may have been considerable overlap between the two groups. Many urban *limes* headquarters may actually have been located in a fort, as yet undiscovered, inside or beside the city, perhaps a survivor from the 2nd or 3rd centuries. Indeed *Gemellae* is an example of just such a case, the Hadrianic fort being surrounded by a town which eventually gained the status of a *municipium* (CIL VIII 2450 = 17950 – *decurio municipi(i) Gemell(ensis)*, cf. CIL VIII 18218; Trousset 1978, 559). There is no guarantee that *Badias* (*AAA* 49:51), which likewise achieved the status of a *municipium* (CIL VIII 2451 = 17945), but has seen virtually no investigation, or *Tubunae* (*AAA* 37:10), where later occupation may have destroyed earlier traces, were not similar with a continuous military presence from the early 2nd century through to the late empire. Certainly, a road was being driven westward towards Badias from the Trajanic fort of Ad Maiores at the beginning of the 2nd century, to judge from surviving milestones (CIL VIII 22348–9), and a convincing case has been made that Trajanic or Hadrianic forts were established at both these pre-existing native centres (Fentress 1979, 70–72, 92, 111). Military occupation may well have continued without a break through to the 4th century. In Mauretania Caesariensis, *Auzia* (Sour el-Ghozlane), probably *Columnata* (Ain Zerla, 1–2 km south of Sidi Hosni) and perhaps even *Bida*, may represent similar instances.

Thus *Auzia* lay at a major crossroads, with routes heading off in as many as seven directions, some being

A - Zebaret et Tir
B - Tamuda (Tingitana)
C - Bourada
D - Aqua Viva
E - Gasr Bularkan
F - Benia bel-Recheb
G - 'Castellum Schneider', Doucen
H - Aquae Herculis
I - Fort Parallelogramme Seba Mgata
J - Hr. Temassine
K - Hr. Rjijila
L - Zavia et-Tailmun (Cyrenaica)
M - El Benia et-Tailmun
N - Ain Gréga

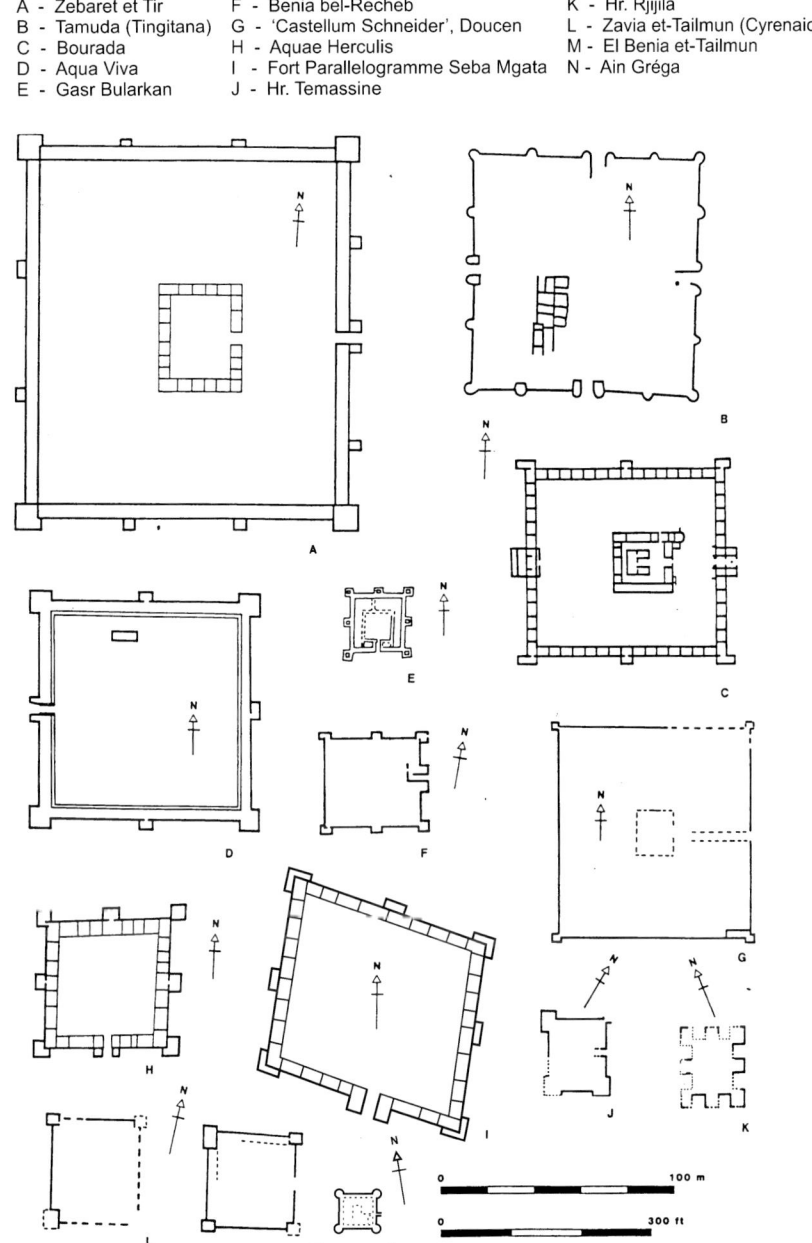

Fig. 10.2: Late Roman forts and fortlets in North Africa. Credit: after Daniels 1987 with modifications

of major importance (Salama 1951, carte). Its crucial strategic importance, surrounded by mountain passes and commanding one of the rare natural routes which leads right through from the Mediterranean coast to the interior steppe to the south, has been underlined by Lassère (1981, 317). Salama (1977, 582, 593 carte 3) has argued that this crucial position was one of the earliest points occupied by the Romans in the interior of eastern Caesariensis. It was sufficiently important to retain a garrison throughout the Roman period. It was the base of the *cohors I Aelia Singularium* from the early / mid-2nd century onwards (Benseddik 1982, 63–64 and 233–234). In the 3rd century, when the surrounding area was the scene of considerable unrest, the cohort was joined by a *vexillatio equitum Maurorum*. This combined force, *in territorio Auziensi praetendentium*, was commanded by a prominent member of the local elite, Gargilius Martialis, during the 250s, playing an instrumental role in tracking down the rebel chieftain Faraxen (CIL VIII 9047 = ILS 2767; cf. also CIL VIII 9045 = ILS 2766, and Pavis d'Escurac Doisy 1966 = AE 1966, 597, for other indications of 3rd-century military activity at *Auzia*). By 301, authority over the surrounding district had been entrusted to a *praepositus limitis*, again a local notable (CIL VIII 9025). The remains of town walls protected by closely spaced projecting rectangular towers were recorded by the early French colonists, however the fort housing the *cohors I Singularium* and the *equites Mauri* has not been located (AAA 14:105; Robert 1901; and see Rushworth 1992, 177–178 for more extensive discussion of the *limes Auziensis*).

Further north, *Bida* (Djemaa Saharidj) formed the headquarters of a command covering the Grande Kabylie (Rushworth 1992, 178–180; for the site see AAA 6:104; Martin 1969, 4–7; Gascou 1982, 253–254). In all probability *Bida* was the site of a 1st- or 2nd-century fort, like *Auzia*, since it forms the major settlement in the interior of the Grande Kabylie and military activity is attested in the area, but it is less easy to postulate unbroken evolution from an earlier base than was the case with *Auzia*. There may well have been a gap in military occupation, perhaps after the Severan advance to *nova praetentura*, or conceivably from an even earlier date. As yet, however, very little is known regarding the subjugation of this particular region of Caesariensis, during the Principate. The formation of the *limes Bidensis* probably did not occur until the aftermath of the campaigns against the *Quinquegentanei* in the 250s or those waged during the reign of Diocletian, first by the governor, Aurelius Litua, and then by the Augustus, Maximian. *Bida* itself may have been a *municipium*, if the itineraries are to be trusted (*Itin. Ant.* 39.4: *Bida municipium*; *Tab. Peut. Seg* II.3: <S>*yda municipium*), but the survival of tribal institutions was particularly marked in the surrounding districts. It is possible that considerable reliance was placed on the support of tribal levies and chieftains to back up a force of regular troops (see Rushworth 1992, 51–52, 215–216).

Likewise, *Columnata* was clearly an administrative hub in the frontier zone as early as the Severan period, when troops were first pushed forward into this part of Caesariensis, and this would imply a garrison fort was established there (see Salama 1953/1955; 1973). Thus a milestone of Macrinus, discovered at Ain Ouaba (CIL VIII 22587; AAA 23:14), was inscribed *a Columnata m(ilia) p(assuum) XV*, which corresponds with the distance to Ain Zerla, whilst general roadworks are documented in the area under Caracalla (AE 1912, 173 = Fabre 1912, 127). The site was strategically located on the interface between the interior, high, arid steppes, known as the High Plateaux, to the south, and the Ouarsenis massif, to the north, which forms one link in the chains of well-watered mountain ranges known as the Tell, running parallel with the coast. The civil settlement was also clearly quite important, to judge from the recorded remains (AAA 22:127 add and 33:15; Gsell 1928, 25; Albertini 1928, 34–35; Cadenat 1953, 167–168; 1957, 90–97; 1958; Lawless 1970 II, 125–131 no 47; Salama 1973, 348 no. 59), and may have attained the status of *civitas*. Perhaps most significantly, military activity is recorded during Diocletian's reign, when a victory dedication was set up at *Columnata* by the governor (*praeses*) Aurelius Litua (AE 1912, 24, *cf.* CIL VIII 9324), and indeed it is possible that the *limes* district was established in connection with these events.

In other cases, however, the army may well have taken over a quarter of a town, as occurred at *Dura Europos* and *Palmyra* on the Eastern frontier in the 3rd century. There is an especially strong likelihood of this occurring when a command was established in a district in the interior previously devoid of military infrastructure.

All this makes the assumption that the site named in the title of each *praepositus limitis* formed his headquarters, rather than simply representing the most sizeable place in the district for which the officer was responsible. It is conceivable that a city may have given its name to a command whilst the *praepositus* was actually ensconced in a fort elsewhere. The fort of Zebaret et Tir would certainly be a candidate for such a role, based on its size, though it must be emphasized how unique it is in that respect. To take the case of one particular command, the *limes Gemellensis*, for example, the fort at *Gemellae* has not yielded any epigraphic evidence or diagnostic traces of architectural refurbishment, such as projecting towers or barracks set against the curtain wall, which would demonstrate late imperial occupation. Moreover, some of the new forts that were distributed along the linear barrier (*fossatum*) screening the oases around *Gemellae*, do contain buildings which could conceivably imply a command function, notably the basilica in the eastern fort at Drah Souid and the central courtyard building at Bourada. Indeed central courtyard buildings can be found in many late African forts (see below).

On balance, however, a more straightforward interpretation of the *Notitia* lists remains preferable. The most important towns in a given area would usually lie at the hub of the local road network, a vital consideration for any military base. As was the case at *Gemellae*, the defences of Ras el-Ain (*Talalati*) in Tripolitania similarly show no indication of late imperial modernisation, but in this instance surviving epigraphic evidence makes it abundantly clear that the site was still in military use and was kept in good repair during the 4th century (*ND Occ.* XXV 31, XXXI 18; cf. CIL VIII 22766 + 22767 = ILAf 11 and CIL VIII 22768). Clearly, it was not felt necessary to upgrade the defences of the larger, older bases. This may have been particularly so when, as in the case of *Gemellae*, the fort was enclosed within a walled *municipium*, itself equipped with projecting towers. Moreover centrally placed buildings, perhaps associated with administration and officer's accommodation, were also a feature of 3rd-century fortlets as well as many 4th-century forts, suggesting they were a normal component of African fortlets and small forts. Hence their appearance in *Gemellae* sector forts like Bourada need not imply any district-wide command function, whilst alternative explanations can also be advanced to account for the presence of a basilica at Drah Souid East (see below: Typology – Numidian forts).

Furthermore, in two instances when the *limes*' title itself was geographically imprecise, care was taken to add the name of the command centre to the *Notitia* entry – the *praepositus limitis Montensis in castris [N]eptitanis* (*ND Occ.* XXV 22) and the *praepositus limitis secundae [A]f[r] orum in castris Tilliba[r]ensibus* (*ND Occ.* XXV 33), both listed under the *comes Africae*. This suggests that when this was not done – the vast majority of cases – the named location represented the headquarters. The second of these entries incidentally confirms that the *praepositus limitis Tillibarensis*, listed in the Tripolitanian chapter in a less elaborate duplicate record (*ND Occ.* XXXI 21), was indeed based in the fort at Remada (*Tillibari*). Similarly, the fact that the *milites munifices* were stationed *in castris Madensibus* (ND Occ. XXXI 30) suggests that the *praepositus limitis Madensis* (*ND Occ.* XXXI 22) was also based in that fort (*castra*).

However, even if we may accept the lists of *praepositi limitum* in three chapters of the *comes Africae*, *dux et praeses Mauretaniae Caesariensis* and the *dux Tripolitanae* as providing a reasonably accurate summary of the location of the local frontier district headquarters, as argued here, it is evident that they do not comprehensively record the distribution of the frontier troops and their associated infrastructure within each military district. Moreover, the *Notitia* shows the military structure of late Roman Africa in its later phase, at the beginning of the 5th century. To gain a clearer impression of the internal organisation of the *limites* and the development of the frontier in the late 3rd and 4th centuries it is necessary to turn to the archaeological record.

Site hierarchy: II, the forts and fortlets

Ranking below the headquarters centres are the smaller forts and fortlets where late imperial occupation can be demonstrated. Many were newly built during the late Roman period. They are particularly useful elements of the military site hierarchy since they show where troops were actually stationed within each *limes* and it is on the relationship between these sites and the main bases that the remainder of this section will focus.

Typology
The Numidian forts

There is considerable homogeneity about the newly built forts of the *limites Gemellensis* and *Tubuniensis*. These have been discussed by Daniels (1987, 260, 262–263, fig.10.19) and Fentress (1979, 105–108). Those located along, or to the west of, the two barriers tend to be square or almost square in plan, with their curtain wall faces ranging around 60–90 m in length and enclosing areas of roughly 0.35–0.75 ha. Examples include: *Centenarium Aqua Viva* (Ain Namia) – 86m square, 0.74 ha; Seba Mgata ("Fort Parallelogramme"), perhaps 60 x 64 m and 0.38 ha; Doucen – perhaps 65 m square and 0.42ha (*cf.* Fentress 1979, 85; but Daniels 1987 plots out a larger fort perhaps 85 x 90 m and 0.765 ha); and Bourada – 77 x 88 m and 0.68 ha. In contrast the forts situated on the road network in the rugged hinterland behind the *fossatum* tend to be smaller, Hammam Sidi el Hadj (*Aquae Herculis*), for example, covers *c*. 0.27 ha, with walls 52 m in length along each side, though the fort is not exactly square. All of these sites feature angle and interval towers, single gateways flanked by twin gatetowers and rooms set against the inner face of the enceinte.

Central courtyard buildings, presumably for administration, storage and housing the officer in charge, are known in the centre of Bourada and Zebaret et Tir, whilst a basilica has been uncovered in Drah Souid East (*cf.* Guey 1939), as noted above. Indeterminate central structures are also recorded at the following forts (*cf.* Baradez 1949): Esdeit; Drah Souid West (Guey 1939, 191: "au centre, éminence"); Doucen; *Mesarfelta* "castrum"; Seba Mgata; the Daya "castellum"; and "Castrum du Confluent" (perhaps the *principia* of the original fort most probably of 2nd-century date). The interior of *Aqua Viva* contains a small building in the northern half, whilst, on the air photograph, the centre is occupied by a large, dark, roughly rectangular area – a *principia*? *Aquae Herculis*, a somewhat smaller site, lacks any central structure.

There may be other ranges of buildings in the interior of the forts, as argued by Baradez in the case of the Fort Parallelogramme at Seba Mgata (1949, 11, 244 and 247), for example. These are far more difficult to spot on the air photos, but this may be because they were built of mud brick alone rather than mud brick on stone footings. The ranges set against internal face of the curtain wall were presumably used to provide barrack and stabling accommodation and storage capacity. The ranges may have been two-storey but so far the evidence on this point is inconclusive as regards 4th-century North African forts, though it is a well attested feature of contemporary military sites elsewhere in the Empire.

It should also be noted that ranges of rooms set against the back of the enceinte and centrally placed administrative buildings were already established features of 2nd- and 3rd-century fortlets like Ksar Rhilane (*Tisavar*), Henchir Mgarine (*Agarlabas?*) and Henchir Medeina (*Thebelami?*). In other words, much of what may be considered the characteristic repertoire of the African frontier's later Roman military architecture had long been present and it is really only the widespread use of projecting towers that distinguishes the late fortifications from their predecessors (see Mattingly 1995, 98–102).

Anomalous sites

The group contains several unusual sites which require further comment. One is Zebaret et Tir. It differs from the pattern outlined above in only one respect, its size. With dimensions of 154 x 142 m it covers 2.19 ha. This puts it on a par with the larger forts typical of the Principate and makes it unique amongst the late Roman fortifications of the region. It is tempting, therefore, to interpret the fort as a forward base designed to accommodate the *praepositus limitis Tubuniensis* during seasonal operations.

The presence of a basilica inside the *Gemellae* sector fort of Drah Souid East also appears to be without parallel in the region's contemporary fortifications and therefore requires some explanation. The possibility that the fort possessed a wider command function, encompassing the *limes Gemellensis*, was noted above, but the absence of appropriate accommodation for an officer, comparable to the courtyard building at Bourada, for instance, would appear to rule that out. Instead, the basilica might simply belong to a later period, after military use of the site had ceased and it had perhaps been converted into a monastery (see Arce, this volume, for the frequency of this occurrence in the Near East). However, if the basilica did form an integral part of the fort, the building could conceivably have had a very specialised function, such as hosting occasional oath-swearing ceremonies, involving imperial officers and pastoralist chieftains, during seasonal transhumant migrations.

A third site requiring comment is the Fort Parallelogramme at Seba Mgata. The ground plan of this site takes the form of a parallel-sided quadrilateral. Baradez records the dimensions of Seba Mgata as 84 x 60 m (1949, 244) although examination of his vertical air photographs casts some doubt on the accuracy of these measurements. The north-west and south-east faces of the fort appear only marginally shorter than its north-east and south-west faces. The discrepancy may be due to a simple typographical error and the text should perhaps have read either 84 x 80 m or, more probably, 64 x 60 m, which would give the fort proportions very like those of other late Roman forts in Numidia, such as *Aqua Viva*, Bourada, Doucen and Zebaret et Tir. The smaller dimensions are to be preferred, based on the number of rooms – *c*. 10–12 – along each side, compared with those in forts of known dimensions such as Bourada, with 14–16.

The rhomboidal form of Seba Mgata is not without parallel. Fentress (1979, 106–108) was inclined to include it amongst the supposed Valentinianic series of trapezoidal forts which she believed could be identified in North Africa, drawing on a parallel with *Alta Ripa* (Altrip) on Rhine. However the other supposed members of this trapezoidal group, *Thabudeos* (Thouda) and Mdila, are better interpreted as 6th-century forts (Trousset 1985, 371–373; Rushworth 1992, 271–272). Both are located in the southern pre-desert margin of Numidia, south of the Aures-Nemenchas mountains, where there is evidence for Byzantine military activity in the 6th century, and are essentially relatively narrowly proportioned oblong rectangles in plan, like the impressive and thoroughly investigated Justinianic fort surviving at Timgad (*cf.* Lassus 1981; Pringle 1981, 232–236, 546–547, fig. 2). Daniels (1982, 120) noted that it is in fact very doubtful whether *Thabudeos* was trapezoidal at all, whilst Baradez' vertical air photograph demonstrates (1949, 126A) that Mdila was so marginally so as to have no tactical benefit, its form being more likely the result of slightly defective military surveying. In any case there are no convincing grounds for including Fort Parallelogramme, with its rhomboidal ground plan, amongst a collection of trapezoidal or more narrowly oblong sites. It would be preferable to compare Seba Mgata with the 4th-century forts at Yverdon and Burg bei Stein (*Taesgaetium*) in modern Switzerland (Schonberger 1969, 179, 185; Von Petrikovits 1971, 181, 185, 195; Drack 1980, 44–46; Johnson 1983, 162–165). These sites are not a distinct group designed to achieve specific advantages in terms of defensive tactics. They are a sub-group of the square/nearly square forts produced by defective Roman surveying, perhaps most aptly entitled the "bent groma" sites. In other words Fort Parallelogramme has a deformed, nearly square plan and falls into the same overall category of Numidian *centenaria* as *Aqua Viva* or Bourada.

Tripolitania

This overall picture contrasts with that presented by the new Tripolitanian forts, which were far smaller than their Numidian counterparts. The table published by Mattingly in his monograph *Tripolitania* (1995, 191, table 10.3) shows that even the largest, Ksar Tabria, was no more than 0.36 ha in area (60 x 60 m). Moreover, that exceeds any other members of the group by a considerable margin, so Mattingly (1995, 101) may be correct in suggesting Tabria was an earlier fort reoccupied or refurbished in the late empire; the next largest, Sdada and Benia Guedah Ceder, only covered 0.27 and 0.24 ha respectively. These alone are comparable in size with the late forts of the *limites Gemellensis* and *Tubuniensis*. The remainder range from 0.16 ha and 0.15 ha, in the cases of Benia bel Recheb and Henchir el Hadjar, to a mere 0.05 ha and 0.04 ha for the diminutive Gasr Bularkan and Henchir Rjijila (later Roman forts in Tripolitania: Mattingly 1995, 193–194, fig. 10.2; Goodchild 1950 = 1976, 38–41; Trousset 1974, 53 (Hr. Temassine), 59–60 (Hr. el Hadjar), 67–68 (Benia Guedah Ceder), 73–75 (Ksar Tabria), 95–96 (Benia bel Recheb), 105–106 (Hr. Rjijila), 133–135 (discussion); Trousset 1978, 134 (Henchir Chenah); Feuille 1938–1940, 260–261 (Henchir Kedama); Rebuffat 1972, 323 (Chawan)).

In plan, however, the Tripolitanian sites do share many of the features of the Numidian forts, notably single gateways and projecting, usually rectangular, towers. Ksar Tabria is unusual in having circular angle towers and D-shaped gate towers (Trousset 1974, 73–75; Mattingly 1995, 99, fig. 5.8, 101). As regards internal buildings, the characteristic ranges set against the inner face of the curtain wall survive at Gasr Bularkan and Sdada and were previously recorded at Benia bel Recheb and Benia Guedah Ceder, but have since been robbed out. Sdada also features a barrack like range in the courtyard (see Mattingly 1995, 192–194, fig. 10.2). Tabria contains a central structure (Trousset 1974, 74), whilst Benia Guedah Ceder incorporates a courtyard building set back against the northwest wall of the circuit (Trousset 1974, 68), both of which have been labelled "reduits". The interpretation of central structures within Roman fortifications on the North African *limes* as 'redoubts' was a common and dubious feature of earlier French colonial studies, and still makes its way into modern literature. They should generally be interpreted as headquarters buildings. Where reduction can actually be shown to have taken place, at sites outside Africa such as *Capidava* on the Lower Danube (Crow 1981, 99, 102–103, and fig 1.1) or *Abusina* (Eining) in Raetia (Baatz 1975, 274), for instance, the new fortification tends to occupy one corner of the site, with the remainder being abandoned.

Mauretania

The evidence from Mauretania Caesariensis and Sitifensis is less clear. The structural evidence for late imperial military architecture in these two provinces has never properly been collated (but see Salama 1984, 130, 135). The preference for round towers rather than the rectangular variety favoured further east is noteworthy. These are recorded at *Ala Miliaria*-Benian (AAA 32:93; De La Blanchère 1883, 67, pl. V; Gsell 1899, 8–9, fig. 2; 1901 I, 87–88, fig. 26; Lawless 1970 II, 104–106; Lenoir 1986), *Cohors Breucorum*-Henchir Souik, the tiny site of Ain Grega (just south of Aioun Sbiba), Ain Grimidi (AAA 24:155 and add; Desrayaux 1911, 475–477, 482), *Aras*-Tarmount (AAA 25:10; Christofle 1938, 276–285) and Ferme Romanette (AAA 34:57; Joly 1898; Benseddik 1980, 981–983, 985–987; 1982, 176). The reliability of some of these records is not beyond doubt. De La Blanchère's plan of *Cohors Breucorum*, for example, is very odd (1883, 69–70 with pl.VII fig. 1; *cf.* AAA 33:23 and add; Lawless 1970 II, 148–152). The dimensions are appropriate to a cohort fort of the Principate, which it was in origin. It has a circular tower at each angle but those at the north-east and south-east corners are both combined with a D-shaped tower to form two gateways sited at either end of the east face of the fort. Judging from the dotted lines employed by De La Blanchère to denote the D-shaped towers these were less certain on the ground than the angle towers. At 15 m square (0.023 ha), Ain Grega is so small that it may simply represent a rather elaborate civilian gasr (courtyard tower) with circular angle turrets in addition to the basic form (AAA 33:36 add; Fort 1908a, 26, and pl. V.1; 1908b, 273; Lawless 1970 II, 158). Fan-shaped angle towers, characteristic of refurbished forts on the Danubian and Eastern frontiers, have been reported at the Antonine outpost fortlet of Medjedel (Salama 1991, 95–97). Rectangular towers are not absent however. They are a feature of the large fort near Ain Bessem, north-east of *Auzia* (AAA 14:28, De Caussade 1851, 242–243; Masqueray 1882–1883, 225–232, with plan; De Cardaillac 1890, 165, plan; Robert 1903, plan; Cagnat 1913, 637–638), the small (95 x 45 m) citadel or fort at the core of Tiaret (AAA 33:14; Azéma de Montgravier 1843, 665–667, 675, plan; Fabre 1900, with plan; Cagnat 1913, 660–661; Lawless 1970 II, 143–147), and the fortlet of Ain Sidi Taieb just west of Ain Grimidi (AAA 24:155 add; Desrayaux 1911, 483).

The lack of excavation or published air photography hampers our understanding of the internal arrangements of the forts, though access to newly declassified modern satellite imagery offers the prospect of future progress (Mattingly *et al.* 2013; Mattingly and Sterry 2014). There is no evidence that the ranges of rooms set against the enceinte, which are such a pronounced feature of later Roman castramentation in Numidia and Tripolitania, are also to be found in the Mauretanias, except in the case of Ain Grega which is perhaps too small to be relevant. Bearing in mind the ease with which similar structures have been robbed out at Benia bel Recheb and Benia Guedah Ceder in Tripolitania this absence may not be significant. At Ferme Romanette something resembling a traditional free-standing barrack block is marked on Joly's plan (1898; republished by Benseddik – 1980, 982 fig. 66.1; 1982, 176, fig. 33), but again the veracity of this record would require confirmation by modern survey or excavation.

Furthermore, little can be deduced from the meagre epigraphic sources regarding the deployment of the regiments, apart from the continued presence of the *numerus Syrorum* at Lalla Maghnia (CIL VIII 9964; CIL VIII 9967 and p. 976; *cf.* Rushworth 1992, 8–11). Milestones which continue to record the distance from *Coh(ors) Breuc(orum)* in the late 3rd century (CIL VIII 22598: AD 270; CIL VIII 22599: AD 282–283), mark the distance from the site, not necessarily the unit. Striking evidence of the changes which may have taken place in these "military" centres, during the course of the 3rd century, is furnished by the example of *Ala Miliaria*. There, a dedication was made in honour of Diocletian and his three colleagues by one Atius Crescens, *ob hono]rem IIvi(ratus) Al(ae) M(iliariae)* (AE 1936, 64 = Leschi 1936, 110–111; *cf.* Gascou 1982, 244–245 and Lepelley 1981, 520–521). The settlement around the fort had obviously acceded to the rank of *municipium* or *colonia* during the previous hundred years. It was not unique in achieving such self-governing civic status. *Altava*, further to the west, was already a *civitas* in 220, as indicated by a dedication to Elagabalus made by the *ordo et vet(erani et) populares Alt(avensium)* (revised reading of CIL VIII 21723

= AE 1889, 150 by Pflaum, followed by Marcillet-Jaubert 1968, 24, no 8). This would suggest that there was already a quasi-urban settlement at *Altava* when the garrison troops of the *cohors II Sardorum equitata* were first installed *c.* 201 (*cf.* Pouthier 1956; Marcillet-Jaubert 1968, 122, 273, 317; Lawless 1970, II, 51–65; Lepelley 1981, 522–534).

Nevertheless, despite its rise in civic status, it appears that *Ala Miliaria* may not yet have bid farewell to its homonymous regiment. Lenoir (1986) has persuasively argued that the 5th-century Donatist basilica situated at the east end of the walled site was not built *de novo* but in fact was constructed from the remains of a second phase *principia* of the fort. After comparing it with other known 3rd- or 4th-century *principia*, Lenoir favoured a date in the third quarter of the 3rd century for its construction, which must have formed part of a fundamental reorganisation of the fort's internal arrangements. A somewhat later date might be preferable. Lenoir's argument that the *Ala Miliaria* basilica formed a stage halfway between the basilica with adjacent courtyard type of headquarters, represented for example by the Severan phase at *Thamusida*, on the one hand, and free-standing or axial street basilica represented by Drah Souid-East (on the *Gemellae fossatum*), *Drobeta* or *Dionysias* is unconvincing. The relocated headquarters must have lain at the very end of an axial street running the entire length of the fort. The parallels for this are late-3rd-century or early 4th-century in date, for example *Dionysias* (Qasr Qarun) in Egypt (AD 306), Palmyra in Syria and *Iatrus* on the lower Danube (Bidwell 1996; Schwartz and Wild 1950; Von Bülow 2007, 463–466, fig. 3). It appears that the *principia* was actually located on the site of the former east gateway, which had perhaps been rendered redundant by the action of the Oued Traria. Indeed it may be possible to detect one or two traces of the former gate-towers on the plan published by Gsell (1899, 19, fig. 5 and 1901, 176, fig. 117). Its subsequent conversion into a Donatist church, to house the relics of Robba, martyred in 434, and several others, may account for some of the differences that are visible. Lenoir himself is justifiably cautious in assessing just what the precise form of the original military structure was, and which elements are to be attributed to the 5th-century conversion work.

Such a major reconstruction indicates the army had no intention of leaving *Ala Miliaria*. Nor did the *municipium* or *colonia* feel the need to build defences of its own to complement those of the fort. The only circuit at Benian is quite plainly that of the fort, itself measuring 235 x 195 m. Evidently the presence of the troops was sufficient defence, and was expected to remain so.

Ala Miliaria is not the only site where the fort circuit is the only one apparent; *Cohors Breucorum* and *Kaputtasaccura* (AAA 31:76, Berbrugger and Capitaine A. 1857–1858, 87, Lawless 1970 II, 75) also fall into this category. In contrast, at Kherba des Ouled Hellal (AAA 23:35, Lt. B. and MacCarthy 1857–1858, Salama 1953, 255–256, and 1973, 347 no. 1, Lawless 1970 II, 180–181), the *hiberna* of the *ala Pia Gemina Sebastena* was surrounded by a town, itself protected by a circuit wall (the same is of course also true of *Gemellae* and *Ad Maiores* in Numidia and Bu Ngem in Tripolitania). At *Numerus Syrorum* (AAA 41:1; Azéma de Montgravier 1841–1847, 335; Callier and Letronne 1844, 182; Cagnat 1913, 628; Salama 1966–1967, 216; Lawless 1970 II, 24–30), *Pomaria*-Tlemcen (AAA 31:56, Canal 1889, plans facing pp. 272 and 320; Lawless 1970 II, 48–49, fig. 10; Dahmani 1983 (1985), 439–441, figs.1–2) and Ain Toukria (AAA 23:27; Gavault 1883, 232; Lawless 1970 II, 171–174; Salama 1973, 347 no 37.) there is no trace of the Severan forts, only large defensive urban circuits have been identified. Two conflicting versions of the defended enclosure at *Numerus Syrorum* are cited by Gsell in the Atlas – a rectangular circuit 400 x 250 m (Azéma de Montgravier), and a triangular area 250 x 225 m (Callier and Letronne) – the former being generally preferred. Azéma de Montgravier notes the enceinte featured numerous, projecting rectangular towers, spaced at 10 m intervals. This feature recurs on the urban defences at *Auzia*, and is somewhat similar to those recorded at Tiaret, but none of these circuits can be dated, unfortunately. Likewise, an urban enceinte can be traced on air photos of *Altava*, and has been partially excavated, but a smaller (120 x 70 m) enclosure can also be discerned in the south-west corner of the town (AAA 31: 68; Pouthier 1956, 221 – plan; Marcillet-Jaubert 1968, 9 – air-photograph). This is probably the *castrum* built, or perhaps restored, by the agents of king Masuna in 508 (AE 1935, 86 = Marcillet-Jaubert 1968, no 67). Lawless (1970 II, 60–61) interpreted it as a late citadel, built *de novo*, rather than the fort of the *cohors II Sardorum*, but at 0.84 ha, it could just about have held the full regiment (Ras el-Ain in Tripolitania was 0.86 ha).

This is a very disparate assemblage of sites. Many were refurbished 3rd-century posts, notably *Ala Miliaria, Cohors Breucorum, Aras,* and Ain Grimidi (Salama 1953/1955; 1977, 585–586, 595). Medjedel was even older, an Antonine creation (AE 1938, 51 – AD 149; Leschi 1938–1940 = 1957, 45–46; Salama 1991). The extent to which projecting towers were added to earlier forts in Caesariensis stands in marked contrast to the situation in Tripolitania and Numidia, where only the Castrum du Confluent and perhaps Ksar Tabria are comparable. Some of the larger sites named above may well be *limes* headquarters, their identity masked in the *Notitia Dignitatum* by a rhetorical title such as the *limes Augustensis* or the *limes Fortensis*. *Ala Miliaria* is a particularly strong candidate for such a role given the evidence for its continued occupation represented by the reorganisation of its headquarters buildings.

Dating

The homogeneity of the Numidian forts may suggest they were all built around the same time. Guey argued that

Bourada was built under Constantine between 324–337, on the basis of a damaged inscription, coins and oil lamps from the site (1939, 206–208, 214–219, 245–247). In contrast, the coinage from nearby Drah Souid East was too worn to indicate more than a late Roman date, also indicated by the Christian motifs on oil lamps from the site, one of which can be dated to the beginning of the 5th century by comparison with a coin type of the period (Guey 1939, 205–206; Rebuffat 1977–1979, 259–260). Epigraphy provides the remaining evidence. *Centenarium Aqua Viva* can be assigned a construction date of 303 on the basis of its dedicatory inscription (AE 1942–1943, 81; *cf.* Leschi 1941 and 1943). Two *centenaria*, built further north, in Sitifensis, also fall within this Tetrarchic-Constantinian timespan, *Aqua Frigida* having been erected in 293 (CIL VIII 20215 = ILS 6886; Rushworth 1992, 181–182) whilst *Centenarium Solis* was constructed in 313–314 (CIL VIII 8913). Unfortunately the descriptions of these sites are too vague to say whether the structures conform to the type outlined above. The same can also be said of the *centenarium* built in 328 by the chieftain, Masaisilen, at or near Ourthi n'Taroummant in the rugged Grande Kabylie region of Mauretania Caesariensis (CIL VIII 9010; the site: AAA 6: 97–99; *cf.* Rushworth 1992, 178–179, 215–216, 282–283). In Tripolitania, there is no detailed evidence from any of the new style forts, but the dedicatory inscription from a small courtyard tower outpost, *Centenarium Tibubuci* (Ksar Tarcine), indicates a Diocletianic construction date (CIL VIII 22763 = ILS 9352). The inscription shows there was official military building activity in the province during the early 4th century (see Rushworth 1992, 145–147 for discussion of *Tibubuci* and a series of virtually identical sites, Bir Mahalla and Ksar Chetaoua, along the same route).

One should not imagine that every fort in North Africa of later Roman type was built during the Tetrarchy or the following period of Constantine's reign. The reigns of Constantine's sons and the Valentinianic dynasty are also represented. The gateways erected at Kherba of the Aouisset, near *Columnata*, in 346, may have belonged to a military installation, though it is perhaps more likely that the *portas ac valvas* formed part of a small town's defences (Cadenat 1953, 169; Salama 1954, 205–229 = AE 1955, 139). More useful are the inscriptions from Ras el-Ain, which reveal refurbishment was underway at that *limes* headquarters fort between 355–360 (CIL VIII 22766 + 22767 = ILAf 11 and CIL VIII 22768). Similarly, a fort (*castra*) was built at El Bahira (now Salah Bey) just north of the Hodna Mountains between 375 and 378 (CIL VIII 10937 = 20566). Unfortunately no archaeological trace of this installation has been identified.

Despite these later phases the assemblage is clearly weighted towards the earlier third of the 4th century. Although predominantly based on epigraphic evidence there is some reason to believe that this may fairly accurately reflect the chronological pattern of later Roman military building activity in North Africa. It seems not unreasonable to connect the construction of these new forts with the administrative reorganisation of the African frontiers, which took place during the Tetrarchy, its subdivision into a series of small territorial commands (*limites*). The Constantinian building work might also be associated with this, since it might be expected that the process of reorganisation took a considerable time to implement, with the *Gemellae* sector perhaps being treated later than the *limes Tubuniensis*.

Frontier commands and troop deployment

The relationship between the headquarters and the subordinate forts within each district needs careful study to establish the respective roles of each. By definition every headquarters base will have housed the *praepositus*, the administrative staff and records for the frontier sector, but beyond that there is little certainty.

Tripolitania

The *limes Talalatensis* is in many ways representative of military dispositions in western Tripolitania. Two sites in particular, Ras el-Ain and Benia bel-Recheb (Fig. 10.3), can be ascribed to this command. They, and their associated watchtowers and valley blocking walls (*clausurae*) in the Jebel Demmer, all form an interconnected group of installations. The two fortifications were of very different sizes. Ras el-Ain encompassed 0.865 ha whilst Benia bel Recheb was a mere 0.16 ha. Nor were they contemporary constructions. Whereas Ras el-Ain was a mid-3rd-century creation, Benia bel Recheb was built in the style typical of 4th-century fortifications. The explanation for these differences is straightforward. Despite some residual doubt over the site of the headquarters of the *limes Talalatensis* it is reasonably certain that Ras el-Ain held a fair proportion, if not all, of the troops based in the area. Recheb, on the other hand, was a much later and less important addition – a small fortlet probably constructed to house the troops outposted to the northernmost *clausurae* of the Demmer chain, which are over 20 km from Ras el-Ain (Ras el-Ain: Trousset 1974, 98–102, no 109; Mattingly 1995, 98; Benia bel Recheb: Trousset 1974, 95–96, no 105; Mattingly 1995, 194; see Rushworth 1992, 153–155 for further discussion).

This pattern is typical of late imperial Tripolitania (Fig. 10.4). The difference in size between the newly built and the retained forts is so very great that it must reflect a difference in function and importance. The most plausible explanation for this phenomenon is that the *quadriburgia* were in every sense supplementary to, rather than replacements of, the pre-existing 2nd- and 3rd-century forts such as Ras el-Ain and Remada. The latter not only served as the local headquarters

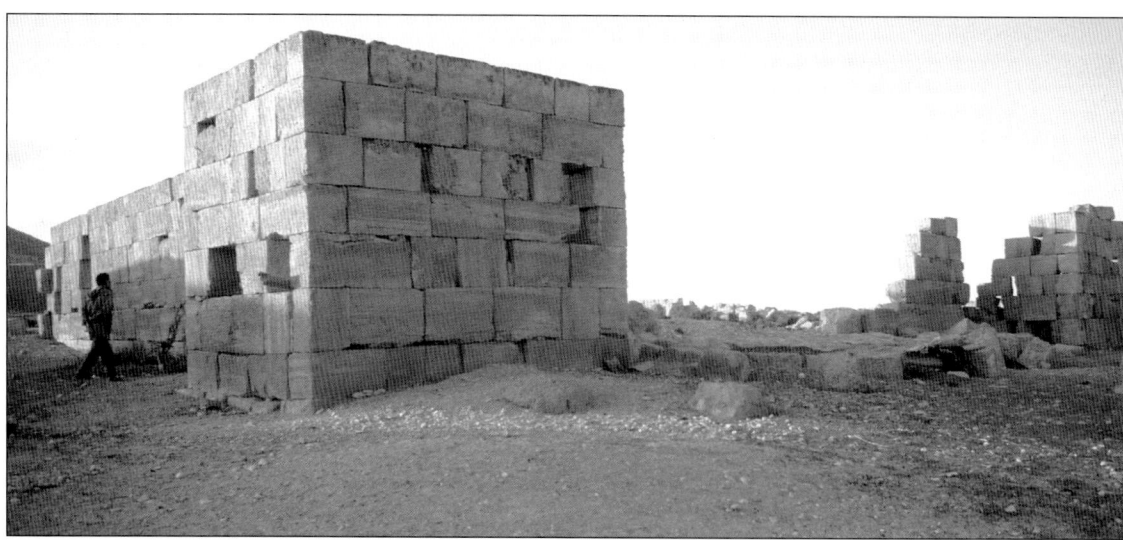

Fig. 10.3: The Tripolitanian fortlet of Benia bel-Recheb

and supply bases for the new *limites* but also retained their function as the principal accommodation for the frontier troops. The new forts were most probably nothing more than outlying police stations, sometimes associated with nearby *clausurae*.

Numidia

The same does not seem to have been the case in the *limites Tubuniensis* and *Gemellensis* of Numidia. Although the new forts there were not as large as the regimental bases of the Principate (Zebaret et Tir apart) sites like Bourada, Doucen, Aqua Viva and Seba Mgata were clearly able to hold significant detachments. The fort of *Aqua Viva* is described as a *centenarium* and, at 0.74 ha, was certainly large enough to hold a hundred men, so the label may be valid in this case (see below: The *centenaria* for further discussion). Given the broadly similar size of so many of the forts in these two sectors, it appears a policy was adopted of breaking the regiments up into 50–150 man detachments and outposting them, either beyond the line of the *fossatum* or right onto the barrier. In other words, the new forts may have taken over the role of accommodating the local garrison from the older sites, though not replacing the latter entirely. The smaller forts and fortlets, such as *Aquae Herculis*, on the other hand, presumably housed far less sizeable detachments, concerned only with policing the roads.

The Mauretanias

The pattern in the two Mauretanias is less clear because of the limited amount of archaeological research carried out there, but what evidence there is suggests that Caesariensis more closely resembled Tripolitania than Numidia. On the other hand the epigraphically attested existence of a *centenarium* and a *castra* as well as the small forts recorded by Baradez may imply that the *limes Thamallulensis* in Sitifensis reproduces the Numidian form of deployment.

Storage and Supply

The new forts may well have continued to rely on their *limes* headquarters to serve as their main storage depot, drawing supplies at intervals and transporting them to the relevant *centenarium*. Certainly no *horrea* have yet been identified in any of the newly built 4th-century forts, though the lack of modern excavation means this observation must be treated with some caution.

In contrast, an olive press uncovered in one of the chambers set against the enceinte of Fort Parallelogramme may point towards local supply (Baradez 1949, 247, plates 68B, 204C). This may simply relate to some secondary, post-military use of the site, but the possibility that it signifies the garrison was receiving its oil ration, or part of it, unprocessed from farms in the immediate neighbourhood and crushing the olives in the fort cannot be excluded. The same may be the case with other items of the soldiers' rations when abundant supplies were available locally. From the reign of Valentinian I a proportion of the frontier army's supplies was commuted to cash, the balance of the soldiers' supplies presumably being bought locally by the quartermasters (*actuarii*). By the late 4th century the *limitanei* received all their *annona* in cash. The olive press may represent one scheme devised by the *actuarii* to make the ration allowance go further for the benefit of their unit, and doubtless their own purse. Southern Numidia was a region of abundant olive production. Two presses have been identified in the adjacent village, for instance (Baradez 1949,

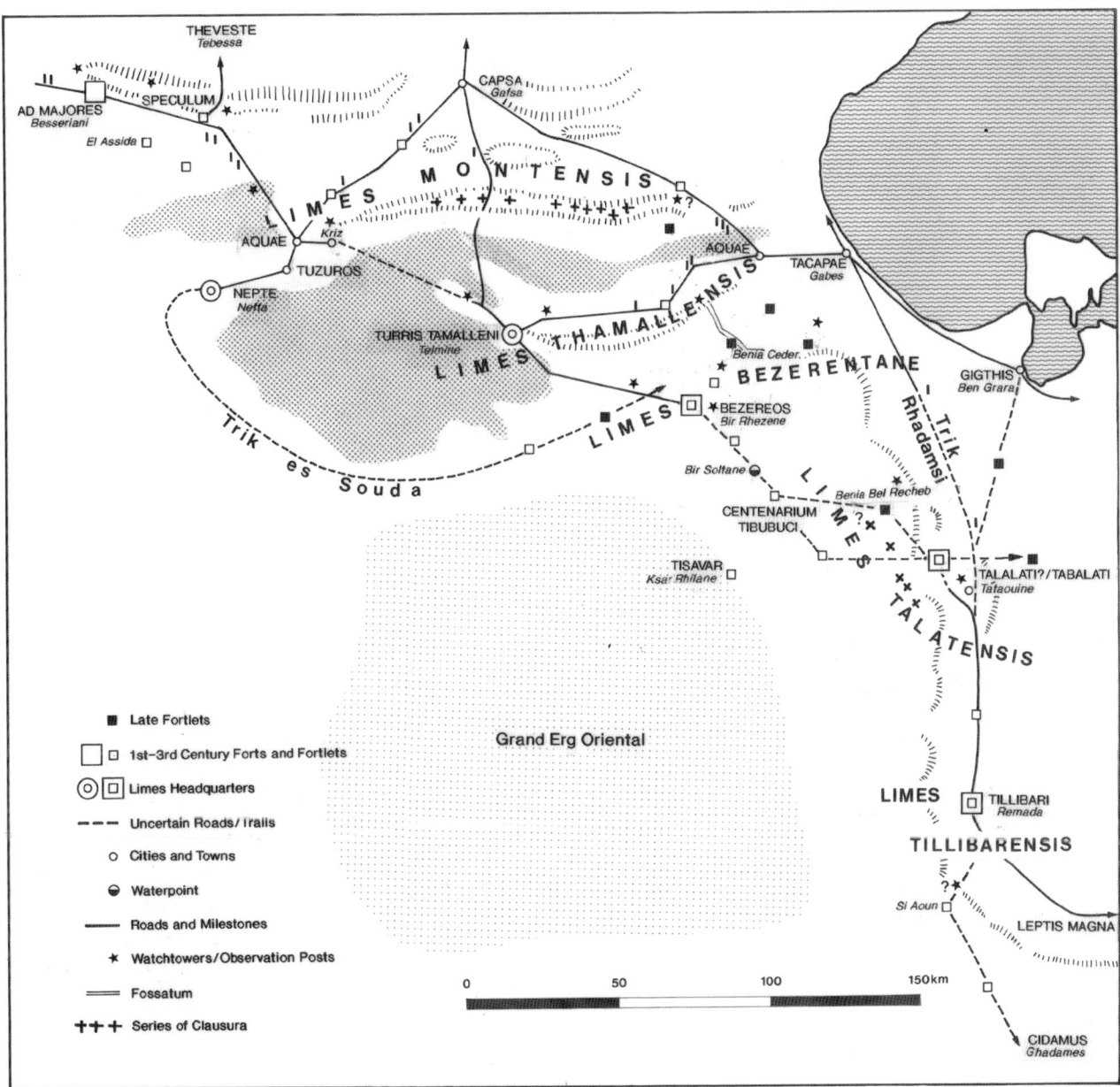

Fig. 10.4: The disposition of forts and fortlets in the limes commands of western Tripolitania and southern Byzacena

200, 247 and pl. 209C). Perhaps it was cheaper to obtain raw olives rather than processed oil from nearby farms and then crush the fruit in the fort, with soldiers' own labour effectively being uncosted (for a fully referenced summary of the legislation relating to the commutation and transport of the rations assigned to the *limitanei* see Jones 1973, 626–630, 1260–1262).

The role of the *limes* headquarters as supply bases is underlined by an inscription discovered at *Tubusuctu* (Tiklat near El Kseur; *cf*. AAA 7: 27). Dating to 304–307 it records the building of granaries (*horrea*) after the revolt of the *Quinquegentanei* (CIL VIII 8836 = ILS 645). This work may well have been associated with the establishment of the *limes Tubusuctitani* and mark the formalisation of an emergency base established during the campaigns of the preceding decade:

[DD(omini) nn(ostri) Diocletianu]s et Maximianus seniores Aug(usti) et /
[dd(omini) nn(ostri) Constantius et Maximianus in]victi imperatores et /
[Severus et Maximinus nobili]ssimi Caesares, /
[quo tempore d(omini) n(ostri) Maxim]ianus invictus senior Aug(ustus) feliciter /
[comprimens turbas Quinquege]ntaneorum ex Tubusuctitana /

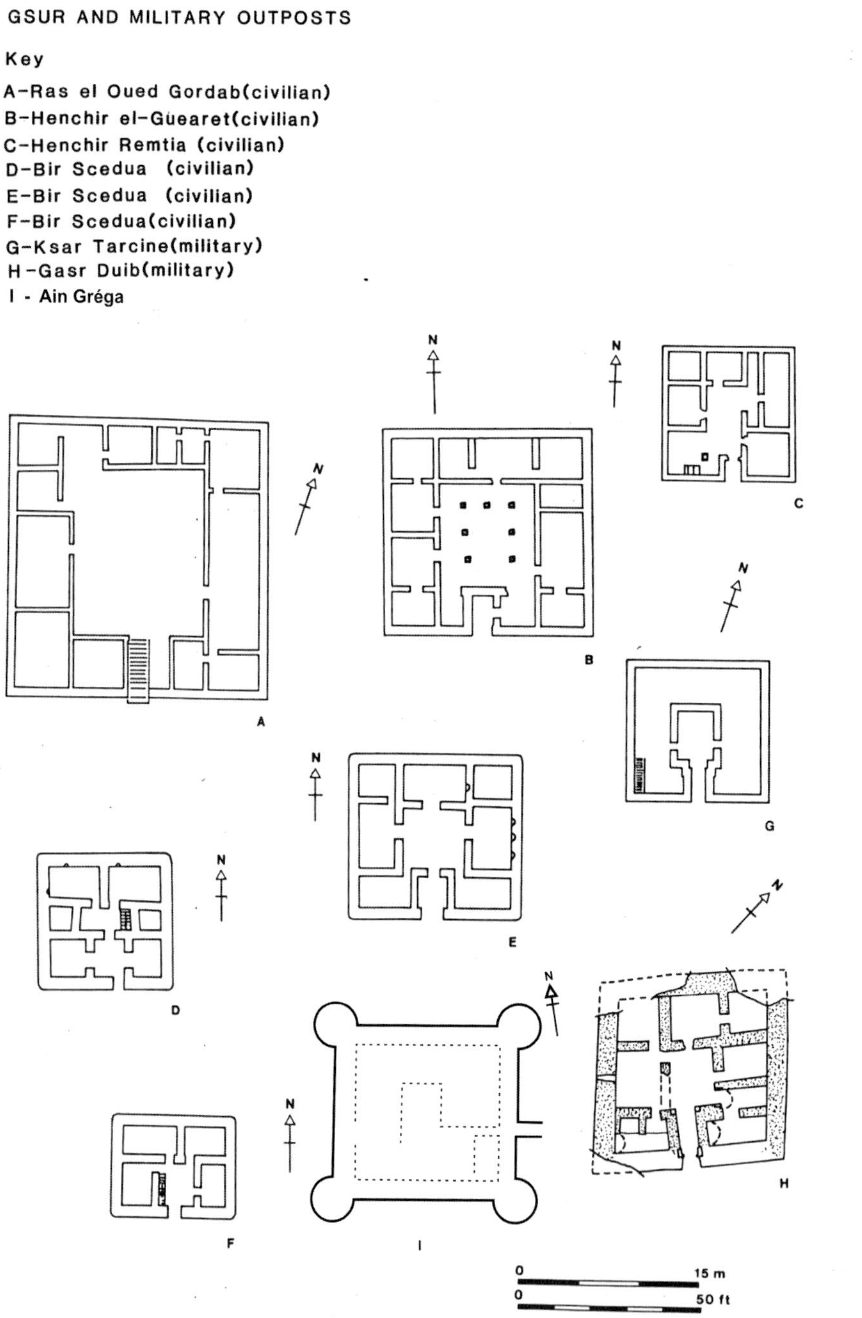

GSUR AND MILITARY OUTPOSTS

Key

A – Ras el Oued Gordab (civilian)
B – Henchir el-Guearet (civilian)
C – Henchir Remtia (civilian)
D – Bir Scedua (civilian)
E – Bir Scedua (civilian)
F – Bir Scedua (civilian)
G – Ksar Tarcine (military)
H – Gasr Duib (military)
I – Ain Gréga

Fig. 10.5: Plans of a range of courtyard towers (gsur). Credit: after Daniels 1987 with additions

[regione copiis iuva]retur, horrea in Tubusuctitana / [civitate fieri] praeceperunt, anno pro(vinciae) cclxv.

The restorations by Poulle, reproduced in CIL, filling the lost portions of the inscription, should obviously be treated with caution, though they reproduce the typically florid style of the Tetrarchy in an authentic fashion and probably reflect the general sense of the original text. Thus it might be preferable to restore *limite* in place of *regione* at the beginning of line 6. The instruction to initiate the work was given in 304, as indicated by the provincial era but not completed until after the abdication of Diocletian and Maximian and their elevation to the figurehead status of *seniores Augusti* in 305. *[Quinquege]ntaneorum* is surely an allusion to the warfare of 297 (cf. Seston 1946, 115–128; Cagnat 1913, 66–70; Salama 1954, 225–226; 1959, 347–350).

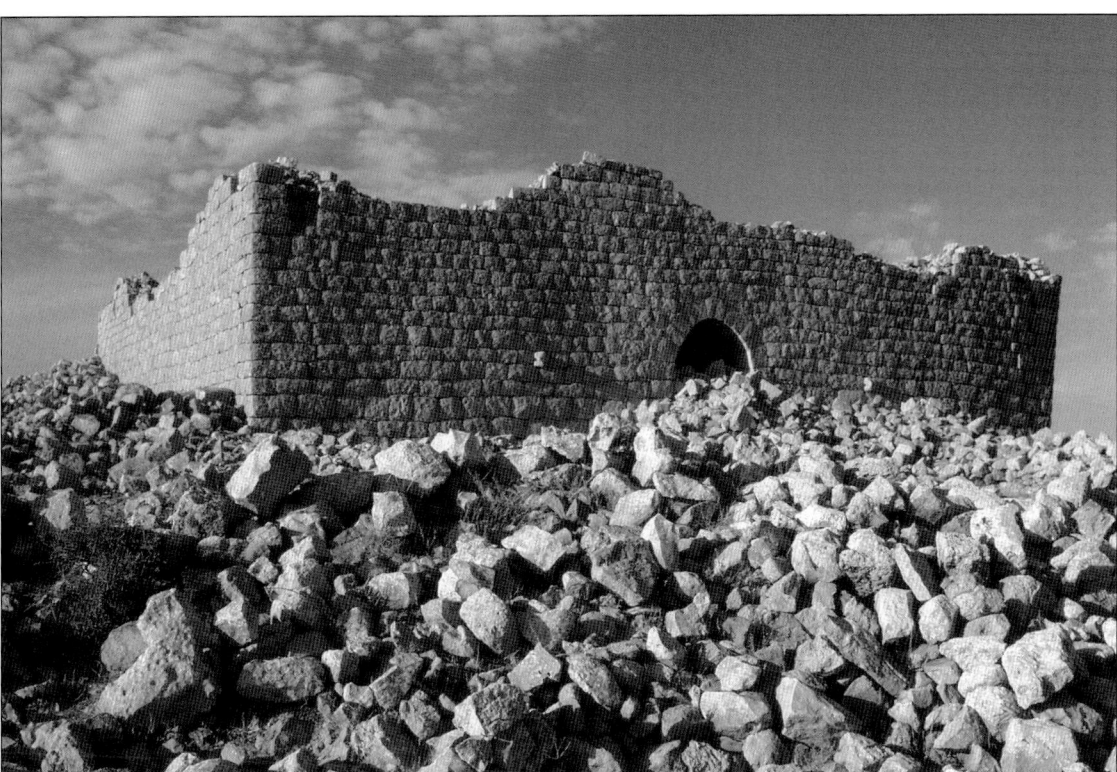

Fig. 10.6: A typical courtyard tower: Gasr Kh 41 in the Wadi Kharab in the Tripolitanian pre-desert. Credit: photograph by J. N. Dore

Site terminology – *centenarium*

One further point that must be considered is the significance of the term *centenarium* and the different types of sites to which the label could be applied, as this represents one of the more confusing aspects of the North African frontier. It might logically be assumed that *centenaria* were military installations designed to hold around 100 men or perhaps those housing detachments under the command of a centurion. Legionary centurions were often used in the 2nd and 3rd centuries as commanders (*praepositi*) of outposted detachments in Numidia and Tripolitania. These could vary in size from the 480 to 800 man vexillations, accommodated in large forts like Gheriat el-Garbia or Bu Njem, to the smaller complements, perhaps ranging from 80 to 160 men, which fortlets like *Bezereos* (Bir Rhezene/Sidi Mohammed ben Aissa), *Tisavar* (Ksar Rhilane) and *Thenadassa* (Ain Wif) could conceivably have held (Mattingly 1995, 84–86, table 4.2). However, judging from the surviving remains of the sites in question, neither garrison size nor commanding officer rank can appropriately explain all of the fortifications epigraphically designated as *centenaria*. Early in the 4th century it was clearly being used to describe a fort like *Aqua Viva*, which would certainly have been capable of housing 100 men, but the term had originated somewhat earlier and its first recorded use, in the mid-3rd century, relates to the courtyard tower, Gasr Duib, built in the *limes Tentheitanus* in 246–247 (IRT 880 = AE 1950, 128; Mattingly 1991; *cf.* Smith 1971; Goodchild and Ward-Perkins 1949, 24–25). It was still being used by the official hierarchy to designate to this type of site at the beginning of the next century when *Centenarium Tibubuci* was erected (CIL VIII 22763 = ILS 9352, *c.* 303) at the very same time as it was also being applied to the much larger site of *Aqua Viva*.

Sites like Gasr Duib were typically of two storeys with rooms arranged around a courtyard or lightwell (Fig. 10.5). In addition to its use by the army as a type of outpost fortlet, the courtyard tower form was widely adopted by the civil communities of the frontier zone from the 3rd century onwards, to provide defensible farms and residences (Barker *et al.* 1996). Today these structures are known locally by the Arabic term *gasr* ("castle" – plural *gsur*), which has also been adopted in the specialist literature (Fig. 10.6). It is conceivable that 100 soldiers or at any rate an infantry century, could be squeezed into such courtyard towers, particularly if the flat roof was also used as a sleeping area. In practice, however, the accommodation would have been extremely cramped and it is unlikely that such sites were ever that full other than in exceptional circumstances. The ground floor of Ksar Tarcine contained 22 water troughs, presumably for cavalry horses, which gives a better idea of the typical complement and even that might allow for overnight accommodation for the mounts of travelling officials or soldiers. More probably *centenarium* acquired the connotation of "outpost" from an early stage, an alternative to using *turris* or *burgus*, which were perhaps both felt to be associated more closely with simple, freestanding watchtowers. At any rate, though its use by the army, the label *centenarium* must have become sufficiently closely attached to such courtyard towers to be adopted as by the local populace of the Tripolitanian frontier zone as one of the Latin terms, along with *turris*, which they used to designate the similar structures they themselves erected as defensible dwellings (IRT 877, 889, perhaps 875; *cf.* Mattingly 1995, 103, 232 n. 24).

Although it clearly acquired much broader connotations, it is possible that when it was first coined *centenarium* did apply specifically to century-sized fortlets. We don't know what term was used to describe the fortlets of *Tisavar* or *Bezereos/Vezereos*, for instance, when they were first established, probably under Commodus. *Praesidum* was the label commonly given to small forts and fortlets throughout the 2nd century and into the Severan era. One example attested by inscriptions is the 0.12 ha fortlet of Si Aoun, just over 30 km south of Remada-*Tillibari*, built in 198 (AE 1909, 104 = ILS 9177 = ILAf 9). Similarly the Antonine Itinerary lists *Ballene Praesidium* and *Tamariceto Praesidium* amongst an alternating sequence of full size garrison forts (*castra*) and intermediate small forts/fortlets (*praesidia*) along the 2nd-century military highway in Mauretania Caesariensis (*Itin Ant.* 36.3–39.1; Rushworth 1996, 312). However *praesidium* does not occur in later official military inscriptions from the region and it is possible that it was supplanted by *centenarium* as the preferred term for smaller forts and fortlets.

Finally, whether or not it did initially relate to fortlets like *Tisavar* or *Bezereos*, the labelling of small forts like *Aqua Viva* as *centenaria* at the beginning of the 4th century may represent a deliberate adoption (or re-adoption) of a more technical usage of the term. This would be associated with the Tetrarchic-Constantinian reorganization of the Numidian frontier zone, involving the formal introduction of the district *praepositi limitum* and the division of individual frontier units into several detachments, which were then deployed away from their headquarters base, along or in advance of the respective stretches of linear barriers, as discussed above.

Conclusions

To summarise, the old regimental bases in Tripolitania probably functioned much as they had done during the Principate, with only small detachments outposted to police stations in the surrounding countryside. In contrast, a more radical shift can be observed in Numidia, where the late forts established along or beyond the linear barriers were capable of holding much larger detachments, perhaps as many as 100 men each. This may imply the headquarters bases relinquished, at least partially, the role of accommodating the local garrison, leaving just a core administrative and logistics presence there. The precise form this took is uncertain. The new forts may have housed permanent units in the manner of the regimental forts of the preceding era, but an alternative possibility is that detachments were rotated out from the main base, with the troops of each *limes* retaining a common identity and perhaps even some elements of the regimental structure, as hinted at by the epigraphic evidence. There is a clear earlier parallel for such a process in the shape of the many legionary vexillations stationed in the Saharan Atlas and Tripolitania during the 3rd century.

In short, in Numidia full advantage was taken of the new territorial system of command to spread troops out more evenly throughout the frontier zone by breaking units down into smaller detachments. This presumably produced benefits in terms of more effective policing.

It is worth asking why this policy was adopted in Numidia but not, for example, in Tripolitania. The explanation is probably the traditional pre-eminence of the Numidian command within Roman Africa (Egypt excluded). During the Principate it had been a senatorial command and home of *legio III Augusta*. This military pre-eminence was continued during the late empire with the creation of the post of *comes Africae*, the only dedicated military command in the African diocese until the very late 4th century. In Tripolitania and Caesariensis military and civil powers were usually combined in the person of the provincial governor. Consequently, it was in Numidia and neighbouring Mauretania Sitifensis that the bulk of the new legions and cavalry *vexillationes* were stationed alongside *III Augusta* (see Rushworth 1992, 93–99).

These units form the core of the field army listed in the *Notitia Dignitatum* under the authority of the *comes Africae*. Their presence in the central provinces and their exclusion from the structure of local frontier commands meant that the *comes* (and previously, under the Tetrarchy, the *praeses Numidiae Militianae*) always had at his disposal sizeable forces unhampered by routine policing duties. These could readily be used in the *limites* to mount punitive operations or suppress unrest which the local territorial troops could not cope with. The Numidian commander could therefore deploy his *limitanei* without having to worry about keeping some in reserve to respond to such problems. The province's two long running barriers may have benefitted from the dispersal of troops along their length. His counterparts in Tripolitania and Mauretania Caesariensis were less well furnished and would have had to request assistance of the *comes* if they needed major reinforcements. This may explain the less pronounced dispersal of troops in the two provinces, as significant numbers of men were retained at the various *limes* headquarters to enforce imperial authority in the frontier zone. To some extent such headquarters forces may have taken the place of legions and cavalry *vexillationes*.

It is unfortunate that the pattern in Mauretania Sitifensis (especially the *limes Zabensis* and the *limes Thamallulensis*) is so unclear. That province contained the other very long linear barrier in North Africa, and moreover it fell under the authority of the *comes* at a relatively early date. By the time the *Notitia* was drawn up it was obviously considered as part of the core of his command. A similar pattern of deployment may therefore have been implemented there, which might be revealed by field research along the Hodna barrier.

Bibliography

Albertini, E. (1928) La route-frontière de la Maurétanie Césarienne entre Boghar et Lalla Maghnia. *Bulletin de la Société de Géographie et d'Archéologie d'Oran* 48, 33–48.

Azéma de Montgravier (1841–1847) Report in: *Mémoires de la Société archéologique du Midi de la France* 5, 335.

Azéma de Montgravier (1843) Observations sur les antiquités militaires de la province d'Oran et en particulier sur les ruines de Tiaret. *Le Spectateur militaire* 35, 662–678 (with plans 1–2 at end of vol.).

Baatz, D. (1974) *Der Römische Limes: Archäologische Ausflüge zwischen Rhein und Donau*. Berlin, Gebr. Mann Verlag.

Baradez, J. (1949) *Fossatum Africae: recherches aériennes sur l'organisation des confins sahariens a l'époque romaine*. Paris, Arts et Metiers Graphiques.

Barker, G., Gilbertson, D., Jones, B. and Mattingly, D. (eds) (1996a/b) *Farming the Desert: The UNESCO Libyan Valleys Archaeological Survey, Vol. 1: Synthesis* and *Vol. 2: Gazetteer and Pottery*. London, Society for Libyan Studies.

Benseddik, N. (1980) La Ferme Romanette, Ain Benia, Ain bent Soltaine: Fortins ou fermes fortifiées? In W. S. Hanson and L. J. F. Keppie (eds) *Roman Frontier Studies 1979*, 977–998. BAR International Series 71, iii, Oxford, BAR.

Benseddik, N. (1982) *Les troupes auxiliaires de l'armée romaine en Maurétanie Césarienne sous le Haut-Empire*. Algiers, SNED.

Berbrugger, A. and Capt. A. (1857–1858) Sidi Ali Ben Youb (Albulae). *Revue Africaine* 2, 86–90.

Bidwell, P. (1996) Some aspects of the development of later Roman fort plans. *The Arbeia Journal* 5, 1–18.

Cadenat, P. (1953) Inscriptions latines de la région de Tiaret. *Libyca* 1, 167–179.

Cadenat, P. (1957) Vestiges paléo-chrétien dans la région de Tiaret. *Libyca* 5, 77–103.

Cadenat, P. (1958) Fouilles à Columnata 1956–1957. *Libyca* 6, 89–98.

Cagnat, R. L. V. (1913) *L'armée romaine d'Afrique et l'occupation militaire de l'Afrique sous les empereurs*. Paris, E. Leroux.

Callier and Letronne (1844) Découverte de deux colonnes milliaires sur la frontière du Maroc. *Revue Archéologique* 1, 182–187.

Canal, J. (1889) Pomaria: Tlemcen sous la domination romaine. *Bulletin de la Société de Géographie et d'Archéologie d'Oran* 9, 257–325.

Christofle, M. (1938) *Rapport sur les travaux de fouilles et consolidations effectuées en 1933, 1934, 1935, 1936 par le service des monuments historiques de l'Algérie*. Algiers, J. Carbonel.

Courtot, P. (1936) Essai historique sur Altava d'après l'épigraphie. *Revue Africaine* 79, 401–429.

Crow, J. G. (1981) *Late Roman Fortifications in the Lower Danube Provinces*. Unpublished M.Litt thesis, University of Newcastle upon Tyne.

Dahmani, S. (1983) Note sur un exemple de permanence de l'habitat et de l'urbanisme de l'époque antique à l'époque musulmane: Agadir – Tlemcen. *Bulletin Archéologique du Comité des Travaux Historiques et Scientifiques* ns 19b, 439–449.

Daniels, C. M. (1982) Review of E. W. B. Fentress, *Numidia and the Roman Army* (Oxford, 1979). *Libyan Studies* 13, 119–121.

Daniels, C. M. (1983) Town Defences in Roman Africa: A tentative historical Survey. In J. Maloney and B. Hobley (eds.) *Roman Urban Defences in the West*. CBA Research Report No 51. London, CBA.

Daniels, C. M. (1987) The Frontiers: Africa. In J. S. Wacher (ed.) *The Roman World* I, 223–265.

De Cardaillac, F. (1890) A travers l'Algérie romaine. *Bulletin de la Société de Géographie et d'Archéologie d'Oran* 10, 161–167 and plan.

De Caussade, (1851) Notice sur les traces de l'occupation romaine dans la province d'Alger. *Mémoires de la Société Archéologiques de l'Orléanais*. 234 ff.

De La Blanchère, M. R. (1883) Voyage d'étude dans une partie de la Maurétanie Césarienne. *Archives des missions scientifiques et littéraires* 10, 1–129.

Desrayaux, H. (1911) Description géographique et topographique des ruines romaines de Ain-Grimidi. *Revue Africaine* 55, 471–483.

Drack, W. (1980) *Die spätrömische Grenzwehr am Hochrhein (Archäologische Führer der Schweiz 13)*. Zurich, Schweizerische Gesellschaft für Ur- und Frühgeschichte.

Euzennat, M. and Trousset, P. (1978) Le camp de Remada: Fouilles inédites du Commandant Donau (mars–avril 1914). *Africa* 5–6, 111–190.

Fabre, S. (1900) Note sur la ville romaine de Tiaret. *Bulletin de la Société de Géographie et d'Archéologie d'Oran* 20, 45–46 and plan.

Fabre, S. (1912) Une nouvelle inscription à Waldeck-Rousseau. *Bulletin de la Société de Géographie et d'Archéologie d'Oran* 32, 127.

Fentress, E. W. B. (1979) *Numidia and the Roman Army: Social, Military and Economic Aspects of the Frontier Zone*. BAR International Series 53, Oxford, BAR.

Feuille, G. L. (1938–1940) Notes sur les ruines de l'Henchir Kedama. *Bulletin Archéologique du Comité des Travaux Historiques et Scientifiques* (1938–1940), 260–265.

Fort, Lt. (1908a) Les ruines romaines d'Ain Sbiba. *Bulletin de la Société de Géographie et d'Archéologie d'Oran* 28, 21–36 and plates I–VII.

Fort, Lt. (1908b) Notes pour servir à la restitution de la frontière romaine au sud de la Maurétanie Césarienne. *Bulletin Archéologique du Comité des Travaux Historiques et Scientifiques* 1908, 261–284 and plate XIX.

Gascou, J. (1982) La politique municipale en Afrique du Nord

II: Après la mort de Septime-Sévère. In H. Temporini (ed.) *Aufstieg und Niedergang der römischen Welt.* II (*Principat*), 10.2, 231–320. Berlin, De Gruyter.

Gavault, P. (1883) Note sur les ruines antiques de Toukria. *Revue Africaine* 27, 231–240 (with 2 plates. facing p. 244).

Goodchild, R. G. (1950) The *Limes Tripolitanus* II. *Journal of Roman Studies* 40, 30–38 = Goodchild 1976, 35–45.

Goodchild, R. G. (1976) *Libyan Studies: Select Papers of the late R.G. Goodchild.* (ed. J. M. Reynolds) London, Elek.

Goodchild, R. G. and Ward-Perkins J. B. (1949) The *Limes Tripolitanus* in the light of recent discoveries. *Journal of Roman Studies* 39, 81–95 = Goodchild 1976, 17–34.

Gsell, S. (1899) *Fouilles de Bénian (Ala Miliaria).* Paris.

Gsell, S. (1911) *Atlas Archéologique de l'Algérie.* Algiers, Adolphe Jourdan.

Gsell, S. (1928) La Christianisme en Oranie avant la conquête arabe. *Bulletin de la Société de Géographie et d'Archéologie d'Oran* 48, 17–32.

Guey, J. (1939) Note sur le *limes* romain de Numidie et le Sahara au IVe siècle. *Mélanges d'Archéologie et d'Histoire de l'Ecole Française de Rome* 56, 178–248.

Haensch, R. and Mackensen, M. (2011) Das tripolitanische Kastell Gheriat el-Garbia im Licht einer neuen spätantiken Inschrift: Am Tag. als der Regen kam. *Chiron* 41, 263–286.

Johnson, J. S. (1983) *Late Roman Fortifications.* London, Batsford.

Joly, A. (1898) Ruines romaines de l'Oued-Ouerq, près de Chellala (Algérie). *Bulletin Archéologique du Comité des Travaux Historiques et Scientifiques* (1898), 188–191.

Jones, A. H. M. (1973) *The Later Roman Empire 284–602: A Social, Economic and Administrative Survey.* (1st publ. 1964 in 3 vols. and maps; repr. 1973 in 2 vols.) Oxford, Blackwell.

Lassère, J. M. (1981) La colonia Septimia Aurelia Auziensium. *Ktema* 6, 317–331.

Lassus, J. (1981) *La forteresse byzantine de Thamugadi, I: Fouilles à Timgad 1938–1956.* Paris, CNRS: Etudes d'Antiquités Africaines.

Lawless, R. I. (1970) *Mauretania Caesariensis: An Archaeological and Geographical Survey.* Unpublished PhD thesis, University of Durham.

Lenoir, M. (1986) Une martyre près des *Principia*: A propos du camp et de la basilique d'*Ala Miliaria.* *Mélanges d'Archéologie et d'Histoire de l'Ecole Française de Rome, Antiquité* 98.2, 643–664.

Lepelley, C. (1979/1981) *Les cités de l'Afrique romaine au Bas-Empire.* Paris, Études Augustiniennes (vol. i, 1979 and vol. ii, 1981).

Leschi, L. (1936) Inscriptions d'Ala Miliaria (Benian). *Bulletin de la Société de Géographie et d'Archéologie d'Oran* 57, 107–111.

Leschi, L. (1938–1940) Une inscription romaine de Medjedel. *Bulletin Archéologique du Comité des Travaux Historiques et Scientifiques* 1938–1940, 162–165 = Leschi 1957, 45–46.

Leschi, L. (1941) Centenarium quod Aqua Viva appelatur. *Comptes-Rendus de l'Académie des Inscriptions et Belles-Lettres* 1941, 163–176.

Leschi, L. (1943) Le "centenarium" d'Aqua Viva près de M'doukal (Commune mixte de Barika). *Revue Africaine* 87, 5–22 = Leschi 1957, 47–57.

Leschi, L. (1957) *Etudes d'épigraphie d'archéologie et d'histoire africaines.* Paris, Arts et metiers graphiques.

Mac-Carthy, O. and Lieutenant. B. (1857–1858) Kherba des Oulad Hellal. *Revue Africaine* 2, 412–413.

Mackensen, M. (2012) New fieldwork at the Severan fort of Myd(---)/Gheriat el-Garbia on the *limes Tripolitanus*. *Libyan Studies* 43, 41–60.

Marcillet-Jaubert, J. (1968) *Les inscriptions d'Altava.* Aix en Provence, Annales de la Faculte des Lettres 65.

Martin, J. (1969) *Bida municipium en Maurétanie Césarienne (Djemaa Saharidj): Notes historiques.* (Fichier de documentation berbère 101) L'Arbaa Naït Iraten (ex Fort National), Algeria, Fort National.

Masqueray, E. (1882–1883) Sour Djouab (Rapidi) – Ain Bessem – Ain bou Dib. *Bulletin de Correspondance Africaine* 1, 206–270.

Mattingly, D. J. (1991) The Constructor of Gasr Duib, Numisius Maximus, *Trib(unus cohortis I Syrorum sagittariorum)*. *Antiquités Africaines* 27, 75–82.

Mattingly, D. J. (1995) *Tripolitania.* London, Batsford.

Mattingly, D. J., Rushworth, A., Sterry, M., and Leitch, V. (2013) *Frontiers of the Roman Empire: The African Frontiers.* Edinburgh.

Mattingly, D. J. and Sterry, M. (2014) The frontiers of Roman North Africa in the satellite age. Unpublished paper given at the Roman Archaeology Conference, Reading 2014.

Pavis d'Escurac-Doisy, H. (1966) Un soulèvement en Maurétanie sous Sévère Alexandre. In R. Chevallier (ed.) *Mélanges d'archéologie et d'histoire offerts à Andre Piganiol* 2, 1191–1204.

Petrikovits, H. von (1971) Fortifications in the North-western Roman Empire from the Third to the Fifth Centuries AD. *Journal of Roman Studies* 61, 178–218.

Poulle, A. (1879–1880) Le centenarium d'Aqua-Frigida et le praeses T. Aurelius Litua. *Recueil des Notices et Mémoires de la Société archéologique du Département de Constantine* 20, 255–265.

Pouthier, P. (1956) Evolution municipale d'Altava aux IIIe et IVe siècles ap. JC. *Mélanges d'Archéologie et d'Histoire de l'Ecole Française de Rome* 68, 205–245.

Pringle, D. (1981) *The Defence of Byzantine Africa from Justinian to the Arab Conquest.* BAR International Series 99, 2 vols, Oxford, BAR.

Rebuffat, R. (1972) Nouvelles recherches dans le Sud de la Tripolitaine. *Comptes-Rendus de l'Académie des Inscriptions et Belles-Lettres* (1972), 319–339.

Rebuffat, R. (1977–1979) Sur le fort oriental de Drah-Souid. *Bulletin d'Archéologie Algérienne* 7.1, 259–270.

Robert, A. (1901) Auzia: Place forte. *Recueil des Notices et Mémoires de la Société archéologique du Département de Constantine* 35, 135–140 (with 3 plates. and 2 plans).

Robert, A. (1903) Notes sur les ruines de Castellum-Auziense (Ain Bessem). *Recueil des Notices et Mémoires de la Société archéologique du Département de Constantine* 37, 49–50.

Rushworth, A. (1992) *Soldiers and Tribesmen: The Roman Army and Tribal Society in Late Imperial Africa.* Unpublished PhD thesis, University of Newcastle upon Tyne.

Rushworth, A. (1996) North African deserts and mountains: comparisons and insights. In D. Kennedy (ed.) *The Roman Army in the East*, 297–316. JRA supplement 18, Ann Arbour, JRA.

Salama, P. (1951) *Les voies romaines de l'Afrique du Nord.* Algiers, Imprimerie officielle du Gouvernement General de l'Algerie.

Salama, P. (1953/1955) Nouveaux témoignages de l'oeuvre des Sévères dans la Maurétanie Césarienne. *Libyca* 1, 231–261 and 3, 329–365.

Salama, P. (1954) A propos d'une inscription maurétanienne de 346 après JC. *Libyca* 2, 205–229.

Salama, P. (1959) Bornes milliaires et problèmes stratégiques du Bas-Empire en Maurétanie. *Comptes-Rendus de l'Académie des Inscriptions et Belles-Lettres* 1959, 346–354.

Salama, P. (1966) Occupation de la Maurétanie Césarienne occidentale sous le Bas-Empire romain. In R. Chevallier (ed.) *Mélanges d'archéologie et d'histoire offerts à Andre Piganiol*, 1291–1311. III, Paris, S.E.V.P.E.N.

Salama, P. (1966–1967) La voie romaine de la vallée de la Tafna. *Bulletin d'Archéologie Algérienne* 2, 183–217.

Salama, P. (1973) Un point d'eau du limes maurétanien. In *Maghreb et Sahara: Etudes géographiques offertes à Jean Despois*, 339–349. Paris, Société de géographie.

Salama, P. (1978) Les déplacements successifs du *limes* en Maurétanie Césarienne (Essai de synthèse). In J. Fitz (ed.) *Limes: Akten des XI Internationalen Limeskongresses*, 577–595. Budapest, Akadémiai Kiadó.

Salama, P. (1984) Masque de parade et casque d'Ain Grimidi: précisions sur le *Limes* de Maurétanie Césarienne centrale. *Bulletin de la Societé nationale des Antiquaires de France* (1984), 130–142.

Salama, P. (1991) Quelques incursions dans la zone occidentale du *limes* de Numidie. *Antiquités Africaines* 27, 93–105.

Schonberger, H. (1969) The Roman Frontier in Germany: An Archaeological Survey. *Journal of Roman Studies* 59, 144–197.

Schwartz, J. and Wild, H. (1950) *Fouilles franco-suisses. Rapport I: Qasr Qarun-Dionysias*, 1948. Cairo, IFAO.

Seston, W. 1946. *Dioclétien et la tétrarchie, I, Guerres et réformes (284–300)*. Paris.

Smith, D. J. (1971) The Centenaria of Tripolitania and their Antecedents. In F. F. Gadallah (ed.) *Libya in History*, 299–320, Libya.

Trousset, P. (1974) *Recherches sur le limes Tripolitanus du Chott el-Djérid à la frontière tuniso-libyenne*. Paris, CNRS: Etudes d'Antiquités Africaines.

Trousset, P. (1978) Le camp de Gemellae sur le *limes* de Numidie d'après les fouilles du colonel Baradez (1947–1950). In J. Fitz (ed.) *Limes: Akten des XI Internationalen Limeskongresses*, 559–576. Budapest, Akadémiai Kiadó.

Trousset, P. (1985) Les 'fines Africae' et la reconquête byzantine en Afrique. *Bulletin Archéologique du Comité des Travaux Historiques et Scientifiques* ns. 19b, 361–376.

Von Bülow, G. (2007) The fort of Iatrus in Moesia Secunda: Observations on the late Roman defensive system on the lower Danube (fourth–sixth centuries AD). In A. G. Poulter (ed.) *The Transition to Late Antiquity on the Danube and Beyond*. Proceedings of the British Academy 141, Oxford, Oxford University Press.

11

IN DEFENCE OF THE LATE EMPIRE

David J. Breeze

The 4th century presents a particular problem to the student of the Roman army. It is not only different from the army of the Principate, but we have to try to understand the changes from earlier years through the fog of the 3rd century. In many ways, it is far better to place on one side the army of Augustus and his successors and start again with the army of Diocletian and his successors, and then work backwards, as Connor Whately has done in his contribution to this volume. The late Roman army also requires the use of a different language. Legions, cohorts and *alae* may still exist, but now we have *comitatenses*, *scholae*, *cunei*, and *milites*. And the names of the enemies of Rome have changed, from Cherusci and Chatti to Vandals, Goths and Huns.

We have lost some types of evidence such as inscriptions, which helped us understand the army of the Principate. Yet, for the 4th century, we have the incomparable Ammianus Marcellinus, whose value is heightened by his service as an army officer, and the archive of Flavius Abinnaeus from Egypt, a record only matched by the Vindolanda writing tablets. As Whately points out, we have different types of sources too: in the *Notitia Dignitatum*, the law codes, and Christian hagiography. Actually, the problems inherent in dealing with Christian hagiography are not unique to such sources. The great writers of the empire all focussed on the leaders and rulers rather than the ruled, and had their own views about them.

One of the most significant questions of the late Roman army is its size, or rather the size of the individual units. Were these units similar to those before, or smaller, perhaps much smaller? Whately points out that in the Moesian provinces there were in the 4th century 20 locations for only eight legions. This obviously suggests division of each legion amongst two or more forts, but the situation is more complicated for two legionary detachments had previously been sent to Egypt and stayed there. There were also many more auxiliary units in the 4th century than earlier. The same process of fragmentation is recognised by Alan Rushworth in Numidia, as is the addition of new installations to the earlier pattern of military deployment. It is difficult not to accept the proposition that the regiments all contained fewer soldiers than previously (for a different view see Hodgson 1999).

The military architects of the 4th century created forts with high and thick walls, but against what? An enemy that came by water and carried no siege engines? Tall towers were erected on the high cliffs of Yorkshire, but for what purpose? To spy on an enemy who came by sea? What were the Romans frightened of? And how did they expect their new 'systems' of defence to work?

These questions are addressed by Matt Symonds. Helpfully, in his study of fortlets, he reminds us that some military considerations continued throughout the empire: fortlets built in the 4th century were largely in the same sort of locations as those erected two or three centuries earlier. But when we consider specific locations, several fortlets, such as those along the Yorkshire coast, are in new places. And these are highly visible places. Is Symonds right in suggesting that the fortlets and their towers were meant to intimidate the enemy? And, if so, can this proposal be extended to the forts of the Saxon Shore? Yet, Symonds also suggests that these late forts and fortlets with their strong stone walls may reflect the inability of the 4th century army to strike at the source of the raiding and thereby eradicate the threat.

On the west coast of Britain there are also fortlets in new locations, and facing a new threat, raiding from Ireland first recorded in 297 (*Panegyric of Constantius*, 11, 3). Sites such as Caer Gybi and Hen Waliau in north-west Wales as well as those on the Yorkshire coast are in the main stream of contemporary military architecture, though some with their own idiosyncratic features, and this is a useful reminder that Britain remained an integral part of the empire.

Symonds also probes another problem, the links between the coastal sites and the internal military bases. He brings together evidence from north-western England to propose a chain of fortlets between York and Carlisle over the Stainmore Pass.

Were all these sites military? Are we too prepared to assign a military purpose to any enclosure which has produced a scrap of military metalwork? And if we are, how do we recognise military as opposed to civilian enclosures? Certainly in North Africa and the East, the same kind of defensive enclosures were constructed by civilians as well as by soldiers. Excavation has not always been helpful in providing answers about the nature of the occupants; hence the importance of the investigations at Oudenburg in Belgium. Here, as at other late forts, a bath-house was built within the defended enclosure in the 4th century, only to be abandoned before the end of the century, possibly owing to the different cultural habits of a new garrison. The area then appeared to have been used as a penning area for animals, possibly horses owing to the discovery of horse equipment.

Sophie Vanhoutte relates these two events to the reduction in unit size and therefore the availability of space within forts for activities relating to the army that had previously been undertaken beyond the walls. She also argues from her analysis of the small finds that there were women and children within Oudenburg during the 3rd century and that their numbers increased during the following century. By 270, the extra-mural settlement had been abandoned, possibly under pressure from hostile action though at the same time coastal change affected the availability of land for settlement. Interestingly, the same date is claimed for the abandonment of several civilian settlements on Hadrian's Wall (Bidwell 1985, 90–92).

There are certain similarities, too, between Oudenburg and Binchester. At the latter site, the commanding officer's house and bath-house fell out of use in the late 4th century and the area turned over to the butchery of animals and some industrial use. Changes, perhaps of a similar nature, took place in one of the barrack-blocks. Yet, occupation of the fort probably continued into the early 5th century.

These are not the only trends that occur along the northern frontiers of the empire. Late Roman Vienna experienced the insertion of underfloor heating in certain barracks, perhaps for civilians. This in turn has been linked to the reduction in the size of the legion and abandonment of the extra-mural settlement, with the movement of civilians into the legionary fortress being accompanied by the spread of cemeteries across the former civil settlement. At the same time, at least one other barrack-block and a workshop appear to have continued in military use. In the second half of the 4th century, the fort wall was strengthened. At Novae, Martin Lemke sees a straightforward relationship: less space in the legionary fortress was occupied by the army and therefore the civilians simply moved into the newly available areas, changing the character of the place from a military establishment into a fortified town. This process was encouraged by the unsettled conditions on the frontier, which led to the gradual abandonment of the countryside. At the same time, across the empire, what we conceive as un-military activities were taking place in forts.

The fact that the Hadrian's Wall forts maintained their essential characteristics into the 4th century has caused a certain amount of puzzlement. Does this, for example, tell us anything about the nature of the enemy? Collins has scraped beneath the surface and analysed the granaries in these forts, noting that several were demolished or had reduced storage capacity in the second half of the 4th century. He considers the possible reasons for this: the reduced size of the military force in each fort or changes in supply mechanisms through the introduction of the *annona* and payment in kind, with any civilians within the fort looking after their own food. Rushworth, with caution, draws attention to the lack of storage facilities in late forts in North Africa and tentatively suggests a system of local supply.

Rushworth touches on other aspects of the internal planning of late Roman fortifications. He acknowledges that the 4th-century characteristic features of fortlets in North Africa were already present in the 2nd and 3rd centuries, thus emphasising the continuity noted by Symonds elsewhere. On the other hand, there were changes as indicated by the small size of the 4th-century fortlets in Tripolitania, compared to those built earlier in Numidia. He also asks whether the buildings erected against the tall internal walls of these fortlets were two stories high or only one, a question not answerable on present evidence.

Are there any significant trends? One is the abandonment of extra-mural settlements outside forts in the late 3rd century. This has been recognised in Britain, in Belgium, and on the middle Danube. In Belgium, Sofie Vanhoutte has argued that this was due to the attacks of Germanic invaders. But in Britain, there is no such evidence, though this may reflect the paucity of our sources. Other reasons for the phenomenon are possible. This period witnessed both civil wars and invasions. It is unlikely that any part of the empire survived without some impact. Some soldiers are likely to have been withdrawn from the frontiers for service in the mobile armies. At the same time, the currency declined in value. This will have affected not only the military, but everyone dependent upon the army. There are several reasons, therefore, for the decline, perhaps even the abandonment, of extra-mural settlements: unsettled conditions in the frontier areas; the reduction in the size of the units on the frontiers; inflation and the decline in military pay; payment in kind to the soldiers; changing methods of supply, all more likely to be operating together to bring about a changed situation. Changes in supply may have had an impact on the interiors of forts, as discussed by

Collins, but also on wider military deployment in the form of the location of defended granaries.

The outward and visible signs of a changed world were the high walls that now surrounded many forts. The construction of new-style military installations took place across the whole empire, as Ignacio Arce has indicated; the *quadriburgium* was now ubiquitous. As much as anything these new defences reflected the move of the initiative away from the Roman army. Along every frontier its enemies snapped like hyenas, and while it could still operate effectively along its borders, the Roman army no longer appears to have had the capacity to strike deep into the territory of its enemies. Changes within those walls are a different matter. We understand these less clearly. Most historians and archaeologists are agreed that unit sizes were smaller in the late empire, but the effects on the internal buildings are another matter. Very few late Roman forts have been completely excavated to allow us to understand even one site. Here is a challenge for the archaeologists of the 21st century.

Running beneath so many issues is the simple fact that the Roman Empire sought to protect itself. It tended to build its military installations in the same place, or at least with the same basic considerations in mind, and even though they might look different, they served the same purpose. This is the *longue durée* of the Roman Empire, its Grand Strategy, at which it was so successful for so long.

Underlying so many papers in this volume is the *Notitia Dignitatum*. It is surely time that we had a new analysis of this most important document, which does not simply consider the late 4th century but reviews the evidence for the earlier history of the army units enumerated in its pages. This leads onto another requirement, a research strategy for the army and frontiers of the late Roman Empire. Useful as all these papers are, they do not include an overview of military deployment in all its ramifications. To date, in Roman army studies, the major period of concentrated research has been the 2nd century, the hey-day of frontiers; it is time that the late empire received similar detailed treatment. We all tend to work in our own modern country or Roman province, but the empire was far wider. To take but one example; the Emperor Valentinian I ordered the construction of military installations in regions ranging from Britain to the eastern frontier. We too often consider these structures on a provincial, diocese, or area basis, but to understand his work more thoroughly, we need to raise our sights. The advantage for all of us is that such an approach will help us understand our own immediate research interested more clearly.

Bibliography

Bidwell, P. T. (1985) *The Roman Fort of Vindolanda*. London, English Heritage.

Hodgson, N. (1999) The late-Roman plan at South Shields and the size and status of units in the late-Roman army. In N. Gudea (ed.) *Roman Frontier Studies XVII/1997*, 547–554. Zalau, County Council of Zalau.